Introductory
Accounting

Tutorial

WITHDRAWN

AAT Diploma Pathway Unit 30

David Cox

Michael Fardon

osborne
BOOKS

© David Cox, Michael Fardon, 2006.

Published by Osborne Books Limited
Unit 1B Everoak Estate
Bromyard Road
Worcester WR2 5HP
Tel 01905 748071
Email books@osbornebooks.co.uk
Website www.osbornebooks.co.uk

Design by Richard Holt
Cover image from Getty Images

Printed by the Bath Press, Bath

British Library Cataloguing in Publication Data
A catalogue record for this book is available from the British Library

ISBN 1 905777 00 0

Contents

34611 3

Introduction

Process sales and receipts (Element 30.1)

Process purchases and payments (Element 30.2)

Process petty cash, reconcile accounts and prepare an initial trial balance (Element 30.3)

Acknowledgements

The publisher wishes to thank the following for their help with the reading and production of the book: Debbie Board, Janet Brammer, Jean Cox, John Elliott, Mike Gilbert, Claire McCarthy, and Jon Moore. Thanks are also due to Roger Petheram for his excellent and patient editorial work, and to Richard Holt for his designs.

The publisher is indebted to the Association of Accounting Technicians for its generous help and advice and for permission to reproduce extracts from the AAT Diploma Pathway Specifications. The publisher would also like to thank Bob Oakley of HSBC Bank and Penny Pritchard of The Royal Bank of Scotland plc for advice on the latest developments in bank payment systems. Thanks also go to Barclays Bank Plc, The Royal Bank of Scotland, Marks & Spencer plc, Microsoft and Sage PLC for permission to use illustrations reproduced within the text. The publisher is grateful to the Inland Revenue for the provision of tax forms, which are Crown Copyright and are reproduced here with the permission of Her Majesty's Stationery Office.

Authors

David Cox has more than twenty years' experience teaching accountancy students over a wide range of levels. Formerly with the Management and Professional Studies Department at Worcester College of Technology, he now lectures on a freelance basis and carries out educational consultancy work in accountancy studies. He is author and joint author of a number of textbooks in the areas of accounting, finance and banking.

Michael Fardon has extensive teaching experience of a wide range of banking, business and accountancy courses at Worcester College of Technology. He now specialises in writing business and financial texts and is General Editor at Osborne Books. He is also an educational consultant and has worked extensively in the areas of vocational business curriculum development.

Introduction

Osborne tutorials

Introductory Accounting Tutorial has been written to provide a study resource for students taking courses based on the AAT Diploma Pathway Unit 30. *Introductory Accounting Tutorial* contains:

- a clear text with worked examples and case studies
- chapter summaries and key terms to help with revision
- a wide range of student activities

Introductory Accounting Tutorial provides the student with the theoretical background to the subject while at the same time including plenty of opportunity to put theory into practice. Our aim has been to introduce the right amount of material at the right level, and not to overload the student with unnecessary detail. The text is appropriate both for classroom use and also for distance learning students. It is with the latter type of student in mind that the answers to the student activities have been included at the back of the book.

Osborne Workbooks

Osborne Workbooks contain practice material which helps students pass their assessments. *Introductory Accounting Workbook,* which accompanies this tutorial text, contains extended student activities and practice Examinations.

If you would like a copy of the *Introductory Accounting Workbook*, please telephone the Osborne Books Sales Office on 01905 748071 for details of mail ordering, or visit the 24-hour online shop at www.osbornebooks.co.uk

Osborne Tutor Packs

The answers to the student activities and Examination tasks in the *Workbook* are available in a separate *Tutor Pack,* which also includes a range of photocopiable documents. Contact the Osborne Books Sales Office on 01905 748071 for details of how to obtain the *Tutor Pack*.

surfing with www.osbornebooks.co.uk

The Osborne Books website is constantly developing its range of facilities for tutors and students. Popular features include the free downloadable resources and the on-line shop. Log on and try us!

Before studying the financial transactions and documents involved in buying, selling and making payments it is important to obtain an overall picture of the accounting system in which they operate.

Every organisation is different, and no single accounting system will be exactly the same as another. This chapter provides a brief introduction to the different types of business organisation, the types of transactions they will carry out and the different ways in which they set up their accounting systems.

Set out below are the AAT Unit 30 Knowledge & Understanding requirements covered by this chapter.

UNIT 30
KNOWLEDGE AND UNDERSTANDING REQUIREMENTS COVERED

12   Relationship between the accounting system and the ledger.

24   Understanding that the accounting system and administration systems and procedures will be affected by the nature of the organisation's business transactions.

BUSINESS ORGANISATIONS

There are three main types of business organisation:

sole trader

A sole trader is an individual trading in his/her own name, or under a trading name.

The majority of businesses are sole traders. A sole trader is likely to be a 'jack of all trades'; he or she will be in charge of buying and selling goods and services, hiring and firing of staff and will often, unless an outside book-keeper is employed, 'keep the books' – ie maintain the accounts. This is important because if the sole trader becomes bankrupt – ie s/he owes more than s/he has – the sole trader's personal belongings may have to be sold to pay off the business debts.

partnership

A partnership is a group of individuals trading in business, aiming to make a profit.

The partnership is clearly a step up from the sole trader: more people are involved in the business and so more expertise and money will be available. Examples of partnerships (normally from 2 to 20 people) include solicitors, accountants, dentists and small building firms. Like sole traders, partners in a partnership (unless they are limited partners) are fully liable for business debts. If the business becomes bankrupt, so do all the partners. The need for maintaining the accounts therefore becomes very important. Often one of the partners will take responsibility for the financial management of the business. As with a sole trader, a book-keeper may also be employed.

limited company

A limited company is a separate legal body, owned by shareholders and managed by directors.

The largest business organisations are usually limited companies. A limited company is quite different from a sole trader and a partnership in that it exists as a business in its own right. It exists separately from its owners, the shareholders, who will not be called upon to pay up if the company goes into liquidation (goes 'bust'). The shareholders have what is known as *limited liability*: all they can lose is the money they have invested in the company. The need for the keeping of accounting records by limited companies is strictly regulated in law. Many limited companies will have an Accounts Department which will carry out all the accounting functions.

OTHER TYPES OF ORGANISATION

Businesses form part of the 'private sector' – they are owned by private individuals. Other types of organisation include 'public sector' organisations which are owned or controlled by the Government, for example local authorities, corporations such as the BBC, and health trusts which run hospitals. Another type of organisation is the charity or club which forms part of the 'voluntary sector'. All these organisations have one thing in common: they need accountants!

ORGANISATIONAL STRUCTURES AND ACCOUNTING

In a small sole trader business, the owner is likely to have to carry out all the 'bookwork' as well as all the other functions of running the business. This is why small business owners work such long hours and also why they are motivated by their work – it is so varied.

The organisational structure of a larger business such as a limited company is far more complex, and as you will see from the diagram below, involves many more staff. Accounting jobs in a larger organisation may therefore be less varied but will allow greater specialisation. Nevertheless, as we will see in the Case Study on the next page, the transactions carried out are essentially the same: buying, selling, settling expenses, paying wages.

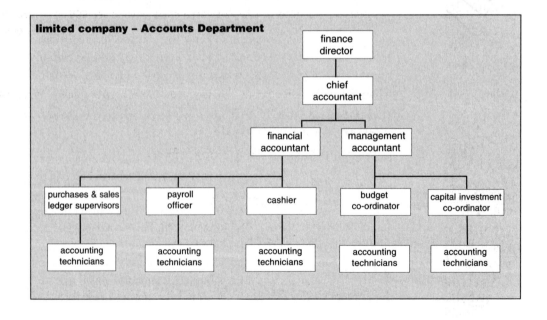

ACCOUNTING TRANSACTIONS

All businesses carry out transactions which need to be recorded in some form of manual or computerised accounting system. The most common transactions include:

*   selling goods and services
*   making purchases and paying expenses
*   paying money into the bank and making payments from the bank account
*   paying wages

If you consider all the activities undertaken during a working day, you will see that there are many different transactions taking place, all of which need recording accurately. Read through the following Case Studies which present two businesses: Stan Taylor Plumbing – a small 'one-person' business (which employs two assistants) and Osborne Electronics Limited – a larger limited company business which supplies computers and business machines and employs eight people.

Case Study

STAN TAYLOR PLUMBING

sale of goods and services

*   installation of toilet for Fred Lush, £250 paid in cash, receipt given by Stan
*   repair of burst pipe at City Architect's office, invoice for £95.50 issued to City Council, payment to be made in 30 days' time (normally a cheque will be posted to Stan)

purchases and payment of expenses

*   settle account with builders merchant, a £1,750 cheque issued by Stan for items bought over the last six weeks
*   buy new van, pay £12,000 by cheque
*   buy diesel fuel for van, pay £18.50 by cheque

visit to the bank

*   pay in cheques totalling £1,753.95
*   cash a cheque, £250, for wages for employees
*   query charges on the bank statement

pay wages

*   complete documentation, including wage slips, and pay employees £250

OSBORNE ELECTRONICS LIMITED

sale of goods and services

- sale of fax machine to Merton Textiles, for £750, cheque received with order
- installation of photocopier for Mereford Tourist Office, cost £2,450, invoice issued to Tourist Office, payment to be made in 30 days' time (normally a cheque will be posted to Osborne)

purchases and payment of expenses

- pay for colour laser printer for use in the office, a £2,750 cheque is issued by Osborne Electronics
- settle account with Nippon Importers for computer software, a £5,675 cheque issued
- issue cheque for £3,500 for insurance premium due

visit to the National Bank plc

- pay in cheques totalling £10,645.50, money received from customers
- cash a cheque, £2,500, for the week's wages

pay wages

- complete documentation, make up pay packets, totalling £2,500

RECORDING FINANCIAL TRANSACTIONS

Although the two businesses in the Case Study are very different in size and in what they do, the types of transactions fall into distinct categories:

- *Cash transactions* – transactions which involve immediate payment, eg Fred Lush's 'loo' and the sale of a fax machine to Merton Textiles. Note that 'cash' payment means 'immediate' payment and can include payment by cheque as well as payment using banknotes.
- *Credit transactions* – transactions which involve payment at a date later than the original transaction, eg the City Architect's burst pipe and the installation of the photocopier for Mereford Tourist Office.

The following transactions can be for cash or for credit:

- *Capital transactions* – the purchase (or sale) of items which are permanently used by the business, eg Stan's van and Osborne's colour laser printer.
- *Revenue transactions* – items of income or expense which occur on a day-to-day basis, eg Stan's diesel bill, Osborne's insurance premiums.

As you will see from the very varied items in the Case Study, recording financial transactions is a complex business. You have to keep track of:

• who owes you what, and when the payment is due

• amounts that you owe, and when the payment is due

You have to record what you pay into the bank and what you draw out. You need to record the amounts paid in wages to each employee. We will not at this stage explore in any detail how these transactions are recorded – such areas will be covered later in the book – but it is worth noting that if these transactions are not recorded accurately, the owner of the business and other interested parties such as the bank manager and the tax authorities will not know how the business is progressing!

ACCOUNTING SYSTEMS

The accounting system of a business is the system for recording information from documents (such as invoices and receipts) into the accounting records, checking that the information has been recorded correctly, and then presenting the information in a way which enables the owner(s) of the business and other interested people to review its progress.

Most businesses use an accounting system based on the double-entry book-keeping system, whereby each financial transaction is recorded in the accounts *twice*. Some small businesses will use a single-entry system, where each transaction is entered once only in a cash book, which records receipts and payments of money. Accounting records are usually kept in one of two forms: handwritten (manual) records or on a computer system.

handwritten accounts – the integrated ledger

This is the traditional method of keeping 'the books', particularly for the smaller business. It is relatively straightforward and cheap to operate. The main record is the *ledger* – a book into which each business transaction is entered by hand into individual accounts. This collection of accounts is known as the *integrated ledger*.

double-entry book-keeping and coding

Double-entry book-keeping involves making two entries in the accounts for each transaction: for instance, if you sell some goods and receive a cheque, you will make an entry in the sales account to record the sale, and an entry in the bank account to record the receipt of a cheque.

If you are operating a manual accounting system you will make the two entries by hand, if you are operating a computer accounting system you will make one entry on the keyboard, but indicate to the machine where the other entry is to be made, by means of a numerical code. Accurate coding is important in the efficient operation of any accounting system.

accounts

The sources for the entries you make are the financial documents. The ledger into which you make the entries is divided into separate accounts, eg a separate account for sales, purchases, each type of business expense, each customer, each supplier, and so on. Each account is given a specific name, and a number code for reference purposes. In a computer system, the accounts are held as data files on a disk, and each account becomes a computer record with its own reference number code.

division of the integrated ledger

Because of the number of accounts involved, the *integrated ledger* is divided into different ledgers, both in manual systems and also in computer systems:

- *sales ledger* – records of sales made to customers, and payments received at a later date (ie not cash sales) – each record shows the amount owed by a particular customer (debtor)

- *purchases ledger* – records of purchases from suppliers, and payments made at a later date (ie not cash purchases) – each record shows the amount owed to a particular supplier (creditor)

- *cash book* – a record of cash and bank transactions (a cash book is the main accounting record for the single-entry system mentioned earlier)

- *main ledger* – records all other transactions of the business, such as assets (things owned), expenses (the overheads of the business, eg wages, rent paid), drawings (the amount taken out of the business by the owner), loans to the business (eg by a bank), and the owner's capital (the amount invested in the business by the owner) – the *main ledger* is sometimes also known as the 'general' ledger or the 'nominal' ledger

integrated ledger – all the accounts			
MAIN LEDGER also known as 'general' or 'nominal' ledger accounts for income, costs, expenses, assets, loans and capital	**CASH BOOK** cash book for all cash and bank transactions	**SALES LEDGER** accounts for customers who buy on credit	**PURCHASES LEDGER** accounts for suppliers who supply on credit

trial balance

Double-entry book-keeping, because it involves making two entries for each transaction, is open to error. What if the book-keeper writes £45 in one account and £54 in another? The trial balance effectively checks the entries made over a given period of time and will pick up most errors. The trial balance sets out the balances of all the double-entry accounts, ie the totals of the accounts for a certain period. As well as being an arithmetic check, it is used to help in the preparation of financial statements – the final accounts of the business.

financial statements (final accounts)

The financial statements (final accounts) of a business comprise the profit and loss account and the balance sheet.

WHAT THE PROFIT AND LOSS ACCOUNT SHOWS

income	*minus*	**expenses**	*equals*	**profit**

The profit and loss account of a business shows the day-to-day ('revenue') income a business has received over a given period for goods sold or services provided. It also sets out the expenses incurred – the cost of producing the product, and the overheads (eg wages, administration, rent, and so on). The difference between income and expenses is the profit of the business. If expenses are greater than income, then a loss has been made. The profit (or loss) belongs to the owner(s) of the business. The figures for sales, purchases, and expenses are taken from the double-entry system.

WHAT THE BALANCE SHEET SHOWS

assets what a business owns	*minus*	**liabilities** what a business owes	*equals*	**capital** how a business has been financed

The balance sheet of a business gives a 'snapshot' of the business at a particular date – eg the end of its accounting period. The balance sheet is prepared from the accounting records and shows:

assets	what the business owns – eg premises, vehicles, computers, stock of goods for resale, debtors (money owed by customers), money in the bank
liabilities	what the business owes – eg bank loans, creditors (money owed to suppliers)
capital	where the money to finance the business has come from – eg the owner's investment, profits made by the business

The equation shown on the previous page –

assets minus liabilities equals capital

is known as the 'accounting equation.' Now study the diagram below which summarises the way the *accounting system* operates from documents through to profit and loss account and balance sheet.

source documents

processing of financial documents relating to purchases, sales, payments and receipts

accounting records

recording financial transactions in the accounting system using books of prime entry (eg day books) and the double-entry book-keeping system

trial balance

the extraction of figures from all the double-entry accounts to check their arithmetical accuracy in the form of a list, known as the trial balance

financial statements

production from the double-entry accounts of:

• profit and loss account

• balance sheet

together known as the 'final accounts'

computer accounting systems

So far in this chapter we have described manual accounting systems because these will form the basis of your studies. Many organisations now use computer accounting systems; you probably use one yourself. Unit 31 'Accounting Work Skills' covered by Osborne Books' *Accounting Work Skills Tutorial* provides a practical introduction to computer accounting.

ACCOUNTING SYSTEMS – CHECKING AND AUDITING

checking manual and computer data

Complete accuracy is essential in accounting. Mistakes in money amounts can result in suppliers being paid too much, the record of the bank balance in the cash book being wrong and, very importantly, employees' wages being wrong! An efficient business will therefore insist on setting up checking procedures for all calculations and listings of figures. Checking is equally important if a computer accounting system is used. Computers are very accurate, but only as accurate as the input data: the 'garbage in, garbage out' principle applies!

The checking may be carried out by employees at the same level of seniority, or it may be carried out by a supervisor. This type of checking will form part of the day-to-day procedures of the business, and will often be shown by the initials of the checker and date of checking.

auditors

Another form of checking is *auditing*. This is carried out by *auditors* – people who do not normally carry out the job in question, and may not even be employees of the business. Auditors are normally employed by larger limited companies and similar-sized organisations, eg local authorities, because they are required to do so by law. Smaller businesses such as sole traders, partnerships and smaller limited companies do not have this legal obligation and so they rarely use auditors.

There are two types of auditor:

• internal auditors

• external auditors

Internal auditors are employees of the business being audited. They are concerned with the internal checking and control procedures of the business: for example control of cash, signing of cheques, authorising of purchases. In a limited company the internal auditors normally report directly to the Finance Director.

External auditors are independent of the business which is being checked (audited). External audit is still the 'bread and butter' business of many firms of accountants. The most common form of external audit is the audit of larger limited companies which is required by the Companies Acts.

The auditors, when they have completed the audit, have by law to sign a declaration stating that the accounts represent a 'true and fair view' of the state of the company. The external auditors report to the shareholders (owners) of the limited company, and are appointed by them.

Auditing is covered fully in the AAT Diploma Pathway (Diploma Level) Unit 17 'Implementing Auditing Procedures'.

Chapter Summary

- There are three main types of business organisation: sole trader, partnership and limited company.

- Larger businesses tend to have more complex structures than small businesses – the accounting jobs will be carried out by a greater number of specialised staff.

- All types of business carry out the same basic types of financial transaction – buying, selling, banking, paying wages; all these transactions need to be accurately recorded and coded.

- Accounting systems within a business may be handwritten (manual) or computerised; they may be single entry (for the smaller business) or, more commonly, double-entry – which involves two entries being made for each transaction.

- Financial transactions are recorded in separate 'accounts' which are grouped in 'ledgers'; this system is true of both handwritten and computerised accounts. The accuracy of the system is checked in a listing of balances known as the 'trial balance'.

- The accounting system is used to produce the financial statements of the business – the profit and loss account and the balance sheet.

- The accuracy of the accounting records should be checked regularly by the accounting staff. In the case of larger businesses it may also be checked by internal and external auditors.

Key Terms		
sole trader		an individual trading on his or her own
partnership		a group of individuals trading in business
limited company		a separate legal body, owned by shareholders
cash transactions		transactions which involve immediate payment
credit transactions		transactions which involve payment at a later date
capital transactions		purchase (or sale) of items which are in permanent use by the business
revenue transactions		items of income or expense which occur on a day-to-day basis
double-entry book-keeping		an accounting system which involves two entries being made in the accounts for every transaction
coding		an identifying reference number or letter code given to accounting transactions, eg an account number, a supplier reference
ledger		a sub-division of the accounting system (strictly speaking a 'ledger' is a book, but the term is still used in computer accounting systems)
trial balance		a listing of the accounts in the accounting system, used to check the accuracy of that system
profit and loss account		a financial statement showing the profit or loss made by the business in a given period
balance sheet		a financial statement showing what a business owns and owes
assets		items the business owns
liabilities		items the business owes
capital		where the money used to finance the business comes from
accounting equation		assets minus liabilities equals capital
auditor		a person who independently checks the accuracy of the accounting records

Student Activities

1.1 A business which is owned by shareholders is known as:

(a)   a sole trader business

(b)   a partnership

(c)   a limited company

(d)   a limited partnership

Answer (a) or (b) or (c) or (d)

1.2 In each of the following cases, state whether the transaction is a **capital** transaction or a **revenue** transaction:

(a)   payment of wages by a bus company

(b)   purchase of a car by an advertising company

(c)   purchase of a car for a customer by a Ford dealer

(d)   sale of a table by a furniture store

(e)   sale of office furniture by a Ford dealer moving premises

1.3 State whether the following are **cash** transactions or **credit** transactions:

(a)   an office buys stationery and settles immediately by cash

(b)   an office buys stationery and settles immediately by cheque

(c)   an office buys stationery and pays thirty days later on an invoice

(d)   a petrol station sells petrol and is paid by cheque

(e)   a business sells goods and is paid thirty days later in cash

1.4 A person starting a new business is not clear about the meaning of the word 'ledger'. What exactly does it mean?

1.5 Write out the accounting equation. Explain the items which make up the two sides of the equation. What would happen to the capital of the business if the assets increased and the liabilities stayed the same (eg if a company revalued its premises)?

1.6 Explain in two short paragraphs:

(a) why it is important to check financial transactions

(b) what auditors do

1.7 The three examples set out below are mistakes that can and do happen in business. Read them through and state in each case what the consequences of each error might be.

(a) The overtime sheet given to the accounting assistant who calculates the wages has not been checked. Jo Isback's fifteen hours of overtime have not been recorded on it.

(b) Because of a computer input error a customer has been billed for 1,000 computer disks instead of 100 computer disks.

(c) The bank has deducted £5,000 from the business bank account by mistake and has not noticed the error.

Documents for goods and services supplied

This chapter examines the procedures involved when a business sells goods or services on credit. The essential point here is that the business wants to get its money on time and it wants to get the right amount. It can achieve these aims through the efficient use and monitoring of financial documents. The chapter covers the areas of:

- the use of business documents – quotations, purchase order, invoice, delivery note, returns note, credit note, statement

- the calculation of document totals and discounts

- the calculation of Value Added Tax (VAT)

- the coding of documents

- the checking and authorisation of documents

This chapter concentrates on the manual completion of documents. Processing sales transactions using computer accounting is dealt with in Osborne Books' **Accounting Work Skills Tutorial** for Unit 31 (Chapter 13).

PERFORMANCE CRITERIA COVERED

unit 30: INTRODUCTORY ACCOUNTING

element 30.1

process sales and receipts

A   prepare sales invoices from source documents

B   prepare sales credit notes from correspondence or other relevant source documents and ensure authorisation

C   code sales invoices and credit notes

J   produce statements of account for debtors

FINANCIAL DOCUMENTS

When a business sells goods or services it will use a number of different documents (mentioned in the diagram below). A single sales transaction of course involves both seller *and* buyer. In this chapter we look at the situation from the point of view of the *seller* of the goods or services. The transaction from the point of view of the buyer is dealt with in Chapter 9. Documents which are often used in the *selling* process include:

- the price *quotation* which the seller may be asked to provide
- the *purchase order* which the seller receives from the buyer
- the *delivery note* which goes with the goods from the seller to the buyer
- the *invoice* which lists the goods and tells the buyer what is owed
- the *credit note* which is sent to the buyer if any refund is due
- a *returns note* which is sent with any goods that are being returned
- the *statement* sent by the seller to remind the buyer what is owed

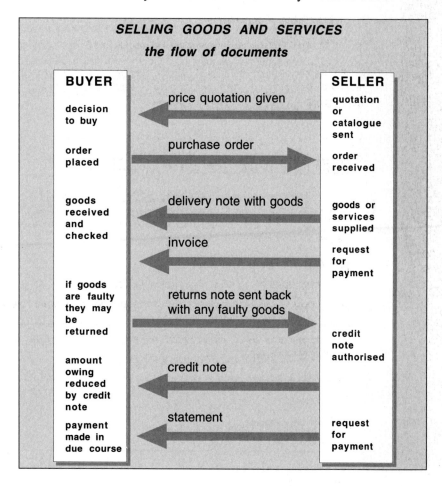

the flow of documents

Before you read the Case Study, examine the diagram set out on the previous page. Down the columns representing the buyer and the seller are various activities which lead to transactions which in turn generate documents.

Case Study

COOL SOCKS – A SALES TRANSACTION

situation

Cool Socks Limited manufactures fashion socks in a variety of colours. It supplies a number of different customers, including Trends, a fashion store in Broadfield. In this Case Study, Trends places an order for 100 pairs of socks with Cool Socks. The socks are delivered, but some are found to be faulty, so some of the socks have to be returned. The Case Study looks in detail at the documents involved.

THE PRICE QUOTATION

Before placing the order, the buyer at Trends will need to find out the price of the socks. This can be done by consulting Cool Socks' catalogue, or by means of a written or telephoned enquiry, or, if Cool Socks has a website, by an on-line enquiry. Cool Socks *may* provide a written quotation for the socks if they are requested to do so, although this procedure is more common with higher value orders. A written quotation might look like this:

QUOTATION

COOL SOCKS LIMITED

Unit 45 Elgar Estate, Broadfield, BR7 4ER
Tel 01908 765314 Fax 01908 765951 Email toni@cool.u-net.com
VAT REG GB 0745 4672 76

| Trends
4 Friar Street
Broadfield
BR1 3RF | date | 19 09 2007 |

Thank you for your enquiry of 17 September 2007. We are pleased to quote as follows:

100 pairs Toebar socks (blue)@ £2.36 a pair, excluding VAT.

M Arnold

Sales Department

PURCHASE ORDER – THE SOCKS ARE ORDERED

The buyer at Trends, once she has accepted the quoted price will post or fax the authorised purchase order shown below, or she might send an online order. The order will have been processed manually, or produced on a computer accounting program.

Note the following details:

- each purchase order has a specific reference number – this is useful for filing and quoting on later documents such as invoices and statements; this reference number is an example of *coding* in accounting

- the catalogue number of the goods required is stated in the product code column – this number can be obtained from the supplier's catalogue – this number is a further example of coding

- the quantity of the goods required is stated in the quantity column – socks are obviously supplied in pairs!

- the description of the goods is set out in full

- the price does not need to be stated, although some purchase orders will include a price

- the purchase order is signed and dated by the person in charge of purchasing – without this authorisation the supplier is unlikely to supply the goods (the order will probably be returned!)

- if Trends had a separate warehouse for storage of its clothes the purchase order will state the address of the warehouse so that the goods could be sent there; in this case the socks will be delivered direct to the shop

- Cool Socks may respond to the purchase order with an *acknowledgement of order*

Trends

4 Friar Street
Broadfield
BR1 3RF

Tel 01908 761234 Fax 01908 761987
VAT REG GB 0745 8383 56

PURCHASE ORDER

Cool Socks Limited,	purchase order no	47609
Unit 45 Elgar Estate,	date	25 09 07
Broadfield,		
BR7 4ER		

product code	quantity	description
45B	100 pairs	Blue Toebar socks

AUTHORISED signature....*D Signer*................................date.....*25/09/07*....

DELIVERY NOTE - THE SOCKS ARE DELIVERED

A delivery note is despatched with the goods when the order is ready. It is either processed manually in the office or printed out by a computer accounting program, often at the same time as the invoice (see next page). Sometimes an *advice note* with the same details is posted to the customer to advise that the goods have been sent.

In this case, the delivery note travels with the socks, and a copy will be signed by Trends on receipt. Note the following details:

- the delivery note has a numerical reference, useful for filing and later reference if there is a query – this is an example of coding

- the method of delivery is stated – here the delivery is by parcel carrier

- the delivery note quotes the purchase order number – 47609 – this enables the buyer to 'tie up' the delivery with the original purchase order – this is another example of the use of coding

- the delivery note quotes

  - Cool Socks' catalogue reference 45B

  - the quantity supplied

  - the description of the goods, but no price – it is not needed at this stage

  these details will be checked against the goods themselves straightaway so that any discrepancies can be reported without delay

- the delivery note will be signed and dated by the person receiving the goods

- a signed copy of the delivery note is normally retained by the carrier as proof of delivery; this is so that the buyer cannot say at a later date "We are not paying for these goods, we never received them!"

── DELIVERY NOTE ──

COOL SOCKS LIMITED

Unit 45 Elgar Estate, Broadfield, BR7 4ER
Tel 01908 765314 Fax 01908 765951 Email toni@cool.u-net.com
VAT REG GB 0745 4672 76

Trends 4 Friar Street Broadfield BR1 3RF		
delivery note no		68873
delivery method		Lynx Parcels
your order		47609
date		02 10 07

product code	quantity	description
45B	100 pairs	Blue Toebar socks

Received

signature...... *V Williams* ......name (capitals)... *V WILLIAMS* ......date *6/10/07*

INVOICE – THE SELLER REQUESTS PAYMENT

The invoice is the trading document which is sent by the seller to the buyer stating how much is owed by the buyer of goods or services. Note that 'goods' can include revenue (day-to-day) expenses or capital items which are to be kept in the business long-term.

The invoice, like the delivery note, is prepared in the supplier's (seller's) office, and is either processed manually or produced on a computer printer using a computer accounting program.

Invoices produced by different organisations will vary to some extent in terms of detail, but their basic layout will always be the same. The invoice prepared by Cool Socks Limited – illustrated on page 27 – is typical of a modern typed or computer printed document. An invoice will normally be printed as part of a multiple set of documents which might include the delivery note, possibly an advice note sent by post to the buyer, and always a copy invoice for the seller's own records. The copy invoice will normally be filed in numerical order (see 'references' below). If a computer accounting program is used, the invoice can, of course, be called up on screen, referenced by its invoice number.

Note the following details, and refer to the invoice on page 27.

addresses
The invoice shows the address:

- of the seller/supplier of the goods – Cool Socks Limited
- where the invoice should be sent – to Trends
- where the goods are to be sent – if it is different from the invoice address

references
There are a number of important references on the invoice:

- the numerical reference of the invoice itself – 787923
- the account number allocated to Trends by the seller – 3993 – possibly for use in the seller's computer accounting program
- the original reference number on the purchase order sent by Trends – 47609 – which will enable the shop to 'tie up' the invoice with the original order
- the VAT registration number (if the business is registered for VAT)

date
The date on the invoice is important because the payment date (here one month) is calculated from it. The invoice date is often described as the 'tax point' because it is the transaction date as far as VAT calculations are concerned, ie it is when the sale took place and the VAT was charged.

Note: VAT (Value Added Tax) is a tax on the supply of goods and services. At the time of writing the VAT rate is 17.5%.

the goods

As the invoice states the amount owing, it must specify accurately the goods supplied. The details – set out in columns in the body of the invoice – include:

- *product code* – this is the catalogue number which appeared on the original purchase order and on the delivery note
- *description* – the goods must be specified precisely
- *quantity* – this should agree with the quantity ordered
- *price* – this is the price of each unit shown in the next column
- *unit* is the way in which the unit is counted and charged for, eg
  - boxes of tights
  - single items, eg designer dresses
- *total* is the unit price multiplied by the number of units
- *discount %* is the percentage allowance (often known as 'trade' discount) given to customers who regularly deal with the supplier, ie they receive a certain percentage (eg 10%) deducted from their bill (see page 34 for further explanation of discounts)
- discounts are also given for *bulk purchases* – 'bulk discount' will also be shown in the discount column
- *net* is the amount due to the seller after deduction of trade or bulk discount, and before VAT is added on (see pages 34 to 36 for details about Value Added Tax)

totals and VAT

Further calculations are made in the box at the bottom of the invoice:

- *Goods Total* is the net amount due to the seller (the total of the net column)
- *Value Added Tax (VAT),* here calculated as 17.5% of the total after deduction of any cash discount. VAT is added to produce the invoice final total
- Total is the VAT added to the Goods Total; it is the amount due to the seller

terms

The terms of payment are stated on the invoice. In this case these include:

- *Net monthly* – this means that full payment of the invoice should be made within a month of the invoice date
- *Carriage paid* means that the price of the goods includes delivery
- *E & OE* stands for 'errors and omissions excepted' which means that if there is a error or something left off the invoice by mistake, resulting in an incorrect final price, the supplier has the right to rectify the mistake and demand the correct amount

Other terms (not shown here) include:

- *COD* stands for 'cash on delivery' – payment is due when the goods are delivered
- *Settlement Discount* (also known as *Cash Discount)* – a further discount given when payment is made early, eg '2.5% settlement discount for payment within 7 days'. See page 32 for further details
- *Ex-Works* – the price of the goods does not include delivery

——— INVOICE ———

COOL SOCKS LIMITED
Unit 45 Elgar Estate, Broadfield, BR7 4ER
Tel 01908 765314 Fax 01908 765951 Email toni@cool.u-net.com
VAT Reg GB 0745 4672 76

invoice to

Trends	
4 Friar Street	
Broadfield	
BR1 3RF	

invoice no	787923
account	3993
your reference	47609
date/tax point	02 10 07

deliver to

as above

product code	description	quantity	price	unit	total	discount %	net
45B	Blue toebar socks	100	2.36	pair	236.00	0.00	236.00

terms
Net monthly
Carriage paid
E & OE

goods total	236.00
VAT	41.30
TOTAL	277.30

CREDIT NOTE – A REFUND IS DUE TO THE BUYER

A *credit note* is a 'refund' document. It reduces the amount owed by the buyer. The goods, remember, have not yet been paid for. The credit note is prepared by the supplier and sent to the buyer. For example:

- the goods may have been damaged, lost in transit or they may be faulty
- not all the goods have been sent – this is referred to as 'shortages'
- the unit price on the invoice may be too high

In this Case Study, when the staff of Trends unpack the socks in the stock room they find that ten pairs are faulty. They telephone Cool Socks to report the problem and Cool Socks authorise the return of the socks for credit. These socks will be sent back to Cool Socks with a returns note (see page 191) asking for credit – ie a reduction in the bill for the 10 faulty pairs. Cool Socks will have to issue the credit note for £27.73 shown below. Note the following details:

- the invoice number of the original consignment is quoted
- the reason for the issue of the credit note is stated at the bottom of the credit note – here 'damaged' goods
- the details are otherwise exactly the same as on an invoice

---

———— CREDIT NOTE ————
COOL SOCKS LIMITED
Unit 45 Elgar Estate, Broadfield, BR7 4ER
Tel 01908 765314 Fax 01908 765951 Email toni@cool.u-net.com
VAT REG GB 0745 4672 76

to

Trends
4 Friar Street
Broadfield
BR1 3RF

credit note no	12157
account	3993
your reference	47609
our invoice	787923
date/tax point	10 10 07

product code	description	quantity	price	unit	total	discount %	net
45B	Blue Toebar socks	10	2.36	pair	23.60	0.00	23.60

Reason for credit
10 pairs of socks received damaged
(Your returns note no. R/N 2384)

GOODS TOTAL	23.60
VAT	4.13
TOTAL	27.73

STATEMENT – THE SELLER REQUESTS PAYMENT

A supplier will not normally expect a buyer to pay each individual invoice as soon as it is received: this could result in the buyer having to make a number of payments during the month. Instead, a *statement of account* is sent by the supplier to the buyer at the end of the month.

This statement, which can be typed out, or printed by the seller's computer accounting program, shows what is owed by the buyer to the seller. It contains details of:

- any balances (amounts owing) at the beginning of the month – these appear with the wording 'balance b/f' in the details column ('b/f' stands for 'brought forward')
- any payments received from the buyer
- invoices issued for goods supplied – the full amount due, including VAT
- refunds made on credit notes – including VAT
- the final total of all the items

The statement issued by Cool Socks to Trends for the period covering the sale and refund is shown below. Note that the balance of £150 owing at the beginning of the month has been paid off in full by a cheque on 2 October.

STATEMENT OF ACCOUNT

COOL SOCKS LIMITED

Unit 45 Elgar Estate, Broadfield, BR7 4ER
Tel 01908 765314 Fax 01908 765951 Email toni@cool.u-net.com
VAT REG GB 0745 4672 76

TO

Trends
4 Friar Street
Broadfield
BR1 3RF

account   3993

date   31 10 07

date	details	debit £	credit £	balance £
01 10 07	Balance b/f	150.00		150.00
02 10 07	Cheque received		150.00	00.00
02 10 07	Invoice 787923	277.30		277.30
10 10 07	Credit note 12157		27.73	249.57
	TOTAL			249.57

DISCOUNTS

The invoice in the Case Study (see page 27 and also the opposite page) shows a column for *discount*.

We also saw that the terms at the bottom of the invoice can allow for *settlement discount* (also known as *cash discount*).

We will now explain these terms and show how the discount is calculated.

trade discount and bulk discount

It is common practice for suppliers to give businesses that order from them on a regular basis an agreed discount – a percentage reduction in the invoiced amount. This is known as *trade discount* because it applies to businesses 'in the trade' rather than to the general public. Discount may also be given by sellers to buyers who purchase in large quantities; this is known as *bulk discount*.

In the example on the next page 10% discount has been given to Trends. Note how the discount percentage is shown in the discount column and the net amount is the amount after deduction of the discount.

The calculations on the invoice are as follows:

Step 1	Calculate the total price before discount
	100 x £2.36 = £236.00
Step 2	Calculate the trade discount
	£236.00 x 10% (ie 10/100) = £23.60
Step 3	Calculate the net price before VAT
	£236.00 - £23.60 = £212.40
Step 4	Calculate the VAT
	£212.40 x 17.5% (ie 17.5/100) = £37.17
Step 5	Calculate the total invoice price
	£212.40 + £37.17 = £249.57

INVOICE

COOL SOCKS LIMITED

Unit 45 Elgar Estate, Broadfield, BR7 4ER
Tel 01908 765314 Fax 01908 765951 Email toni@cool.u-net.com
VAT Reg GB 0745 4672 76

invoice to

Trends 4 Friar Street Broadfield BR1 3RF	

invoice no	787923
account	3993
your reference	47609
date/tax point	02 10 07

deliver to

as above

product code	description	quantity	price	unit	total	discount %	net
45B	Blue toebar socks	100	2.36	pair	236.00	10.00	212.40

terms
Net monthly
Carriage paid
E & OE

goods total	212.40
VAT	37.17
TOTAL	249.57

an invoice with 10% trade discount deducted

settlement (cash) discount

Settlement discount (also known as *cash discount*) is a discount offered by the seller to the buyer to encourage the buyer to settle up straightaway or in a short space of time rather than waiting the thirty or more days specified on the invoice. For example, the terms on the bottom of the invoice may include the phrase: *"Settlement discount of 2.5% for settlement within seven days"*. This means that the seller will allow 2.5% off the net invoice price (ie the price before VAT is added on) if the invoice is settled within seven days of the invoice date.

There are two important points to remember:

1   VAT charged on an invoice with settlement (cash) discount offered is calculated *on the invoice amount after deduction of settlement discount.*

2   The invoice total is the sum of this reduced amount of VAT and *the goods total before deduction of settlement discount.*

If we take the Cool Socks invoice on the previous page, the calculations for a cash discount of 2.5% are as follows:

Step 1	Calculate the total price before trade discount 100 x £2.36 = £236.00
Step 2	Calculate the trade discount (as before) £236.00 x 10% (ie 10/100) = £23.60
Step 3	Calculate the net price/Goods Total (as before) £236.00 - £23.60 = £212.40
Step 4	NOW calculate the settlement discount £212.40 x 2.5% (ie 2.5/100) = £5.31
Step 5	Calculate the reduced goods total (this is not written on the invoice) £212.40 - £5.31 = £207.09
Step 6	Calculate the VAT on this lower amount £207.09 x 17.5% (ie 17.5/100) = £36.24
Step 7	Calculate the total invoice price (using the goods total before deduction of settlement discount) £212.40 + £36.24 = £248.64

INVOICE

COOL SOCKS LIMITED

Unit 45 Elgar Estate, Broadfield, BR7 4ER
Tel 01908 765314 Fax 01908 765951 Email toni@cool.u-net.com
VAT Reg GB 0745 4672 76

invoice to

Trends
4 Friar Street
Broadfield
BR1 3RF

deliver to

as above

		invoice no	787923
		account	3993
		your reference	47609
		date/tax point	02 10 07

product code	description	quantity	price	unit	total	discount %	net
45B	Blue toebar socks	100	2.36	pair	236.00	10.00	212.40

terms

2.5% settlement discount for settlement within 7 days, otherwise net monthly

Carriage paid

E & OE

goods total	212.40
VAT	36.24
TOTAL	248.64

an invoice with 10% trade discount deducted and 2.5% settlement discount allowed for quick settlement

VALUE ADDED TAX (VAT)

VAT (Value Added Tax) is a government tax on the selling price charged to buyers at every level of sales, from the first supplier to the final consumer.

As we have seen on some of the business documents illustrated in this chapter, VAT is added to the purchase price of items sold. VAT is a tax on the consumer and, along with income tax, is an important source of revenue for the government.

registering for VAT

In Britain most businesses with a sales turnover (ie the total amount of sales in a given period) of more than a certain figure (increased from time-to-time by the government's budget) must be registered for VAT.

Once registered, a business is issued with a VAT registration number which must be quoted on all invoices and on other business documents. It charges VAT at the standard rate (currently 17.5 per cent) on all taxable supplies, ie whenever it sells goods, or supplies a service. From the supplier's viewpoint the tax so charged is known as *output tax*.

Businesses registered for VAT must pay to the VAT authorities (HM Revenue & Customs):

• the amount of VAT collected on sales (output tax)

• less the amount of VAT charged to them (input tax) on all taxable supplies bought in

If the amount of input tax is larger than the output tax, the business claims a refund of the difference from HM Revenue & Customs.

Every three months a form known as a VAT return (Form VAT 100) has to be completed, either on paper or on-line, although some smaller businesses submit a VAT return on an annual basis. Payment of VAT due (if the business is not claiming a refund) is made with the VAT return.

zero-rated and exempt supplies

A number of items are *zero-rated* and no tax is charged when they are supplied: for example, food and children's clothing are zero-rated.

Some goods and services (such as postal services, loans of money, sales or lettings of land) are neither standard-rated nor zero-rated for VAT: instead they are *exempt*. The effect of this is that the supplier of such goods cannot charge VAT on outputs (as is the case with zero-rated goods) but cannot claim back all the tax which has been paid on inputs.

VAT – a tax on the final consumer

VAT is a tax which is paid by the final consumer of the goods. If we take, for example, a member of the public buying a computer for £705, the amount paid includes VAT of £105 (ie 17.5% of £600). The buyer stands the cost of the VAT, but the VAT is actually *paid* to HM Revenue & Customs by all those involved in the manufacturing and selling process. This procedure is illustrated by the flow chart shown below. You will see that the right hand column shows the amount of VAT paid to HM Revenue & Customs at each stage in the process.

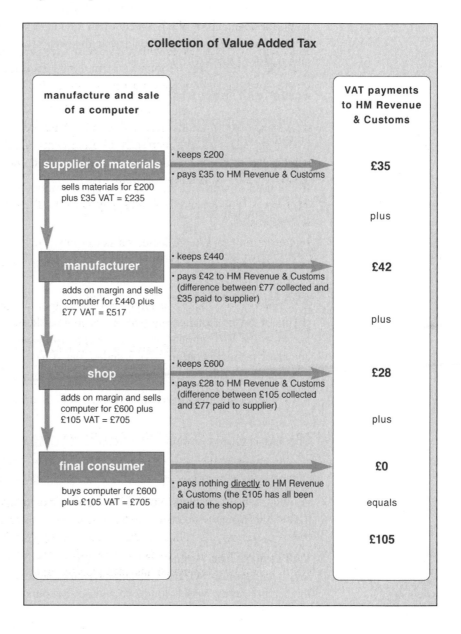

collection of Value Added Tax

manufacture and sale of a computer

VAT payments to HM Revenue & Customs

supplier of materials
- keeps £200
- pays £35 to HM Revenue & Customs

£35

sells materials for £200 plus £35 VAT = £235

plus

manufacturer
- keeps £440
- pays £42 to HM Revenue & Customs (difference between £77 collected and £35 paid to supplier)

£42

adds on margin and sells computer for £440 plus £77 VAT = £517

plus

shop
- keeps £600
- pays £28 to HM Revenue & Customs (difference between £105 collected and £77 paid to supplier)

£28

adds on margin and sells computer for £600 plus £105 VAT = £705

plus

final consumer
- pays nothing <u>directly</u> to HM Revenue & Customs (the £105 has all been paid to the shop)

£0

buys computer for £600 plus £105 VAT = £705

equals

£105

VAT records

Organisations must keep careful records of VAT paid and collected. This means filing documents such as invoices and credit notes for a minimum period of six years. HM Revenue & Customs VAT inspectors visit businesses from time-to-time to ensure that:

- VAT is being charged and claimed correctly
- there are no VAT 'fiddles' taking place
- VAT records are being maintained correctly

If, for example, a business has been trading and not charging VAT, the VAT authorities can claim back payment of all the tax that should have been paid. Traders have been put out of business in this way because they have not been able to afford the VAT due.

some VAT calculations

You may be asked to carry out a variety of calculations involving VAT. Here are some of the more common ones.

what is the VAT to be charged?

If you need to work out the VAT on a given amount you apply the formula:

$$\text{amount} \times \frac{17.5}{100} \text{ (ie the VAT rate)} = \text{VAT payable}$$

VAT chargeable on £100 is therefore $£100 \times \frac{17.5}{100} = £17.50$

what is the amount before VAT is added on?

If you are given a total amount, for an example a shop till receipt which does not show the VAT amount, you may need to work out both the VAT content and also the amount before VAT is added (the 'VAT exclusive' amount). The formula for working out the amount before VAT is added is

$$\text{total amount including VAT} \times \frac{100}{117.5} = \text{amount excluding VAT}$$

The VAT exclusive amount in a receipt for £117.50 is therefore

$$£117.50 \times \frac{100}{117.50} = £100$$

A quick way to calculate the VAT exclusive amount on a calculator is to divide the total amount by 1.175.

VAT amounts – rounding down

When calculating VAT, the VAT amounts should always be rounded *down* to the nearest penny. VAT amounts should not be rounded up.

AUTHORISING INVOICES

credit limits

A credit limit of a customer is the maximum amount which the seller will allow the customer to owe at any one time.

Part of the accounting control system of a business is to set credit limits for its established customers and to establish limits for new customers. Each time therefore that an invoice is issued, a check should be made against the credit limit of that customer.

authorisation of invoices

Most invoices issued will be within the credit limit and processed with the authority of the person in charge of invoicing. What if the credit limit will be exceeded? No business is going to be foolish enough to refuse to supply a good customer. It may be that a cheque will soon come in from the buyer, or the amount involved is relatively small. In these cases the invoice will need authorisation from a more senior person in the accounts department. It is quite possible that a credit limit may have to be raised if a customer is buying more goods or services, and, of course, is paying invoices on time.

checking invoices

Few things are more annoying to a buyer than an incorrect invoice – the wrong goods, the wrong price, the wrong discount, and so on. It wastes the buyer's time and often leads to an adjusting credit note being issued. It is essential that the following details are checked by the seller before invoices are sent out:

- is the correct customer being invoiced? – there are often customers with similar names
- are the correct goods being sent? – the product coding on the purchase order must be checked carefully against the description – it is quite possible that the buyer has quoted an incorrect code!
- is the quantity correct?
- are the goods being sent to the correct place? – sometimes the delivery address can be different from the address normally held on file
- is the price right?
- is the discount allowed to the customer (if any) right? – do any special terms apply?
- are the calculations on the invoice correct? – this is especially relevant to invoices which are not produced on a computer

checking invoices – manual accounting

As you will see from the above list, the person processing the invoice will need to consult:

- the purchase order (this is very important)
- the seller's own record of any price quoted (this may be as simple as looking at a catalogue or stock list)
- the seller's file record of the buyer (which will normally give the credit limit and the discount allowed)
- a calculator!

checking and coding – computer accounting

Clearly, if the business uses a computer, many of these processes, particularly the calculations, will be automated. If a computer is used, *checking of coding* will be very important. There will be codes for

- the buyer (which will bring up the buyer's address on the invoice screen)
- the buyer's purchase order number (normally input in a 'reference' field on the invoice screen)
- the seller's product code (which is normally quoted in the catalogue and which will be input on the invoice screen to bring up the product details and price)

You will see from this that computerised invoicing is much easier than producing the documents manually. Accurate checking, however, is critically important.

the importance of customer communications

You will see from all these procedures that accounts staff need to communicate regularly with customers:

- providing information relating to prices, discounts and terms
- answering queries and dealing with problems
- coping with complaints
- politely chasing up overdue invoices
- putting the pressure on bad payers to avoid them becoming bad debts (if a customer cannot pay due invoices – perhaps because he or she has gone 'bust' – the seller loses the money, which becomes a *bad debt* which will reduce the seller's profits)

We will deal with the various forms of communication in detail in Chapter 15, which presents a number of situations commonly encountered in an accounts department and suggests practical solutions, giving examples of communication methods.

Chapter Summary

- When a business sells goods or services on credit it will deal with a number of business documents, including the quotation, purchase order, delivery note, invoice, credit note and statement (see key terms below).

- The seller of the goods or services will request payment by means of an invoice and then remind the buyer by means of a regular statement (normally monthly).

- A refund due to the buyer will be acknowledged by means of a credit note.

- All documents and goods and services are normally coded (given a numerical or alphanumeric code) both for reference purposes and also for input into the accounting systems of the seller and the buyer.

- All documents should be checked carefully both by the originator and by the recipient to make sure that the right goods or services have been supplied, and at the right price. It is essential that items such as discounts, VAT and totals are calculated correctly.

- All documents generated in the sales transaction are normally filed away for reference purposes.

- Some documents, eg the purchase order, will need to be authorised before issue – this is part of the control system of the accounting function.

Key Terms

purchase order	a document issued by the buyer of goods and services, sent to the seller, indicating the goods or services required
delivery note	a document sent by the seller with the goods
invoice	a document issued by the seller of goods or services indicating the amount owing and the required payment date
credit note	a document issued by the seller of the goods or services reducing the amount owed by the buyer
statement	a document issued by the seller to the buyer summarising invoices and credit notes issued and payments received
trade discount	a percentage reduction in the selling price given to the buyer because of the trading relationship
bulk discount	a discount given for bulk purchases
settlement (cash) discount	a percentage reduction in the selling price given to the buyer if the buyer pays within a short space of time
Value Added Tax (VAT)	a government tax on spending, often calculated on invoices and credit notes

Student Activities

2.1   What type of business document would normally be used when goods are sold on credit:

    (a)   to accompany goods from the seller to the buyer?

    (b)   to accompany faulty goods sent back by the buyer?

    (c)   as a formal notification of the amount owed?

    (d)   to remind the buyer of the amount owed to the seller?

    (e)   as a formal notification from the seller of a refund made to the buyer?

    (f)   to order the goods from the seller in the first place?

2.2   Compudisc sells computer floppy disks and has a special sales offer. A box of ten formatted disks normally sells at £8.00 (excluding VAT). Compudisc is offering to give a 20% discount for orders of ten boxes or more. It receives in the post one morning the following orders:

    (a)   20 boxes ordered by Osborne Electronics Limited

    (b)   50 boxes ordered by Helfield College

    (c)   5 boxes ordered by Jim Masters

    (d)   1000 boxes ordered by Trigger Trading Limited

    Calculate in each case

       - the total cost before discount

       - the discount

       - the cost after discount

       - the VAT at the current rate

       - the total cost

2.3   Recalculate the totals in Activity 2.2 allowing for a settlement (cash) discount of 2.5%.

2.4   Explain what is meant by the invoice terms 'net monthly' and 'E & OE' and 'carriage paid'.

2.5   Give three examples of coding on business documents. Why is coding important?

2.6   You work as one of three assistants in an accounts office. Your supervisor is off sick. You receive an urgent and large purchase order and find that the product code and goods description do not match up. The goods have to be despatched on the same day. What *exactly* is the problem and what would you do about it?

2.7   •   Check the invoice extracts shown below.

   •   State what is wrong with them.

   •   Calculate the correct final totals.

   Note: VAT is always rounded down to the nearest penny.

invoice (a)

description	quantity	price	total	discount %	net
Cotton shirts (red)	10	9.50	95.00	20	85.50

goods total	85.50
VAT @ 17.5%	14.96
TOTAL	100.45

invoice (b)

description	quantity	price	total	discount %	net
'Crazy Surfin' T-shirts (yellow)	50	5.00	225.00	10	202.50

goods total	202.50
VAT @ 17.5%	35.44
TOTAL	237.94

2.8   The following amounts include VAT. What is the VAT content and the amount before VAT is added in each case? Remember that VAT must be rounded down to the nearest penny.

   (a)   £47.00

   (b)   £40,670.98

   (c)   £39.98

   (d)   £94.00

   (e)   47p

   (f)   £1.20

2.9 You work in the Accounts Department of Pool Cleaning Services Limited, a business which maintains swimming pools, spa baths and jacuzzis.

It is 31 July 2007 and you are looking through the file for the account of Mr Henry Simpson. Your file shows that you issued an invoice on 8 July (shown below) and a credit note on 14 July for a 10% trade discount which should have been deducted from the invoice.

You also note from last month's statement that Mr Simpson still owed you £58.75 on 1 July for a call out charge he had not yet paid. You received a cheque for this amount on 4 July.

You are to prepare a statement for Mr H Simpson as at 31 July 2007. It should show opening and closing balances and transactions for the month.

INVOICE

Pool Cleaning Services Limited

Unit 5 Neptune Estate, Mereford, MR7 4EF
Tel 01908 352456 Fax 01908 352466 Email mail@poolcleaning-services.com
VAT Reg GB 0745 4872 21

invoice to

H Simpson 45 Bishops Avenue Marston Hackett MR7 9JH	

invoice no	**10982**
account	**234**
your reference	**verbal**
date/tax point	**08 07 07**

description	total	discount %	net
Annual swimming pool service, 27 June 2007	290.00	0.00	290.00

Net Total	290.00
VAT	50.75
TOTAL	340.75

terms
Net monthly

extract from credit note No. 2378 dated 14 July

description		total	discount	net
Annual swimming pool service		29.00	0.00	29.00

Reason for credit
10% discount allowable on invoice
10982

NET TOTAL	29.00
VAT	5.07
TOTAL	34.07

STATEMENT OF ACCOUNT
Pool Cleaning Services Limited

Unit 5 Neptune Estate, Mereford, MR7 4EF
Tel 01908 352456 Fax 01908 352466 Email mail@poolcleaning-services.com
VAT Reg GB 0745 4872 21

TO

account

date

date	details	debit £	credit £	balance £
			TOTAL	£

3 Accounting for credit sales and sales returns

this chapter covers . . .

The previous chapter looked at the documents and procedures involved in selling on credit. In this chapter we examine the principles of the accounting system which is used to record the details of invoices and credit notes.

We then apply these principles to credit sales (sales invoices) and sales returns (credit notes) and see how they are entered in the books of prime entry (sales day book and sales returns day book).

This information is then transferred from the day books into the ledger accounts of the double-entry system.

PERFORMANCE CRITERIA COVERED

unit 30: INTRODUCTORY ACCOUNTING

element 30.1

process sales and receipts

D   enter sales invoices and credit notes into sales day book and sales returns day book

E   post sales invoices and credit notes into the subsidiary (sales) ledger and main (general) ledger

THE ACCOUNTING SYSTEM

We have seen earlier in Chapter 1 (page 14) that the accounting system comprises a number of stages of recording and presenting financial transactions:

- prime documents (also known as 'source' documents)
- books of prime entry (eg day books)
- double-entry book-keeping
- trial balance
- financial statements

In this chapter we look at the principles of recording documents relating to credit sales transactions in the books of prime entry and the entries to be made in the double-entry accounts. Later in the book we will see how a list of the balances of the double-entry accounts is used to form the trial balance (Chapter 20). Financial statements – the profit and loss account and balance sheet – are the end result of the accounting system; they will be covered at later levels of your Diploma Pathway studies.

ACCOUNTING FOR CREDIT SALES TRANSACTIONS

This chapter focuses on credit sales transactions; the recording of transactions for cash sales will be covered when we study the receipts side of the cash book – Chapter 7.

In accounting, the term 'sales' has a specific meaning:

the sale of goods in which the business or organisation trades

Thus an office stationery shop will record as sales things such as photocopier paper, ring binders, etc; however, if the shop sells off its old cash till when it is replaced with a new one, this is not recorded as sales but, instead, is accounted for against the original cost of the till.

The accounting system starts its recording process from prime documents. The prime documents used to record different aspects of credit sales are:

- sales invoices
- credit notes issued

The diagram on the next page shows the order in which the accounting records are prepared for credit sales transactions. You will see that the steps for recording credit sales transactions in the accounting system are:

- start with a *prime document* (the source document for the accounting records)

- enter it in the appropriate *book of prime entry* (the first accounting book in which the prime document is recorded and summarised)
- transfer the information from the book of prime entry into the *double-entry accounts*

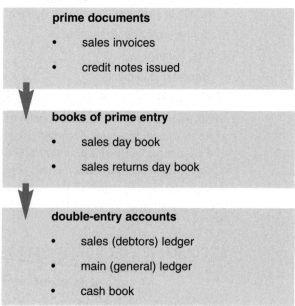

accounting for credit sales transactions

prime documents

- sales invoices
- credit notes issued

books of prime entry

- sales day book
- sales returns day book

double-entry accounts

- sales (debtors) ledger
- main (general) ledger
- cash book

We will now look in more detail at the mechanics of the books of prime entry and the double-entry system. We shall then apply the accounting system to the recording of credit sales and sales returns.

BOOKS OF PRIME ENTRY

The books of prime entry include a number of *day books* which list money amounts and other details taken from prime documents.

The day books used for credit sales and sales returns are:

- sales day book
- sales returns day book

These are called books of prime entry because they are the first place in the accounting system where prime documents are recorded.

A sales day book is set out in the following way with sample entries shown (a sales returns day book uses the same layout):

Sales Day Book						SDB 21
Date	Customer	Invoice No	Folio	Total	VAT*	Net
2007				£	£	£
5 Jan	Doyle & Co Ltd	901	SL 58	141.00	21.00	120.00
8 Jan	Sparkes & Sons Ltd	902	SL 127	188.00	28.00	160.00
13 Jan	T Young	903	SL 179	94.00	14.00	80.00
15 Jan	A-Z Supplies Ltd	904	SL 3	235.00	35.00	200.00
21 Jan	Sparkes & Sons Ltd	905	SL 127	141.00	21.00	120.00
31 Jan	Totals for month			799.00	119.00	680.00

* VAT = 17.5 per cent

Notes:

- The day book is prepared from prime documents – sales day book from sales invoices (or copies of sales invoices), and sales returns day book from credit notes (or copies) issued.
- The reference 'SDB 21' is used for cross-referencing to the book-keeping system: here it indicates that this is page 21 of the sales day book.
- The *folio* column is also used for cross-referencing purposes: 'SL' refers to Sales Ledger, followed by the account number.
- The *total* column records the amount of each prime document, ie after VAT has been included.
- The day book is totalled at appropriate intervals – daily, weekly, or monthly (as here) – the total of the *net* column tells the business the amount of credit sales (as here), or sales returns for the period.
- The amounts from the day books are recorded in the book-keeping system.
- When control accounts (see Chapter 4) are in use, the total for the month from the 'total' column is entered into the sales ledger control account from both the sales day book and the sales returns day book.

day books and Value Added Tax

Many businesses and other organisations are registered for Value Added Tax (VAT). When a business is registered for VAT:

- VAT is charged on invoices issued to customers
- an allowance for VAT is made on credit notes issued
- VAT charged on invoices received from VAT-registered suppliers and allowed on credit notes issued is set off against VAT charged on invoices issued (any surplus which cannot be set off in this way can be reclaimed from HM Customs and Excise, the VAT authority)

When writing up day books from VAT invoices and credit notes:

- enter the total amount of the invoice or credit note into the total column
- enter the VAT amount in the VAT column
- enter the net amount of the invoice or credit note, before VAT is added

When a business is not registered for VAT, it cannot charge VAT on invoices issued and it cannot reclaim VAT charged on invoices received from suppliers. In such circumstances the total amount of the invoice is recorded in both the net and total columns; a dash may be inserted in the VAT column. Likewise, VAT cannot be allowed on credit notes issued (nor recorded for credit notes received).

In this chapter we shall see how the VAT columns from the sales and sales returns day books are entered into the double-entry accounts. Chapter 11 shows how VAT on purchases and purchases returns is recorded in the accounts.

DOUBLE-ENTRY SYSTEM

The accounting system is organised on the basis of a number of *accounts* which record the money amounts of financial transactions: collectively these accounts are known as 'the ledger'.

Accounts are kept in the names of customers and of suppliers of the business, and also for other transactions such as the receipt and payment of money for various purposes. Accounts can be kept in the form of:

- handwritten records
- computer records

In a handwritten system, accounts are maintained either in a bound book or a series of separate sheets of paper or card – each account occupying a separate page. The business can set up its own manual system, or can buy one ready-made from a business supplies shop.

In a computerised system each account is held as data in a computer file. Whether a handwritten or computerised system is being used, the principles remain the same. For the moment we will concentrate on handwritten accounts.

A handwritten system can either use specially ruled accounting paper – known as ledger paper – which can be purchased from a business supplies shop, or a suitable layout can be ruled as follows:

Debit   **Name of Account, eg Sales Account**   Credit

Date	Details	£ p	Date	Details	£ p
↑ of trans-action	↑ name of other account	↑ amount of trans-action			

Note the following points about the layout of this account:

- the name of the account is written at the top (often followed by the account number)

- the account is divided into two identical halves, separated by a central double vertical line

- the left-hand side is called the 'debit' side ('debit' is abbreviated to 'Dr' – short for <u>D</u>ebto<u>R</u>)

- the right-hand side is called the 'credit' (or 'Cr') side

- the date, details and amount of the transaction are entered in the account

- in the 'details' column is entered the name of the other account (or book of prime entry) involved – this acts as a cross reference; as a further cross reference, a 'folio' column is often incorporated on each side of an account – to the left of the money amount columns

In practice, each account would occupy a whole page in a handwritten book-keeping system but, to save space when doing exercises, it is usual to put several accounts on a page. In future, in this book, the account layout will be simplified to give more clarity as follows (example transaction shown):

Dr   **Sales Account**   Cr

2007	£	2007	£
		31 Jan Sales Day Book SDB 21	680

This layout is often known in accounting jargon as a 'T' account; it is used to illustrate accounts because it separates in a simple way the two sides – debit and credit – of the account. An alternative style of account has three money columns: debit, credit and balance. This type of account is commonly used for bank statements, building society passbooks and computer accounting statements. Because the balance of the account is calculated after every transaction, it is known as a *running balance account.*

debits and credits

The principle of double-entry book-keeping is that two entries are made, for every financial transaction, usually in different accounts:

- one account is *debited* with the money amount of the transaction, and
- one account is *credited* with the money amount of the transaction

The principle is often known as the *dual aspect* of book-keeping, ie each transaction has a dual effect on the accounts – one account gains, while another account gives value by recording a payment or a liability.

Debit entries are on the left-hand side of the appropriate account, while credit entries are on the right. The rules for debits and credits are:

- *debit entry* – the account which gains value, or records an asset, or an expense
- *credit entry* – the account which gives value, or records a liability, or an income item

division of the ledger

Accounts, as mentioned above, are normally written on separate pages of a book known as 'the ledger'. In practice, several separate ledgers are kept: for credit sales transactions we shall be making use of the following ledgers:

- sales ledger, also known as the debtors ledger, containing the accounts of the firm's debtors (customers)
- cash book, containing the bank account and cash account records of the business
- main ledger (also often referred to as the general ledger or nominal ledger) containing sales account, sales returns account, Value Added Tax account, together with other accounts kept by the business

The following diagram shows how ledgers and accounts are used in connection with sales:

SALES (DEBTORS) LEDGER	MAIN (GENERAL) LEDGER
separate accounts for each *debtor,* ie customers who owe money to the business	• *sales account* – to record sales invoices issued • *sales returns account* – to record credit notes issued • *Value Added Tax account* – to record the VAT amounts of credit sales and sales returns

Note that main ledger contains a number of other accounts in connection with purchases (see Chapter 10), expenses, receipts and payments, and the assets and liabilities of the business.

METHODS OF CODING IN ACCOUNTING SYSTEMS

As a business grows, methods of coding need to be used to trace transactions through the accounting system, ie:

- prime documents
- books of prime entry
- double-entry accounts
- trial balance

Uses of coding in the stages of the accounting system are:

prime documents

- each document, eg invoice, credit note, is numbered
- goods listed on invoices have reference numbers, eg catalogue number, which, if a computer accounting system is used, will enable the business to analyse sales by product

books of prime entry

- each page of the day books is numbered
- the number of the document, eg invoice, credit note is recorded
- the number of the debtors or creditors account is recorded in the folio column, eg 'SL' for sales ledger, followed by the account number (or short name – see below)

double-entry accounts

- the accounts system is divided into sections, the division of the ledger: sales ledger, purchases ledger (see Chapter 10), cash book (Chapters 7 and 14), and main ledger

- each account is numbered eg 'SL 58' (or some accounting systems use an abbreviated name, or short name, eg the account of Peterhead Trading Company might be coded as 'PETER')

- main ledger accounts are numbered and are often arranged in a particular order, for example

0001 – 1299	Assets
2100 – 2399	Liabilities
3000 – 3099	Capital
4000 – 4999	Sales
5000 – 5299	Purchases
6000 – 8299	Expenses

ACCOUNTING SYSTEM FOR CREDIT SALES

The accounting system for credit sales fits together in the following way:

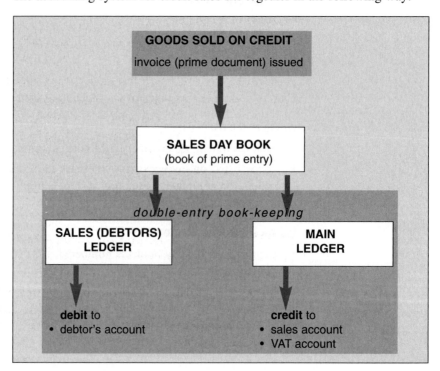

We shall now look in more detail at the sales day book and the double-entry accounts for credit sales. In the examples which follow we will assume that the business is registered for Value Added Tax and so:

- VAT is charged on invoices issued to customers
- VAT charged on invoices received from suppliers is either set off against VAT charged on invoices issued, or is reclaimed from HM Revenue & Customs

The VAT rate used in the examples is 17.5%.

WRITING UP THE SALES DAY BOOK

The sales day book lists the credit sales made by a business. Following the issue of an invoice for each transaction, the sales day book is prepared from sales invoices (or copies of sales invoices). Please refer back to the example of a sales day book which was shown earlier in this chapter on page 47.

In order to write up the sales day book we take sales invoices or copy invoices – that have been checked and authorised – for the period and enter the details:

- date of invoice
- name of customer
- sales invoice number
- cross reference to the customer's account number in the sales ledger, eg 'SL 58'
- enter the total amount of the invoice into the total column
- enter the VAT amount shown on the invoice – don't be concerned with any adjustments to the VAT for the effect of any settlement (cash) discounts (see page 32), simply record the VAT amount shown
- enter the net amount of the invoice (often described as 'goods or services total'), before VAT is added

DOUBLE-ENTRY BOOK-KEEPING FOR CREDIT SALES

After the sales day book has been written up and totalled, the information from it is transferred into the double-entry system. The accounts in the sales ledger and main ledger to record the transactions from the sales day book, seen earlier on page 47, are as follows:

SALES (DEBTORS) LEDGER

Dr		A-Z Supplies Ltd (account no 3)			Cr
2007			£	2007	£
15 Jan	Sales SDB 21		235		

Dr		Doyle & Co Ltd (account no 58)			Cr
2007			£	2007	£
5 Jan	Sales SDB 21		141		

Dr		Sparkes & Sons Ltd (account no 127)			Cr
2007			£	2007	£
8 Jan	Sales SDB 21		188		
21 Jan	Sales SDB 21		141		

Dr		T Young (account no 179)			Cr
2007			£	2007	£
13 Jan	Sales SDB 21		94		

MAIN LEDGER

Dr		Sales Account (account no 4001)		Cr
2007		£	2007	£
			31 Jan Sales Day Book SDB 21	680

Dr		Value Added Tax Account (account no 2200)		Cr
2007		£	2007	£
			31 Jan Sales Day Book SDB 21	119

Note that from the sales day book:

- the amounts from the total column *for each separate sale* have been debited to the accounts of the customers, ie the business has a debtor for the amounts shown
- the total of the VAT column, £119, has been credited to VAT account (which has given value)
- the total of the net column, £680, has been credited to sales account (which has given value)

- the sales day book incorporates a folio column which cross-references each transaction to the personal account of each debtor in the sales ledger (SL); this enables a particular transaction to be traced from prime document (invoice issued), through the book of prime entry (sales day book), to the debtor's ledger account

- each entry in the sales ledger and main ledger is cross-referenced back to the page number of the sales day book; here the reference is 'SDB 21'.

ACCOUNTING SYSTEM FOR SALES RETURNS

A credit note (see page 28) is the document issued by a business when it makes a refund to a customer who has bought goods on credit. A credit note reduces the amount owed by the debtor. *Sales returns* (or returns in) are when goods previously sold on credit are returned to the business by its customers.

The accounting procedures for sales returns involve:

- *prime documents* – credit notes issued to customers
- *book of prime entry* – sales returns day book
- *double-entry accounts* – sales ledger (accounts for each debtor) and main ledger (sales returns account, which records the totals of credit notes issued, and Value Added Tax account, which records the VAT amount of sales returns)

The accounting system for sales returns is summarised as follows:

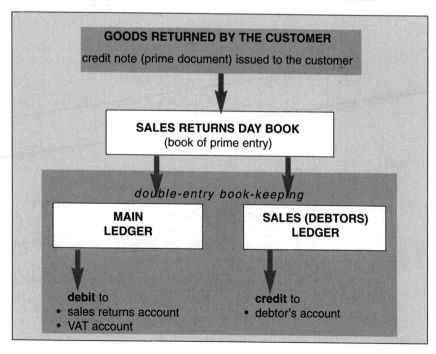

We shall now look in more detail at the sales returns day book and the double-entry accounts for sales returns. Note that the business is registered for Value Added Tax.

SALES RETURNS DAY BOOK

The sales returns day book uses virtually the same layout as the sales day book seen on page 47 of this chapter. It operates in a similar way, storing up information about sales returns until such time as a transfer is made into the double-entry accounts system. The prime documents for sales returns day book are credit notes (or copies of credit notes) issued to customers.

example transactions

2007

| 15 Jan | T Young returns goods, £40 + VAT, credit note no CN702 issued |
| 27 Jan | A-Z Supplies Ltd returns goods, £120 + VAT, credit note no CN703 issued |

The sales returns day book is written up as shown below:

Sales Returns Day Book						SRDB 5
Date	Customer	Credit Note No	Folio	Total	VAT*	Net
2007				£	£	£
15 Jan	T Young	CN702	SL 179	47.00	7.00	40.00
27 Jan	A-Z Supplies Ltd	CN703	SL 3	141.00	21.00	120.00
31 Jan	Totals for month			188.00	28.00	160.00

* VAT = 17.5 per cent

Notes:

- The sales returns day book is prepared from credit notes (or copies of credit notes) issued to customers.
- The day book is totalled at appropriate intervals – weekly or monthly.
- The VAT-inclusive amounts from the total column are credited to the debtors' personal accounts in the sales ledger.

- The total of the VAT column is transferred to the debit of the VAT account in the main ledger.
- The total of the net column tells the business the amount of sales returns for the period. This amount is transferred to the debit of sales returns account in the main ledger.
- The total column records the amount of each credit note issued, ie after VAT has been included. When control accounts (see Chapter 4) are in use, the total for the month of the 'total' column is entered into the sales ledger control account.

DOUBLE-ENTRY BOOK-KEEPING FOR SALES RETURNS

After the sales returns day book has been written up and totalled, the information from it is transferred into the double-entry system. The accounts in the sales ledger and main ledger to record the transactions from the above sales returns day book (including any other transactions already recorded on these accounts) are:

SALES (DEBTORS) LEDGER

Dr	A-Z Supplies Ltd (account no 3)		Cr
2007	£	2007	£
15 Jan Sales SDB 21	235	27 Jan Sales Returns SRDB 5	141

Dr	T Young (account no 179)		Cr
2007	£	2007	£
12 Jan Sales SDB 21	94	15 Jan Sales Returns SRDB 5	47

MAIN LEDGER

Dr	Sales Returns Account (account no 4010)		Cr
2007	£	2007	£
31 Jan Sales Returns Day Book SRDB 5	160		

Dr	Value Added Tax Account (account no 2200)		Cr
2007	£	2007	£
31 Jan Sales Returns Day Book SRDB 5	28	31 Jan Sales Day Book SDB 21	119

THE USE OF ANALYSED SALES DAY BOOKS

As well as the layout of the day books we have seen in this chapter, a business can use analysed day books whenever it needs to analyse its sales and sales returns between

- different departments, eg a store with departments for furniture, carpets and curtains, hardware
- different categories of goods sold, eg paint, wallpaper, brushes, or services supplied

For example, a wholesaler of decorators' supplies may decide to write up its sales day book as shown below.

Sales Day Book								SDB 48
Date	Customer	Invoice No	Folio	Total	VAT*	Net	Paint	Wallpaper	Brushes
2007				£	£	£	£	£	£
9 Aug	DIY Sales Limited	1478	SL 59	235.00	35.00	200.00	75.00	125.00	–
12 Aug	T Lane Decorators	1479	SL 108	141.00	21.00	120.00	–	100.00	20.00
16 Aug	Colour Painters Limited	1480	SL 38	329.00	49.00	280.00	150.00	100.00	30.00
23 Aug	Southern Decorators	1481	SL 211	188.00	28.00	160.00	100.00	60.00	–
31 Aug	Totals for month			893.00	133.00	760.00	325.00	385.00	50.00

* VAT = 17.5 per cent

Notes:

- The references in the folio column are to 'SL' (Sales Ledger), followed by the customer's account number.

- The analysis columns – here paint, wallpaper, brushes – show the amount of sales net of VAT (ie before VAT is added).

- The analysis columns analyse the net amount from sales invoices of products sold or services supplied.

In using analysed sales day books and sales returns day books, a business adapts the accounting records to suit its own particular requirements for information. There is not a standard way in which to present the books of prime entry – the needs of the user of the information are all important. By using analysed day books, the owner of the business can see how much has been sold by departments, or categories of goods and services.

BATCH CONTROL SYSTEMS

A variation on the use of day books is often used – particularly with computer accounting programs. With batched data entry a series of transactions for a day, week or month relating to, say, sales invoices is entered into the accounts in one 'run'. By batching, the computer operator concentrates on entering one type of transaction without the need to keep changing from one area of the computer program to another. Before entering a batch of transactions they are pre-listed on a separate batch control form such as that shown below for a batch of sales invoices:

Batch Control: sales invoices

Customer		Invoice		Total	VAT*	Net
Account No	Name	Date	No	£	£	£
		2007				
SL 58	Doyle & Co Ltd	5 Jan	901	141.00	21.00	120.00
SL 127	Sparkes & Sons Ltd	8 Jan	902	188.00	28.00	160.00
SL 179	T Young	13 Jan	903	94.00	14.00	80.00
SL 3	A-Z Supplies Ltd	15 Jan	904	235.00	35.00	200.00
SL 127	Sparkes & Sons Ltd	21 Jan	905	141.00	21.00	120.00
Check list totals				799.00	119.00	680.00

Prepared by	*Gill Pate*	Date	*31 Jan 2007*
Checked by	*Karan Hopwood*	Date	*31 Jan 2007*
Posted by	*Ian Turner*	Date	*31 Jan 2007*

* VAT = 17.5 per cent

The sales invoice batch form is completed from invoices (or copy invoices) which have been prepared and checked. The transactions are then entered into the sales ledger section of the computer accounting program. The computer screen shows the total money amount of sales invoices and this is compared with the check list total from the sales invoice batch control form; if there is a discrepancy, the error must be located and corrected.

Note that businesses often use batch control forms in place of day books. Also, when a sales ledger control account (see Chapter 4) is in use, the total from the batch control form is recorded in the control account.

Case
Study

WYVERN TRADERS

To bring together the material covered in this chapter, we will look at a comprehensive Case Study which makes use of:

- **books of prime entry**

  - sales day book

  - sales returns day book

- **double-entry accounts**

  - sales (debtors) ledger

  - main ledger

The Case Study also includes a diagram (see page 63) which summarises the procedures for recording credit sales and sales returns transactions in the accounting system.

situation

Wyvern Traders is a wholesaler of stationery and office equipment. The business is registered for VAT. The following are the credit sales and sales returns transactions for April 2007:

2007	
2 Apr	Sold goods to P Woodhouse, £200.00 + VAT, invoice no 2416
9 Apr	P Woodhouse returns goods, £60.00 + VAT, we issue credit note no CN12
14 Apr	Sold goods to Blackheath Limited, £80.00 + VAT, invoice no 2417
21 Apr	Blackheath Limited returns goods, £10.00 + VAT, we issue credit note no CN13
26 Apr	Sold goods to Butterworth Limited, £160.00 + VAT, invoice no 2418

The day books and double-entry accounts are illustrated on the next two pages: arrows indicate the transfers from the day books to the individual accounts. Note that some accounts have been represented on both pages in order to show, on the same page, the accounts relating to a particular day book: in practice a business would keep all the transactions together in one account.

Sales Day Book

SDB 30

Date	Customer	Invoice No	Folio	Total		VAT		Net	
2007				£	p	£	p	£	p
2 Apr	P Woodhouse	2416	SL 248	235	00	35	00	200	00
14 Apr	Blackheath Ltd	2417	SL 27	94	00	14	00	80	00
26 Apr	Butterworth Ltd	2418	SL 35	188	00	28	00	160	00
30 Apr	Totals for month			517	00	77	00	440	00

SALES (DEBTORS) LEDGER

Dr   **Blackheath Ltd** (account no 27)   Cr

Date	Details		£	p	Date	Details	£	p
2007					2007			
14 Apr	Sales	SDB 30	94	00				

Dr   **Butterworth Ltd** (account no 35)   Cr

Date	Details		£	p	Date	Details	£	p
2007					2007			
26 Apr	Sales	SDB 30	188	00				

Dr   **P Woodhouse** (account no 248)   Cr

Date	Details		£	p	Date	Details	£	p
2007					2007			
2 Apr	Sales	SDB 30	235	00				

MAIN LEDGER

Dr   **Value Added Tax Account** (account no 2200)   Cr

Date	Details	£	p	Date	Details	£	p
2007				2007			
				30 Apr	Sales Day Book SDB 30	77	00

Dr   **Sales Account** (account no 4001)   Cr

Date	Details	£	p	Date	Details	£	p
2007				2007			
				30 Apr	Sales Day Book SDB 30	440	00

Sales Returns Day Book

SRDB 4

Date	Customer	Credit Note No	Folio	Total		VAT		Net	
				£	p	£	p	£	p
2007									
9 Apr	P Woodhouse	CN 12	SL 248	70	50	10	50	60	00
21 Apr	Blackheath Ltd	CN 13	SL 27	11	75	1	75	10	00
30 Apr	Totals for month			82	25	12	25	70	00

SALES (DEBTORS) LEDGER

Dr   **Blackheath Ltd** (account no 27)   Cr

Date	Details		£ p	Date	Details		£ p
2007				2007			
14 Apr	Sales	SDB 30	94 00*	21 Apr	Sales Returns	SRDB 4	11 75

Dr   **P Woodhouse** (account no 248)   Cr

Date	Details		£ p	Date	Details		£ p
2007				2007			
2 Apr	Sales	SDB 30	235 00*	9 Apr	Sales Returns	SRDB 4	70 50

MAIN LEDGER

Dr   **Value Added Tax Account** (account no 2200)   Cr

Date	Details		£ p	Date	Details		£ p
2007				2007			
30 Apr	Sales Returns Day Book	SRDB 4	12 25	30 Apr	Sales Day Book SDB 30		77 00*

Dr   **Sales Returns Account** (account no 4010)   Cr

Date	Details		£ p	Date	Details		£ p
2007				2007			
30 Apr	Sales Returns Day Book	SRDB 4	70 00				

* transactions entered previously

The diagram below summarises the material we have studied in this chapter. It shows the procedures for recording transactions in the accounting system for

- credit sales
- sales returns

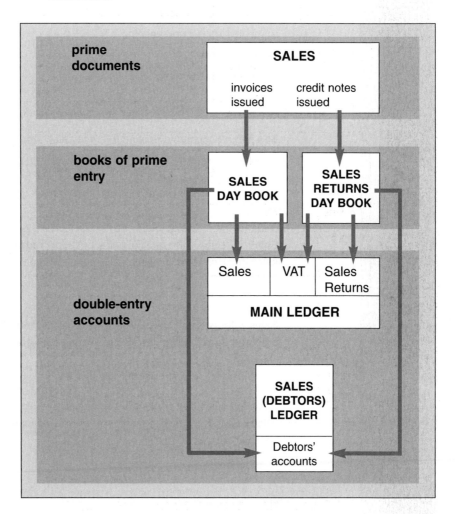

BALANCING ACCOUNTS

Where there is only one transaction recorded on an account, the amount of the transaction is the balance of the account, ie the total of the account to date. With several transactions recorded on an account it is necessary to work out the balance more formally from time-to-time. Such balancing of accounts is usually carried out at the end of each month, sometimes more often. We will look in more detail at balancing accounts in the next chapter.

- The accounting system comprises a number of specific stages of recording and presenting financial transactions:
  - prime documents (also known as source documents)
  - books of prime entry (eg day books)
  - double-entry book-keeping
  - trial balance
  - financial statements

- The prime documents relating to credit sales are:
  - sales invoices
  - credit notes issued

- Sales day book is the book of prime entry for credit sales. It is prepared from sales invoices (or copy invoices) sent to customers.

- Sales returns day book is the book of prime entry for sales returns. It is prepared from credit notes (or copy credit notes) issued to customers.

- Analysed sales day books are used when a business wishes to analyse its sales between different departments or different categories of goods sold or services supplied.

- Recording credit sales in the double-entry system uses:
  - prime documents, sales invoices
  - book of prime entry, sales day book
  - double-entry accounts, sales ledger and main ledger

- Recording sales returns in the double-entry system uses:
  - prime documents, credit notes issued to customers
  - book of prime entry, sales returns day book
  - double-entry accounts, sales ledger and main ledger

H/W (HOME) by heart the definitions

Key Terms		
	prime documents	source documents for the accounting records
	books of prime entry	the first accounting books in which transactions are recorded
	folio	a form of cross-referencing used in the accounting system
	ledger	collection of accounts; a sub-division of the accounting system
	debit entry	records a gain in value, an asset, or an expense
	credit entry	records the giving of value, a liability, or an income item
	sales	the sale of goods in which the business or organisation trades
	sales day book	book of prime entry prepared from sales invoices (or copy invoices)
	sales returns	goods sold on credit which are returned by customers
	credit note	the prime document for returned goods – issued by the business allowing credit to the customer
	sales returns day book	book of prime entry prepared from credit notes (or copy credit notes) issued to customers
	analysed sales day book	day book which incorporates analysis columns, for example between
		– different departments
		– different categories of goods sold, or services supplied
	sales (debtors) ledger	division of the ledger which contains the accounts of the firm's debtors (customers)
	main (general) ledger	division of the ledger which includes
		– sales account
		– sales returns account
		– Value Added Tax account

Student Activities

3.1   Which one of the following is a book of prime entry?

(a)   sales day book

(b)   sales account

(c)   account of T Smith, a debtor

(d)   profit and loss account

Answer (a) or (b) or (c) or (d)

3.2   Which one of the following is in the right order?

(a)   sales invoice; sales day book; sales account; debtor's account

(b)   sales day book; debtor's account; sales account; sales invoice

(c)   sales day book; sales invoice; debtor's account; sales account

(d)   sales account; debtor's account; sales invoice; sales day book

Answer (a) or (b) or (c) or (d)

3.3   Explain in note format:

(a)   the principles of recording a credit sales transaction in the accounting system

(b)   the principles of recording a sales returns transaction in the accounting system

---

In the Activities which follow, the rate of Value Added Tax is to be calculated at the current rate (17.5% at the time of writing). When calculating VAT amounts, you should ignore fractions of a penny, ie round down to a whole penny.

For Activities 3.4 and 3.5 use a cross-referencing system incorporating the following:

- *sales day book*   – *SDB 50*
  sales returns day book – *SRDB 8*

- *sales ledger account numbers*
  A Cox   – *account no 32*
  Dines Stores   – *account no 48*
  E Grainger   – *account no 55*
  M Kershaw   – *account no 90*
  D Lloyd   – *account no 95*
  Malvern Stores   – *account no 110*
  Pershore Retailers   – *account no 145*
  P Wilson   – *account no 172*

- *main ledger account numbers*
  sales account   – *account no 4001*
  sales returns account   – *account no 4010*
  Value Added Tax account– *account no 2200*

3.4 Wyvern Wholesalers sells office stationery to other businesses in the area. During April 2007 the following credit transactions took place:

2007

2 Apr	Sold goods to Malvern Stores £55 + VAT, invoice no 4578
5 Apr	Sold goods to Pershore Retailers £65 + VAT, invoice no 4579
7 Apr	Sold goods to E Grainger £28 + VAT, invoice no 4580
9 Apr	Sold goods to P Wilson £58 + VAT, invoice no 4581
12 Apr	Sold goods to M Kershaw £76 + VAT, invoice no 4582
14 Apr	Sold goods to D Lloyd £66 + VAT, invoice no 4583
19 Apr	Sold goods to A Cox £33 + VAT, invoice no 4584
22 Apr	Sold goods to Dines Stores £102 + VAT, invoice no 4585
23 Apr	Sold goods to Malvern Stores £47 + VAT, invoice no 4586
26 Apr	Sold goods to P Wilson £35 + VAT, invoice no 4587
29 Apr	Sold goods to A Cox £82 + VAT, invoice no 4588

You are to:

(a)   enter the above transactions in Wyvern Wholesaler's sales day book for April 2007

(b)   record the accounting entries in Wyvern Wholesaler's sales ledger and main ledger

3.5 The following details are the sales returns of Wyvern Wholesalers for April 2007. They are to be

(a)   entered in the sales returns day book for April 2007

(b)   recorded in the sales ledger and main ledger (use the ledgers already prepared in the answer to Activity 3.4)

2007

8 Apr	Pershore Retailers returns goods £20 + VAT, we issue credit note no CN572
12 Apr	E Grainger returns goods £28 + VAT, we issue credit note no CN573
16 Apr	D Lloyd returns goods £33 + VAT, we issue credit note no CN574
28 Apr	Malvern Stores returns goods £20 + VAT, we issue credit note no CN575
30 Apr	A Cox returns goods £40 + VAT, we issue credit note no CN576

4 Balancing accounts and control account for sales

this chapter covers . . .

In the previous chapter we saw how to record credit sales and sales returns transactions in the ledger accounts of the double-entry system.

When you use the 'traditional' form of double-entry account (the 'T' account), it is necessary to calculate the balance of each account from time-to-time, according to the needs of the business. The balance of an account is the running total of that account to date, eg the amount of sales made, the amount due for VAT. In this chapter we shall see how this balancing of accounts is carried out.

We also develop the double-entry system by seeing how control accounts are used to record, by means of totals, the transactions passing through the accounts that they control. In particular, we shall be looking at how sales ledger control account and the subsidiary (sales) ledger accounts fit into the double-entry system.

PERFORMANCE CRITERIA COVERED

unit 30: INTRODUCTORY ACCOUNTING

element 30.1

process sales and receipts

E   post sales invoices and credit notes into the subsidiary (sales) ledger and main (general) ledger

BALANCING ACCOUNTS

At regular intervals, often at the end of each month, accounts are balanced in order to show the running total of the account to date, for example:

- the amount of sales made
- the amount of sales returns
- the amount owing by each debtor
- the amount of VAT due to or from HM Revenue & Customs

When accounts are produced using a computer accounting system, there is no need to balance each account – the balance is calculated automatically after each transaction and shown in a third money column (after debit and credit).

METHOD OF BALANCING ACCOUNTS

Set out below is an example of a debtor's account which has been balanced at the month-end:

Dr			**Keene and Company**			Cr
2007		£	2007			£
1 Jun	Balance b/d	110	14 Jun	Sales Returns		190
8 Jun	Sales	460	21 Jun	Sales Returns		130
17 Jun	Sales	240	30 Jun	Balance c/d		630
29 Jun	Sales	140				
		950				950
1 Jul	Balance b/d	630				

The steps involved in balancing accounts are set out below.

Step 1

The entries in the debit and credit money columns are totalled; these totals are not recorded in ink on the account at this stage, but can be recorded either as sub-totals in pencil on the account, or noted on a separate piece of paper. In the example above, the debit side totals £950, while the credit side is £320.

Step 2

The difference between the two totals is the balance of the account and this is entered on the account:

- on the side of the smaller total
- on the next available line
- with the date of balancing (often the last day of the month)
- with the description 'balance c/d', or 'balance carried down'

In the account of Keene and Company above, the balance carried down is £950 – £320 = £630, entered in the credit column.

Step 3

Both sides of the account are now totalled, including the balance which has just been entered, and the totals (the same on both sides) are entered on the same line in the appropriate column, and bold-underlined or double-underlined. The underline indicates that the account has been balanced at this point using the figures above the total: the figures above the underline should not be added in to anything below the underline.

In the debtor's account on the previous page the totals on each side of the account are £950.

Step 4

As we are using double-entry book-keeping, there must be an opposite entry to the 'balance c/d' calculated in Step 2. The same money amount is entered on the other side of the account below the underlined totals entered in Step 3. We have now completed both the debit and credit entry. The date is usually recorded as the next day after 'balance c/d', ie often the first day of the following month, and the description can be 'balance b/d' or 'balance brought down'.

Balance b/d

In the example above, the balance brought down on the account of 1 July 2007 is £630 debit; this means that, according to the accounting records, Keene and Company owes £630, ie is a debtor of the business. (You will note that the first item on the debit side of the account is '1 Jun Balance b/d £110': this shows that the account was balanced in May, with the balance brought down to June.)

Credit sales transactions for July for this customer will be recorded on the debit side of the account, below the balance brought down; any sales returns transactions will be recorded on the credit side.

a practical point:

When balancing accounts, use a pen and not a pencil (except for Step 1). If any errors are made, cross them through neatly with a single line, and write the corrected version on the line below. Do not use correcting fluid: at best it conceals errors, at worst it conceals fraudulent transactions.

FURTHER EXAMPLES OF BALANCING ACCOUNTS

Dr		£		Temeside Traders	Cr £
2007		£	2007		£
1 Apr	Balance b/d	500	30 Apr	Balance c/d	1,100
9 Apr	Sales	250			
16 Apr	Sales	200			
23 Apr	Sales	150			
		1,100			1,100
1 May	Balance b/d	1,100			

The above debtor's account has transactions on one side only, but is still balanced in the same way. This account shows that, according to the accounting records, Temeside Traders owes £1,100, ie is a debtor of the business.

Dr		£		B Lewis Limited	Cr £
2007		£	2007		£
1 Aug	Balance b/d	350	9 Aug	Sales Returns	350
12 Aug	Sales	150	20 Aug	Sales Returns	150
		500			500

This debtor's account has a 'nil' balance after the transactions for August have taken place. The two sides of the account are totalled and, as both debit and credit side are the same amount, there is nothing further to do, apart from entering the bold- or double-underlined total.

Dr		£		Sales Account	Cr £
2007		£	2007		£
			31 Jan	Sales Day Book	680

This account has just the one transaction and, in practice, there is no need to balance it. It should be clear that the account has a credit balance of £680, which is probably the sales for the first month of the new financial year.

Dr	Malvern Manufacturing Company		Cr
2007	£	2007	£
1 Nov Balance b/d	250	4 Nov Sales Returns	250

This debtor's account has a 'nil' balance, with just one transaction on each side. All that is needed here is to bold- or double-underline the amount on both sides.

CONTROL ACCOUNTS

The previous chapter looked at the basics of the double-entry book-keeping system for credit sales and sales returns. This system uses a main ledger – which contains the accounts for sales, sales returns and VAT – and a sales ledger which contains the accounts of the debtors to whom the business has sold goods on credit terms. We are now going to develop the book-keeping system by introducing control accounts – these are featured in all but the smallest manual systems and are used by all computer accounting systems. We will look firstly at the concept of control accounts, and will then focus on the sales ledger control account which fits in with the book-keeping for credit sales and sales returns.

THE CONCEPT OF CONTROL ACCOUNTS

Control accounts are 'master' accounts which control a number of subsidiary accounts. Control accounts work in the following way:

The control account (also known as a *totals account*) is used to record the totals of transactions passing through the subsidiary accounts. In this way, the balance of the control account will always be equal to the total balances of the subsidiary accounts, unless an error has occurred. Two commonly-used control accounts are:

- **sales ledger control account**, which controls the subsidiary (sales) ledger
- **purchases ledger control account** (see Chapter 11), which controls the subsidiary (purchases) ledger

In the illustration above we have seen how a control account acts as a master account for a number of subsidiary accounts. The principle is that, if the total of the opening balances for subsidiary accounts is known, together with the total of amounts increasing these balances, and the total of amounts decreasing these balances, then the total of the closing balances for the subsidiary accounts can be calculated.

For example:

	£
Total of opening balances	50,000
Add increases	10,000
	60,000
Less decreases	12,000
Total of closing balances	48,000

The total of the closing balances can now be checked against a separate listing of the balances of the subsidiary accounts to ensure that the two figures agree. If they do, it proves that the ledgers within the section are correct unless an error has occurred. Let us now apply this concept to one of the divisions of the ledger – sales ledger.

The diagram on the next page shows the personal accounts which form the subsidiary (sales) ledger of a particular business – in practice there would, of course, be more than four accounts involved ('bank' and 'discount allowed' transactions will be explained fully in Chapter 7). The sales ledger control account acts as a totals account, which records totals of the transactions passing through the subsidiary accounts which it controls. Notice that transactions appear in the control account *on the same side* as they appear in the subsidiary accounts. The sales ledger control account can be reconciled with the balances of the subsidiary accounts which it controls (see below). Thus, control accounts act as an aid to locating errors: if the control account and subsidiary accounts agree, then the error is likely to lie elsewhere. In this way the control account acts as an intermediate checking device – proving the arithmetical accuracy of the ledger section.

Normally the whole of a subsidiary ledger section is controlled by one control account, eg sales ledger control account. However, it is also possible to have a number of separate control accounts for sections of the subsidiary

Dr	Sales Ledger Control Account		Cr
2007		£	2007	£
1 Jan	Balance b/d	500	31 Jan Bank*	443
31 Jan	Sales	700	31 Jan Discount allowed*	7
			31 Jan Sales returns	70
			31 Jan Balance c/d	680
		1,200		1,200
1 Feb	Balance b/d	680		

Dr	A Ackroyd		Cr
2007		£	2007	£
1 Jan	Balance b/d	100	12 Jan Bank*	98
6 Jan	Sales	150	12 Jan Discount allowed*	2
			31 Jan Balance c/d	150
		250		250
1 Feb	Balance b/d	150		

Dr	B Barnes		Cr
2007		£	2007	£
1 Jan	Balance b/d	200	13 Jan Bank*	195
6 Jan	Sales	250	13 Jan Discount allowed*	5
			27 Jan Sales returns	50
			31 Jan Balance c/d	200
		450		450
1 Feb	Balance b/d	200		

Dr	C Cox		Cr
2007		£	2007	£
1 Jan	Balance b/d	50	20 Jan Bank*	50
15 Jan	Sales	200	29 Jan Sales returns	20
			31 Jan Balance c/d	180
		250		250
1 Feb	Balance b/d	180		

Dr	D Douglas		Cr
2007		£	2007	£
1 Jan	Balance b/d	150	30 Jan Bank*	100
20 Jan	Sales	100	31 Jan Balance c/d	150
		250		250
1 Feb	Balance b/d	150		

* Note that the book-keeping transactions for 'bank' and 'discount allowed' will be explained fully in Chapter 7.

ledger, eg sales ledger control account A-K, sales ledger control account L-Z. It is for a business – the user of the accounting system – to decide what is most suitable, taking into account the number of accounts in the subsidiary (sales) ledger, together with the type of book-keeping system – manual or computerised.

From the diagram on the previous page the sales ledger control account and subsidiary (sales) ledger accounts will be agreed at the beginning and end of the month, as follows:

Reconciliation of sales ledger control account		
	1 January 2007	*31 January 2007*
	£	£
A Ackroyd	100	150
B Barnes	200	200
C Cox	50	180
D Douglas	150	150
Sales ledger control account	500	680

The business will decide how often to reconcile (agree) the control account with the subsidiary accounts – weekly, monthly, quarterly or annually. Any discrepancy should be investigated immediately and the error(s) traced.

SALES LEDGER CONTROL ACCOUNT

The set-out of a sales ledger control account (also known as a debtors control account) is shown below. Study the layout carefully and read the text which explains the additional items, some of which have not yet been covered but which will be dealt with in later chapters.

Dr		Sales Ledger Control Account		Cr
	£			£
Balance b/d		Cash/cheques received from debtors		
Credit sales		Settlement (cash) discount allowed		
Returned cheques		Sales returns		
Interest charged to debtors		Bad debts written off		
		Set-off/contra entries		
		Balance c/d		
Balance b/d				

balance b/d

The figure for balance b/d on the debit side of the control account represents the total of the balances of the individual debtors' accounts in the sales ledger. This principle is illustrated in the diagram on page 74. Remember that, at the end of the month (or other period covered by the control account), the account must be balanced and carried down (on the credit side) on the last day of the month, and then brought down (on the debit side) on the first day of the next month.

Note that it is possible for a debtor's account to have a credit balance, instead of the usual debit balance. This may come about, for example, because the debtor has paid for goods and then returned them, or has overpaid in error: the business owes the amount due, ie the debtor has a credit balance for the time being. Most accounting systems 'net off' any such credit balances against the debit balances to give an overall figure for debtors.

credit sales

Only credit sales – and not cash sales – are entered in the control account because only credit sales are recorded in the debtors' accounts. The total sales of the business may well comprise both credit and cash sales.

returned cheques

If a debtor's cheque is returned unpaid by the bank, ie the cheque has 'bounced', then authorisation for the entries to be made in the book-keeping system must be given by the accounts supervisor. These entries are:

– *debit* debtor's account

– *credit* cash book (bank columns)

As a transaction has been made in a debtor's account, then the amount must also be recorded in the sales ledger control account – on the debit side. Note that the returned cheque is the prime document for the adjustment – like other prime documents it should be stored securely for future reference.

interest charged to debtors

Sometimes a business will charge a debtor for slow payment of an account. The accounting entries, which must be authorised by the supervisor, are:

– *debit* debtor's account

– *credit* interest received account

As a debit transaction has been made in the debtor's account, so a debit entry must be recorded in the control account. The documentation which shows how the interest has been calculated should be stored for future reference.

bad debts written off

The book-keeping entries after a bad debt has been authorised for write off (see Chapter 17) are:

– *debit* bad debts written off account

– *credit* debtor's account

A credit transaction is entered in a debtor's account. This is because the control account 'masters' the subsidiary (sales) ledger and so the transaction must also be recorded as a credit transaction in the control account.

set-off/contra entries

These entries occur when the same person or business has an account in both the subsidiary (sales) ledger and the subsidiary (purchases) ledger, ie they are both buying from, and selling to, the business whose accounts we are preparing.

Set-off contra entries will be looked at in more detail in Chapter 11 when we cover the purchases ledger control account; there we will see the book-keeping entries which affect the control accounts.

CONTROL ACCOUNTS AS AN AID TO MANAGEMENT

When the manager of a business needs to know the figure for debtors (or creditors) – important information for the manager – the balance of the appropriate control account will give the information immediately. There is no need to add up the balances of all the individual debtors' (or creditors') accounts.

If a computer accounting system is used it will automatically post entries to the control accounts. It can print out the balances of the control accounts at any time.

The use of control accounts makes fraud more difficult – particularly in a manual accounting system. If a fraudulent transaction is to be recorded on a subsidiary account, the transaction must also be entered in the control account. As the control account will be either maintained by a supervisor, or checked regularly by the manager, the control accounts add another level of security within the accounting system.

Control accounts can also help in locating errors. Remember, though, that a control account only proves the arithmetical accuracy of the subsidiary accounts which it controls – there could still be errors within the subsidiary ledger section.

CONTROL ACCOUNTS AND BOOK-KEEPING

A business must decide how to use control accounts in its book-keeping system. The usual way of doing this is to incorporate the control accounts into double-entry book-keeping.

The control accounts therefore form part of the double-entry system in the main ledger. This means that the individual accounts of debtors (and creditors) are not part of double-entry, but are *subsidiary accounts* which record how much each debtor owes (and how much is owed to each creditor). From time-to-time, the balances of the subsidiary accounts are agreed with the balance of the appropriate control account, and any discrepancies investigated.

The diagram which follows shows how the sales ledger control account is incorporated in the main ledger of the double-entry book-keeping system, with the individual debtors' accounts kept in the form of a subsidiary (sales) ledger.

When a sales ledger control account is in use and journal entries are made (eg for correction of errors – see Chapter 20), transactions involving debtors' accounts must be recorded in:

- the sales ledger control account in the main ledger
- the subsidiary (sales) ledger

INFORMATION SOURCES FOR SALES LEDGER CONTROL ACCOUNT

Control accounts use totals (remember that their other name is 'totals accounts') for the week, month, quarter or year – depending on what time period is decided upon by the business. The totals for sales ledger control account come from a number of sources in the accounting system:

- total credit sales (including VAT) – from the 'total' column of the sales day book
- total sales returns (including VAT) – from the 'total' column of the sales returns day book
- total cash/cheques received from debtors – from the cash book (see Chapter 7)
- returned cheques – from the cash book
- total settlement discount allowed – from the discount allowed column of the cash book (see Chapter 7), or from discount allowed account
- bad debts – from the journal, or bad debts written off account (see Chapter 17)
- set-off/contra entries (see page 224) – from the journal (see Chapter 19)

Chapter Summary

- The traditional 'T' account needs to be balanced at regular intervals – often the month-end.

- The 'balance b/d' is the account balance at the start of the next period.

- Control accounts (or totals accounts) are 'master' accounts, which control a number of subsidiary accounts.

- Two commonly used control accounts are:
  - sales ledger control account
  - purchases ledger control account

- Transactions are recorded on the same side of the control account as on the subsidiary accounts.

- Control accounts are an aid to management:
  - they give up-to-date information on the total of debtors (or creditors)
  - by making fraud more difficult
  - in helping to locate errors

- Control accounts are normally incorporated into the main ledger of the double-entry book-keeping system. The subsidiary accounts, eg for debtors, are in a separate subsidiary ledger – subsidiary (sales) ledger.

Key Terms

balance of account	the running total of the account to date
control account	a 'master' account which controls a number of subsidiary accounts
sales ledger control account	a 'master' account which controls the subsidiary (sales) ledger

Student Activities

4.1 Balance the following accounts at 30 April 2007, bringing down the balances on 1 May:

Dr		Sales Account		Cr
2007		£	2007	£
			1 Apr Balance b/d	12,555
			30 Apr Sales Day Book	4,640

Dr		Sales Returns Account		Cr
2007		£	2007	£
1 Apr Balance b/d		527		
30 Apr Sales Returns Day Book		200		

Dr		Value Added Tax Account		Cr
2007		£	2007	£
30 Apr Sales Returns Day Book		35	1 Apr Balance b/d	1,233
			30 Apr Sales Day Book	812

Dr		T Johnson		Cr
2007		£	2007	£
1 Apr Balance b/d		496		
5 Apr Sales		198		
20 Apr Sales		467		
26 Apr Sales		302		

Dr		Doyle Traders		Cr
2007		£	2007	£
1 Apr Balance b/d		183	14 Apr Sales Returns	47
8 Apr Sales		221		
22 Apr Sales		395		

4.2 You have the following information:

- opening debtor balances at start of month £18,600
- credit sales for month £9,100
- sales returns for month £800

What is the figure for closing debtor balances at the end of the month?

(a) £10,300

(b) £26,900

(c) £27,700

(d) £28,500

Answer (a) or (b) or (c) or (d)

4.3 A friend has recently started work as an accounts clerk for a large electrical wholesalers. He asks you the following questions about control accounts:

- "What are the principles of control accounts?"
- "I've heard it said that control accounts help the management of the business. How is this?"
- "In our double-entry system we have a sales ledger control account in the main ledger, with an account for each debtor kept in the subsidiary (sales) ledger. I thought you told me earlier that debtors' accounts were part of double-entry ..."

Write answers to your friend.

4.4 Prepare a sales ledger control account for the month of June 2007 from the following information:

2007		£
1 Jun	Debit balance brought down	17,491
30 Jun	Credit sales for month	42,591
	Sales returns	1,045
	Payments received from debtors	39,024

Balance the account at 30 June 2007.

4.5 The main ledger of Shire Traders contains the following accounts on 1 February 2007:

sales, balance £5,097.24 credit

sales returns, balance £346.97 debit

Value Added Tax, balance £452.31 credit

The subsidiary (sales) ledger contains the following accounts on 1 February 2007:

Arrow Valley Retailers, balance £826.40 debit

B Brick (Builders) Limited, balance £59.28 debit

Mereford Manufacturing Company, balance £293.49 debit

Redgrove Restorations, balance £724.86 debit

Wyvern Warehouse Limited, balance £108.40 debit

The following transactions, which have been authorised by the accounts supervisor, took place during February 2007:

3 Feb Sold goods on credit to Arrow Valley Retailers £205.75 + VAT, invoice no 2731

5 Feb Sold goods on credit to Mereford Manufacturing Company £112.37 + VAT, invoice no 2732

6 Feb Redgrave Restorations returned goods £85.90 + VAT, credit note no CN127 issued

10 Feb Sold goods on credit to Wyvern Warehouse Limited £412.96 + VAT, invoice no 2733

12 Feb Sold goods on credit to Redgrove Restorations £258.21 + VAT, invoice no 2734

17 Feb Mereford Manufacturing Company returned goods £45.27 + VAT, credit note no CN128 issued

19 Feb Sold goods on credit to B Brick (Builders) Limited £275.36 + VAT, invoice no 2735

23 Feb Sold goods on credit to Redgrove Restorations £204.47 + VAT, invoice no 2736

27 Feb B Brick (Builders) Limited returned goods £28.40 + VAT, credit note no CN129 issued

You are to:

(a) prepare the accounts in the main ledger – including a sales ledger control account – and subsidiary (sales) ledger of Shire Traders and record the balances at 1 February 2007.

(b) enter the above transactions in Shire Traders' sales day book and sales returns day book for February 2007.

(c) from the books of prime entry, record the accounting entries in the main ledger and subsidiary (sales) ledger, balancing all accounts at the month-end (28 February 2007).

(d) reconcile the control account balance with the subsidiary accounts at 1 February and 28February 2007.

This chapter explains the different ways in which money is received by an organisation and then sets out the procedures it follows in recording those payments. It covers:

- receiving money in the form of cash, cheques and similar items, inter-bank transfers and payment by debit and credit card

- the legal meaning of cheque crossings and endorsements

- checking of the money against covering documentation where appropriate

- checking cash, giving change and issuing receipts

- recording incoming payments on remittance lists, cash books and cash registers

- dealing with problem payments – incorrect cheques, suspicious cards, situations where the money received does not tally with the accompanying documentation

This chapter concentrates on the manual recording of receipts. Recording receipts using computer accounting is dealt with in is dealt with in Osborne Books' **Accounting Work Skills Tutorial** for Unit 31 (Chapter 15).

PERFORMANCE CRITERIA COVERED

unit 30: INTRODUCTORY ACCOUNTING

element 30.1

process sales and receipts

F   check receipts against records

G   deal with discrepancies

INCOMING PAYMENTS

Payments can be received by an organisation in a variety of ways:

- cash
- cheque
- credit card and debit card transactions (which can be manually or electronically processed)
- direct to the bank by inter-bank transfer: BACS and CHAPS

It depends on the nature and the size of the organisation how the payments are received and processed. In the retail sector, for example, a newsagent will depend to a great extent on cash transactions and the cash register, a large supermarket on the other hand will use electronic tills and accept cash, cheques, and credit and debit card payments.

CASH

Cash is still used for most small transactions, and we are still nowhere near the 'cashless society' which is often talked about.

As far as the organisation accepting payments in cash is concerned, the main disadvantage of cash is the security problem, and there is a risk of receiving forged notes.

receiving payment in cash

For a business receiving sums of money in the form of cash it is necessary for an employee to count the cash received and check it against the amount due. Notes should be checked for forgeries (held against the light or viewed on special machines). Change will need to be given when the exact amount is not tendered (given). For example:

Sale	£3.64
Amount tendered (given) by customer	£10.00
Change to be given	£6.36

The amount of change is the difference between the amount tendered (handed over) and the amount of the sale. When a cash till is in use, most types of till will indicate the amount of change to be given after the amount tendered has been entered through the keypad. A more traditional method is for a cashier to count out the change starting with the amount of the sale and working to the amount tendered, but this is becoming increasingly rare.

Often when payment is made in cash, a receipt is given: this can take the form of a machine-produced receipt, such as is given in a shop, or a handwritten receipt. Look at these examples:

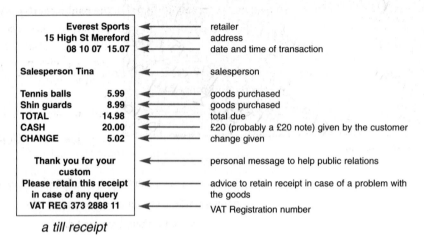

Everest Sports		retailer
15 High St Mereford		address
08 10 07 15.07		date and time of transaction
Salesperson Tina		salesperson
Tennis balls 5.99		goods purchased
Shin guards 8.99		goods purchased
TOTAL 14.98		total due
CASH 20.00		£20 (probably a £20 note) given by the customer
CHANGE 5.02		change given
Thank you for your custom		personal message to help public relations
Please retain this receipt in case of any query		advice to retain receipt in case of a problem with the goods
VAT REG 373 2888 11		VAT Registration number

a till receipt

ENIGMA MUSIC LIMITED   *receipt*   958

13 High Street, Mereford MR1 2TF
VAT Reg 343 7645 23

Customer ....*R V Williams*...date ..*3 Oct 2007*....

'*Golden Oldies*' *by J Moore*	£20.00
	£20.00
VAT @ 17.5%	£3.50
Total	£23.50

a hand-written receipt

tills and cash floats

At the end of the day it will be necessary to 'cash up' by balancing the amount of cash held. As most cash tills start each day with a float of cash (to enable change to be given, if necessary, to the first customers), the amount in the till at the end of the day will be:

cash float at start

plus sales made during the day (listed on the till roll)

equals amount of cash held at end of day

an electronic till

A cash float will be kept back for the following day, and the surplus will be transferred to the safe for paying into the bank next day. Alternatively, a bank paying-in slip (see the next chapter) might be made out, and the cash, together with the paying-in slip and any cheques received placed in a 'wallet' to be deposited in the bank's night safe (see the next chapter).

A typical calculation would be:

cash float at start	£150.00
plus sales made during the day (listed on the till roll)	£2,608.50
equals amount of cash held at end of day	£2,758.50
less cash float retained for next day	£150.00
amount transferred to safe or bank's night safe	£2,608.50

If the cash in the till does not agree with the total on the till roll, the discrepancy needs investigation. Regular discrepancies for significant amounts, eg £5 or £10, will lead to urgent investigations – there could be pilfering taking place if the till is often short at the end of the day, or it could be caused by poor cashiering – giving the wrong change.

guidelines for cash handling

Those who handle cash in an organisation are responsible for its safekeeping. Cash is often a target for theft – and regrettably not only from people outside the organisation. General security guidelines for looking after cash received will vary according to the size and type of organisation:

- cash should be kept in a cash till or in a cash box which should be kept locked when not in use
- keys should be retained under the control of the cashier
- as little cash as is practically possible should be kept in tills
- cash should be paid into the bank as soon as possible

'topping up' the petty cash

The organisation may also operate a petty cash system for making small payments (see Chapter 16). The cash will be kept in a locked tin and will need to be 'topped up' from time-to-time to what is known as the 'imprest amount'. Care will have to be taken when transferring money from the main cash fund to the petty cash tin: security precautions should be observed and the transaction recorded.

CHEQUES

Cheques are issued by banks to their personal and business account customers. Building societies also issue cheques on current accounts – their customers are mainly personal. Payment by cheque is a common method of making payment through the post. A specimen cheque is shown below (there is more on how to write out a cheque in Chapter 12).

what is a cheque?

A cheque, as used in normal business practice, may be defined as

a written order to the bank (known as the 'drawee') signed by its customer (known as the 'drawer') to pay a specified amount to a specified person (known as the 'payee')

Some organisations – large retail stores, for example – have machines which print out their customers' cheques on the till. A large number of cheques, however, are still written by hand, and great care must be taken both when writing out cheques and also when receiving cheques in payment. The cheques must be examined to ensure that all the details and signatures are correct. The vast majority of cheques are 'crossed' – they have two parallel lines, known as a 'crossing' on the front of the cheque.

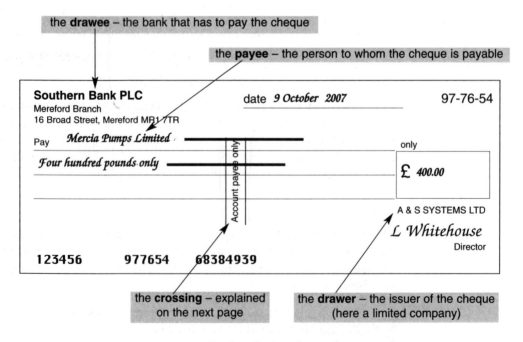

the 'parties' and crossing on a cheque

examining the cheque

If you are receiving payment by cheque, whether it is direct from the customer over the counter or through the post on a remittance advice, there are a number of basic checks to carry out:

- is the cheque signed? – it is invalid if it is not
- is the payee's name correct? – it should be changed and initialled by the drawer (issuer) if it is not
- is the cheque in date? – a cheque becomes out of date ('stale') and invalid after six months; note that if the date is missing, it may be written in
- do the words and figures agree? – the cheque may be returned by the bank if they do not

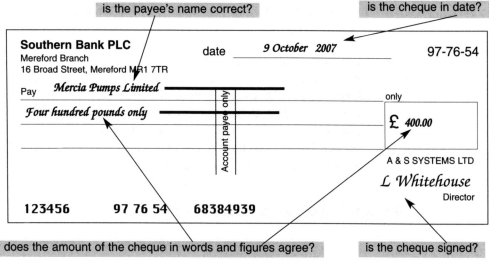

checking the cheque

If the organisation accepting payment by cheque is inefficient and does not carry out these precautions, the cheque concerned may be returned to the organisation's bank after it has been paid in, and the amount of the cheque deducted from the organisation's bank account. If the cheque is guaranteed by a bank card, different conditions apply (see page 92).

crossings

Cheques are normally *crossed* – they are printed with two parallel lines across the face of the cheque. Often there are words printed or written in the crossing. If a cheque is not crossed, it is an *open* cheque. Open cheques are very rare.

A crossed cheque may only be paid into a bank account. The crossing says in effect: 'this cheque must be paid into a bank account'.

types of crossing

If you are receiving cheques you will need to know the different types of crossing, as the type of crossing may affect whether or not the cheque can be paid into the organisation's bank account. These are the basic types of crossing:

crossing		*effect*
_____ & co _____	or _____	A *general* crossing – the cheque can be paid into the bank
_____ HSBC Bank Pershore _____		This crossing is known as a *special* crossing – the cheque can *only* be paid into HSBC Bank in Pershore
_____ account payee _____		An *account payee* crossing' – this cheque should only be paid into the payee's account

endorsements – a historical note

Traditionally the payee of a cheque was entitled to sign it on the back – *endorse* it – so that it could be passed on to another person who could pay it into his or her bank account and receive payment. This signature on the back was known as an *endorsement,* which means 'written on the back'. Owners of a driving licence with an 'endorsement' may be familiar with this term!

The Cheques Act 1992 has, in effect, made cheque endorsements redundant. The Act states that a cheque which has an 'account payee' or 'a/c payee' crossing is 'not transferable'. This means it cannot change hands after the payee has received it – except, of course, when it is paid into the bank. As most cheques are now crossed 'account payee' the idea of the payee endorsing the cheque has become largely meaningless. Banks generally nowadays *only accept cheques for the account of the payee.*

PAYMENT BY MULTIFUNCTION CARD

Banks issue 'multifunction cards' which combine a number of different services for their customers. These services include:

- giving cash from cash machines in the UK and abroad
- guaranteeing payment of customers' cheques up to a certain amount, usually £100 or (more commonly) £250
- acting as debit cards – enabling customers to make payment without issuing a cheque

Businesses which accept payment from customers using these cards either over the counter, by telephone or through mail order must be familiar with the procedures for accepting payment.

The details shown below describe The Royal Bank of Scotland 'Highline' multifunction card. They also explain how the customer's photograph can be incorporated into the card as an added security measure.

The symbols which are also shown below relate to the functions of the card.

On the pages which follow we describe how businesses deal with:

- the cheque guarantee function
- the debit card function

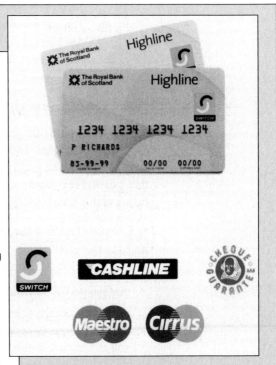

The Royal Bank of Scotland's multi-function Highline card combines five services in one card:

- **Switch debit card** – pay for goods and services without writing a cheque wherever you see the Switch symbol – and even get cash where you see the cashback sign
- **Cashline card** – access Britain's widest cash dispensing network – use your card not only in Royal Bank Cashline machines, but in cash machines belonging to any major bank or building society throughout Great Britain
- **Cheque guarantee card** – guarantee your cheques up to the limit shown on your card
- **Cirrus card** – access your money in local currency at thousands of cash dispensers worldwide – wherever you see the Cirrus symbol
- **Maestro debit card** – access to your money in local currency as well as paying for goods and services worldwide – wherever you see the Maestro symbol.

Photocard for security

For added security you can have your photograph and signature laser-etched onto your card. The Royal Bank of Scotland was the first bank in the UK to introduce this system – and it still gives you added peace of mind against fraud.

a card used to guarantee cheques

The rules for the use of a multifunction card used to guarantee a customer's cheques may be set out in the agreement form signed when the card is issued, or may be available at the bank. Here are some typical conditions:

> XYZ Bank plc guarantees in any single transaction the payment of one cheque taken from one of its own cheque books for up to £250 provided the cheque is not drawn on the account of a Limited Company, and
>
> (1) The cheque bears the same name and code number as this card.
>
> (2) It is signed, before the expiry of the card, in the United Kingdom of Great Britain and Northern Ireland, the Channel Islands or the Isle of Man in the presence of the payee by the person whose signature appears on this card.
>
> (3) The card number is written on the back of the cheque by the payee.
>
> (4) The card has not been altered or defaced.

receiving payment by cheque and guarantee card

If you have read the guarantee card conditions set out above you will appreciate that when you accept payment by cheque and cheque guarantee card you must take great care that all the conditions are met. If you do not, the purchaser's bank may not 'honour' (pay) the cheque, and your organisation stands to lose the money. Also, because of the large number of stolen and fraudulent cards in circulation, you must be on your guard against suspicious-looking cards and customers. The procedure is therefore as follows:

- if there is a photograph of the customer on the card, check it to make sure that the person in front of you is that customer
- examine the card to make sure it is not defaced – has the photograph or signature been tampered with? – be suspicious if the card is handed to you in a plastic wallet – it may be a forgery
- examine the card for
  - expiry date
  - amount of the guarantee (if it is stated)
  - name agreeing with the name on the cheque
  - bank details agreeing with those on the cheque
- examine the cheque for
  - signature (this should agree with the signature on the card)
  - date
  - payee's name
  - amount in words and figures (they should agree)

- write the card number on the back of the cheque – an essential procedure, adding any other details which your organisation requires (some businesses use a rubber stamp on the back of the cheque to list the required details)

cheque card limits – a common mistake

Bank customers sometimes think that if the cost of the item being purchased is above the cheque guarantee limit, then a number of cheques may be issued and payment is guaranteed. This is not correct – the cheque card guarantee covers only *one cheque per transaction*.

DEBIT CARDS

Debit cards are issued to personal customers by banks and building societies to enable their customers to make payments from their bank accounts by Electronic Funds Transfer (see page 98). *No cheque is written out.*

Debit cards are issued to selected customers of the bank; they enable a payment to be made from the person's bank account electronically. A debit card has the obvious advantages of being quicker to use and more convenient. Examples of debit cards are Barclays' Connect (see below) and Royal Bank of Scotland Highline cards.

From a seller's point of view, when a customer wishes to pay by debit card in person, the transaction is handled in a similar way to a credit card, (see next page) using either

- a manually completed sales voucher on an imprinter, or, more commonly
- an electronic terminal, either 'standalone' and linked by telephone (used by smaller organisations), or connected to an electronic 'card swipe' till (as in the big supermarkets)

CREDIT CARDS

Credit cards provide a means of obtaining goods and services immediately, but paying for them later. The commonest credit cards used in the UK use the names Visa and Mastercard. The card illustrated below is a Visa Barclaycard.

Credit cards are issued, upon application, to customers of banks, building societies, retail chains and an increasingly wide variety of businesses and other organisations. Goods and services can be obtained at shops and other outlets having computer terminals. Credit cards can also be used for mail order, telephoned and internet sales.

Retailers use a *card merchant* to process all their card payments, and pay a set percentage (up to 5%) of each transaction amount for the use of the credit card facility. An example of a card merchant is Streamline.

Each month a cardholder is sent a statement of the purchases made and can choose to pay off the balance of the account, or to pay part only (subject to a certain minimum amount), carrying forward the remaining balance to next month. Interest is charged on balances owing to the credit card company. An annual flat fee is sometimes charged to the cardholder for the use of the card.

ACCEPTING CARD PAYMENTS – 'OVER THE COUNTER' SALES

A business will offer one of three methods of receiving payment by credit card or debit card by a customer who calls in person:

- *'chip and PIN'* – the customer authorises payment on a terminal using a four digit number known as a 'PIN' (Personal Identification Number)
- an electronic till or terminal, linked to the card merchant by telephone line, requiring a *customer signature,* a process rapidly being replaced by 'chip and PIN'
- a mechanical imprinter machine, which imprints the embossed details from the credit card onto a sales voucher – this method is now very rare

terminal sales – chip and PIN

This method of accepting payment by credit and debit cards involves the card holder's card being inserted in a card reader device with a keypad, eg in a supermarket or a restaurant. The customer then authorises the sales transaction (or the bill for the meal) by keying in a four digit number (PIN) which should only be known to the card holder. If there is any problem (eg the card is stolen or the limit exceeded) authorisation will be refused. Also if the PIN is incorrectly entered three times, the system will 'lock out' and refuse the card. In this case an alternative means of payment will have to be requested.

'Chip and PIN' was introduced for two main reasons:

• it greatly increases the efficiency of checkouts because it saves time

• it cuts down on card fraud because it is a far more secure method of making payment

It is true to say that this system has been very successful on both counts. Note that a chip and PIN transaction avoids the retailer having to carry out all the security checks needed when a signature is required (see below). There are, of course, some common sense precautions which should be taken by the retailer, for example making sure that other customers (or employees) cannot easily watch the PIN being entered.

terminal sales requiring a signature

This older method of using a terminal to process card payments is rapidly being superseded by 'chip and PIN'. Before reading the next two sections you should check with your tutor in case the system is in fact no longer used. With this system the assistant operating the terminal should:

• in the case of a shop till, 'swipe' the card through the card reader – this 'captures' the details encoded in the magnetic stripe on the reverse of the card or in the chip embedded in the card

• in the case of a business using a 'standalone' terminal, the details are input manually when the terminal is connected to the card merchant by telephone line

• in both cases, the card merchant's system checks automatically that
   - the card number is valid
   - the card has not been lost or stolen
   - there is enough money (or limit) available to pay for the transaction

• if all is well, each transaction will be allowed to pass through; if it is not, the customer will be asked to pay another way, eg cash!

• if the amount is above the 'floor limit', a telephone call to the card merchant will be required to authorise the transaction

- the till prints a two-part receipt which includes space for the cardholder's signature
- the customer signs, and the signature is compared with that on the card
- the customer is handed the top-copy of the receipt, and the other copy is kept in the event of a query in the future
- the amount of the transaction is automatically debited (deducted)
  - in the case of a credit card from the cardholder's credit card account
  - in the case of a debit card from the cardholder's bank account
- the amount of the transaction is automatically credited (added) to the bank account of the business
- the business will receive a regular schedule of amounts automatically paid into the bank account; this will be checked with the bank statement when it is received

checks when accepting a card on a terminal

There are a number of checks that should be made when accepting payment when operating an electronic terminal. These apply equally to debit cards and to credit cards. You should make sure that:

- the card has an appropriate logo, eg 'Switch' – you will probably have a list against which you can compare the logo
- the card has a magnetic stripe on the reverse or an embedded chip
- the card has not expired
- the start date on the card is not in the future
- the card holder title is appropriate (eg a card issued to Miss Helen Jones is not used by a man!)
- the signature on the card is consistent and has not been tampered with
- the card has not been defaced or mutilated in any way
- any photograph on the card looks like the customer

mechanical imprinter machine

This system is now very rarely used. The procedure is as follows:

- check any photograph on the card and make sure that the card has not been defaced or tampered with
- check that the card has not expired
- imprint the sales voucher (see illustration below)
- complete the sales voucher with date, details of goods, and total money amount

- the customer signs the imprinted sales voucher, and the signature should be compared with that on the card
- the list of stolen cards is checked
- if the payment is above a certain amount – the *floor limit* (which varies according to the type of business) it will be necessary to telephone the card merchant company to obtain an authorisation code for the transaction to go ahead – the authorisation code is recorded on the sales voucher
- the top copy of the sales voucher is handed to the customer, and the other three copies are retained
- of the three copies of the sales voucher which are retained, the white copy is treated in the same way as a cheque, and is kept in the till and added to the cheques and cash received to give the total sales figure; the other two copies (yellow and blue) are kept in the event of a query in the future
- the white copy of the sales voucher kept in the till is then banked along with the cash and cheques

mail order and telephone sales

Buying goods and services by credit card and debit card over the telephone, and by mail order is very common. When accepting payment by this means, the organisation must exercise the same degree of care as a shop accepting an 'over the counter' transaction. Some organisations will complete the same type of sales voucher used for an 'over the counter' transaction and send the top copy to the customer as a receipt; some organisations will use an electronic terminal, and send a copy of the receipt to the customer. Organisations which have a large volume of transactions will not use vouchers but instead record the details of sales on a Mail Order Schedule, a form which will provide space for recording ten transactions or more.

When accepting payment by credit card by telephone or mail order, the following details must be obtained:

- the card number
- the expiry date of the card
- the issue number and/or start date of any debit card
- the name and initials of the cardholder as shown on the card
- the cardholder's address
- the cardholder's signature (mail order only)

Any authorisation of amounts over the 'floor limit' must be carried out in the normal way.

Internet sales are also booming – these are described on page 99.

floor limits and authorisations

As we have seen, it may be necessary from time-to-time for a business accepting a debit or credit card payment to seek authorisation for the transaction from the card merchant company (the company that deals with all the payments). Authorisation can be given over the telephone or in some cases electronically. Authorisation may be needed in a number of situations:

- when the amount of the transaction exceeds the Floor Limit – this limit is a transaction amount set by the card merchant company – it can vary
- the terminal indicates that the card is not valid for some reason or other (it may be out of date)
- when the cashier is suspicious about the signature
- when the cashier is suspicious about the customer
- the terminal indicates that the cashier should contact the card merchant company (it may be a stolen card!)

These authorisations are important because if they are not carried out the business accepting payment may lose the money – it will not be a guaranteed payment. Many retail businesses give rewards to vigilant cashiers who recover a stolen card used by a suspicious customer – who normally runs out of the store when the cashier decides to ask for authorisation!

ELECTRONIC FUNDS TRANSFER AT POINT OF SALE (EFTPOS)

EFT stands for 'Electronic Funds Transfer'. Credit card and debit card transactions which go through an electronic terminal (eg 'chip and PIN') are processed by a system known as *Electronic Funds Transfer at Point Of Sale* (EFTPOS). This allows a retail outlet to debit the bank account or credit card account of the purchaser at the point of sale and, at the same time, to credit the retailer's bank account. Besides removing the need to carry a lot of cash, the system reduces paperwork, eg writing out cheques.

Details of the transaction are transmitted electronically by means of a computer link to a central computer either immediately, or, normally, at the end of the day.

The benefits of EFTPOS to a retail business are:

- greater efficiency, with less time taken by customers to make payment
- reduced queuing time
- less cash to handle (giving fewer security risks)
- guaranteed payment once acceptance has been made

INTERNET PAYMENT TRANSACTIONS

Businesses which have on-line facilities for selling their products from their websites carry out these sales on a 'remote control' basis. They do not deal with these customers personally. The customers order and pay for the goods on-line using a credit or debit card and all the business has to do is to despatch the goods (eg an on-line shop) or provide the service (eg a holiday company). The money is credited (added) directly to the bank account of the business.

The business will receive a schedule of the payments received which it can check against its bank statement.

The buying public is naturally concerned about the security of this system. Stories abound of people hacking into shop and bank websites and obtaining names and credit card numbers and then going on spending sprees. Businesses setting up on-line selling facilities have to ensure that the security of the system is as watertight as it can be. Software companies are constantly working to improve levels of security and methods of encoding data ('encryption') so that payment details – including card numbers – remain secret.

The mechanics of how the payment from an internet purchase reaches the bank account of the seller is explained in detail on page 99.

PAYABLE ORDERS

Sometimes a business will receive documents similar to cheques as a means of payment. These *payable orders* include

- *Postal orders* – money orders purchased from the Post Office, often used by people who do not have bank accounts and who wish to send money through the post.

- *Bank drafts* – these are cheques issued by a *bank* and are as good as cash. They are bank cheques so they will not 'bounce' – the bank is both drawer (issuer) and drawee (the bank that pays). Drafts are often used by people wanting to pay large amounts, eg for a house or car purchase.

- *Building society cheques* – these work on the same principle as bank drafts, except that the drawer (issuer) is a building society and the drawee (the organisation who has to make payment) is a bank. Like bank drafts, they are often accepted for large purchases.

If you receive payment in the form of a postal order, bank draft or building society cheque, it can be paid into the bank account like a cheque.

CHECKING PAYMENTS AGAINST DOCUMENTATION

It is important that incoming payments received from customers are checked against any documentation that the supplier receives. This is to ensure that the correct amount is received and that no future disputes can arise – for example 'We sent you £450, that's what it says on our advice" ... "No you didn't, you only sent us £405, that's what it shows on your account.'

The most common type of document which advises the amount of a payment is a *remittance advice* (see page 235 for an explanation of this document).

Payments from customers can be received either through the post, or through the bank as inter-bank transfers. A remittance advice will be issued in both instances by the person paying.

postal payments

Any cheque received through the post should be checked carefully against the accompanying remittance advice, which can be:

- a special form prepared by the person paying, setting out the amount of the cheque, the date and the item(s) the cheque is covering, or
- a tear-off slip sent with the statement of account by the seller; often the items being paid are ticked off by the buyer, but the amount of the cheque may not be written down

In both cases (and particularly the second) the organisation receiving payment *must* check that the total of the items being paid less any credit due equals the amount of the cheque. Failure to carry out this simple check could cause problems later on if there is a discrepancy. Any differences should be marked on the remittance advice which is then normally queried with the customer by telephone.

inter-bank transfers – BACS

An increasing number of payments are now made automatically from bank account to bank account, normally on the instructions of the payer, through the BACS system (BACS stands for Bankers Automated Clearing Services). As no cheque is issued, payment is made more quickly and more cheaply. The problem of how the seller is to *know* that payment is made is solved by the buyer sending a BACS advice – essentially a remittance advice for a BACS payment.

BACS payments are made in a number of situations:

- by customers who buy from a business regularly, settling up invoices
- by people paying standing orders (a regular payment) – the BACS payment is originated by the person sending the money

- by people paying direct debits – a regular payment from bank account to bank account where the payment is originated by the business receiving the money

The organisation receiving payment will have to check each advice carefully against the bank statement when it arrives to ensure that the correct amount has been received. In the case of the direct debit, the business receiving the money has also originated the transfer, so the bank statement will be checked against the payment schedule produced internally by the business.

Examples of remittance advices are shown below.

TO	**REMITTANCE ADVICE**	FROM	
Cool Socks Limited Unit 45 Elgar Estate, Broadfield, BR7 4ER		**Trends** **4 Friar Street** **Broadfield** **BR1 3RF** Tel 01908 761234 Fax 01908 761987 VAT REG GB 0745 8383 56	

Account 3993		6 November 2007	

date	your reference	our reference	payment amount
01 10 07	INVOICE 787923	47609	277.30
10 10 07	CREDIT NOTE 12157	47609	(27.73)
		CHEQUE TOTAL	249.57

remittance advice sent with a cheque payment

BACS REMITTANCE ADVICE			FROM: Trends 4 Friar Street Broadfield BR1 3RF
TO Cool Socks Limited Unit 45 Elgar Estate, Broadfield, BR7 4ER			06 11 07

Your ref	Our ref		Amount
787923	47609	BACS TRANSFER	249.57
		TOTAL	249.57

THIS HAS BEEN PAID BY BACS CREDIT TRANSFER DIRECTLY INTO YOUR BANK ACCOUNT AT ALBION BANK NO 11451226 SORT CODE 90 47 17

remittance advice sent to advise of a BACS payment

RECORDING MONEY RECEIVED

The individual amounts of money received should be recorded by the organisation. The *way* in which they are recorded will depend on the way in which they are received. The fact that the amounts are recorded will help security by discouraging employees from being tempted to raid the till and steal money.

cash tills

Money received over a counter is likely to be recorded on a cash till tally roll or electronic till memory – the totals on the till roll or memory can then be checked with the actual money received, ready for paying into the bank. The security of cash tills is tightly controlled: they are operated by a security key and any transfer of change is recorded. The more modern cash registers (supermarket tills, for example) are linked to a central computer and automatically change the stock level records as items are sold.

remittance lists (postal items)

Cheques and other money received may be recorded manually on a *remittance list*. 'Remittance list' just means a list of what you have been sent. It can record items received through the post by a business, or it can be used at the counter of old-fashioned shops instead of a cash register. A remittance list for items received through the post is likely to include columns for the date, sender, the nature of the 'remittance' amount, and, as a security measure, the signature of the person opening the post.

date	sender	remittance	amount	signature
12.3.07	Travers Toys Ltd	cheque	234.50	G Palmer
12.3.07	Grampian Traders	bank draft	10,500.00	G Palmer
12.3.07	Mrs D Dodds	cash	14.50	R Patel
12.3.07	Mercia Foods	cheque	450.00	G Palmer

example of a remittance list for items received through the post

remittance lists/cash received lists

A remittance list is also used to record payments received over the counter. It is an old-fashioned method, but it serves its purpose very well. The person at the till will record each sale as it occurs; the cash and cheques are likely to be kept in a locked cash box, as there is no cash register. The total of the remittance list (or *cash received list*) should be agreed with the takings at the end of each day.

The items can either be written on a separate piece of paper or they may be entered in a book. The example below shows the sales made by a second-hand bookshop during the course of day.

FOLIO BOOKS   takings for *22 January 2007*

Milton, Paradise Lost, 1793	*cash*	*£45.00*
Hardy, Mayor of Casterbridge, 1896	*cheque*	*£65.00*
Graham Greene, The End of the Affair	*cash*	*£1.75*
Punch selections	*cheque*	*£25.00*
T S Eliot, 4 Quartets	*cheque*	*£12.50*
Haynes, Worcester within the Walls	*cheque*	*£14.95*
Culpeper, Tudor Remedies	*cash*	*£4.95*
W English, Alvechurch - a History	*cheque*	*£9.95*
TOTAL CASH		*£51.70*
TOTAL CHEQUES		*£127.40*
Total Takings		*£179.10*

---

example of a remittance list for items received over the counter

cash book

The cash book is the central record of money amounts received and paid out by the organisation either in the form of cash, or as items passed through the bank account. All the receipts referred to in this chapter will eventually pass through the cash book. It will be dealt with in detail in Chapter 7.

Chapter Summary

- Incoming payments can be received in a number of ways: cash, cheque, credit and debit card, inter-bank transfer from BACS and internet sales.

- Receipts are often issued for cash payments; either till receipts or handwritten receipts.

- Cash in a till will be counted up at the end of each day; the amount should equal the takings for the day plus any 'float' held in the till.

- Cheques should be examined carefully when taken in payment, either over the counter or through the post. Normally they are crossed, and should only be paid into the account of the payee.

- Cheques received over the counter are normally only accepted with a bank multi-function card which has a cheque guarantee. When this occurs, the card and the cheque should be carefully inspected together.

- Debit cards are commonly accepted as a means of payment in place of cash or cheques. They are normally processed using a 'chip and PIN' electronic terminal.

- Payment can also be accepted by credit card – normally using a 'chip and PIN' electronic terminal. A credit card enables payment to be made to the credit card company by the buyer at a later date.

- If a business uses an electronic terminal, the money will be transferred electronically from the customer's bank account or credit card account to the business bank account. This system is known as EFTPOS (Electronic Funds Transfer at Point Of Sale).

- Sales transactions over the Internet are processed under secure conditions and the money transferred automatically to the seller's bank account.

- When payments are evidenced by documentation such as a remittance advice, the payment should be checked against the documentation. Payment in this case can be by cheque or by inter-bank transfer.

- When money is received it should be recorded, both for security purposes and also as part of the operation of the accounting system. Forms of recording include the cash till roll, remittance lists and the cash book.

Key Terms

cash float — the amount of cash kept in a till at the end of the day to provide change when the till is next used

cheque — a written order to the bank, signed by its customer, instructing it to pay a specified amount to a specified person

drawer of a cheque — the person who signs the front of the cheque – the customer from whose account the money is to be paid

drawee of a cheque	the bank which has to make payment – its name and address normally appears at the top of the cheque
payee of a cheque	the person to whom the cheque is payable – normally specified on the first line of the cheque amount
cheque crossing	two parallel lines on the front of a cheque, with or without writing in them – they mean that the cheque has to be paid into a bank account
'account payee' crossing	two parallel lines on the face of the cheque with the words 'account payee' between them – the cheque cannot be endorsed over – it must be paid into the account of the payee
debit card	a plastic card which enables customers to make payment for purchases without having to write out a cheque – payment is made electronically from the bank account straightaway
credit card	a plastic card issued by a credit card company which enables customers to make purchases and pay for them at a later date
chip and PIN	the technology for accepting payments by debit and credit cards where the customer enters a four digit number (PIN) into an electronic terminal
EFTPOS	Electronic Funds Transfer at Point Of Sale – the electronic transfer of payments between the bank accounts of buyer and seller which is originated at a till
BACS	BACS stands for Bankers Automated Clearing Services, a body (owned by the banks) which organises computer payments between bank accounts
remittance advice	a document sent to the recipient of a payment, advising that a payment is being made
remittance list	also known as a 'cash received list' – a record of money amounts received, either through the post, or over the counter
cash book	the central record kept by a business of cash and bank transaction

Student Activities

5.1   You operate the cash till at the firm where you work. The following are the sales for one day:

		Amount of sale £	Notes and/or coin tendered
Customer	1	8.50	£10 note
	2	3.30	£10 note
	3	2.51	£5 note
	4	1.79	£5 note
	5	0.34	£1 coin
	6	6.22	£10 note
	7	12.76	£20 note
	8	1.42	two £1 coins
	9	6.54	£10 note
	10	3.08	£5 note

Calculate
(a) the amount of change to be given to each customer
(b) the notes and/or coins that will be given in change, using the minimum number possible

5.2   If the cash till in activity 1 had a float of £28.71 at the start of the day, how much cash should be held in the till after the sales from activity 1 had been made? Present your answer in the following form:

	£
cash float at start	28.71
plus sales made during the day	
equals amount of cash held at end of day	

5.3   You work as a shop counter assistant at New Era Lighting. You make a number of sales during the day (use today's date) which require the completion of a handwritten receipt. Complete the receipts set out on the next page. Include VAT on all purchases at the current rate. All prices quoted here are catalogue prices and exclude VAT.

(a) 2 flexilamps @ £13.99, 2 60w candlelight bulbs @ 85p, to Mr George Ohm

NEW ERA LIGHTING 977

17 High Street Mereford MR1 2TF
VAT reg 141 7645 23

CASH RECEIPT

Customer...date............................

	VAT
	TOTAL

(b) 1 standard lamp @ £149.95, 1 3amp plug @ 99p, to Mr Alex Bell

NEW ERA LIGHTING 978

17 High Street Mereford MR1 2TF
VAT reg 141 7645 23

CASH RECEIPT

Customer...date............................

	VAT
	TOTAL

(c) 2 external Georgian lamps @ £35.99, to Tom Edison

NEW ERA LIGHTING 979

17 High Street Mereford MR1 2TF
VAT reg 141 7645 23

CASH RECEIPT

Customer...date............................

	VAT
	TOTAL

5.4   Examine the cheque shown below and state who is

(a)   the drawer

(b)   the drawee

(c)   the payee

In each case, explain what the term means.

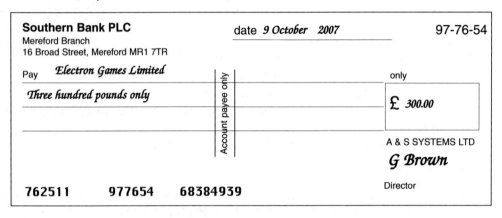

5.5   What difference does a crossing on a cheque make to the payee?

5.6   What are the following cheque crossings called, and what do they mean?:

(a)   _____

(b)   __Barclays Bank, Hanover Square__

(c)   _____& co_____

(d)   _____account payee_____

5.7   Henry Enfield is the payee of a cheque for £100 which has the following crossing:

_____account payee_____

What would you do if Sandra Lobb sent you the cheque for £100 in payment of an outstanding invoice on her acount. She says 'Henry has endorsed the cheque over to me – so all you have to do is to pay it into your bank account and it will be OK.' Give reasons for your answer.

Pay Sandra Lobb
Henry Enfield

5.8   List three checks a cashier should make to a cheque when receiving it in the post for payment of an outstanding invoice.

5.9   List three checks a cashier should make when accepting a cheque over the counter when the cheque is supported by a bank guarantee card.

5.10   What is the main security risk when a customer uses a 'chip and PIN' card at a store checkout?

5.11   What should a cashier do if the amount of a purchase being made by a customer (£500) exceeds the cheque guarantee amount of £250 on the customer's card?

    (a)   Refuse to allow the purchase to go ahead.

    (b)   Ask for two cheques for £250, all dated differently.

    (c)   Ask the customer to use the credit card which the cashier has spotted in the customer's card wallet.

    (d)   Request the customer to go and get a bank draft for £500.

    Choose *one* answer.

5.12   What should a store using a 'chip and PIN' system do if a customer using a credit card forgets her PIN, causing the system to 'lock out' after three attempts to input the number?

5.13   The advantage to a shop of accepting payment by debit card is that

    (a)   All cheques are automatically guaranteed.

    (b)   There is no cheque.

    (c)   The cheque is automatically debited to the customer' bank account.

    (d)   The signature on the cheque is automatically verified.

    Choose *one* answer.

5.14   EFT stands for:

    (a)   Electronic Foreign Transfer

    (b)   Electronic Financial Transaction

    (c)   Electronic Funds Till

    (d)   Electronic Funds Transfer

    Choose *one* answer.

5.15   List three advantages to a shop of using EFTPOS.

5.16   (a)   Who is the drawer and the drawee of a bank draft?

    (b)   Give examples of two transactions for which a bank draft would be suitable.

5.17   Give two examples of situations where a remittance list would be used.

6 Paying into the bank

this chapter covers . . .

This chapter explains the relationship between banks and their customers and sets out the procedures for paying money into the bank. The chapter covers the areas of:

- the legal relationship between the bank and its customers

- banking services available to customers

- the bank clearing system

- paying money into the bank using paying-in slips

- banking documents, including sales voucher summaries and statements

- security procedures used when handling cash

PERFORMANCE CRITERION COVERED

unit 30: INTRODUCTORY ACCOUNTING

element 30.1

process sales and receipts

I   prepare paying in documents

BANKS AND CUSTOMERS

By way of introduction we will look briefly at the legal background to the bank and customer relationship, the main types of accounts offered by banks to their personal and business customers, and the bank clearing system.

a legal relationship

It is important to appreciate when studying and practising banking procedures that there is a distinct *legal relationship* between a bank and its customer. Normally this relationship does not give much cause for concern; it is only when something goes wrong – for example when a bank pays a cheque which its customer has stopped – that the legal relationship becomes particularly important.

bank and customer contract

In law there is said to be a *contract* between the customer and the bank. A contract may be defined as:

a legally binding agreement which is recognised in a court of law

You may wonder why a contract between a bank and a customer is important in business dealings. The answer is that the bank/customer contract means that the customer has certain rights and duties to perform, including keeping the bank account in credit (not overdrawn, unless by arrangement) and taking care when writing out cheques so that they cannot be altered by a fraudster.

If the customer fails in any of these duties and the bank loses a substantial amount of money, it has the right in law under the contract to take the customer to court to recover its money.

Similarly, the bank has certain rights and duties to perform under the contract, and if it fails to do so and the customer suffers a loss (money or reputation), the customer can take the bank to court. Examples of the bank's duties include:

- paying the customer's cheques when there is sufficient money in the account
- keeping details of the customer's account secret
- sending statements of account to the customer

Clearly a customer will not take a bank to court if a statement is not sent out! But it may do so if the bank by mistake fails to pay a business cheque issued to a supplier, and the supplier cuts off supplies to the business. This could bankrupt the customer and is a clear *breach of the contract* between the bank and the customer. For further details of the theory of contract see Chapter 8.

BANK/CUSTOMER RELATIONSHIPS

There are a number of different bank/customer relationships:

debtor and creditor

This terminology relates to whether or not the customer has any money in the bank. Remember that:

debtor = a person who owes money

creditor = a person to whom you owe money

Therefore:

customer has money in bank: *customer = creditor (is owed money)*
                                   bank = debtor (owes money)

customer is borrowing: *customer = debtor (owes money)*
                                   bank = creditor (is owed money)

This may seem complicated, but if you think it through, it is logical.

mortgagor and mortgagee

If the customer has a mortgage with the bank (a mortgage is a legal document which secures a loan), the customer is a *mortgagor* and the bank is a *mortgagee.*

bailor and bailee

If the customer deposits valuable items in the bank's safe, the customer is a *bailor* and the bank a *bailee.*

principal and agent

If the customer uses the bank to carry out a transaction, eg to arrange an insurance policy, to sell shares, then the customer is known as the *principal* and the bank the *agent.* Note that the word 'agent' is also used in 'travel agent' and 'estate agent' – businesses that arrange travel and property deals.

TYPES OF ACCOUNT

There are three main types of accounts offered by banks to its customers:

- current account/overdraft
- deposit (savings) account
- loan accounts

current account/overdraft

With this type of account a customer is issued with a cheque book and card and may make use of most of the services of the bank. Bank customers use a current account as a 'working account' into which receipts are paid and out of which expenses are paid by means of cheques and automated computer payments. Many current accounts now pay interest.

An **overdraft** is borrowing from the bank on a current account.

If a business thinks that it will need an overdraft, it should contact the bank and seek agreement for an overdraft 'facility' up to a certain limit for a specified time. Interest will be charged on overdrawn balances and an arrangement/renewal fee is normally payable.

deposit (savings) account

A deposit account is used for savings by personal customers, or excess money held by a business, and interest is paid by the bank. Current account facilities such as cheque books, standing orders, direct debits, and overdrafts are not normally allowed on deposit accounts for business customers. Notice of withdrawal may need to be given to the bank. Other types of account may need a longer period of notice of withdrawal, perhaps one month or three months.

Many business customers have both a current and a deposit account. A business can use a deposit account as a temporary 'home' for surplus money, where it can earn interest. When the money is needed it can be transferred on request – or sometimes automatically – to the firm's current account.

loan accounts

Whereas an overdraft is a means of borrowing on an ordinary current account and will cover day-to-day running (*revenue*) expenses of the business, loan accounts are long-term loans for items of *capital* expenditure, eg machinery and new projects. Different banks will offer different types of loan account. Some typical examples include:

business loan

A loan for three to ten years to cover large items of expense such as new plant, premises expansion, a new project.

commercial mortgage

A loan for up to twenty five years to cover the purchase of property (the business equivalent of a 'home loan' mortgage to an individual).

CHEQUE CLEARING

Every working day each bank branch receives cheques paid in by customers. These cheques take a defined time to 'clear'. The term to 'clear' means that the cheque must have passed to the bank of the issuer of the cheque for payment before the money amount of the cheque – the amount paid in – can be used by the customer. This requirement for the cheque to be physically be passed to the issuer's (drawer's) bank is based in law dating back to the Victorian era! The clearance times are normally:

- cheques paid in and issued by customers of the same branch – same day clearance

- cheques paid in by customers of other banks and branches – three working days' clearance

This means that if you are given a cheque by someone who has an account at your branch and you pay it in on Monday, you can draw against it, ie you can use the money on the account, on Monday, the same day. This assumes, of course, that the cheque does not 'bounce'. On the other hand, if you are given a cheque which is issued by someone who banks at another bank (or another branch of your bank), then if you pay it in on Monday, you will have to wait three working days, ie until Wednesday before the cheque is cleared, and you can use the money.

The reason for this delay is that the cheque will have to be sent through the bank's processing centre via a central exchange centre (in Milton Keynes or Edinburgh) and then physically to the bank of the issuer of the cheque, where it arrives on day three. If that cheque is returned ('bounces') your bank will receive it back again through the post on day four or five and the money will be deducted from your account.

It is also possible to get a 'next day' or 'special' clearance by asking your bank to send the cheque by first class post to the issuer's bank. This could cost you £10 or more.

PAYING-IN SLIPS

Business customers are issued with a *paying-in* book by the bank. These books are pre-printed and encoded with the customer's name and account number together with details of the bank branch where the money will be paid in.

Details to be completed before paying in at the bank are:

- a summary of the different categories of notes or coins being paid in, the amount of each category being entered on the slip

- amounts and details of cheques being paid in, usually entered on the reverse of the slip, with the total entered on the front
- the cash and cheques being paid in are totalled to give the amount being paid in
- the counterfoil is completed (some counterfoils do not require the breakdown of cash)
- the person paying-in will sign the slip and get it checked in the office

A completed paying-in slip (with counterfoil) is illustrated below.

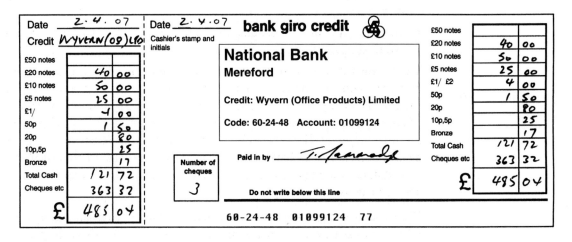

paying-in slip and counterfoil (front)

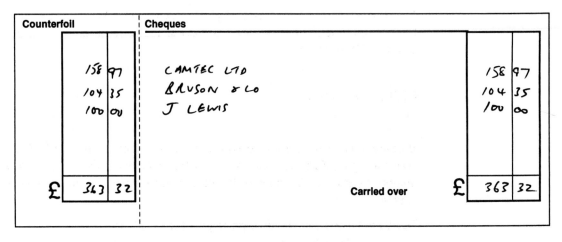

paying-in slip and counterfoil (back)

PROCEDURES FOR PAYING IN

the accounting process

Cash and cheques paid in at the bank will normally have been received by the business as cash sales and on remittance advices from debtors, and so form part of the accounting process. We will see how they are entered in the cash book in Chapter 7.

preparing the cash

The notes should be counted, checked and sorted so that they all face the same way, but should be kept separate. Defaced (damaged) notes, and notes from Scotland and Northern Ireland are normally accepted by banks. Coins should normally be sorted into denominations, eg £2, £1, 50p and so on, and placed in plastic money bags.

preparing the cheques

The cheques must first be examined carefully for any irregularities, such as

- **signatures** – has the drawer (issuer) signed the cheque?
- **payee** – if the name on the payee line is not the same as the name of the account into which it is being paid, the cheque will not be accepted
- **crossings** – if the cheque has the 'account payee' wording in the crossing and your organisation is not the payee, it will not be possible to pay it in (Cheques Act 1992) – see also 'payee' above
- **date** – is it out of date (over six months old)? is it post-dated? – if so, it cannot be paid in (but note that you can fill in a missing date and pay in the cheque)
- **words and figures** – do they agree?

The details of the cheques – the amounts and the customer names – may then be listed on the back of the paying-in slip, as in the illustration on the previous page.

If the volume of cheques paid in is very large, there will not be room on the paying-in slip, so the cheque details may be listed on a separate schedule. Some banks accept instead a calculator tally-roll listing the amounts, the number of cheques, and the total money amount transferred to the front of the paying-in slip.

The important point is that the organisation paying in the cheques must keep a record of the cheque details in case of future queries, and in the unfortunate event of any of the cheques 'bouncing' – ie being returned unpaid.

reconciliation with the financial records

It is important that the paying-in slips are reconciled with the relevant financial and accounting records before the slips are taken to the bank. For example, the total of the paying-in slip should be agreed with the subtotal of receipts shown in the cash book (see page 134). Further reconciliations could be carried out between the cheque total and the remittance list and the cash total with the total taken from the cash tills. These reconciliations will highlight any errors – either in the records or on the paying-in slip.

paying in at the bank

At the bank the completed paying-in book is handed to the bank cashier together with the notes, coins, and cheques. The cashier counts the cash, ticks off the cheques and, if everything is correct, receipt stamps and initials the paying-in slip and counterfoil. The slip is retained by the bank for the amount to be credited to the account-holder, while the paying-in book is handed back, complete with the receipted counterfoil. A business paying-in book is sometimes larger than the paying-in slip illustrated, and sometimes there is a carbon copy which acts as a counterfoil.

security measures for cash handling – night safes

Care must be taken when taking large amounts of cash to the bank. If possible two staff members should visit the bank. If the amount is very large, for instance the takings from a department store, a security firm may be employed to carry the cash. If the cash is received by an organisation over the weekend or, late in the day, it may be placed in a special wallet and lodged in the bank's *night safe* – a small lockable door leading to a safe in the wall of the bank.

When a business pays in money to the bank, it will record the amount in its own records, called the cash book (see Chapter 7).

card voucher clearing – card merchant services

As we saw in the last chapter, the sales voucher is the basic document produced when a debit card and a credit card transaction are processed manually (although this is now comparateively rare). The sales voucher may be produced as a result of an 'over the counter' sale or from a mail order or telephone sale. The details recorded on it will enable the card company to charge the amount to their customer's bank account (debit card transaction) or credit card account. The voucher like a cheque, is paid in at the bank and sent to the card company and 'cleared'.

Although there are a number of different card companies – Mastercard and Visa for example – the normal practice is for the organisation accepting payment to sign an agreement with a separate company – a card merchant –

which will accept all vouchers from cards issued by different companies. For example, a customer of The Royal Bank of Scotland may sign an agreement with a company called Streamline (owned by The Royal Bank of Scotland) and accept payment by Mastercard and Visa and other cards.

The customer will pay in all credit card vouchers on the one paying-in slip and schedule (see below) at the The Royal Bank of Scotland or NatWest (owned by The Royal Bank of Scotland). The bank will pass them to Streamline, which will then process them by sending them to the issuing card company (Mastercard or Visa, for example). Streamline is only one of a number of 'card merchant' companies which will process credit card sales vouchers.

The customer paying in the vouchers is charged a set percentage fee – usually between 2% and 5% – of the total sales amount. Some debit card transactions, Switch for example, are charged at a flat amount 'item charge'.

preparing card sales vouchers for paying-in

The vouchers are paid in after completion of a three-part Retailer Summary, illustrated below and on the next page. In this case three sales vouchers are listed on the back of the summary.

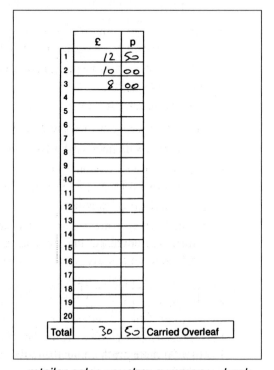

	£	p	
1	12	50	
2	10	00	
3	8	00	
4			
5			
6			
7			
8			
9			
10			
11			
12			
13			
14			
15			
16			
17			
18			
19			
20			
Total	30	50	Carried Overleaf

retailer sales voucher summary – back

Have you imprinted the summary with your Retailer's Card?

VISA

Bank Processing copy of Summary
with your Vouchers in correct order:

1 Summary

2 Sales Vouchers

3 Refund Vouchers

Keep Retailer's copy and
Retailer's Duplicate copy

No more than 200 Vouchers to each Summary

Do not use Staples, Pins, Paper Clips

	Items	Amount	
Sales Vouchers	3	30	50
Less Refund Vouchers			
Date	Total		
28.03.07 £		30 : 50	

MasterCard *E*

Retailer's Signature

Retailer's Copy   Retailer Summary

Retailer Summary

Complete this summary for every Deposit of Sales Vouchers and enter the
Total on your normal Current Account paying-in slip

retailer sales voucher summary – front

The procedure for listing credit card sales vouchers on the retailer's summary is as follows:

- the summary is imprinted with details of the retailer using a plastic card – the Retailer's Card – supplied with the imprinter machine
- the amounts of the sales vouchers are listed on the reverse of the summary and totalled
- the total is carried forward to the front of the summary
- any refund vouchers are listed on the front of the summary
- the summary is dated, signed and totalled
- the summary is separated into its three copies – the top two are retained by the organisation and the bottom copy (the processing copy) is placed in front of the sales vouchers
- the processing copy and sales and any refund vouchers are placed in a transparent envelope and are paid into the bank on a paying-in slip, the total from the summary listed as a single item on the paying-in slip

Organisations which accept sales by mail and telephone may use schedules rather than sales vouchers for recording and listing the credit card transactions. The procedure for paying-in for these organisations is exactly the same, except that the totals of the schedule(s) are listed on the back of the Retailer Summary rather than the individual amounts of the sales vouchers as described above.

THE IMPORTANCE OF PAYING IN PROMPTLY

Organisations are well aware that problems can arise if money is not banked promptly and safely.

theft

Cash is tempting to a thief, and it must be remembered that many instances of theft are carried out by employees of an organisation rather than by criminals with tights over their heads. An organisation will therefore have a security policy, for example:

- cash and cheques being paid in will be kept under lock and key at the place of work, normally in a cash box, under the control of the cashier
- amounts received through the post or over the counter are recorded on remittance lists or on a cash register (or equivalent) as an additional security measure – money, once it is recorded, will be missed when stolen
- larger organisations will have a system of spot checking (internal audit) to identify any theft by employees
- arranging for cash and cheques to be taken to the bank by security firm (appropriate for large businesses)
- arranging for Friday and weekend takings of cash to be lodged in the bank's night safe
- making arrangements for payroll – the organisation will have to arrange the pick up of cash from the bank, using employees or a security firm

timescale – security and cashflow

Organisations will also have a policy for the prompt paying of money into the bank, for two main reasons – *security* and *cashflow*. Money kept on the premises is a security risk: the longer it remains there, the more likely it is that it will be stolen. Also, money not paid in is money that is not available for paying cheques and other items from the organisation's bank account: *cashflow* will be restricted. For example, it may be that the business is borrowing money on overdraft – it could save paying interest if money is banked promptly: a cheque for £50,000 lying around in the office for a week could cost the business up to £50 in interest!

procedures

Because of these factors an organisation will draw up procedures for banking money. These will include the security measures mentioned above and also set timescales for paying in money, eg twice a week, one visit to coincide with the collection of the payroll cash (often a Friday). If you work in an accounts office, you will be familiar with these procedures.

confidentiality

Confidentiality – a topic covered in full in Unit 31 of the Diploma Pathway – means not telling outsiders about your employer's dealings and not revealing personal data held at work. Important aspects of this include not talking to outsiders about your customers, not disclosing secret details of your products, and most importantly to this area of your studies, not disclosing your security arrangements for handling of money. Imagine the consequences of telling a group of friends in the pub that the firm's wages are collected from the bank every Friday at 10.00 in the morning.

AUTOMATED PAYMENTS INTO THE BANK

So far in this chapter we have looked at how a business pays into the bank manually, ie paying in on a paying-in slip. Many payments nowadays come into the bank account by computer transfer from other banks. The business will know about these payments because:

- it will receive notification either through the post or online

- the payments will appear on the bank statement

A business will enter details of cash and cheque payments in the accounts when the money is received. Payments received electronically must also be entered in the accounts when notification is received and checked in due course against the bank statement. The diagram below shows the variety of payments that can be received. The mechanics of *making* these payments are covered in Chapter 12.

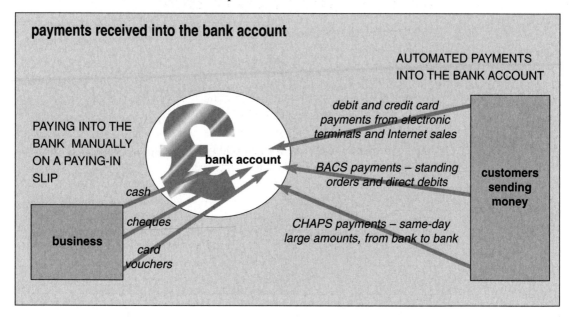

payments received into the bank account

AUTOMATED PAYMENTS
INTO THE BANK ACCOUNT

PAYING INTO THE
BANK MANUALLY
ON A PAYING-IN
SLIP

bank account

debit and credit card payments from electronic terminals and Internet sales

BACS payments – standing orders and direct debits

CHAPS payments – same-day large amounts, from bank to bank

customers sending money

business

cash

cheques

card vouchers

PAYMENTS THROUGH THE INTERNET

the process

If a business has an internet shopping facility, its customers order and pay for goods or services online using a credit or debit card and the money is credited direct to the bank account of the business. The business will receive a schedule of the payments received which it can check against its bank statement. Alternatively, it may be able to view this data online.

The diagram below shows the procedure adopted for this process. There is nothing significantly different from other payment systems about the way the system works – it is merely another way of providing a shopping outlet to customers with debit cards and credit cards.

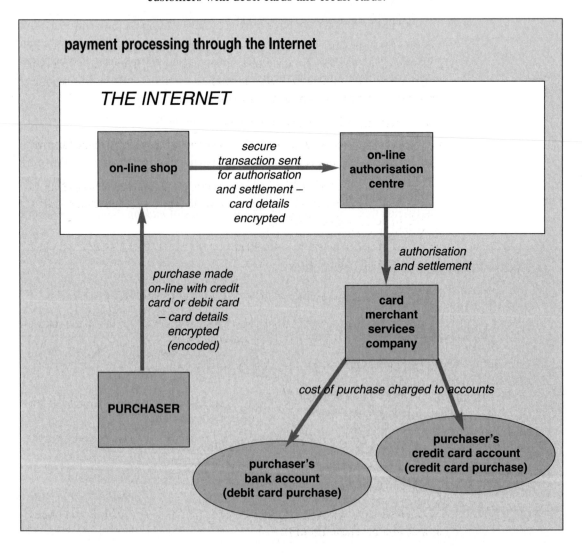

As we noted in the last chapter, the buying public is concerned about the security of giving their names, addresses and card numbers on-line. Businesses setting up selling facilities on-line have to ensure that the security of the system is ensured by using software which encodes the data (data 'encryption') so that payment details remain secret.

This security is no different *in principle* from the security measures adopted by businesses which accept debit and credit card payments over the counter, ie to keep any records of customers and their card numbers under lock and key and not to throw copies of sales vouchers (with card numbers on) in the bin where they can be found by people committing frauds.

BANK STATEMENTS

At regular intervals the bank sends out statements of account to its customers. A business current account with many items passing through it may have weekly statements, while a less active account or a deposit account may have monthly or even quarterly statements.

A bank statement is a summary showing:

- the balance at the beginning of the statement – 'balance brought forward'
- amounts paid into (credited to) the account
- amounts paid out of (debited to) the account – eg cheques issued, cheques returned 'unpaid', bank charges and standing orders and direct debits (automatic computer payments)

The balance of the account is shown after each transaction. A specimen bank statement is shown on the next page.

a note on debits, credits and bank accounts

You should be aware of the fact that the terms 'credit' and 'debit' mean different things to banks and their customers.

In the double-entry system of a business customer

debit = money received

credit = money paid out

Banks see things from the opposite angle. To their accounting system:

debit = money paid out from a customer's account

credit = money paid into a customer's account

In other words a credit to a bank account is the same as a debit in the books of a customer. Think about it!

Albion Bank plc

7 The Avenue, Broadfield, BR1 2AJ

		Account title	Trends
		Account number	11719512
		Statement	85

Date	Details	Payments	Receipts	Balance
2007				
3 Nov	Balance brought down			1,678.90 CR
10 Nov	Credit 109626		1,427.85	3,106.75 CR
10 Nov	238628	249.57		2,857.18 CR
11 Nov	238629	50.00		2,807.18 CR
13 Nov	POS Switch		67.45	2,874.63 CR
17 Nov	Credit 109627		100.00	2,974.63 CR
17 Nov	Albionet Card Services POS 2824242		500.00	3,474.63 CR
21 Nov	238630	783.90		2,690.73 CR
24 Nov	238626	127.00		2,563.73 CR
24 Nov	Albionet Netsales 43182639		1,006.70	3,570.43 CR
25 Nov	BACS ORLANDO 37646		162.30	3,732.73 CR
25 Nov	DD Westmid Gas	167.50		3,565.23 CR
27 Nov	238634	421.80		3,143.43 CR
27 Nov	DD RT Telecom	96.50		3,046.93 CR
28 Nov	Bank charges	87.50		2,959.43 CR

checking the bank statement for payments received

You will see from the specimen bank statement shown above that the balance of the account is followed each time by the abbreviation 'CR'. This means that the customer has a credit balance, ie has money in the bank. The abbreviation 'DR' would indicates a debit balance – an overdraft, ie the customer would owe the bank money and be a 'debtor' of the bank.

Note the following payments that have been received during the month:

- on 10 and 17 November the business has paid in on a paying-in slip
- on 13 November payment is received from debit card transactions
- on 17 November payment is received from credit card transactions
- on 24 November payment is received from Internet sales
- on 25 November payment is received via the BACS electronic transfer system – possibly a customer settling up an invoice

When a bank statement is received it should be checked and compared with the firm's record of bank receipts and payments – the cash book – and a bank reconciliation statement prepared (see Chapter 18).

Chapter Summary

- The legal relationship between a bank and its customer can take a number of forms: debtor and creditor, mortgagor and mortgagee, bailor and baliee, principal and agent.

- Banks offer a wide range of accounts: current accounts (including overdraft) deposit accounts and loan accounts.

- When a cheque is paid into a bank it normally takes three days to clear. When a cheque is cleared the person who has paid it in can normally draw on the money.

- Organisations pay money into their bank account on a paying-in slip which lists the cash and cheques paid in and totals the amounts.

- Cash and cheques must be checked and listed before they are paid in.

- Credit and debit card vouchers may also be paid into the bank account on a retailer summary form which lists all of the vouchers.

- Organisations should set up procedures to ensure that cash, cheques and card vouchers are kept safely on the premises and in transit to the bank.

- Money should be paid into the bank as soon as possible, both for security reasons and also to help the cashflow of the organisation.

- Automated payments – BACS, CHAPS and card payments processed electronically over-the-counter and through the Internet are also received into the bank account and will be advised to the business.

- Businesses should keep records of automatically processed card payments secure for security reasons – card numbers are valuable to thieves.

- Bank statements are sent regularly to customers and should be checked on receipt for manual and automatically processed payments received.

- To a bank, money paid in is a 'credit' and money paid out is a 'debit.'

Key Terms

contract	a legally binding agreement which is recognised in a court of law
mortgagor/mortgagee	when a mortgage is signed the borrower is the mortgagor and the bank the mortgagee
bailor/bailee	when a customer deposits items of value for safe keeping with a bank the customer is the bailor and the bank the bailee
principal/agent	when a customer asks the bank to carry out something on its behalf (eg arrange insurance) the customer is the principal and the bank the agent
cheque clearing	a system used by the banks to clear cheques paid in – the process takes three working days

paying-in slip	a paper slip listing cash and cheques paid into a bank
retailer summary	a form listing credit card sales vouchers paid into a bank account
night safe	a wallet or bag containing cash and cheques lodged with a bank (when it is closed) through an opening in the wall of the bank – used by shops and clubs banking their takings
card merchant	a company which handles all the payments by debit card and credit card received by a business over-the-counter or through the Internet
encryption	the encoding for security reasons of debit and credit card details sent over the Internet
BACS	Bankers Automated Clearing Services – used for sending computer payments from bank to bank
CHAPS	Clearing House Automated Payment System – used for sending same-day high value payments
bank statement	a document sent by the bank to its customer setting out transactions on the bank account

Student Activities

6.1 State two duties of a bank to its customer.

6.2 State two duties of a customer to the bank.

6.3 If a customer has an overdraft with a bank, the customer is a creditor of the bank. True or false?

6.4 If a customer has a credit balance with a bank, the customer is a debtor of the bank. True or false?

6.5 Write out and complete the following sentences:

(a) When a customer signs a mortgage to the bank, the customer is a .... and the bank is a ....

(a) When a customer deposits items of value with a bank, the bank is a .... and the customer is a ....

(c) A bank that arranges an insurance policy for a customer is known as an...............................

6.6 What type of bank account would be appropriate in the following circumstances?

(a) A business needs finance for the purchase of a new machine (capital expenditure).

(b) A business needs finance for day-to-day expenses (revenue expenditure).

(c) A business needs an account which will pay interest on a large sum of money.

6.7 A business receives a large cheque from a customer for a purchase, but wants to make sure that the cheque will be paid before releasing the goods. The business bank account is at HSBC Bank, Holborn Circus and the cheque bears the name of Barclays Bank, Finsbury Circus. How long will it take to obtain clearance

(a) through the normal bank clearing system?

(b) by means of special clearance?

Would it make any difference if the cheque bore the name of HSBC Bank, Holborn Circus?

6.8 State two advantages to the customer of using a night safe.

6.9 State two reasons why cash should not be kept on the business premises for a long period of time.

6.10 State whether the following entries are debits or credits – from the viewpoint of the bank:

(a) an amount paid into a bank account

(b) an amount paid out of the bank account

6.11 The firm you work for is Eveshore Traders Ltd., which has a bank account at Barclays Bank, Eveshore. You are required to prepare the paying-in slip (below) and counterfoil (see next page) as at today's date. The cheques are to be listed on the back of the paying-in slip. The items to be banked are:

Cash		*Cheques*	
two £20 notes		£20.00	Maytree Enterprises
five £10 notes		£18.50	Bakewell Catering
eight £5 notes		£75.25	Henderson & Co
two £1 coins		£68.95	Musgrave Fine Art
six 50p coins			
four 10p coins			
two 2p coins			

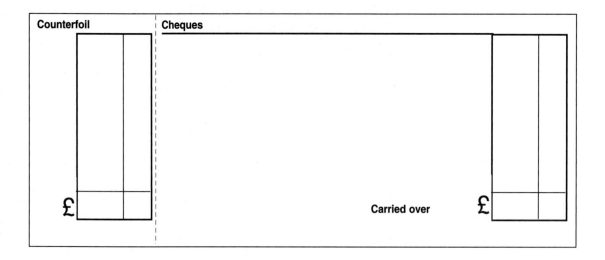

6.12 The firm you work for is Buxton Fine Wines, which has a bank account at Western Bank, Grantminster. Using today's date you are required to prepare the Retailers Summary and paying-in slip for ten credit card sales vouchers and a refund voucher. The documents are shown below and on the next page. The items to be banked are:

Sales vouchers	£45.60	£56.85
	£10.00	£56.00
	£15.50	£45.00
	£25.99	£49.50
	£67.50	£25.00
Refund voucher	£13.50	

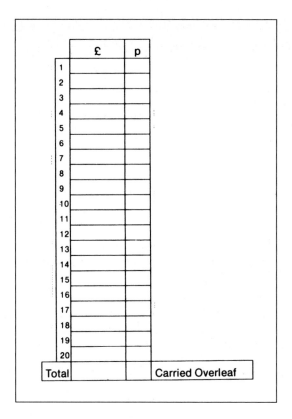

	£	p	
1			
2			
3			
4			
5			
6			
7			
8			
9			
10			
11			
12			
13			
14			
15			
16			
17			
18			
19			
20			
Total			Carried Overleaf

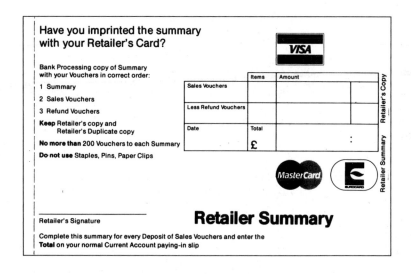

Have you imprinted the summary with your Retailer's Card?

VISA

Bank Processing copy of Summary with your Vouchers in correct order:

1 Summary

2 Sales Vouchers

3 Refund Vouchers

Keep Retailer's copy and Retailer's Duplicate copy

No more than 200 Vouchers to each Summary

Do not use Staples, Pins, Paper Clips

	Items	Amount		Retailer's Copy
Sales Vouchers				
Less Refund Vouchers				
Date	Total			Retailer Summary
	£		:	

MasterCard   EUROCARD

_____
Retailer's Signature

Retailer Summary

Complete this summary for every Deposit of Sales Vouchers and enter the **Total** on your normal Current Account paying-in slip

7 Cash book – recording receipts

this chapter covers . . .

In this chapter we look at the way in which the cash book records money received in the form of cash, cheques and other bank transfers.

The cash book is used to record the money side of book-keeping transactions and is part of the double-entry system.

This chapter focuses on the receipts (debit) side of the cash book; we will see also how the opposite credit entry is recorded in debtors' and other accounts.

PERFORMANCE CRITERIA COVERED

unit 30: INTRODUCTORY ACCOUNTING

element 30.1

process sales and receipts

H   enter receipts into the cash book, subsidiary ledger and main ledger

THE CASH BOOK IN THE ACCOUNTING SYSTEM

For most businesses, accounting for cash – including both bank and cash transactions – takes place in the cash books which comprise:

- *cash book,* for receipts and payments in cash and through the bank (cheques and BACS transfers)
- *petty cash book* (see Chapter 16), for low-value expense payments

The cash books combine the roles of books of prime entry and double-entry book-keeping. Cash books are:

- books of prime entry for cash and bank transactions
- double-entry accounts for cash and bank accounts

In this chapter we look at how the cash book is used to record receipts; the recording of payments made through the cash book is covered in Chapter 14; petty cash payments are dealt with in Chapter 16.

USES OF THE CASH BOOK

The cash book brings together the cash and bank transactions of a business. Thus it is used to record the money side of book-keeping transactions such as:

- cash transactions
  - all receipts in cash
  - most payments for cash, except for low-value expense payments (which are paid through petty cash book: see Chapter 16)
- bank transactions
  - all receipts through the bank (including the payment of cash into the bank)
  - all payments through the bank (including the withdrawal of cash from the bank)

Note that receipts are dealt with in this chapter, whilst payments are considered in Chapter 14.

The cash book is usually controlled by a cashier who:

- records receipts and payments through the bank and in cash
- makes cash payments, and prepares cheques and other bank transfers for signature by those authorised to sign
- pays cash and cheques received into the bank
- has control over the firm's cash, in a cash till or cash box

- issues cash to the petty cashier who operates the firm's petty cash book (see Chapter 16)
- checks the accuracy of the cash and bank balances at regular intervals

It is important to note that transactions passing through the cash book must be supported by documentary evidence. In this way an audit trail is established which provides a link that can be checked and followed through the accounting system:

- prime document
- book of prime entry
- double-entry accounts

Such an audit trail is required both as a security feature within the business (to help to ensure that false and fraudulent transactions cannot be made), and also for taxation purposes – for HM Revenue & Customs.

The cashier has an important role to play within the accounting function of a business – most business activities will, at some point, involve cash or cheque transactions. Thus the cash book and the cashier are at the hub of the accounting system. In particular, the cashier is responsible for:

- issuing receipts for cash (and sometimes cheques) received
- making authorised payments in cash, and by cheque and other bank transfers against documents received (such as invoices and statements) showing the amounts due
- checking expenses claims (see Chapter 14) and seeking authorisation before making payment

With so many transactions passing through the cash book, accounting procedures must include:

- accuracy – in writing up the cash book, in cash handling, and in ensuring that payments are made only against correct documents and appropriate authorisation
- security – of cash and cheque books, correct authorisation of payments
- confidentiality – that all cash/bank transactions, including cash and bank balances, are kept confidential

If the cashier has any queries about any transactions, he or she should refer them to the accounts supervisor.

RECORDING RECEIPTS – LAYOUT OF THE CASH BOOK

In this chapter we focus on the debit side of the cash book, which is used for recording receipts. The credit side of the cash book – used for recording payments is covered in Chapter 14.

A cash book can be set out in a variety of formats to suit the requirements of a particular business. One format that can be used is a columnar cash book incorporating several money columns. An example of the receipts side of a three-column cash book (with three money columns) is shown below:

Debit		Cash Book: Receipts				CBR
Date	Details		Folio	Discount allowed	Cash	Bank
				£	£	£

points to note

- The cash book receipts (CBR) is the debit side (the payments side is the credit side – see Chapter 14); thus the cash book is part of the double-entry system.

- The cash book shown here has separate money columns for cash receipts and for bank receipts, eg cheques, BACS transfers received. Note that the cash column does not always appear in the cash book – it is most often used by businesses, such as shops, which have a high volume of cash receipts. Many businesses use a cash book which just has a bank column to record receipts such as cheques, BACS transfers and any cash received – all paid straight into the bank. Whatever the format of the cash book, the basic principles will remain the same.

- A third money column is used to record any settlement (cash) discount allowed to customers (that is, an allowance offered to customers for quick settlement of the amount due, eg 2% discount for settlement within seven days).

- As the cash book is part of the double-entry system, each entry on the receipts side (the debit side) of the cash and bank columns must have an opposite entry on the credit side of another account elsewhere.

- The discount allowed column is not part of the double-entry system – it is used in the cash book as a listing device or memorandum column. We will see later in this chapter how amounts from this column are transferred into the double-entry system.

Case Study

SEVERN TRADING COMPANY – CASH BOOK RECEIPTS

situation

The cashier at the firm for which you work, Severn Trading Company, is away on a training course this week. You are required, in her absence, to take over as cashier. The following receipts are to be entered into the firm's three column cash book:

2007

5 Apr	Balances at start of week: cash £300, bank £1,550
5 Apr	Cash sales £235 (including VAT of £35)
6 Apr	Received a cheque from S Wright, a debtor, for £98 – we have allowed her £2 settlement discount
6 Apr	Received a bank giro credit from Peter Singh Limited, a debtor, for £205 (no settlement discount)
7 Apr	J Jones settles her account of £80, by cheque, after deducting 5% settlement discount
7 Apr	Cash sales £94 (including VAT of £14), a cheque received
9 Apr	Received a cheque for £45 from D Whiteman Limited in full settlement of the account of £48
9 Apr	Received a monthly standing order payment for £110 from Natasha Lloyd and Co, a debtor (no settlement discount)

Note: all cheques are banked on the day of receipt

solution

The receipts side of the cash book records these transactions as shown below:

Debit		Cash Book: Receipts			CBR 24
Date	Details	Folio	Discount allowed	Cash	Bank
2007			£	£	£
5 Apr	Balances brought down			300	1,550
5 Apr	Sales	ML 4001/2200		235	
6 Apr	S Wright	SL 295	2		98
6 Apr	Peter Singh Limited (CR)	SL 147			205
7 Apr	J Jones	SL 86	4		76
7 Apr	Sales	ML 4001/2200			94
9 Apr	D Whiteman Limited	SL 278	3		45
9 Apr	Natasha Lloyd and Co (SO)	SL 121			110
			9	535	2,178

notes

- The cash book receipts page is numbered – here 'CBR 24'.

- The cash book forms a part of the double-entry book-keeping system. The receipts side of the cash book records the debit entry for cash and bank transactions – in the section which follows we shall see how the credit entry for each transaction is recorded in order to complete double-entry. (The discount allowed column is not part of double-entry – we will see how it is transferred into the accounts in the next section.)

- The balances brought down on 5 April are the amounts of cash held and the amount of money in the bank account as shown by the cash book at the beginning of the week. The cash book, like other accounts, is balanced at regular intervals – eg weekly or monthly – and we shall look at how it is balanced in Chapter 18.

- The folio column has been completed to show in which division of the ledger and to which account number(s) the opposite book-keeping entry appears:

  ML = main ledger

  SL = sales ledger, ie subsidiary (sales) ledger

- Where receipts have been transferred direct into the bank account, for example here on 6 April by bank giro credit and on 9 April by standing order, the transactions have been indicated – this information will help when the firm's bank statement is received (see page 362).

- Where two or more cheques are banked on the same day and on the same paying-in slip, it is possible to sub-total the cash book in order to show that the cheques total on the paying-in slip agrees with the sub-total of the cash book. This is a very useful checking device.

- For cash sales, the amount of cash (or cheques) received and recorded in the cash book includes VAT; when recording the entries to be shown on the credit side of the accounts, we need to distinguish between the sales amount and VAT – see the section which follows. This is the reason why two main ledger account numbers are shown in the folio column against cash sales – the first number refers to sales account, the second to VAT account.

- The money columns of the cash book have been sub-totalled – this helps as we take information forward into other accounts within the double-entry system, and also when we balance the cash book (see Chapter 18).

COMPLETING DOUBLE-ENTRY TRANSACTIONS

We have seen how the debit side of the cash book is used to record receipts in the form of cash or through the bank account. In this section we look at how to complete the double-entry accounts for

- cash sales

- receipts from debtors

recording cash sales

By 'cash sales' we mean where a customer buys goods or services and pays immediately either in cash or by cheque (or other payment method such as BACS, debit card, credit card). The double-entry book-keeping entries are:

- payment received in cash
    - *debit* cash column of the cash book
    - *credit* sales account (or *credit* cash sales account – some businesses prefer to separate cash sales from credit sales)
    - *credit* VAT account (with the amount of VAT)
- payment received by cheque (or other banking payment method)
    - *debit* bank column of the cash book
    - *credit* sales account (or *credit* cash sales account)
    - *credit* VAT account

Note that such 'cash' customers do not have credit accounts.

The credit entries from the Case Study for the cash sales transactions of 5 April and 7 April are recorded in the double-entry accounts as follows:

MAIN LEDGER

Dr		**Sales Account** (account no 4001)		Cr
2007	£	2007		£
		5 Apr	Cash CBR 24	200
		7 Apr	Bank CBR 24	80

Dr		**Value Added Tax Account** (account no 2200)		Cr
2007	£	2007		£
		5 Apr	Cash CBR 24	35
		7 Apr	Bank CBR 24	14

recording receipts from debtors

When customers (debtors) pay for goods or services that have been sold to them on credit, the method of payment is:

- either by cheque, or other payment method such as BACS, debit card, credit card
- or, less commonly, in cash

The double-entry book-keeping entries are:

- payment received by cheque (or other banking method)
  - *debit* bank column of the cash book
  - *credit* sales ledger control account (in the main ledger)
  - and a credit to the debtor's account in the subsidiary (sales) ledger
- payment received in cash
  - *debit* cash column of the cash book
  - *credit* sales ledger control account (in the main ledger)
  - and a credit to the debtor's account in the subsidiary (sales) ledger

As well as the credit to sales ledger control account, remember that a credit must be recorded on the debtor's account in the subsidiary (sales) ledger. Note that no entry is needed in VAT account as it will have been made when the credit sale was recorded in the accounting system (see Chapter 3).

Where cash discount allowed for prompt settlement has been taken by the debtor, ie settlement discount has reduced the amount of the payment, entries must be made in the double-entry system as follows:

- *debit* discount allowed account (in the main ledger)
- *credit* sales ledger control account (in the main ledger)
- and a credit to the debtor's account in the subsidiary (sales) ledger

The credit entries from the Case Study for the receipts from debtors are as follows, starting with the subsidiary (sales) ledger. It is suggested that you 'tick back' each transaction.

Note: for illustrative purposes an amount for sales has been debited to each debtor's account (with the cross-reference to SDB 98).

SUBSIDIARY (SALES) LEDGER

Dr				**S Wright** (account no 295)			Cr
2007			£	2007			£
15 Mar	Sales	SDB 98	100	6 Apr	Bank CBR 24		98
				6 Apr	Discount Allowed ML 6501		2

Dr				**Peter Singh Limited** (account no 147)			Cr
2007			£	2007			£
15 Mar	Sales	SDB 98	400	6 Apr	Bank	CBR 24	205

Dr			**J Jones** (account no 86)		Cr
2007		£	2007		£
15 Mar	Sales SDB 98	80	7 Apr	Bank CBR 24	76
			7 Apr	Discount Allowed ML 6501	4

Dr			**D Whiteman Limited** (account no 278)		Cr
2007		£	2007		£
15 Mar	Sales SDB 98	48	9 Apr	Bank CBR 24	45
			9 Apr	Discount Allowed ML 6501	3

Dr			**Natasha Lloyd and Co** (account no 121)		Cr
2007		£	2007		£
15 Mar	Sales SDB 98	350	9 Apr	Bank CBR 24	110

Notes:

- In the above accounts amounts for sales have been shown for illustrative purposes – see Chapter 3, which covers accounting for sales.
- In order to complete double-entry book-keeping, discount allowed amounts, which have been credited to the debtors' accounts, must also be debited to discount allowed account in the main ledger (the discount column in the cash book is not part of the double-entry system, but is a memorandum column only). The account is completed by entering the total of the discount column from the cash book, as follows:

MAIN LEDGER

Dr	**Discount Allowed Account** (account no 6501)			Cr
2007		£	2007	£
9 Apr Cash Book CBR 24		9		

- Sales ledger control account (see below) is credited with the amount of discount allowed.
- Once the total of discount allowed has been taken from the cash book, the discount column 'starts again' (ie the amount of £9, above, for this week will not be included in next week's transfer).
- Sales ledger control account is written up as follows at 9 April (the end of the week):

MAIN LEDGER

Dr	**Sales Ledger Control Account** (account no 6001)			Cr
2007		£	2007	£
15 Mar Sales SDB 98		*978	9 Apr Bank CBR 24	**534
			9 Apr Discount Allowed ML 6501	9

*   As the sales day book is not shown here, the sales figure is the total of the debits to the subsidiary debtors' accounts, ie £100 + £400 + £80 + £48 + £350.

** The total bank receipts of £534 comprises cheques and bank transfers from debtors, ie £98 + £205 + £76 + £45 + £110 (the amount does not include receipts from cash sales). Later in this chapter – page 151 – we will see how an analysed cash book can be used to obtain more easily the total of receipts from debtors.

treatment of VAT – cash sales and credit sales

Remember the terminology:

cash sales = *sales where payment (whether in cash, by cheque or debit/credit card) is received straightaway*

credit sales = *sales where payment (whether in cash, by cheque or debit/credit card) is received from the debtor at a later date*

When carrying out the book-keeping entries for receipts from cash sales and receipts from debtors, the treatment of VAT is quite different. It is important to bear these differences in mind. Remember:

The double-entry for a payment received from **cash sales** is:

– *debit* bank column of the cash book (or cash column if it is used)

– *credit* sales account

– *credit* VAT account (with the amount of VAT)

The double-entry for a payment received from **credit sales** (ie from a debtor):

– *debit* bank column of the cash book

– *credit* sales ledger control account (in the main ledger)

There is no entry for VAT here because the VAT has already been accounted for when the sale was first made (see Chapter 3). The entries would then have been: *debit* debtor account and *credit* sales account and *credit* VAT account.

The diagram on the next page illustrates the book-keeping entries for the receipts from sales, which have been described in this section of the chapter.

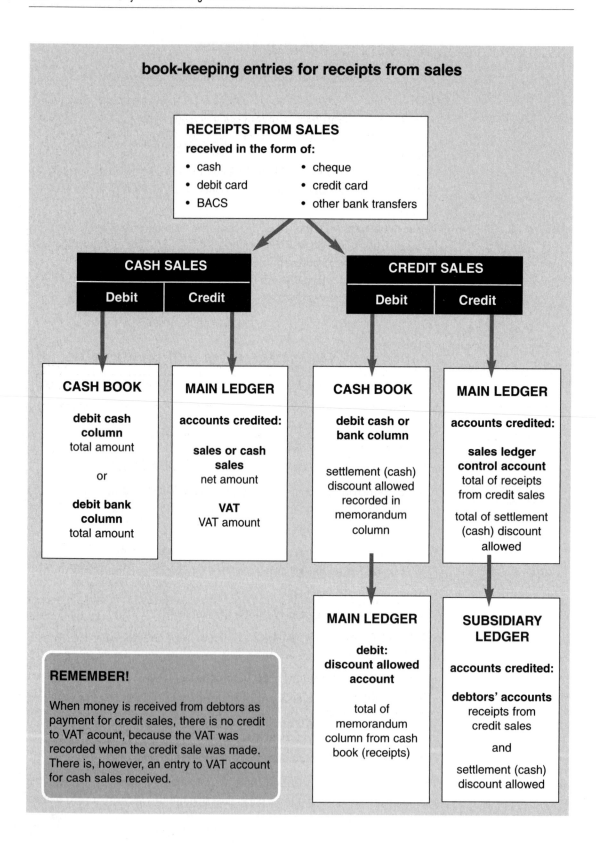

BATCH CONTROL SYSTEMS

Where businesses have a large number of receipts – from cash sales and/or from debtors – they often use batched data entry in order to enter such transactions into the accounts in one 'run'. As we have seen previously in Chapter 3, a batch of transactions for a day, week or month is pre-listed on a batch control form; the example shown below is for a batch of cheques received from debtors:

Batch Control: cheques received from debtors

Customer			Debit	Debit	Credit
Date	Account No	Name	Discount allowed	Bank	Debtors control
2007			£	£	£
6 Apr	SL 295	S Wright	2.00	98.00	100.00
7 Apr	SL 86	J Jones	4.00	76.00	80.00
7 Apr	SL 278	D Whiteman Ltd	3.00	45.00	48.00
		Check list totals	9.00	219.00	228.00

Prepared by	*Neil Ford*	Date	*9 Apr 2007*
Checked by	*Barbara Smith*	Date	*9 Apr 2007*
Posted by	*Dan Ryan*	Date	*9 Apr 2007*

Note that receipts from customers by BACS and other bank transfers have not been shown on the batch control form – only cheques received are listed. A business that has a lot of cash sales or receives large numbers of payments from customers by BACS or other methods – such as credit and debit cards – will use batch control systems for each type of receipt. As always, in accounting, businesses adapt systems to suit their own circumstances.

Totals are taken from the batch control form and transferred to sales ledger control account. It is probably better practice to credit the two separate amounts, ie £9.00 and £219.00, rather than the total credit of £228.00.

Payments received by methods other than by cheque – such as BACS, debit card and credit card receipts – will also be credited to sales ledger control account.

THE CASH BOOK IN THE ACCOUNTING SYSTEM

The cash book performs two functions within the accounting system:

- it is the book of prime entry for cash/bank transactions
- it forms part of the double-entry system (note that the cash book can, alternatively, be represented in the main ledger by a cash control account – see page 387)

For the receipts side of the cash book these functions are illustrated in the diagram which follows:

CASH AND BANK RECEIPTS

PRIME DOCUMENTS
- receipts issued
- bank paying-in slips
- BACS and other bank transfers received
- debit and credit card vouchers

BOOK OF PRIME ENTRY
AND DOUBLE-ENTRY BOOK-KEEPING

DEBIT cash book receipts

DOUBLE-ENTRY BOOK-KEEPING
either
- CREDIT sales ledger control account (money received), and debtors' accounts in the subsidiary (sales) ledger
or
- CREDIT other account, eg sales account (for cash sales), VAT account (for VAT on cash sales)

CASH BOOK INCORPORATING VAT

A cash book can be adapted to suit the needs of a business – already we have seen how a cash book incorporates a memorandum column for settlement discount. Another common layout uses a money column for VAT, as shown in the Case Study which follows. The VAT column acts as a memorandum column and, at the end of the week or month, is transferred to VAT account.

CASH BOOK INCORPORATING VAT

situation

On Monday 7 June 2007, the cash book of Eveshore Growers showed a balance of £248 in the bank. Receipts for the week were:

7 June Received a cheque for £470 from a debtor, Sisco Systems

7 June Cash sales of £282, including Value Added Tax, paid direct into the bank

8 June Received a cheque for £230 from a debtor, P Leech, who was settling his account balance of £235 after deducting £5 settlement discount

9 June Cash sales of £423, including Value Added Tax, paid for by cheque

The rate of Value Added Tax is 17.5%.

All cheques are banked on the day of receipt.

As cashier to Eveshore Growers, you are to:

• write up page 54 of the receipts side of the cash book for the week commencing 7 June 2007, using separate columns for discount, VAT and bank (note that no cash column is required in this cash book – all cash is paid straight into the bank)

• sub-total the cash book at 11 June 2007

• explain how the totals for the discount and VAT columns will be entered in the main ledger of Eveshore Growers

solution

Debit		Cash Book: Receipts				CBR 54
Date	Details	Folio	Discount allowed	VAT	Bank	
2007			£	£	£	
7 Jun	Balance brought down				248	
7 Jun	Sisco Systems	SL			470	
7 Jun	Sales	ML		42	282	
8 Jun	P Leech	SL	5		230	
9 Jun	Sales	ML		63	423	
			5	105	1,653	

Notes:

• The folio columns have been completed as follows (account numbers have not been shown)

ML =   main ledger

SL =   sales ledger, ie subsidiary (sales) ledger

- For transactions involving sales ledger (eg Sisco Systems), no amount for VAT is shown in the VAT column. This is because VAT has been charged on invoices issued and was recorded in the VAT account (through the sales day book) when the sale was made.

- VAT on cash sales and other transactions is recorded in the VAT analysis column.

- Receipts from debtors (eg Sisco Systems) are credited to sales ledger control account in the main ledger, and to the debtors' accounts in the subsidiary (sales) ledger.

The discount and VAT columns:

- discount allowed column – the total of £5 will be debited to discount allowed account in the main ledger, credited to sales ledger control account in the main ledger and to P Leech's account in the subsidiary (sales) ledger

- VAT column – the total of £105 will be credited to VAT account in the main ledger (alternatively the individual amounts of £42 and £63 could be credited)

Note that, in the cash book, the discount allowed and VAT columns 'start again' from zero after the totals have been transferred to the main ledger accounts.

ANALYSED CASH BOOK

Many businesses use an analysed cash book to provide more information. An analysed cash book divides receipts (and payments – see Chapter 14) between a number of categories.

Receipts could be divided between:

- the main sections of a business, such as (1) furniture, and (2) carpets, for a home furnishing shop

- (1) discount allowed, (2) Value Added Tax (where a business is registered for VAT), (3) cash sales, (4) sales ledger, ie receipts from debtors, (5) sundry receipts

A business will use whatever analysis columns suit it best: the cash book should be adapted to meet the needs of the business in the best possible way.

Case Study

ANALYSED CASH BOOK

situation

Wyvern Auto Spares Limited sells car parts to local garages and to members of the public. The company is registered for Value Added Tax.

The business uses a cash book which analyses receipts as follows:

> **RECEIPTS**
> * discount allowed
> * VAT
> * cash sales
> * sales ledger, ie subsidiary (sales) ledger
> * sundry receipts

The following receipts transactions are to be entered on page 31 of the receipts side of the cash book for the first week of December 2007:

6 Dec	Balances from previous week: cash £255, bank £875
6 Dec	Sales for cash £240 + VAT
7 Dec	A debtor, Main Street Garage, settles an invoice for £195, paying by cheque
7 Dec	Sales for cash £200 + VAT
9 Dec	A debtor, A45 Service Station, settles an invoice for £240, paying £235 by cheque and receiving £5 discount for prompt settlement
9 Dec	Sales £320 + VAT, received by cheque
10 Dec	Sales for cash £200 + VAT

[handwritten: 255 × 17·5 = 100 = 44·625]

The rate of Value Added Tax is 17.5%. All cheques are banked on the day of receipt.

solution

Debit					Cash Book: Receipts					CBR 31
Date	Details	Folio	Cash	Bank	Discount allowed	VAT	Cash sales	Sales ledger	Sundry
2007			£	£	£	£	£	£	£
6 Dec	Balances brought down		255	875					
6 Dec	Sales	ML	282			42	240		
7 Dec	Main Street Garage	SL		195				195	
7 Dec	Sales	ML	235			35	200		
9 Dec	A45 Service Station	SL		235	5			235	
9 Dec	Sales	ML		376		56	320		
10 Dec	Sales	ML	235			35	200		
			1,007	1,681	5	168	960	430	–

notes

- The receipts side of the cash book analyses each receipt between a number of headings. A business will adapt the cash book and use whatever analysis columns suit it best for its receipts.

- References to the ledger sections have been shown in the folio column.

- For transactions involving sales ledger, no amount for VAT is shown in the VAT columns. This is because VAT has been charged on invoices issued and was recorded in the VAT account (through the sales day book) when the sale was made.

- The columns are sub-totalled at the end of the week and the totals of the analysis columns are transferred to other accounts as follows:

  - discount allowed column total of £5 is debited to discount allowed account in the main ledger and credited to sales ledger control account in the main ledger

  - Value Added Tax column, the total of £168 is credited to VAT account in the main ledger

  - cash sales column, the total of £960 is credited to sales account (or cash sales account) in the main ledger

  - sales ledger column, the total of £430 is credited to sales ledger control account in the main ledger

- Individual amounts of receipts from debtors and discount allowed are credited to debtors' accounts in the subsidiary (sales) ledger

- Sundry receipts are dealt with individually by crediting the appropriate account (eg capital, loan, income): see section below

OTHER RECEIPTS

In addition to receipts from debtors and from cash sales, the debit side of the cash book is used to record other receipts of the business. These include:

- capital introduced by the owner(s)

- loans made to the business, such as a bank loan, or from a relative or friend

- income, such as rent received, commission received

We will look at further aspects of these transactions in more detail in Chapter 17 and see how they fit into the double-entry system. For the moment we will see how they are recorded in the double-entry system of cash book and ledger accounts:

- capital introduced

  - *debit* cash book

  - *credit* capital account

The owner of the business pays in capital (or more capital) in the form of cash or a cheque.

- loans received
  - *debit* cash book
  - *credit* loan account, eg bank loan, loan from J Smith

  The amount of the loan is received in the cash book, by cheque or through the bank.

- income received
  - *debit* cash book
  - *credit* income account (using the appropriate account, eg rent received, commission received)

  Business income, other than from sales, may be received in the form of cash, a cheque or by bank transfer.

example transactions

2007

16 Jun	The owner of the business pays in additional capital of £1,000, by cheque
17 Jun	Received a loan of £500, by cheque, from A Friend (no VAT)
18 Jun	Rent received from tenant, £150 by cheque (no VAT)

The cash book (receipts) records these transactions as follows:

Debit		**Cash Book: Receipts**				**CBR 10**
Date	Details		Folio	Discount allowed	Cash	Bank
2007				£	£	£
16 Jun	Capital		ML			1,000
17 Jun	Loan: A Friend		ML			500
18 Jun	Rent received		ML			150

The credit entries are shown in the main ledger (in which all of these accounts are contained) as follows:

MAIN LEDGER

Dr		**Capital Account**		Cr
2007	£	2007		£
		16 Jun Bank CBR 10		1,000

Dr		**Loan Account: A Friend**		Cr
2007	£	2007		£
		17 Jun Bank CBR 10		500

Dr		**Rent Received Account**		Cr
2007	£	2007		£
		18 Jun Bank CBR 10		150

Chapter Summary

- The cash book records receipts (debits) for cash and credit transactions.

- The basic layout for a cash book (receipts) includes a money column for bank transactions, together with a column for discount allowed. Cash books for businesses which receive substantial amounts of cash (eg shops) may have a further money column to record cash (notes and coins) transactions.

- Another common cash book layout incorporates a VAT column.

- An analysed cash book is used to provide more information: it divides receipts between a number of categories.

Key Terms

cash book	records bank (and in some cases cash) transactions; it combines the roles of book of prime entry and double-entry book-keeping
columnar cash book	commonly-used layout for cash books which incorporates several money columns, eg for settlement discount, VAT, cash, bank
analysed cash book	cash book which divides receipts (and payments) between a number of categories, eg the main sections of the business

Student Activities

7.1 The cash book is:

(a) a prime document

(b) a book of prime entry only

(c) part of double-entry book-keeping only

(d) combines book of prime entry and double-entry book-keeping

Answer (a) or (b) or (c) or (d)

7.2 You work as the cashier for Wyvern Publishing, a company which publishes a wide range of travel and historical books. As cashier, your main responsibility is for the firm's cash book.

Explain to a friend what your job involves and the qualities required of a cashier.

7.3 The following are the receipts transactions of Metro Trading Company for August 2007:

1 Aug   Balances from previous month: cash £276, bank £4,928

3 Aug   Received a cheque from a debtor, Wild & Sons Limited, £398

6 Aug   Sales for cash, £160 + VAT   28

16 Aug   Received a cheque for £1,755 from A Lewis Limited in full settlement of their account of £1,775

18 Aug   Sales for cash, £240 + VAT 42

20 Aug   Received a cheque for £261 from Harvey & Sons Limited, a debtor

23 Aug   Received a loan of £750 from the bank (no VAT)

24 Aug   Sales £400 + VAT, received half in cash, and half by cheque 70

26 Aug   Rent received from tenant, £100 in cash (no VAT)

27 Aug   Received a cheque for £595 from Wild & Sons Limited in full settlement of their account of £610

The rate of Value Added Tax is 17.5%

All cheques are banked on the day of receipt

Account numbers are to be used – see below

You are to:

*   Enter the above receipts on page 45 of the three column cash book of Metro Trading Company. This cash book has columns for discount allowed, cash and bank.

*   Sub-total the money columns at 31 August.

*   Show the entries to be made in the following accounts:

    subsidiary (sales) ledger

    Wild & Sons Limited (account no 843)

    A Lewis Limited (account no 531)

    Harvey & Sons Limited (account no 467)

    main ledger

    sales ledger control account (account no 6001)

    discount allowed account (account no 6501)

    bank loan (account no 2210)

    rent received account (account no 4951)

    sales account (account no 4001)

    VAT account (account no 2200)

7.4 The following are the receipts transactions of Johnson Brothers for April 2007:

1 Apr   Balance at bank from previous month, £718

8 Apr   J Bowen, a debtor, settles an invoice for £90, paying £85 by cheque and receiving £5 discount for prompt settlement

9 Apr   Cash sales £470 (including Value Added Tax) received by cheque

12 Apr   Rent received from tenant, £250 by cheque (no VAT)

16 Apr	Cash sales of £94 (including Value Added Tax) received by cheque
19 Apr	Received a cheque for £575 from J Burrows, a debtor, in full settlement of an invoice for £600
20 Apr	Cash sales of £188 (including Value Added Tax) paid direct into the bank
26 Apr	Received a cheque for £245 from Wilson Limited, a debtor, in full settlement of an invoice for £255

The rate of Value Added Tax is 17.5%

All cash and cheques are banked on the day of receipt

Account numbers are to be used – see below

You are to:

* Enter the above receipts on page 88 of the cash book of Johnson Brothers. The cash book has columns for date, details, discount allowed, VAT and bank.

* Sub-total the money columns at 30 April.

* Show the entries to be made in the following accounts:

    subsidiary (sales) ledger
    J Bowen (account no 117)
    J Burrows (account no 125)
    Wilson Limited (account no 855)

    main ledger
    sales ledger control account (account no 6001)
    discount allowed account (account no 6501)
    rent received account (account no 4951)
    sales account (account no 4001)
    VAT account (account no 2200)

7.5 David Lewis runs a shop selling carpets to the public on cash terms and also to a few trade customers – such as carpet fitters – on credit terms. His business is registered for VAT.

He uses an analysed cash book which has columns for:
* bank
* discount allowed
* VAT
* sales
* sales ledger
* sundry

The following transactions take place during the week commencing 17 May 2007:

17 May	Balance at bank from previous week, £825.30
17 May	Sales £534.62 (including VAT), cheque received
17 May	Rent received from tenant of flat above the shop, £255.50 by cheque (no VAT)
18 May	Sales £164.50 (including VAT), cash received and paid direct into the bank
18 May	A debtor, T Jarvis, settles an invoice for £157.50, paying £155.00 by cheque, £2.50 discount being allowed for prompt settlement
19 May	David Lewis' brother, Terry, makes a loan to the business of £500.00 by cheque (no VAT)

19 May   Sales £752.00 (including VAT), cheque received

20 May   Sales £264.37 (including VAT), cash received and paid direct into the bank

21 May   David Lewis pays in additional capital of £1,000.00 by cheque (no VAT)

21 May   A debtor, Wyvern District Council, settles an invoice for £565.45, paying £560.45 by cheque and receiving £5.00 discount for prompt settlement

The rate of Value Added Tax is 17.5%

All cash and cheques are banked on the day of receipt

Account numbers are to be used – see below

You are to:

•   Enter the above receipts on page 96 of the cash book of David Lewis (VAT amounts should be rounded down to the nearest penny).

•   Sub-total the money columns at 21 May.

•   Show the entries to be made in the following accounts:

subsidiary (sales) ledger

T Jarvis (account no 497)

Wyvern District Council (account no 924)

main ledger

capital account (account no 3005)

sales ledger control account (account no 6001)

discount allowed account (account no 6501)

loan account: T Lewis (account no 2220)

rent received account (account no 4951)

sales account (account no 4001)

VAT account (account no 2200)

7.6   Prepare a sales ledger control account for the month of December 2007 from the following information:

2007		£
1 Dec	Debit balances brought down	38,643
31 Dec	Credit sales for month	45,419
	Sales returns	3,210
	Payments received from debtors	43,987
	Settlement discount allowed	695

Balance the account at 31 December 2007.

8 Customer communications and legal issues

This chapter starts by explaining the importance of polite and effective handling of communications between an organisation and its customers. It covers:

- the need for effectiveness – choosing the right means of communication and expressing the facts accurately and in an appropriate way

- an illustration of the wide variety of business communication formats

- practical examples of how those formats are used

- the different forms of written communication – notes, letters and memoranda

This chapter then explains how businesses are affected by the law – both by contract law and by statute law (Acts of Parliament). Specific areas covered are:

- what makes up a legally binding contract

- breach of contract – what to do when things go wrong

- protection given in statute law when someone purchases goods or services

Data Protection law is is dealt with in Osborne Books' **Accounting Work Skills Tutorial** for Unit 31 (Chapter 11).

PERFORMANCE CRITERIA COVERED

unit 30: INTRODUCTORY ACCOUNTING

element 30.1

process sales and receipts

K   write to customers in an appropriate style to request payment of an overdue account

The legal issues explained in this chapter are required by assessable Knowledge & Understanding item 2.

COMMUNICATING WITH CUSTOMERS

When dealing with customers you should communicate withthem *politely* and *effectively*. In other words, you should be pleasant and respectful in your communication and you transfer the necessary message accurately and within the correct timescale. These principles are often set out in an organisation's 'customer charter' scheme or will form part of a general 'quality' policy adopted by a business.

Politeness involves putting the other person first, no matter how stupid or arrogant that person might be – politeness is your mental attitude – it may come naturally, or it may not! *Effectivness* of communication, on the other hand, is less easy to achieve. It means:

- choosing the right means of communication
- getting your facts right
- being able to express those facts in the appropriate way

Effectiveness is a skill that has to be learned over a period of time.

Over the next few pages we will look at the different types of communication used internally in an organisation and externally with customers. You will need to study these carefully. First however, we give some examples of situations relating to customers which will require your communication skills.

examples of customer communications

The types of situation which might arise include:

- answering a customer enquiry about an invoice – eg the terms
- sending back a customer's cheque which has a signature missing
- chasing up debts from customers who are slow in paying

THE MEMORANDUM

format

The memorandum (plural memoranda) is a formal written note used for internal communication within an organisation. It may be word-processed or handwritten, and will often be produced in a number of copies which can be circulated as necessary. A memorandum may be sent by email within an organisation. A memorandum can be used for situations such as:

- giving instructions
- requesting information
- making suggestions
- recording of opinions
- confirming telephone conversations

elements of the memorandum

'to' and 'from'	the name and job title of the sender and the recipient are entered in full, and the formal phrases you find on letters, eg 'Dear......' and 'Yours ....' are not necessary
copies to	memoranda are sometimes sent to a number of people; the recipients will be indicated in this section of the document
subject	the subject matter of the memorandum must be stated concisely
text	the message of the memorandum should be clear and concise
signature	a memorandum can be signed, initialled, or even – as is often the case – left blank
enclosures	if material is circulated with the memorandum, the abbreviation 'enc' or 'encl' should be used

---

MEMORANDUM

To	John Stone, Accounts Supervisor		
From	Tim Blake, Sales Manager	**Ref**	TB/AC/1098
Copies to	n/a	**Date**	23 June 2007
Subject	Bad payers		

Please can you let me have an updated list of our customers who exceed their credit period and pay late.

I need to give this list to the sales reps so that they will not be tempted to extend credit any further to these customers.

Thank you.

a completed memorandum relating to customer accounts

THE NOTE

One of the most common forms of communication within an organisation is the *note*. This can be:

- an informal written note, passing on a message or an instruction
- a telephone message (some organisations use preprinted telephone message pads)

The important elements of a written note are

- the name of the person who is sending the note
- the name of the person who is to receive the note
- the time and date that the note is written
- a clearly stated message
- a clear indication of any action to be taken as a result of the message

Examine the examples set out below and see how they contain all these elements.

To Tim Blackstock,
Order Processing

Please remember to allow PDT Ltd an extra 10% trade discount on invoices this month.

John Tregennick, Sales
03.04.07 10.30

TELEPHONE MESSAGE

TO   Karin Schmidt, Accounts
FROM   H Khan, Sales
DATE   22 April 2007
TIME   12.30

Please ring Jim Stoat at RF Electronics – he is complaining that they have not received a credit note for returned damaged stock (order ref 823423).

Please treat urgently – he is not very happy!

HK

THE FAX

The fax (short for 'facsimile') enables you to transmit electronically an exact copy of the details on a sheet of paper. This can either be done on a computer or on a fax machine. If you use a fax machine you feed the sheet into the machine, dial up the recipient on the inbuilt telephone pad and transmit the document down the line. The machine at the other end will print out an exact copy of the original document.

The fax can be used within an organisation or for external contact with a customer. You normally send a 'fax header' first sheet (see illustration below) and then feed in any further pages/documents as required.

The fax is very useful for sending copies of documents. A frequent excuse given by people who are slow at paying is "I can't pay because I don't seem to have the original invoice". This can be replied to with 'No problem! We can fax you a copy. What is your fax number?' Look at the example below.

Winterborn Electronics Limited

Unit 4 Everoak Estate, Bromyard Road
St Johns, Worcester WR2 5HN
tel 01905 748043 fax 01905 748911

facsimile transmission header

To: Jamie Milne, Accounts Office, Zippo Computers

Fax number: 01350 525504

Number of pages including this header: 2   Date: 17 October 2007

message

Invoice 24375

Further to our recent telephone conversation I am faxing you a copy of invoice 24375 which is now overdue.

I shall be grateful if you will arrange for the £4,678.50 owing to be paid to us as soon as possible.

R Pound

Credit Controller

THE EMAIL

Email is the sending and receiving of electronic messages by means of computer. Emails can be

- external – communications with customers through the Internet, or
- internal – through a network of computers in the business – an intranet

Emails can be sent quickly and cheaply within the UK and overseas.

When someone wants to check an email account, it is necessary to log in. A list of messages is displayed. The user can read them or delete them. When a message is read, it is easy to reply to it. The original message re-appears and comments can be added to the original. If a message is of interest to someone else, it can be forwarded. Computer files – eg spreadsheets – can also be sent by email as 'attachments'.

When composing an email, a screen such as the one illustrated below is used.

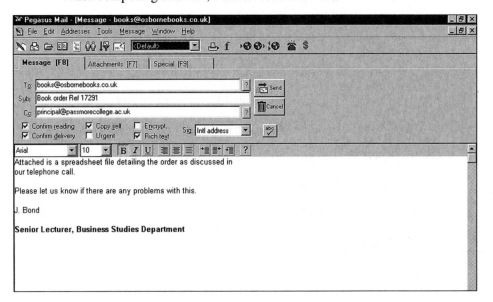

It can be seen that there is:

- space for the message
- a place to type in the email address of where the email has to go (this is not needed if it is a reply or if the address is held in your address book
- a subject box to say what the email is about – this is useful for the person reading a message list to identify which ones are more important
- a CC (carbon copy) box so that a copy of the email can be sent to anyone else who needs to know about the message
- an attachments facility to send attcahed files

THE 'HOUSE STYLE' LETTER

When you deal with business letters you will see that the appearance and format of each letter is in a uniform 'house' style, a style which identifies that business, and is common to all letters that it sends. The letter will normally be on standard printed stationery showing the name, address and details of the business, and will be set out with headings, paragraphs, signatures – the 'elements' of the letter – in a uniform way.

There are a number of different ways of setting out the text of a letter. The most of common of these – the 'fully blocked' style is illustrated and explained on the next two pages.

characteristics of a fully blocked letter

- the most commonly used style of letter

- all the lines start at the left margin

- the use of open punctuation, ie there is no punctuation, except in the main body of the letter, which uses normal punctuation

- paragraphs are divided by a space, and are not indented

- a fully blocked letter is easy to type as all the lines are set uniformly to the left margin

elements of the letter

The explanations which follow refer to the illustration of the letter on page 160.

printed letterhead   The name and address of the business is normally pre-printed, and must be up-to-date.

reference   The reference on the letter illustrated – DH/SB/69 – is a standard format

- DH (Derek Hunt), the writer

- SB (Sally Burgess), the secretary

- 69, the number of the file where Mr Smart's correspondence is kept

If you need to quote the reference of a letter to which you are replying, the references will be quoted as follows: Your ref TR/FG/45 Our ref DH/SB/69.

date	The date is typed in date (number), month (word), year (number) order.
recipient	The name and address of the person to whom the letter is sent. This section of the letter may be displayed in the window of a window envelope, so it is essential that it is accurate.
salutation	'Dear Sir. . . Dear Madam' – if you know the person's name and title (ie Mr, Mrs, Miss, Ms) use it, but check that it is correct – a misspelt name or an incorrect title will ruin an otherwise competent letter.
heading	The heading sets out the subject matter of the letter – it will concentrate the reader's mind.
body	The body of the letter is an area where the message of the letter is set out. The text must be
	• laid out in short precise paragraphs and short clear sentences
	• start with a point of reference (eg referring to an invoice)
	• set out the message in a logical sequence
	• be written in plain English – but avoid 'slang' expressions and, equally, avoid 'posh' words
	• finish with a clear indication of the next step to be taken (eg please telephone, please arrange appointment, please buy our products, please pay our invoice)
complimentary close	The complimentary close (signing off phrase) must be consistent with the salutation:
	'Dear Sir/Dear Madam' followed by 'Yours faithfully'
	'Dear Mr Sutton/Dear Ms Jones' followed by 'Yours sincerely'.
name and job title	It is essential for the reader to know the name of the person who sent the letter, and that person's job title, because a reply will need to be addressed to a specific person.
enclosures	If there are enclosures with the letter, the abbreviation 'enc' or 'encl' is used at the bottom of the letter.

the 'house style' letter

Wyvern Motor Supplies
107 High Street
Mereford
MR1 9SZ
Tel 01605 675365 Fax 01605 765576

reference ➜ Ref DH/SB/69

date ➜ 15 December 2007

name and address
of recipient ➜ Purchasing Department
Osborne Car Accessories
17 Pump Street
Mereford MR6 7ER

salutation ➜ Dear Sir

heading ➜ Invoice 8288 £10,589.50

body of
the letter ➜ We note from our records that we have not yet received payment of our invoice 8288 dated 15 September 2007. Our up-to-date statement of account is enclosed, together with a copy of the invoice.

Our payment terms are strictly 30 days from the date of the invoice. We shall be grateful if you will settle the £10,589.50 without further delay.

We look forward to receiving your cheque.

complimentary
close ➜ Yours faithfully

signature ➜ *D M Hunt*

name and job title
➜ Derek Hunt
Accounts Manager

enclosures ➜ enc

TYPES OF BUSINESS LETTER

Different types of business letter require different treatment. We will look at two situations and in each case give an example of how the text of the letter might read:

- dealing with queries and providing information
- chasing a debt

dealing with queries and providing information

The body of a letter providing information in answer to an enquiry will be structured in a number of stages:

1   Refer to the original enquiry, eg 'Further to your telephone enquiry/visit/letter' and give the enquiry a date ... 'of 1 April.'

2   Provide the information, either in the text, or by enclosing promotional literature, eg a catalogue.

3   Finish the text of the letter on a positive note or 'selling' note, eg 'Please let us know if we can be of further help' ... 'We look forward to your order' ... 'If you wish to order the goods, please contact Mr Eden in our Sales Department, telephone 01908 384983.'

Here is an extract from a letter following a telephone enquiry to a bathroom centre. Note that the text is not particularly lengthy, but is polite and to the point. It follows the three stages set out above.

Dear Mr Knott

Shower Enclosures

Thank you for your telephone enquiry of today.

I am pleased to enclose a brochure and price list for the Niagara range of shower enclosures.

If you require further information, please do not hesitate to give me a call.

Yours sincerely

J Waterman

J Waterman
Sales Manager

---

a letter chasing a debt

This type of letter is used by an accounts department or by a sole trader chasing up overdue invoices. Often the letter will be a 'set' letter, already formatted on the computer. There may be a number of set letters on file: a gentle reminder, a firm reminder, a threat of legal action and a formal demand. Each letter is set out in a number of stages:

1   Details of the amount owing is clearly stated: the amount itself and the date of the original invoice(s). Sometimes a copy invoice(s) will be included in the letter to avoid the common problem of the customer claiming that the original invoice has been lost!

    Mention will often be made of the fact that statements of account have also been sent.

2   The terms of the invoice will be stated and the fact that the terms have not been complied with will be stressed.

3   Payment will be firmly requested – often a time limit will be stated.

4   Sometimes it may be necessary to threaten what will happen if the money is not received, eg 'If we do not receive settlement by this date we regret we will have no alternative but to place the matter in the hands of our solicitors.'

The text of a chaser letter for a long overdue invoice is shown below. Study the text and then read the Case Study which follows.

---

30 April 2007

Dear Mr Khan

Invoice 23846 £1,250

We note from our records that invoice 23846 (copy enclosed)for £1,250, dated 8 January 2007, has not yet been settled.

The terms of this invoice were strictly 30 days and therefore it is well overdue.

We shall be grateful if you will kindly settle this amount by return of post.

Yours sincerely

N Wakefield

N Wakefield
Accounts Manager

VALLEYMORE FOODS

situation

Valleymore Foods Limited produces a variety of foodstuffs – pies, desserts, ready-made meals – which are sold frozen to its customers, who include supermarkets, pubs and local shops.

You work in the Accounts Department of Valleymore Foods and spend some of your time answering customer queries and debt chasing.

This Case Study illustrates some of the more common tasks you have to undertake.

situation 1: a customer overpays

You receive a telephone message on your voicemail from Sid Parks, owner of 'The Pig and Whistle', a local pub which you supply with snack meals.

"Hello there. I have just received my monthly statement of account from you. The balance should be back down to zero, but in fact it is showing a credit balance of £40. Does this mean that you owe me money? If so, can you let me have a refund? Perhaps you can let me know. Bye."

You look into the ledgers and find that Sid's last cheque to you was for £155 rather than the £115 owing on the account. He has overpaid by £40. You speak to Ivor Penny, your Customer Accounts Manager, who agrees that you can issue him with a refund cheque. He asks you to write a covering letter for his signature.

Valleymore Foods Limited
Martley Road, St Gregorys, MR2 5GT
Tel 01908 675234 Fax 01908 675332 email foods@valleymore.com

Mr S Parks
The Pig and Whistle
The Green
Clitteridge
MR4 9YH

3 July 2007

Dear Mr Parks

Account 29847

Further to your recent telephone message left with us we have pleasure in enclosing our cheque for £40. This represents the balance of your account with us. The account had gone into credit because the last settlement cheque you issued was for £155 rather than the £115 owing.

Yours sincerely

Ivor Penny
Customer Accounts Manager

situation 2: an unsigned customer cheque

You receive a cheque through the post from a customer Totley Limited. Unfortunately the cheque is unsigned. Your Manager says that you will have to send it back to the customer with a request for the customer to sign it ...

Accounts Department
Totley Limited
Unit 17 Deepend Estate
Bath
BA2 3BR

4 July 2007

Dear Sirs

Account 28761

I enclose your cheque 564132 for £12,349.50 which was received in our office today. Unfortunately the cheque has not been signed. I shall be grateful if you will arrange for it to be signed by the appropriate signatories and returned to us as soon as possible.

Yours faithfully

Ivor Penny
Customer Accounts Manager

situation 3: a missing credit note

You receive an email from Tredco Limited. The text reads:

> 'We have received your July statement today. It lists a credit note for £1,876.50 which we cannot trace. Please can you let us have a copy.'

You refer it to your Manager who suggests you fax the document with a suitable fax header message...

facsimile transmission header

To: Asaf Patel, Accounts Office, Tredco Limited
Fax number: 01350 525504
Number of pages including this header: 2   Date: 4 July 2007

message

Credit Note 8732
Further to your email of 3 July I am faxing you a copy of credit note 8732 for £1,876.50.

R U Shaw

Sales Ledger,
Accounts Department

situation 4: debt chasing

Every month Valleymore Foods Limited prints out its customer statements from the computer. These list transactions on each customers' account and show the amount(s) which are owing and due to be paid. Valleymore Foods Limited gives a standard 30 days credit to its sales ledger customers.

Every month you also have to send out standard chaser letters to late payers. Some letters are polite reminders, others are stronger in their terms.

You have been given a number of tasks.

Task 1

You have been asked to send 'Letter A' (a polite reminder) to any customers who have not settled within 60 days.

Task 2

You have been asked to send 'Letter B' (a firm reminder) to any customer who is exceeding 60 days.

These letters are to be signed by Ann Dover, the Credit Controller.

Computer analysis of the sales ledger shows that Maxwell Foods are due Letter A and Premier Chef Trading are due Letter B.

The letters produced are shown below and on the next page.

Task 1
Letter A

Valleymore Foods Limited
Martley Road, St Gregorys, MR2 5GT
Tel 01908 675234 Fax 01908 675332 email foods@valleymore.com

The Manager, Accounts Department
Maxwell Foods Limited
Parsons Road
Farmborough
SY3 7YH

4 August 2007

Dear Sir

Account 29613

We note from our records that we have not yet received settlement of due invoices totalling £833.75. Our invoice terms are strictly 30 days and these items are now overdue.

We shall be grateful if you will kindly settle this amount by return of post.

Yours faithfully

Ann Dover
Credit Controller

Task 2
Letter B

Valleymore Foods Limited

Martley Road, St Gregorys, MR2 5GT
Tel 01908 675234 Fax 01908 675332 email foods@valleymore.com

Accounts Manager
Premier Chef Trading
78 High Road
Brimley
BR6 5GF

4 August 2007

Dear Sir

Account 28745

Further to our previous reminders we still have not received settlement of the overdue invoices on your account. We shall be grateful if you will kindly forward us your cheque for £1546.88. If this amount has not been received at this address within seven working days we will have no alternative but to place the matter in the hands of our solicitors.

Yours faithfully

Ann Dover
Credit Controller

LEGAL ISSUES

The remainder of this chapter explores another important aspect of the relationship between an organisation and the customers to whom it sells – the legal issues involved.

The legal context involves two areas:

- the nature of a *contract* – particularly a contract of sale of goods or services
- the *legislation* covering the sale of goods and services

You are likely to be assessed in this area – possibly in relation to some practical problem or other. If you study the text that follows and carry out the related student activities at the end of the chapter you should be well prepared for your assessment.

A CONTRACT DEFINED

Part of your course involves the understanding of the legal framework which enables buying and selling to take place and which states what can happen if there is a dispute. The agreement between the parties is known as a *contract.*

what is a contract?

a contract is a legally binding agreement enforceable in a court of law

Contracts, which may be in writing, or by word of mouth (oral), are agreements between two parties. Examples include:

- a written contract which you sign if you buy a house
- a written contract for a loan agreement if you borrow money
- a written contract of employment
- an oral contract if you buy goods in a shop
- an oral contract if you order goods over the telephone
- an oral contract if you hire a decorator to paint your house

In each case somebody does something for which some kind of payment is made. A contract is *an agreement with legal consequences* because if the work done is not satisfactory, or if the payment is not made, the wronged party can take the other person to court for *breach of contract.*

You may rightly wonder how all this affects you in the workplace. The answer is that the principles of contract affect any person carrying out normal business activities. For example if you quote an incorrect price to a customer, they may be able to hold your business to that price, under the terms of the contract of sale. If you fail to finish a job for a customer, they may be able to go to court to obtain a court order for your business to complete the work under the contract.

the three elements of contract

There are three elements which are common and essential to all contracts:

agreement – an offer and an acceptance

bargain – some value (consideration) passes

intention to create legal relations – the agreement is commercial

THE AGREEMENT – OFFER AND ACCEPTANCE

the offer

A firm and clear offer must be made either to a single party, a group, or to the world at large. In a famous legal case in 1893, a manufacturer of medicines (the Carbolic Smoke Ball Company) advertised a patented smoke ball and promised to pay a £100 reward to any person who contracted a specified illness having used the ball three times a day for two weeks. A Mrs Carlill used the ball for eight weeks and still contracted 'flu. She claimed her £100, the company refused, and she had to take the matter to the court which ruled that she should be granted her £100, as the offer of £100 had been to the "whole world" and needed no communicated acceptance from Mrs Carlill. It formed part of a valid contract which the company had to honour. Note that this is *not* the same situation as an *advertised price* which is not an offer but information which will enable a purchase – the contract – to be made (see below).

invitation to treat

An offer is quite different from an *invitation to treat* which is an invitation for a person to make an offer. Goods on supermarket shelves are an invitation for a customer to take them to the checkout where that customer can offer to purchase them at the price indicated at the checkout, which is where the contract takes place. That is the reason why shop tills indicate the price for each item, normally on an illuminated display; it is also the reason why a shop is not obliged to sell the goods at the price shown on the shelves.

practical example – invitation to treat

problem
Basil sees a holiday advertised in the local paper for £50. He telephones the travel company which tells him that the figure is a printing error – it should have been £500. Basil is angry and insists on booking his week in Menorca for £50. The problem is, does a contract exist on the basis of the £50 quoted?

answer
Basil has no rights here. There is no contract because the £50 quoted is only *an invitation to treat*, an invitation for Basil to make an agreement for booking the holiday. The company will clearly not agree to £50 for a week in Menorca!

termination of an offer

An offer may only be accepted while it is still open for acceptance. An offer may be terminated in the following circumstances:

- the time limit (if there is one) expires; if there is no time limit the offer lapses after a reasonable period of time
- the offeror – the person making the offer – may revoke (cancel) the offer
- an offer may be rejected by the making of a counter-offer; for instance, if you offer your car for sale for £1,500 and someone offers you £1,350, that is a counter-offer
- by acceptance or rejection of the offer

acceptance of an offer

Acceptance of an offer must be firm and unambiguous; it may be in spoken words, written form or even implied by action. Acceptance cannot be assumed from silence on the part of the person to whom the offer is made. For instance, if you say "I offer you my car for £1,500; if I have not heard from you within a week I will assume the deal is done", there is no acceptance. The offeree may go on holiday, or forget it even happened. Acceptance must also be *unconditional*. Any new term introduced – "I will agree to buy your car as long as the wing is resprayed" – amounts to a counter-offer (see above) and revokes the original offer.

practical example – conditional acceptance

problem
Basil works for Martley Garden Centre and has recently sent a quotation for a fountain to Mrs Waters: the cost will be £250.00 plus VAT and the fountain will have to be ordered from an outside supplier. Mrs Waters writes back saying she wants to accept the price, but the fountain must be delivered before the end of the month. Is there a valid contract between Mrs Waters and the garden centre?

answer
No. There is no contract because the acceptance has been conditional. *Acceptance must be unconditional.* Any new term introduced amounts to a counter-offer: "I will pay £250 plus VAT if the fountain is delivered by the end of the month".

The term "subject to contract", often seen on estate agents' boards, means that the terms of the offer to the offeree are acceptable, but have not been finally accepted. The two parties involved have agreed to draw up a formal contract for signature at a later date. There is no binding contract at this point.

communication of acceptance

The rules relating to communication of acceptance are largely dictated by what is required by the offer:

- the acceptance must normally be communicated to the person making the offer

- if the offer requires acceptance by a specific means (letter/fax/verbal message) then that means must be used

the postal rule

An acceptance by post is effective as long as the letter of acceptance is correctly addressed, correctly stamped and actually posted.

The time of acceptance is when the letter is posted (not when it is received). Given that letters may be delayed or lost in the post, this rule may seem unjust to the offeror! The postal rule only applies to an acceptance, it does not apply to a posted offer which must reach the offeree.

---

practical example – acceptance by post

problem
On 1 April Cotheridge Conifers telephones Basil at Martley Garden Centre to offer a job lot of 150 Leylandii trees at a knock-down price of £1.50 each. Basil needs time to think about this and says he will drop a line in the post. On 3 April he posts a reply to Cotheridge Conifers accepting the offer and placing an order for the trees. On 5 April the order is received. The question is, what is the date on which the contract was formed?

answer
3 April. The postal rule states that the date of posting of an acceptance of an offer is the effective date of the contract.

THE BARGAIN: CONSIDERATION

definition of consideration

A valid contract involves a bargain, a passing of value, known in law as consideration. If a business buys goods there is a two way process involved:

- the supplier promises to deliver the goods

- the buyer agrees to pay for them

The parties involved are:

- the promisor, the supplier that promises to supply the goods
- the promisee, the buyer who has to make payment

The consideration here is the payment, the price paid for the service provided. The principle is simple in itself, but there are a number of rules which relate to consideration.

consideration must be sufficient

Consideration must by law be sufficient. This means that:

- it must have value, although the value need not be adequate in some eyes; for example, you could sell this book for 5p; many would consider the amount to be inadequate, but the 5p still has value and is therefore consideration
- it must be sufficient, ie it must be in return for the promise; money due for some other reason or obligation is not sufficient consideration

consideration must move from the promisee

This legal phrase means, in effect, that the person who is promised goods or a service must themselves provide payment if the promise is to be enforceable as a contract. If you buy goods, you must make the payment. If someone else pays for you (an unlikely event!) you cannot take the supplier to court if the goods do not arrive.

consideration cannot be past

This legal phrase means that the consideration should not precede the promise. If you mend someone's car without any mention of payment, and the car owner the following week promises to give you £5, and subsequently refuses to pay you, there is no contract. The promise of payment followed the good turn done, consideration (the repair) was past as it had taken place the previous week.

---

practical example – consideration

problem
Basil promises to cut down some trees for a friend free of charge one weekend. Unfortunately Basil cuts down the wrong trees. His friend is very upset and says he will sue Basil. Can he? Is there a contract?

answer
No. There is no contract because there is no consideration – no money has been paid. Basil has made a mistake but he cannot be sued.

THE INTENTION TO CREATE LEGAL RELATIONS

A contract is an agreement involving consideration which the parties intend to be legally binding. In other words the parties entering a contract can reasonably expect the agreement to be enforced in a court of law if the necessity arises. The law assumes:

• commercial agreements are intended to be legally binding

• social and domestic arrangements are not intended to be legally binding

In short, if a person enters a contract to buy your car and then, without reason, refuses to pay for it, you can take him or her to court. If you ask a friend out for the evening, promising to take him or her out for a meal, and your friend doesn't turn up, you can not take court action. The sale of a car involves the intention to create legal relations, the invitation out does not.

BREACH OF CONTRACT

A contract normally contains certain terms which must be fulfilled as part of the agreement. If a person breaks one of those terms, that person is in *breach of contract*. For example, if a supplier undertakes to supply goods, it must send the goods on the due date, and in turn expects the goods to be paid for by a certain time. If the customer does not pay, he or she is in breach of contract and may be taken to court for damages (money compensation).

Contract terms may be classified as follows:

express terms   explicitly stated terms which are binding on both parties to the contract

conditions   fundamental terms of the contract which, if broken, will enable the injured party to reject the contract and to go to court to sue for damages

warranties   minor terms which if broken can be cause for an action for damages for loss suffered; the contract, however, remains in force

implied terms   terms which are not stated, but which are implied by trade custom or by law; for instance, goods sold should be of "satisfactory quality", in accordance with the Sale of Goods Act

In short:

• express terms are written into the contract; implied terms are not

• conditions are important terms, warranties are less important

> ## practical example – breach of contract
>
> **problem**
> Martley Garden Centre orders 1500 flower arrangements from a London wholesale supplier for delivery two days before Mothers Day. Unfortunately, because of a transport strike they arrive during the week following Mothers Day. Martley Garden Centre threatens to sue the supplier. Is the garden centre within its rights to do so?
>
> **answer**
> There is a clear breach of contract – the delivery date is a term of the contract and has not been met. Martley Garden Centre could sue.

SELLING AND STATUTE LAW

Statute law is law set down in an Act of Parliament.

There are a number of statutes which govern the way in which goods and services are sold, and they obviously affect the way in which businesses operate. The principal statutes are the Trades Descriptions Act, the Sale of Goods Act and the Unfair Contract Terms Act.

Trades Descriptions Act

The Trades Descriptions Act makes it a criminal offence:

- to make false statements about goods offered for sale
- to make misleading statements about services

Examples of offences therefore include:

- stating that a car for sale has clocked up 15,000 miles, when in fact the figure is 150,000 miles
- making a misleading statement about the price of goods, eg saying 'Now only £49.95, was £99.95' when it has only ever sold for £69.95
- making a misleading statement about a service, eg 'our dry cleaning is guaranteed to remove every stain' when it does not, or 'our apartments are within easy reach of the sea' when they are fifteen miles away

Sale of Goods Act

This Act states that you are entitled to expect any goods that you buy from a shop to be:

of 'satisfactory quality'
This means they must meet the standard that a 'reasonable' person would expect given the description and the price.

'fit for the purpose'

The goods must do what they are supposed to do, or what the shop claims they can do: an umbrella should keep the rain out, a watch should keep accurate time.

'as described'

The goods must be what they are claimed to be: a 'leather coat' must be made of leather, a 'digital TV' must be able to decode digital TV signals.

If any of these three conditions is not met, the purchaser is entitled to a full or a part refund, depending on how soon the fault appears, how serious it is and how quickly the matter is taken up. Note also the following practical points:

- the buyer can accept a replacement, but can also insist on a refund if a replacement is not wanted

- the buyer does not have to accept a credit note for spending on other purchases

- a shop is not entitled to put up a notice saying "No Refunds!"

---

practical example – Sale of Goods Act

problem
Jason buys a watering can from Martley Garden Centre but finds that it leaks. He returns it to the Garden Centre, asking for a refund. The sales assistant refuses, pointing to a sign on the counter which states "No refunds given!" What is Jason's position?
answer
Jason *is* entitled to a refund. The Sale of Goods Act clearly states that goods must be of 'satisfactory quality'. The shop has no right to try and avoid statute law.

Unfair Contract Terms Act

Any organisation that tries to insist on *unfair* terms (eg in small print on the back of a sales contract) may be in breach of the Unfair Contract Terms Act. This would protect, for example, holidaymakers who are not put up in the hotel they booked because the small print stated that the holiday company had the right to move them to another resort. This would be seen as an 'unfair term' and would enable the holidaymaker to seek compensation. In short, a business cannot 'contract out' through the small print.

Chapter Summary

- Business communications should be polite and effective – using the appropriate format, and be sent within the appropriate timescale.

- Common reasons for communicating are replying to queries and chasing overdue debts.

- There are a number of different forms of written communication which are used both within an organisation and also when dealing with outsiders:
  - memorandum (plural 'memoranda')
  - notes
  - fax
  - email
  - formal written letter

- A contract is an agreement between two people ('parties') with legal consequences – if something goes wrong with the agreement, the matter can go to court if necessary.

- A contract contains three elements: an agreement made between two parties, a bargain struck involving each party giving up something of value, and an intention that the agreement is a legal one.

- A contract involves an offer being made and accepted. An offer may be made to an individual, a group of people or to everyone. For a contract to exist, an offer must be accepted clearly and without any conditions attached.

- The bargain in a contract – the passing of something of value – must involve both parties and must follow the contract.

- The intention behind a contract should be to form a legal agreement; arrangements such as 'doing someone a favour' do not form a contract.

- If one of the parties breaks the terms of a contract – eg does not pay, does not do the work required – the matter can be taken to court as a breach of contract, either for damages (money compensation) or to ensure the work is done.

- Statute law (laws passed in Parliament) protects buyers of goods and services. Examples include the Trades Descriptions Act and the Sale of Goods Act.

Key Terms		
	memorandum	a formal written communication used internally within an organisation
	fax	short for 'facsimile' – an electronic transmission of an exact image
	email	an electronic message sent from one computer to another
	Internet	a world-wide network of interlinked computers
	intranet	a linked network of computers within an organisation
	attachment	a digital file (text or image, for example) which is sent with an email
	house style letter	a letter produced by a business in a style which has been adopted as standard by the business
	contract	a legally binding agreement enforceable in a court of law
	parties	the people directly involved in a contract
	consideration	value which is passed between the parties to a contract, eg money, doing a job
	invitation to treat	an invitation for someone to make an offer, eg priced goods on a shop shelf
	subject to contract	the stage reached when the terms of an offer are said to be acceptable but the final agreement has not been finalised
	postal rule	if an acceptance of an offer is made by post, the contract comes into being when the acceptance is correctly posted
	breach of contract	the situation where one of the parties to a contract breaks one or more of the terms of the contract
	damages	money compensation awarded in a court of law

Student Activities

In these exercises you may have to make up names, addresses and dates. Unless your tutor states otherwise, make these up as you think appropriate.

8.1   You receive a cheque through the post from a sales ledger customer. The words and figures are different. The words say 'five hundred and fifty pounds' and the figures '£500'. The amount should be £550. Write the text of a suitable letter to the customer.

8.2   One of your sales ledger customers, Adrian Duffe Associates, is well known in your Accounts Department as a bad payer. When telephoned recently about the non-payment of invoices, the assistant said 'We don't seem to have received these invoices. Are you sure they are ours?' You check your records and find that the invoices were sent to Adrian Duffe Associates with the goods. How would you deal with this problem?

8.3   You are an Accounts Supervisor and you need to circulate to all the Sales Managers in the business a list of the customers who are more than 2 months behind in settling their accounts. These customers should be referred to the Accounts Manager before any further credit sales are made. You are to write a suitable memorandum, using your own name and today's date.

Note: you do not need to produce the list (which has been produced on your computer).

8.4   Draft a letter chasing up an overdue invoice. The letter is a 'gentle' reminder and follows previous statements of account. Complete the letter with details of a specimen invoice. The letter is for signature by your Accounts Manager.

8.5   You are an Accounts Supervisor in the Accounts Department of Janus Fabrics. You receive the following email message from your Customer Services Department on 1 April:

'Mrs Joan Pearce of Lizard Designs telephoned. She is furious. She placed an urgent customer order for 25 square metres of Roma velvet curtain fabric, colour burgundy, and has only received 15 square metres. I have sent a further 10 square metres today. Please write to her – she is a valued customer and needs to be kept happy.'

You check your records and find that on her purchase order (no 6234) the figure '25' could be read as '15' because the first digit is indistinct. Write her a suitable letter, using your own name and today's date. Her address is Lizard Designs, 13 Regency Passage, Mereford, MR2 6DA.

8.6   Write down a sentence defining a contract – use your own words.

8.7   State the three elements of a contract, writing down a sentence describing each of the three elements.

8.8   State in each of the following situations whether a contract exists. In each case give reasons for your answer.

(a)   You order goods over the phone and agree a price but do not issue a purchase order.

(b)   You order goods by sending a signed purchase order by fax to the supplier who then despatches them.

(c)   You do a job for someone free of charge and as a favour. She later gives you £10 but then complains that the job has not been done properly.

(d)   You do a job for a friend and agree a price, but after you have done the job he refuses to pay you.

8.9   You go to a local DIY store and see a power drill on the shelves with a price sticker of £39.95. You think it is a good buy and take it to the till. The cashier says that the price is now £49.95; the lower price was for a special offer that has now expired.

Is the cashier right to insist on charging the higher price or can you insist that the contract is based on the lower price being the offer price? Give *legal reasons* for your answer.

8.10   You fill in an order form for some stationery. The order form is contained in the catalogue sent to you by the supplier. At the bottom of the form you write in red "We are only placing this order on the basis that we will receive the goods by 4 April." The order form says "Allow 28 days for delivery." The date is 15 March.

Is this a valid acceptance of the offer for sale made by the stationery company in its catalogue?

8.11   You telephone for a mail order catalogue on 15 March, complete the order form on 16 March and post the order form on 17 March. It is received by the mail order company on 19 March.

On what date is the contract formed?

8.12   You buy a word processor from Zenith Office Supplies. Unfortunately the machine will not work – it appears to be damaged. You take it back to Zenith. The salesman says "Sorry - nothing we can do – you will have to get in touch with the manufacturer!"

Is he right? What is the legal position?

8.13   You buy an office chair from Summit Office Furniture. It is advertised as having an adjustable back. When you get it back to your office, you find it does not. You telephone the supplier to complain and are told "Sorry we can't change it – you saw what it was like when you picked it up."

Is the supplier right? Explain the legal position.

this chapter covers . . .

In Chapter 2 we looked at the selling of goods and services from the point of view of the supplier. This chapter examines the transactions from the point of view of the purchaser and describes the procedures and documents involved. The chapter covers the areas of:

- the use of financial documents – purchase order, invoice, delivery note, goods received note, returns note, credit note, statement, remittance advice

- the checking of the supplier's documents against the purchaser's documents

- the calculation of document totals, including discounts and VAT

- the coding and filing of documents

- the checking and authorisation of documents and dealing with discrepancies

This chapter concentrates on the manual completion of documents. Processing purchases transactions using computer accounting is dealt with in Osborne Books' **Accounting Work Skills Tutorial** *for Unit 31 (Chapter 14).*

PERFORMANCE CRITERIA COVERED

unit 30: INTRODUCTORY ACCOUNTING

element 30.2

process purchases and payments

A   check suppliers invoices for accuracy and against source documents

B   check calculations, including discounts, on suppliers invoices and credit notes

C   check suppliers credit notes against correspondence or other relevant source documents

D   code purchase invoices and credit notes

BUSINESS DOCUMENTS – THE PURCHASER'S POINT OF VIEW

When a business *sells* goods and services its main concern is that it provides what has been ordered and that it gets paid on time. When a business, on the other hand, *orders* goods and services it will want to ensure that:

- the correct goods and services are provided
- they are provided on time
- they are charged at the right price

Businesses vary in the way they achieve this. The normal procedure is for the purchaser to accumulate on file – normally stapled together – a series of documents which will be checked against each other as they are produced or come into the office, eg copy purchase order, delivery note, invoice, a copy of any returns note, any credit note, statement, and so on. These will often be kept in a 'pending invoices' file until payment is finally made, when they will go into a 'paid invoices' file. The diagram below shows this flow of documents.

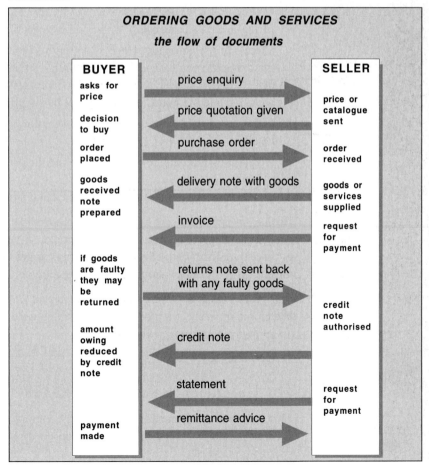

ORDERING PROCEDURES

the traditional method

The diagram on the previous page shows the traditional method of ordering goods and services: a paper purchase order is issued, the goods (or services) are delivered (or provided) and an invoice is sent which is eventually paid by cheque. There are of course, many variations on this procedure, particularly with the introduction of e-commerce where buying and selling and settlement takes place on-line.

In this book and in your studies the emphasis is on the traditional method of ordering and paying because the principles of this method underlie all the other methods. You should however be aware of the other methods as you may encounter some of them in your day-to-day work.

other ordering methods – paper based

Businesses can order goods and services in a variety of other ways:

- filling in a catalogue order form and posting off a cheque with the order
- telephoning a company which is selling to you for the first time to ask them to issue you with a 'pro-forma invoice' for the goods or service you need; when you receive this invoice document, you will send it back with a cheque and the goods or service will be supplied by return
- faxing off a catalogue order form and quoting the company credit card details
- telephoning a catalogue order and quoting the company credit card details

other ordering methods – electronically based

Businesses are increasing turning to Internet retailers for purchases of goods and services, eg computers. Ordering goods or services from an Internet site is very straightforward: all you need to do is to get on-line, place your order on one of the virtual 'shopping malls' and quote the company credit card details.

Electronic ordering has produced terms which need some explanation:

- EDI (Electronic Data Interchange)
- e-commerce

EDI – electronic data interchange

This a method of connecting businesses by computer link so that documents such as purchase orders and invoices can be electronically generated and payments made electronically when they are due. The EDI system should *not* be confused with the Internet, which is basically an uncontrolled electronic free-for-all. EDI has been running for many years, the electronic links are private and secure; the system is expensive to set up. A number of supermarkets have adopted EDI: the supermarket is the 'hub' of the system and its suppliers are on 'spokes'. Look at the diagram below.

the 'hub' and 'spokes' of an EDI system

e-commerce

E-commerce is a loose term which is short for 'electronic commerce'. It covers selling and buying on the Internet, both business-to-business and business-to-customer. We have already seen in Chapter 6 how Internet sales receipts are tracked onto the bank account. The screen extract here shows this book for sale on the on-line shop at www.osbornebooks.co.uk

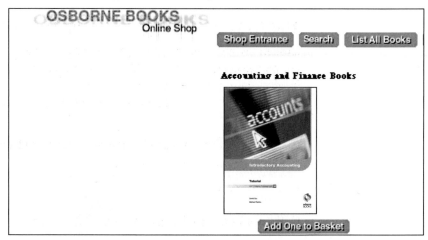

In the rest of this chapter we will look at the traditional method of ordering goods and services which is most likely to feature in your exams and skills tests.

AUTHORISATION OF PURCHASE ORDERS

A purchaser, once the price of the product(s) has been agreed, normally issues a *purchase order*. It is essential that this purchase order is *authorised* by the appropriate person. This authority is shown on the document in the form of a signature and date. Some businesses will insist that more senior staff in the buying department sign larger orders. A business keeps a copy of every purchase order it issues and often files them in numerical order (each order has a numerical code). The purchase order from the Case Study in the last chapter is shown here.

Trends	PURCHASE ORDER
4 Friar Street Broadfield BR1 3RF Tel 01908 761234 Fax 01908 761987 VAT REG GB 0745 8383 56	

| Cool Socks Limited,
Unit 45 Elgar Estate,
Broadfield,
BR7 4ER | purchase order no   47609
date   25 09 07 |

product code	quantity	description
45B	100 pairs	Blue Toebar socks

AUTHORISED signature.......*D Signer*..date........*25 Sept 07*..........

It should be noted that a business may not *always* issue a purchase order: if the order is small, or if the buyer knows the seller well, the order may be made by telephone.

CHECKS AND CONTROLS: PURCHASES

When an organisation purchases goods, it is important that the accounting system includes checks and controls to ensure that:

- the correct goods have been received in an acceptable condition
- the correct terms and price have been applied
- the goods are paid for once only (paying for goods twice does occur!)

The three main documents involved in the checking process are the *purchase order* (a copy of which will be kept by the purchaser), the *delivery note* and the *invoice,* received from the seller.

You should note that some organisations use an internal document known as a *goods received note* on which the buyer records the receipt of the goods and the details set out on the delivery note or advice note sent by the supplier. Most businesses, however, rely on the delivery note as a record of the goods received, and we will concentrate on this document here.

CHECKING INVOICE, DELIVERY NOTE AND PURCHASE ORDER

The checking process involves two separate procedures carried out in the Accounts Department:

- checking the three documents – the invoice, delivery note and copy purchase order – with each other
- checking the calculations on the invoice

We will deal with these in separate stages, starting with the checking of the three documents:

check 1 – goods received and delivery note

When the goods are received they should be checked against the delivery note – the quantities should be counted and the condition of the goods checked. Any discrepancies or damage should be notified immediately to the supplier, usually on a *discrepancy note*, so that replacements can be sent or the buyer credited with the value of the missing or damaged goods (ie the bill reduced by the issue of a credit note).

check 2 – delivery note and purchase order

The delivery note should then be checked in the Accounts Department against a copy of the original purchase order. The illustration on the next page shows the details that should be checked:

- catalogue number (ie the supplier's catalogue) – has the right type of goods been delivered?
- quantity – has the right number been delivered?
- specifications – are the goods delivered to the same specifications as those ordered
- purchase order reference number – do the goods relate to the purchase order being examined?

If all is in order, the delivery note will be filed with the copy purchase order under the purchase order reference number, ready for checking against the invoice when it arrives.

check 3 – invoice, delivery note and purchase order

When the invoice arrives from the supplier, it should be checked against the delivery note and the purchase order (which should be filed together). The specific points to look at are:

- *invoice and delivery note*
  Are the details of the goods on the invoice and delivery note the same? The product code, description and quantity of the goods should agree.

- *invoice and purchase order*

  Has the correct price been charged? The unit price quoted by the supplier or obtained from the supplier's catalogue will be stated on the purchase order, and should agree with the unit price stated on the invoice. If there is a difference, it should be queried with the supplier.

student task

Look at the invoice below and the purchase order and delivery note on the next page. They all relate to the same transaction. Can you spot any discrepancies? The answers are set out at the bottom of the page.

— INVOICE —

Stourford Office Supplies

Unit 12, Avon Industrial Estate, Stourford, SF5 6TD
Tel 01807 765434 Fax 01807 765123 Email stourford@stourford.co.uk
VAT Reg GB 0745 4001 76

invoice to

Martley Machine Rental Limited 67 Broadgreen Road Martley MR6 7TR	invoice no **652771** account **MAR435** your reference **47780** date/tax point **31 03 07**

deliver to

as above

product code	description	quantity	price	unit	total	discount %	net
3564748	80gsm white Supalaser	15	3.50	ream	52.00	0.00	52.00

terms

Net monthly

Carriage paid

E & OE

goods total	**52.00**
VAT	**9.01**
TOTAL	**42.99**

The purchase order and delivery note agree, but the invoice has a number of discrepancies:
- the order reference differs (47700 and 47780)
- the product code differs (3564749 and 3564748)
- the product description differs (100 gsm and 80 gsm)
- the price differs (£4.00 and £3.50 per ream)

Martley Machine Rental

PURCHASE ORDER

67 Broadgreen Road
Martley
MR6 7TR
Tel 01908 546321 Fax 01908 546335
VAT REG GB 0745 8383 56

```
Stourford Office Supplies
Unit 12
Avon Industrial Estate
Stourford SF5 6TD
```

purchase order no   47700
date   13 03 07

product code	quantity	description		
3564749	15 reams	100gsm white Supalaser paper @ £4.00 per ream		

AUTHORISED   signature................*C Farmer*...date *13 March 07*.................

catalogue number	quantity	order specifications	purchase order reference number

---

DELIVERY NOTE

Stourford Office Supplies
Unit 12, Avon Industrial Estate, Stourford, SF5 6TD
Tel 01807 765434 Fax 01807 765123 Email stourford@stourford.co.uk
VAT Reg GB 0745 4001 76

```
Martley Machine Rental Ltd
67 Broadgreen Road
Martley
MR6 7TR
```

delivery note no	26754
delivery method	**Puma Express**
your order	47700
date	**27 03 07**

product code	quantity	description	
3564749	15 reams	100gsm white Supalaser paper	

Received

signature.................*G.Hughes*......................print name (capitals)...*G.HUGHES*................date *31.03.07*

details to check on the purchase order and delivery note

CHECKING THE CALCULATIONS ON THE INVOICE

Another important step is for the Accounts Department to check the calculations on the invoice. If any one of these calculations is incorrect, the final total will be wrong, and the invoice will have to be queried with the supplier, so accurate checking is essential. The checks to be made are:

quantity x unit price   The quantity of the items multiplied by the unit price must be correct. The result – the total price or *price extension* – is used for the calculation of any trade discount applicable.

trade or bulk discount   Any trade or bulk discount – allowances given to approved customers or for bulk purchases – must be deducted from the total price worked out. Trade or bulk discount is calculated as a percentage of the total price, eg a trade discount of 20% on a total price of £150 is calculated

$$£150 \text{ x } \frac{20}{100} = £30$$

The net price charged (before VAT) is therefore

$$£150 - £30 = £120 = \text{net total}$$

settlement discount   Any settlement (cash) discount – an allowance sometimes given for quick payment – is deducted from the net total before VAT is calculated. Settlement discount, when it is offered, is usually included as one of the terms at the bottom of the invoice. It is not normally deducted from the invoice total, so it will be up to the buyer to settle early and to adjust the invoice total down.

VAT   Value Added Tax is currently charged at 17.5%. To calculate VAT, the total after the deduction of any settlement discount is treated as follows

$$\text{Total x } \frac{17.5}{100} = \text{VAT amount}$$

If you are using a calculator, all you need to do is to multiply the total by 0.175 to give the VAT, which is then added to the total.

Remember that any fractions of a penny are ignored. For example if the total price is £55.75, the VAT will be:

£55.75 x 0.175 = £9.75625

£9.75625 then loses the last three digits – the fraction of a penny – to become £9.75.

For the purpose of your studies you must assume that the calculations on all invoices must be checked. In practice, invoicing programs perform the calculations automatically, and in principle should be correct.

Now check the calculations on the invoice on page 186. You should be able to detect a large number of errors:

- quantity x unit price should be £52.50, not £52.00
- the VAT is wrongly calculated £52.00 x 0.175 = £9.10, not £9.01 (it would be £9.18 on £52.50)
- the VAT has been deducted instead of added: the total should be £52.50 + £9.18 = £61.68

AUTHORISING THE INVOICE FOR PAYMENT

In most organisations checked invoices are passed to the person in the Accounts Department who deals with making payments to suppliers. First, however, an invoice will have to be *authorised* for payment. It will then, as long as no credit notes are due, be paid after the statement arrives and the date for payment is reached. Clearly only correct invoices can be passed forward for payment. Invoices with errors will need to be queried with the supplier.

When an invoice is checked and found to be correct, the person carrying out the check will usually mark the document and authorise it for payment. This authorisation can take a number of forms:

- the checker can initial and date the invoice, and tick it or write 'pay' as an authorisation
- the organisation may have a special rubber stamp which can be used in the authorisation process (see next page) – this stamp may also allow provide space for details such as the cost code and the allocation of an internal reference number which can be entered in the purchases day book and used for internal filing purposes

This procedure of authorisation obviously helps the efficiency of the organisation:

- only authorised invoices will be passed forward in the Accounts Department for entry into the purchases day book and double-entry accounts (see Chapter 10); each invoice will be attached to the copy purchase order and will eventually be paid when the due date comes

- the checker's initials will be there in case of any future query on the invoice, eg an undetected error

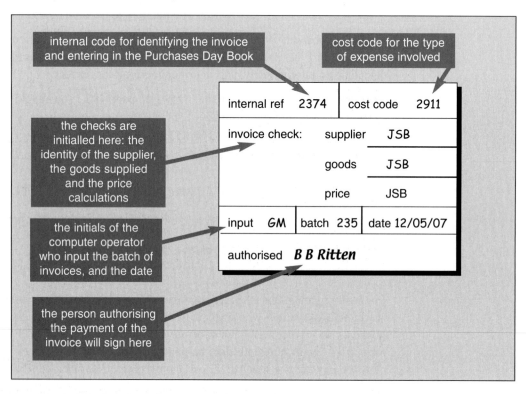

internal code for identifying the invoice and entering in the Purchases Day Book

cost code for the type of expense involved

the checks are initialled here: the identity of the supplier, the goods supplied and the price calculations

the initials of the computer operator who input the batch of invoices, and the date

the person authorising the payment of the invoice will sign here

| internal ref | 2374 | cost code | 2911 |

invoice check: supplier *JSB*

goods *JSB*

price JSB

input *GM* batch 235 date 12/05/07

authorised *B B Ritten*

authorisation stamp placed on an invoice received for checking

GOODS RECEIVED NOTE (GRN)

As mentioned earlier in the chapter some purchasers use a document known as a *goods received note* (GRN). This is essentially a checklist on which is recorded the name of the supplier and details of the goods ordered. As the goods are received and are checked in, the GRN is ticked and initialled to indicate that the right quantity and description of goods has been received. The GRN forms part of the payment authorisation process: only when a completed and correct GRN is approved by the Accounts Department can the relevant invoice be paid. As you will see, the GRN fulfils the same checking function as the entries on the invoice authorisation stamp shown above.

Shown on the next page is the goods received note relating to the Case Study in the last chapter in which the shop 'Trends' ordered some fashion socks from Cool Socks Limited. Note that the receipt of the 100 pairs of socks has been recorded, and also the fact that 10 pairs are damaged.

Trends   **GOODS RECEIVED NOTE**

Supplier

Cool Socks Limited,	GRN no	1871
Unit 45 Elgar Estate,	date	06 10 07
Broadfield,		
BR7 4ER		

quantity	description	order number
100 pairs	Blue Toebar socks	47609

carrier	Lynx Parcels	consignment no	8479347

received by	*V Williams*	checked by	*R Patel*

condition of goods (please tick and comment)	good condition		**copies to**
	damaged ✓ (10 pairs)		Buyer ✓
	shortages		Accounts ✓
			Stockroom ✓

RETURNS

As you can see from the goods received note above, a purchaser will sometimes have to return faulty or incorrect goods and request a credit note from the seller to reduce the amount owed. Note that a purchaser should *never* for this reason change figures on an invoice – this would cause havoc with the accounting records! When the goods are sent back – the socks in the Case Study – they will be accompanied by a *returns note*.

When the goods are received back by the seller and checked, a *credit note* will be issued to reduce the amount owing. This is illustrated on the next page.

Trends   **RETURNS NOTE**
4 Friar Street
Broadfield
BR1 3RF
Tel 01908 761234 Fax 01908 761987
VAT REG GB 0745 8383 56

Cool Socks Limited,	returns note no	2384
Unit 45 Elgar Estate,	date	08 10 07
Broadfield,		
BR7 4ER		

product code	quantity	description
45B	10 pairs	Blue Toebar socks

REASON FOR RETURN: *faulty goods, credit requested*

SIGNATURE   *R SINGH*   DATE   *10 10 07*

─────── **CREDIT NOTE** ───────

COOL SOCKS LIMITED

Unit 45 Elgar Estate, Broadfield, BR7 4ER
Tel 01908 765314 Fax 01908 765951 Email toni@cool.u-net.com
VAT REG GB 0745 4672 76

to

| Trends |
| 4 Friar Street |
| Broadfield |
| BR1 3RF |

credit note no	12157
account	3993
your reference	47609
our invoice	787923
date/tax point	13 10 07

product code	description	quantity	price	unit	total	discount %	net
45B	Blue Toebar socks	10	2.36	pair	23.60	0.00	23.60

Reason for credit
10 pairs of socks received damaged
(Your returns note no. R/N 2384)

GOODS TOTAL	23.60
VAT	4.13
TOTAL	27.73

CHECKING THE CREDIT NOTE

When the credit note is received by the purchaser it will have to be checked carefully to make sure that the quantity of goods, the price, discount and VAT are correctly calculated. If it is correct, the document will be entered into the purchases returns day book and double-entry accounts (see Chapter 10) and then filed with (stapled to) the appropriate copy purchase order, delivery note, invoice and copy returns note, awaiting the arrival of the statement.

PAYING SUPPLIERS' INVOICES

resolving discrepancies

Before an invoice can be authorised for payment, any problems and discrepancies must be resolved. These may be simple problems, which can be resolved at the level at which you are working:

- calculation errors on the invoice which can be put right by requesting the issue of a correct invoice (the incorrect invoice must never be corrected by the organisation to which it is issued)
- duplicated invoices – a duplicate can be disregarded and returned

Other issues may need to be referred to a supervisor before the invoice can be paid, for example:

- the goods or the services have not been supplied – they will have to be chased up by someone elsewhere in the organisation

- an incorrect discount will have to be referred internally so that the problem can be taken up at a higher level with the seller

The guidelines suggested here are not 'cast in stone'. The relative size of the business paying the invoice will dictate what will and will not need referring. A small office is likely to give more decision-making authority to junior employees. Larger businesses are more likely to require referrals.

paying the invoice

There are two common ways of setting up a system for paying invoices:

1 Many businesses pay on receipt of a statement, not on receipt of the invoice. As most statements tend to go out at the end of the month, paying of invoices often then becomes a monthly routine. In this case payments due can be put on diary for a set day of the month, eg the 27th.

2 Some businesses will pay invoices after the maximum number of days allowed – normally 30 days. In this case a diary system will be set up and the checked/authorised invoices filed in payment date order.

MAKING PAYMENT – REMITTANCE ADVICES

The cycle of documents is completed by the issue of a remittance advice by the supplier when payment is made. Payment can either be made by *cheque* or by *electronic transfer* through the bank using a system known as BACS (Bankers Automated Clearing Services). A remittance advice will be issued for both types of transfer.

TO	**REMITTANCE ADVICE** FROM		
Cool Socks Limited Unit 45 Elgar Estate, Broadfield, BR7 4ER		**Trends** 4 Friar Street Broadfield BR1 3RF Tel 01908 761234 Fax 01908 761987 VAT REG GB 0745 8383 56	
Account 3993	6 November 2007		
date	your reference	our reference	payment amount
01 10 07 10 10 07	INVOICE 787923 CREDIT NOTE 12157	47609 47609	277.30 (27.73)
		CHEQUE TOTAL	249.57

a remittance advice sent with a cheque payment

Chapter Summary

- Traditionally, a business placing an order will request the goods or services by means of a paper document – a purchase order. There then follows a 'flow' of paper documents, concluding with payment.
- Although electronic methods of ordering through e-commerce and EDI have become more common, the same traditional principles apply; it is just that the documents are on-screen rather than paper-based.
- A business purchasing goods or services will need to ensure that the right goods have been supplied, at the right price, before payment is made.
- When the goods arrive they should be checked against the delivery note which accompanies the goods. The delivery note is then checked against the purchase order and attached to it.
- Some businesses will prepare a goods received note to check off the goods when they arrive and to record any subsequent returns.
- When the invoice arrives it will be checked against the purchase order and delivery note and attached to the documents.
- The calculations and terms on the invoice will be checked carefully, particularly if it is not a computerised invoice.
- If any goods have to be returned they will be sent back with a returns note.
- Any credit notes issued to the purchaser (including any for returned goods) will have to be checked carefully on receipt.
- When the invoice and any relevant credit notes have been found to be correct the invoice can be authorised for payment.
- Authorised invoices are filed in a diary system until the appropriate payment date (normally after receipt of a statement).
- Payment is normally advised to the seller by means of a remittance advice.

Key Terms

EDI	Electronic Data Interchange is an electronic system of ordering goods and services using secure private computer links
e-commerce	buying and selling on the Internet – business to business and business to customer
purchase order	a document issued and authorised by the buyer of goods and services, sent to the seller, indicating the goods or services required
delivery note	a document listing and accompanying the goods sent to the purchaser
goods received note	a document sometimes used by purchasers to record receipt of stock and any returns made
invoice	a document issued by the seller of goods or services to the purchaser indicating the amount owing and the required payment date

returns note	a document sent with goods returned by the purchaser to the seller, requesting credit
credit note	a document issued by the seller of the goods or services reducing the amount owed by the buyer
statement	a document issued by the seller to the buyer summarising invoices and credit notes issued and payments received
remittance advice	a document sent by the purchaser to the seller advising the amount and date of payment of money due

Student Activities

9.1 What type of business document would normally be used when goods are bought on credit

    (a)   to order the goods from the seller?

    (b)   to accompany goods sent from the seller?

    (c)   to record the receipt and any return of goods at the buyer's premises?

    (d)   to advise the seller of the amount of money being paid on account?

    (e)   to advise the buyer in the first instance of the amount of money due on an order?

    (f)   to accompany faulty goods sent back by the buyer?

9.2 An unsigned purchase order is sent out to a supplier. What is likely to happen to it, and why?

9.3 Which documents would normally be checked by the buyer against the purchase order? Answer (a) or (b) or (c) or (d).

    (a)   the delivery note and the returns note

    (b)   the invoice and the returns note

    (c)   the goods received note and the remittance advice

    (d)   the delivery note and the invoice

9.4 What is the difference between a returns note and a credit note?

9.5 What would be the problem if the seller of goods accidentally forgot to include the normal trade discount on an invoice to a regular customer? What should the customer do?

9.6 Eduservice, an educational consultancy business, ordered some computer disks from Compusupply Limited on purchase order 53659 for courses it runs at Itec College in Broadfield. The goods were delivered to the Eduservice office at 45 The Ridings, Broadfield on 3 February.

You work in the Eduservice office as an administrative assistant. Part of your job is to deal with all the documents, including the accounting work.

You have today (5 February 2007) received an invoice from Compusupply. You are not happy with the service you are receiving from this company and are thinking of going elsewhere for a supplier.

Shown below and on the next page are:
- a list of Compusupply customer trade discounts (for information purposes)
- the original purchase order
- the invoice you receive

You are to write a letter to Compusupply setting out the errors that have been made. Address the letter to the Sales Manager and sign it with your own name as an administrative assistant. The date is 5 February 2007.

Compusupply – Customer discounts and credit limits (extracts)

Customer	Trade discount (%)	Credit limit (£)
Donmar Estates	15	12,000
Dugdale, E	10	5,000
Easifit Ltd	15	10,000
Eduservice	15	12,500
Estima Designs	10	5,000

EDUSERVICE   *PURCHASE ORDER*

45 The Ridings
Broadfield
BR2 3TR
Tel 01908 333691

TO

Compusupply Limited
Unit 17 Elgar Estate,
Broadfield, BR7 4ER

purchase order no   53659

date   27 January 2007

product code	quantity	description
4573	10 disks	Zap 100MB Storage disks @ £95 per box of 10

Authorised   signature......*J Wales*...............................date...*27.1.07*...........

INVOICE

COMPUSUPPLY LIMITED
Unit 17 Elgar Estate, Broadfield, BR7 4ER
Tel 01908 765756 Fax 01908 765777 Email rob@compusupply.u-net.com
VAT Reg GB 0745 4689 13

invoice to

Eduservice
45 The Ridings
Broadfield
BR2 3TR

invoice no	20424
account	242
your reference	53659
date/tax point	30.01.2007

deliver to

J Wales
Itec College
Fairacre
Broadfield BR5 7YT

product code	description	quantity	price	unit	total	discount %	net
4574	Zap 200MB Storage disk	10	125.00	box (10)	125.00	10	112.50

terms
Net monthly
Carriage paid
E & OE

goods total	112.50
VAT	19.68
TOTAL	132.18

9.7 You work for J Hudson & Partners, a wholesaler. You are an accounts assistant and one of your tasks is to process payments to suppliers. The business normally pays on the second and last Friday of each month. In September 2007 these Fridays fall on the 12th and 26th. The company takes full advantage of the credit terms offered by its suppliers.

J Hudson & Partners has recently been having problems with its supplier RMC Import Agency, which supplies on 30 day terms. Orders have been delivered late and wrong goods have been supplied. As a result J Hudson & Partners withheld the July payment until a credit note for £568.00 was received in respect of wrong goods supplied.

The credit note finally arrived on 22 August 2007.

It is 29 August and you have been told that you can now process a payment to RMC Import Agency. The statement is shown below.

You are to calculate the amount owing and complete the remittance advice and cheque shown on the next page. You will not sign the cheque, as it has to be authorised and signed by John Hudson.

STATEMENT OF ACCOUNT

RMC Import Agency
56 Russell Court
London
WC1A 2MS
Tel 0207 764098 Fax 01207 764083 Email mail@rmc.com
VAT Reg GB 0748 4872 99

TO

| J Hudson & Partners |
| 45 Helby Road |
| Mereford |
| MR1 4FG |

account **2941**

date **26 August 2007**

date	details	debit £	credit £	balance £
2007				
1 Aug	Balance b/f			3,650.00
8 Aug	Invoice 23721	1,200.00		4,850.00
11 Aug	Invoice 23788	1,945.00		6,795.00
22 Aug	Invoice 23921	4,560.00		11,355.00
20 Aug	Credit note 3525		568.00	10,787.00
	TOTAL			**£ 10,787.00**

REMITTANCE ADVICE

TO

RMC Import Agency
56 Russell Court
London
WC1A 2MS

FROM

J Hudson & Partners
45 Helby Road
Mereford
MR1 4FG
Tel 01908 761276 Fax 01908 761998
VAT REG GB 0745 8383 01

Account:	2941	Date:	29 Aug	

date	your reference		our reference	payment amount
22 Aug	bw 23921			4560
			CHEQUE TOTAL	4560

Southern Bank PLC
Mereford Branch
16 Broad Street, Mereford MR1 7TR

date 29 Aug 2007   97-76-54

Pay Four thousand
     five hundred and   Sixty pounds   only
                             only   £ 4560

Account payee only

J HUDSON & PARTNERS

989451   97 76 54   87453219

Accounting for credit purchases and purchases returns

this chapter covers . . .

In this chapter we apply the principles of the accounting system to credit purchases and purchases returns.

We shall see how the prime documents for credit purchases (purchases invoices) and purchases returns (credit notes) are entered in the books of prime entry (purchases day book and purchases returns day book).

The information is then transferred from the day books into the ledger accounts of the double-entry system.

PERFORMANCE CRITERIA COVERED

unit 30: INTRODUCTORY ACCOUNTING

element 30.2

process purchases and payments

E   enter purchases invoices and credit notes into the purchases day book and purchases returns day book

F   post invoices and credit notes into the subsidiary (purchases) ledger and main (general) ledger

ACCOUNTING FOR CREDIT PURCHASES TRANSACTIONS

This chapter focuses on credit purchases transactions; the recording of transactions for *cash purchases* will be covered when we study the payments side of the cash book in Chapter 14.

In accounting, the term 'purchases' has a specific meaning:

the purchase of goods with the intention that they should be resold at a profit

Thus an office stationery shop will record as purchases those items – such as photocopier paper, ring binders – which it buys in with the intention of resale at a profit. Other items purchased in connection with the running of the business – eg buildings, shop fittings – are recorded not as purchases but, instead, are accounted for against the name of the item, ie buildings, shop fittings.

The accounting system for credit purchases starts its recording process from prime documents (also known as source documents) – these comprise:

- purchases invoices
- credit notes received

The diagram which follows shows the order in which the accounting records are prepared for credit purchases transactions.

accounting for credit purchases transactions

prime documents

- purchases invoices
- credit notes received

books of prime entry

- purchases day book
- purchases returns day book

double-entry accounts

- purchases (creditors) ledger
- main (general) ledger
- cash book

We will now look in more detail at the use of the books of prime entry and the double-entry system for credit purchases. These are very similar to the system already used for credit sales in Chapter 3 and you may wish to refer to the sections of Chapter 3 which cover books of prime entry (pages 46-48), the double-entry system (pages 48-51), and methods of coding in accounting systems (pages 51-52).

ACCOUNTING SYSTEM FOR CREDIT PURCHASES

The accounting system for credit purchases fits together in the following way:

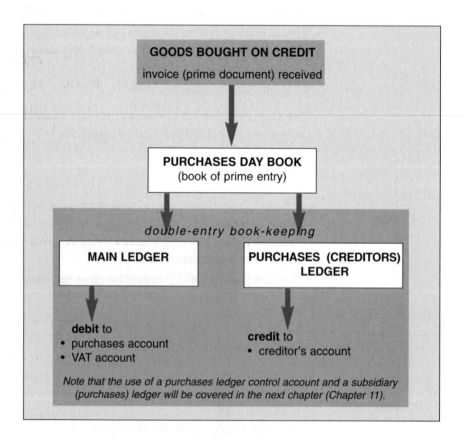

We shall now look in more detail at the purchases day book and the double-entry accounts for credit purchases. In the examples which follow we will assume that the business is registered for Value Added Tax. The rate of VAT used in the example is 17.5%.

PURCHASES DAY BOOK

The purchases day book is a collection point for accounting information on the credit purchases of a business and is set out in the following way (with sample entries shown):

Purchases Day Book						PDB 57
Date	Supplier	Invoice No	Folio	Total	VAT*	Net
2007				£	£	£
5 Jan	P Bond Ltd	1234	PL 125	94.00	14.00	80.00
9 Jan	D Webster	A373	PL 730	141.00	21.00	120.00
16 Jan	P Bond Ltd	1247	PL 125	47.00	7.00	40.00
20 Jan	Sanders & Sons	5691	PL 495	188.00	28.00	160.00
31 Jan	Totals for month			470.00	70.00	400.00

* VAT = 17.5 per cent

Notes:

- The purchases day book is prepared from purchases invoices received from suppliers. The invoice number used is either that of the supplier's invoice (as above) or is a unique number given to each invoice by the buyer's accounts department.
- The reference 'PDB 57' is used for cross-referencing to the book-keeping system: here it indicates that this is page 57 of the purchases day book.
- The *folio* column is also used for cross-referencing purposes: 'PL' refers to Purchases Ledger, followed by the account number.
- The *total* column records the amount of each invoice, ie after VAT has been included.
- The day book is totalled at appropriate intervals – daily, weekly or monthly – and the total of the *net* column will tell the business the amount of credit purchases for the period.
- When control accounts (see Chapter 11) are in use, the total for the month from the 'total' column from the purchases day book is entered into the purchases ledger control account.

Thus, to write up the purchases day book, we take the purchases invoices –

that have been checked and authorised (see pages 188-190) – for the period and enter the details:

- date of invoice

- name of supplier

- purchase invoice number, using either the supplier's invoice number, or a unique number given to each invoice by the buyer's accounts department

- cross-reference to the supplier's account number in the purchases ledger, eg 'PL 125'

- enter the total amount of the invoice into the 'total' column

- enter the VAT amount shown on the invoice – don't be concerned with any adjustments to the VAT for the effect of any settlement discounts, simply record the VAT amount shown

- enter the net amount of the invoice (often described as 'goods or services total'), before VAT is added

DOUBLE-ENTRY BOOK-KEEPING FOR CREDIT PURCHASES

After the purchases day book has been written up and totalled, the information from it is transferred into the double-entry system. The accounts in the purchases ledger and main ledger to record the transactions from the purchases day book seen earlier are as follows:

PURCHASES (CREDITORS) LEDGER

Dr		**P Bond Limited** (account no 125)		Cr
2007	£	2007		£
		5 Jan	Purchases PDB 57	94
		16 Jan	Purchases PDB 57	47

Dr		**Sanders & Sons** (account no 495)		Cr
2007	£	2007		£
		20 Jan	Purchases PDB 57	188

Dr		**D Webster** (account no 730)		Cr
2007	£	2007		£
		9 Jan	Purchases PDB 57	141

MAIN LEDGER

Dr		Purchases Account (account no 5001)		Cr
2007		£	2007	£
31 Jan	Purchases Day Book PDB 57	400		

Dr		Value Added Tax Account (account no 2200)		Cr
2007		£	2007	£
31 Jan	Purchases Day Book PDB 57	70		

Note that from the purchases day book:

- the amounts from the total column *for each separate purchase* have been credited to the accounts of the suppliers, ie the business owes to each creditor the amounts shown

- the total of the VAT column, £70, has been debited to VAT account (which has gained value)

- the total of the net column, £400, has been debited to purchases account (ie the account which has gained value)

- the folio column in the day book gives a cross-reference to the creditors' accounts in the purchases ledger (PL)

- each entry in the purchases ledger and main ledger is cross-referenced back to the page number of the purchases day book; here the reference is to 'PDB 57'.

ACCOUNTING SYSTEM FOR PURCHASES RETURNS

Purchases returns (or returns out) are when goods previously bought on credit are returned by the business to its suppliers. A credit note (see page 192) is requested and, when received, it is entered in the accounting system to reduce the amount owing to the creditor.

The accounting procedures for purchases returns involve:

- *prime documents* – credit notes received from suppliers
- *book of prime entry* – purchases returns day book
- *double-entry accounts* – purchases ledger (accounts for each creditor) and main ledger (purchases returns account, which records the total of credit notes received, and Value Added Tax account, which records the VAT amount of purchases returns)

The accounting system for purchases returns is summarised as follows:

GOODS RETURNED TO THE SUPPLIER
credit note (prime document) received from supplier

↓

PURCHASES RETURNS DAY BOOK
(book of prime entry)

double-entry book-keeping

PURCHASES (CREDITORS) LEDGER   **MAIN LEDGER**

↓   ↓

debit to   **credit** to

• creditor's account   • purchases returns account

                                           • VAT account

Note that the use of a purchases ledger control account and a subsidiary (purchases) ledger will be covered in the next chapter (Chapter 11).

We shall now look in more detail at the purchases returns day book and the double-entry accounts for purchases returns. Note that the business is registered for Value Added Tax.

PURCHASES RETURNS DAY BOOK

The purchases returns day book uses virtually the same layout as the purchases day book seen earlier in this chapter. It operates in a similar way, storing up information about purchases returns until such time as a transfer is made into the double-entry accounts system. The prime documents for purchases returns day book are credit notes received from suppliers.

example transactions

2007

20 Jan   Returned goods, £40 + VAT to D Webster, credit note no 123 received

27 Jan   Returned goods, £80 + VAT to Sanders & Sons, credit note no 406 received

The purchases returns day book is written up as follows:

	Purchases Returns Day Book				PRDB 3	
Date	Supplier	Credit Note No	Folio	Total	VAT*	Net
2007				£	£	£
20 Jan	D Webster	123	PL 730	47.00	7.00	40.00
27 Jan	Sanders & Sons	406	PL 495	94.00	14.00	80.00
31 Jan	Totals for month			141.00	21.00	120.00

* VAT = 17.5 per cent

Notes:

- The purchases returns day book is prepared from credit notes received from suppliers. The credit note number used is either that of the supplier's credit note (as above) or is a unique number given to each credit note by the buyer's accounts department.
- The day book is totalled at appropriate intervals – weekly or monthly.
- The VAT-inclusive amounts from the total column are debited to the creditors' personal accounts in the purchases ledger.
- The total of the VAT column is transferred to the credit of the VAT account in the main ledger.
- The total of the net column tells the business the amount of purchases returns for the period. This amount is transferred to the credit of purchases returns account in the main ledger.
- The total column records the amount of each credit note received, ie after VAT has been included. When control accounts (see Chapter 11) are in use, the total for the month of the 'total' column is entered into the purchases ledger control account.

DOUBLE-ENTRY BOOK-KEEPING FOR PURCHASES RETURNS

After the purchases returns day book has been written up and totalled, the information from it is transferred into the double-entry system. The accounts in the purchases ledger and main ledger to record the transactions from the above purchases returns day book (including any other transactions already recorded on these accounts) are:

PURCHASES (CREDITORS) LEDGER

Dr		Sanders & Sons (account no 495)			Cr
2007		£	2007		£
27 Jan	Purchases Returns PRDB 3	94	20 Jan	Purchases PDB 57	188

Dr		D Webster (account no 730)			Cr
2007		£	2007		£
20 Jan	Purchases Returns PRDB 3	47	9 Jan	Purchases PDB 57	141

MAIN LEDGER

Dr	Purchases Returns Account (account no 5010)			Cr
2007	£	2007		£
		31 Jan	Purchases Returns Day Book PRDB 3	120

Dr		Value Added Tax Account (account no 2200)			Cr
2007		£	2007		£
31 Jan	Purchases Day Book PDB 57	70	31 Jan	Purchases Returns Day Book PRDB 3	21

THE USE OF ANALYSED PURCHASES DAY BOOKS

Businesses use analysed day books whenever they wish to analyse purchases and purchases returns between different categories of purchases:

- goods for resale, perhaps split between types of goods, eg in a clothes shop between ladies wear and mens wear
- other items of expenditure, eg bills for expenses, such as telephone, electricity etc

An example of an analysed purchases day book is shown below.

	Purchases Day Book								PDB 86
Date	Supplier	Invoice ref.	Folio	Total	VAT*	Net	Ladies wear	Mens wear	Other expenses
2007				£	£	£	£	£	£
2 Sep	Fashions Limited	1401	PL 87	129.25	19.25	110.00	50.00	60.00	–
4 Sep	Eastern Telephones	1402	PL 61	175.66	26.16	149.50	–	–	149.50
8 Sep	Mercian Models	1403	PL 102	301.74	44.94	256.80	256.80	–	–
12 Sep	Media Advertising	1404	PL 92	528.75	78.75	450.00	–	–	450.00
15 Sep	Style Limited	1405	PL 379	432.87	64.47	368.40	218.20	150.20	–
19 Sep	Wyvern Motors	1406	PL 423	149.81	22.31	127.50	–	–	127.50
26 Sep	Denim Traders	1407	PL 45	322.36	48.01	274.35	65.50	208.85	–
30 Sep	Totals for month			2,040.44	303.89	1,736.55	590.50	419.05	727.00

* VAT = 17.5 per cent

Analysed purchases day books and purchases returns day books can be adapted to suit the particular needs of a business. Thus there is not a standard way in which to present the books of prime entry – the needs of the user are all important. By using analysed day books, the owner of the business can see how much has been bought for each of the different categories of purchases.

Notes:

- Each purchases invoice has been given a unique number (starting at 1401) by the buyer's accounts department

- The references in the folio column are to the 'PL' (Purchase Ledger) and supplier's account number

- The analysis columns – here ladies wear, mens wear and other expenses – show the amount of purchases net of VAT (ie before VAT is added)

- The analysis columns analyse the net amount – by category of expenditure – from purchases invoices

BATCH CONTROL SYSTEMS

As we have seen with sales ledger (page 59), many firms use batch control systems in place of day books. Batched data entry for purchases enables a computer operator to enter a series of, say, purchases invoices without the need to keep changing from one area of the computer program to another. The pre-list is prepared on a batch control form such as that shown below for a batch of purchases invoices:

Batch Control: purchases invoices

Supplier		Invoice		Total	VAT*	Net
Account No	Name	Date	No	£	£	£
		2007				
PL 125	P Bond Ltd	5 Jan	1234	94.00	14.00	80.00
PL 730	D Webster	9 Jan	A373	141.00	21.00	120.00
PL 125	P Bond Ltd	16 Jan	1247	47.00	7.00	40.00
PL 495	Sanders & Sons	20 Jan	5691	188.00	28.00	160.00
			Check list totals	470.00	70.00	400.00

Prepared by	*Keith Moore*	Date	*31 Jan 2007*
Checked by	Karen Abrahall	Date	31 Jan 2007
Posted by	*Clare McGougan*	Date	*31 Jan 2007*

* VAT = 17.5 per cent

The purchases invoice batch form is completed from invoices which have been received and checked.

The transactions are then entered into the purchases ledger section of the computer accounting program. The computer screen shows the total money amount of purchases invoices and this is compared with the check list total from the purchases invoices batch control form; if there is a discrepancy, the error must be located and corrected.

Where a business uses control accounts (see Chapter 11), the total from the batch control form for purchases invoices is recorded in the purchases ledger control account.

WYVERN TRADERS

To bring together the material covered in this chapter, we will look at a comprehensive Case Study which makes use of

- **books of prime entry**
  - purchases day book
  - purchases returns day book
- **double-entry accounts**
  - purchases (creditors) ledger
  - main ledger

The Case Study also includes a diagram (page 214) which summarises the procedures for recording credit purchases and purchases returns transactions in the accounting system.

situation

Wyvern Traders is a wholesaler of stationery and office equipment. The business is registered for VAT. The following are the credit purchases and purchases returns transactions for April 2007:

2007

1 Apr	Bought goods from Midland Supplies, £120.00 + VAT, their invoice no 12486
9 Apr	Returned goods to Midland Supplies, £20.00 + VAT, credit note no 104 received
14 Apr	Bought goods from National Stationery, £60.00 +VAT, their invoice no A184
28 Apr	Bought goods from Swan Equipment, £160.00 + VAT, their invoice no P102
30 Apr	Returned goods to Swan Equipment, £40.00 + VAT, credit note no X102 received

The day books and double-entry accounts are illustrated on the next two pages: arrows indicate the transfers from the day books to the individual accounts. Note that some accounts have been repeated on both pages in order to show, on the same page, the accounts relating to a particular day book: in practice a business would keep all the transactions together in one account.

The diagram on page 214 summarises the material we have studied in this chapters. It shows the procedures for recording transactions in the accounting system for

- credit purchases
- purchases returns

Purchases Day Book

PDB 19

Date	Supplier	Invoice No	Folio	Total		VAT		Net	
				£	p	£	p	£	p
2007									
1 Apr	Midland Supplies	12486	PL 45	141	00	21	00	120	00
14 Apr	National Stationery	A184	PL 67	70	50	10	50	60	00
28 Apr	Swan Equipment	P102	PL 112	188	00	28	00	160	00
30 Apr	Totals for month			399	50	59	50	340	00

PURCHASES (CREDITORS) LEDGER

Dr   **Midland Supplies** (account no 45)   Cr

Date	Details	£	p	Date	Details		£	p
2007				2007				
				1 Apr	Purchases	PDB 19	141	00

Dr   **National Stationery** (account no 67)   Cr

Date	Details	£	p	Date	Details		£	p
2007				2007				
				14 Apr	Purchases	PDB 19	70	50

Dr   **Swan Equipment** (account no 112)   Cr

Date	Details	£	p	Date	Details		£	p
2007				2007				
				28 Apr	Purchases	PDB 19	188	00

MAIN LEDGER

Dr   **Value Added Tax Account** (account no 2200)   Cr

Date	Details		£	p	Date	Details	£	p
2007					2007			
30 Apr	Purchases Day Book	PDB 19	59	50				

Dr   **Purchases Account** (account no 5001)   Cr

Date	Details		£	p	Date	Details	£	p
2007					2007			
30 Apr	Purchases Day Book	PDB 19	340	00				

Purchases Returns Day Book

PRDB 7

Date	Supplier	Credit Note No	Folio	Total		VAT		Net	
				£	p	£	p	£	p
2007									
9 Apr	Midland Supplies	104	PL 45	23	50	3	50	20	00
30 Apr	Swan Equipment	X102	PL 112	47	00	7	00	40	00
30 Apr	Totals for month			70	50	10	50	60	00

PURCHASES (CREDITORS) LEDGER

Dr   **Midland Supplies** (account no 45)   Cr

Date	Details	£	p	Date	Details	£	p
2007				2007			
9 Apr	Purchases Returns PRDB 7	23	50	1 Apr	Purchases PDB 19	141	00*

Dr   **Swan Equipment** (account no 112)   Cr

Date	Details	£	p	Date	Details	£	p
2007				2007			
30 Apr	Purchases Returns PRDB 7	47	00	28 Apr	Purchases PDB 19	188	00*

MAIN LEDGER

Dr   **Value Added Tax Account** (account no 2200)   Cr

Date	Details	£	p	Date	Details	£	p
2007				2007			
30 Apr	Purchases Day Book PDB19	59	50*	30 Apr	Purchases Returns Day Book PRDB 7	10	50

Dr   **Purchases Returns Account** (account no 112)   Cr

Date	Details	£	p	Date	Details	£	p
2007				2007			
				30 Apr	Purchases Returns Day Book PRDB 7	60	00

* transactions entered previously

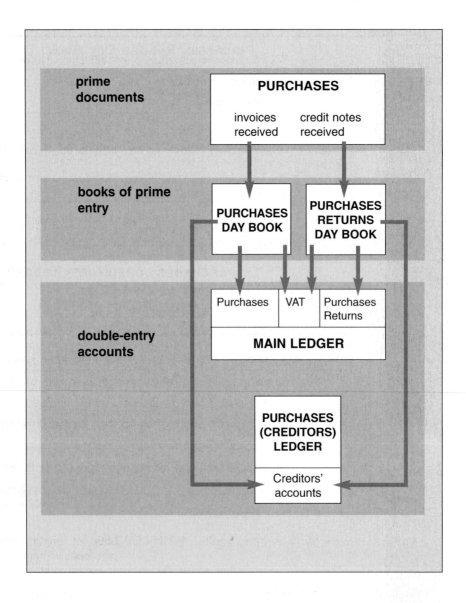

BALANCING ACCOUNTS

Where there is more than one transaction on an account, it is necessary to balance the account at regular intervals – often monthly, sometimes more often.

We have already seen how to balance accounts in Chapter 4, and the technique is summarised at the beginning of the next chapter.

Chapter Summary

- The prime documents relating to credit purchases are:
  - purchases invoices
  - credit notes received

- Purchases day book is the book of prime entry for credit purchases. It is prepared from purchases invoices received from suppliers.

- Purchases returns day book is the book of prime entry for purchases returns. It is prepared from credit notes received from suppliers.

- Analysed purchases day books are used when a business wishes to analyse its purchases between different categories of expenditure.

- Recording credit purchases in the double-entry system uses:
  - prime documents, purchases invoices
  - book of prime entry, purchases day book
  - double-entry accounts, purchases ledger and main ledger

- Recording purchases returns in the double-entry system uses:
  - prime documents, credit notes received from suppliers
  - book of prime entry, purchases returns day book
  - double-entry accounts, purchases ledger and main ledger

Key Terms

purchases	the purchase of goods with the intention that they should be resold at a profit
purchases day book	book of prime entry prepared from purchases invoices
purchases returns	goods purchased on credit which are returned to the supplier
purchases returns day book	book of prime entry prepared from credit notes received from suppliers
analysed purchases day book	day book which incorporates analysis columns between different categories of expenditure
purchases (creditors) ledger	division of the ledger which contains the accounts of the firm's creditors (suppliers)

Student Activities

10.1 Which one of the following is in the right order?

(a) purchases returns day book; credit note issued; purchases returns account; creditor's account

(b) purchases returns account; creditor's account; purchases returns day book; credit note issued

(c) purchases returns day book; purchases returns account; creditor's account; credit note issued

(d) credit note issued; purchases returns day book; purchases returns account; creditor's account

Answer (a) or (b) or (c) or (d)

10.2 Explain in note format:

(a) the principles of recording a credit purchases transaction in the accounting system

(b) the principles of recording a purchases returns transaction in the accounting system

---

In the Activities which follow, the rate of Value Added Tax is to be calculated at the current rate (17.5% at the time of writing). When calculating VAT amounts, you should ignore fractions of a penny, ie round down to a whole penny.

For Activities 10.3 and 10.4 use a cross-referencing system incorporating the following:

- *purchases day book* – *PDB 36*

  purchases returns day book – *PRDB 11*

- *purchases ledger account numbers*

AMC Enterprises	– *account no 520*
S Green	– *account no 574*
I Johnstone	– *account no 604*
Mercia Manufacturing	– *account no 627*
L Murphy	– *account no 659*
Severn Supplies	– *account no 721*

- *main ledger accounts*

purchases account	– *account no 5001*
purchases returns account	– *account no 5010*
Value Added Tax account	– *account no 2200*

10.3 During April 2007, Wyvern Wholesalers had the following credit transactions:

2007

2 Apr	Bought goods from Severn Supplies £250 + VAT, invoice no 6789
5 Apr	Bought goods from I Johnstone £210 + VAT, invoice no A241
9 Apr	Bought goods from L Murphy £185 + VAT, invoice no 2456
15 Apr	Bought goods from Mercia Manufacturing £180 + VAT, invoice no X457
19 Apr	Bought goods from AMC Enterprises £345 + VAT, invoice no AMC 456
26 Apr	Bought goods from S Green £395 + VAT, invoice no 2846

You are to:

(a)   enter the above transactions in Wyvern Wholesaler's purchases day book for April 2007

(b)   record the accounting entries in Wyvern Wholesaler's purchases ledger and main ledger

10.4 The following are the purchases returns of Wyvern Wholesalers for April 2007. They are to be:

(a)   entered in the purchases returns day book for April 2007

(b)   recorded in the purchases ledger and main ledger (use the ledgers already prepared in the answer to Activity 10.3)

2007

7 Apr	Returned goods to Severn Supplies £50 + VAT, credit note no CN225 received
14 Apr	Returned goods to L Murphy £80 + VAT, credit note no X456 received
21 Apr	Returned goods to AMC Enterprises £125 + VAT, credit note no C3921 received
29 Apr	Returned goods to S Green £68 + VAT, credit note no CN/SG247 received

10.5 Jason Smythe owns a business selling furniture and carpets. During April 2007 he received the following invoices from his suppliers:

2007

2 Apr	Invoice for furniture from T Table Limited for £1,247.50 + VAT
7 Apr	Invoice for carpets from Eastern Imports for £796.80 + VAT
9 Apr	Invoice for carpets from Minster Carpets Limited for £1,875.24 + VAT
14 Apr	Invoice for furniture from Pegasus Limited for £498.13 + VAT
16 Apr	Invoice for carpets from United Carpets Limited for £476.22 + VAT
21 Apr	Invoice for furniture from Gerrard Furniture for £831.49 + VAT
23 Apr	Invoice for furniture from T Table Limited for £648.90 + VAT
28 Apr	Invoice for carpets from Eastern Imports for £1,297.31 + VAT

You are to:

(a)   give each invoice a unique number – Jason tells you to start with number 2750

(b)   enter the above transactions into page 21 of the *analysed* purchases day book including columns for VAT, net, furniture, and carpets

(b)   total the day book at 30 April 2007

Notes:

•   folio entries are *not* required.

•   entries in the purchases ledger and main ledger are *not* required

Balancing accounts and control account for purchases

In the previous chapter we saw how to record credit purchases and purchases returns transactions in the ledger accounts of the double-entry system. In this chapter we will develop the double-entry system by using purchases ledger control account in the main ledger with the individual creditors' accounts being held in the subsidiary (purchases) ledger.

Before looking at the use of purchases ledger control account we need to recap on how to balance accounts. This topic has been covered already in Chapter 4 (when we were dealing with Element 30.1 of Introductory Accounting); however, Element 30.2 also requires accounts to be balanced, so it is important to check out your skills again.

PERFORMANCE CRITERIA COVERED

unit 30: INTRODUCTORY ACCOUNTING

element 30.2

process purchases and payments

F   *post invoices and credit notes into the subsidiary (purchases) ledger and main (general) ledger*

BALANCING ACCOUNTS – A RECAP

It is important for you to acquire the skill of balancing accounts in your accounting studies. This topic has been covered already in Chapter 4 (pages 69-72) and you might want to refer back to the practical steps involved in balancing accounts.

The objective of balancing accounts is to show the running total of the account to date, for example:

- the amount of purchases made
- the amount of purchases returns
- the amount owing to each creditor
- the amount of VAT due to or from HM Revenue & Customs

Set out below is an example of a creditor's account which has been balanced at the month-end:

Dr			Phoenix Traders		Cr
2007		£	2007		£
13 Sep	Purchases Returns	50	1 Sep	Balance b/d	530
28 Sep	Purchases Returns	100	8 Sep	Purchases	260
30 Sep	Balance c/d	810	21 Sep	Purchases	170
		960			960
			1 Oct	Balance b/d	810

The four steps to balancing the above account are:

Step 1: in pencil, total the entries in the debit and credit money columns – here they are £150 on the debit side, and £960 on the credit side.

Step 2: calculate the difference between the two amounts in Step 1 – here it is £960 – £150 = £810; enter this amount on the side with the smaller total, using the date of balancing (here 30 September) and the description 'Balance c/d'.

Step 3: total both sides of the account (here £960) and bold – underline or double-underline each total; make sure that the two totals are on the same line on each side of the account

Step 4: complete double-entry book-keeping by recording an equal but opposite entry to the balance c/d; this is entered on the first available line below the totals 'boxes' and is described as 'balance b/d'; the date shown is usually recorded as the next day after 'balance c/d' (here it is 1 October).

FURTHER EXAMPLES OF BALANCING ACCOUNTS

Purchase ledger A/c

Dr		£			Cr £
2007			2007		
30 Apr	Balance c/d	880	1 Apr	Balance b/d	360
			6 Apr	Purchases	170
			14 Apr	Purchases	200
			22 Apr	Purchases	150
		880			880
			1 May	Balance b/d	880

ARJ Limited

The above creditor's account has transactions on one side only, but is still balanced in the same way. This account shows that, according to the accounting records, ARJ Limited is owed £880, ie is a creditor of the business.

Dr		£			Cr £
2007			2007		
3 Sep	Purchases Returns	280	1 Sep	Balance b/d	280
20 Sep	Purchases Returns	110	13 Sep	Purchases	110
		390			390

Harper and Company

This creditor's account has a 'nil' balance after the transactions for September have taken place. The two sides of the account are totalled and, as both debit and credit side are the same amount, there is nothing further to do, apart from entering the bold- or double-underlined total.

Dr		£			Cr £
2007			2007		
			31 Jan	Purchases Returns	
				Day Book	120

Purchases Returns Account

This account has just the one transaction and, in practice, there is no need to balance it. It should be clear that the account has a credit balance of £120 which is the amount of purchases returns for what is probably the first month of a new financial year.

Dr			**D Patel**		Cr
2007		£	2007		£
6 Dec	Purchases Returns	120	1 Dec	Balance b/d	120

This creditor's account has a 'nil' balance, with just one transaction on each side. All that is needed here is to bold- or double-underline the amount on both sides.

PURCHASES LEDGER CONTROL ACCOUNT

The previous chapter looked at the basics of the double-entry book-keeping system for credit purchases and purchases returns. This system uses a main ledger – which contains the accounts for purchases, purchases returns, and VAT – and a purchases ledger which contains the accounts of the creditors from whom the business has bought goods on credit terms. As we did with credit sales, we are now going to develop the book-keeping system by introducing a control account: here it is the purchases ledger control account which fits in with the book-keeping for credit purchases and purchases returns.

The concept of control accounts has been discussed earlier (pages 72-75), so here we will focus on the layout of the purchases ledger control account.

The set-out of a purchases ledger control account (also known as creditors control account) is shown below. The layout is explained on the next page. Note that some of the items have not yet been covered – they will be dealt with in later chapters.

will be entered same as Purchase ledger side.

Dr	**Purchases Ledger Control Account**			Cr
	£			£
Cash/cheques paid to creditors		Balance b/d		
Settlement (cash) discount received		Credit purchases		
Purchases returns		Interest charged by creditors		
Set-off/contra entries		*discount allowed*		
Balance c/d				
	———			———
	═══			═══
		Balance b/d		

balance b/d

The figure for balance b/d on the credit side of the control account represents the total of the balances of the individual creditors' accounts in the purchases ledger. This principle is illustrated in the diagram on the next page.

Note that it is possible for a creditor's account to have a debit balance, instead of the usual credit balance – for example, if the creditor has been overpaid. Most accounting systems 'net off' any such debit balances against the credit balances to give an overall figure for creditors.

credit purchases

Only credit purchases – and not cash purchases – are entered in the control account. However, the total purchases of the business will comprise both credit and cash purchases.

interest charged by creditors

If a creditor charges interest because of slow payment, this must be recorded on both the creditor's account and the control account. The supervisor might well enquire of the creditor why and how the interest has been calculated.

set-off/contra entries

See page 224.

reconciliation of purchases ledger control account

The diagram on the next page shows how a purchases ledger control account acts as a totals account for the creditors of a business. Reconciliation (agreement) of the balances on the purchases ledger control account and subsidiary accounts is made as follows:

Reconciliation of purchases ledger control account

	1 January 2007	31 January 2007
	£	£
F Francis	100	200
G Gold	200	350
H Harris	300	500
I Ingram	400	900
Purchases ledger control account	1,000	1,950

Any discrepancy should be investigated immediately and the error(s) traced.

Dr		Purchases Ledger Control Account			Cr
2007			£	2007	£
31 Jan	Purchases returns		150	1 Jan Balance b/d	1,000
31 Jan	Bank		594	31 Jan Purchases	1,700
31 Jan	Discount received		6		
31 Jan	Balance c/d		1,950		
			2,700		2,700
				1 Feb Balance b/d	1,950

SUBSIDIARY (PURCHASES) LEDGER

Dr		F Francis			Cr
2007			£	2007	£
16 Jan	Bank*		98	1 Jan Balance b/d	100
16 Jan	Discount received*		2	2 Jan Purchases	200
31 Jan	Balance c/d		200		
			300		300
				1 Feb Balance b/d	200

Dr		G Gold			Cr
2007			£	2007	£
15 Jan	Purchases returns		50	1 Jan Balance b/d	200
28 Jan	Bank*		100	9 Jan Purchases	300
31 Jan	Balance c/d		350		
			500		500
				1 Feb Balance b/d	350

Dr		H Harris			Cr
2007			£	2007	£
28 Jan	Purchases returns		100	1 Jan Balance b/d	300
30 Jan	Bank*		200	16 Jan Purchases	500
31 Jan	Balance c/d		500		
			800		800
				1 Feb Balance b/d	500

Dr		I Ingram			Cr
2007			£	2007	£
22 Jan	Bank*		196	1 Jan Balance b/d	400
22 Jan	Discount received*		4	27 Jan Purchases	700
31 Jan	Balance c/d		900		
			1,100		1,100
				1 Feb Balance b/d	900

Note that the book-keeping transactions for 'bank' and 'discount received' will be explained fully in Chapter 14.

SET-OFF/CONTRA ENTRIES

These entries occur when the same person or business has an account in both subsidiary ledgers – sales ledger and purchases ledger – ie they are both buying from, and selling to, the business whose accounts we are preparing. For example, M Patel Limited has the following accounts in the subsidiary sales and purchases ledgers:

SUBSIDIARY (SALES) LEDGER

Dr		A Smith		Cr
		£		£
Balance b/d		200		

SUBSIDIARY (PURCHASES) LEDGER

Dr		A Smith		Cr
		£		£
			Balance b/d	300

From these accounts we can see that:

- A Smith owes M Patel Limited £200 (sales ledger)
- M Patel Limited owes A Smith £300 (purchases ledger)

To save each having to write out a cheque to send to the other, it is possible (with A Smith's agreement) to set-off one account against the other, so that they can settle their net indebtedness with one cheque. The book-keeping entries in M Patel's books will be:

– *debit* A Smith (purchases ledger) £200

– *credit* A Smith (sales ledger) £200

The accounts will now appear as:

SUBSIDIARY (SALES) LEDGER

Dr		A Smith		Cr
		£		£
Balance b/d		200	Set-off: purchases ledger	200

SUBSIDIARY (PURCHASES) LEDGER

Dr		A Smith		Cr
	£			£
Set-off: sales ledger	200	Balance b/d		300

The net result is that M Patel Limited owes A Smith £100. The important point to note is that, because transactions have been recorded in the subsidiary accounts, an entry needs to be made in the two control accounts:

– *debit* purchases ledger control account

– *credit* sales ledger control account

Set-off transactions should be appropriately documented and authorised. The book of prime entry for set-off transactions is the journal (see Chapter 19).

INFORMATION SOURCES FOR PURCHASES LEDGER CONTROL ACCOUNT

Control accounts use totals (remember that their other name is totals accounts) for the week, month, quarter or year – depending on what time period is decided upon by the business. The totals for purchases ledger control account come from a number of sources in the accounting system:

- total credit purchases (including VAT) – from the 'total' column of the purchases day book
- total purchases returns (including VAT) – from the 'total' column of the purchases returns day book
- total cash/cheques paid to creditors – from the cash book (see Chapter 14)
- total settlement discount received – from the discount received column of the cash book (see Chapter 14), or from discount received account
- set-off/contra entries – from the journal (see Chapter 19)

CONTROL ACCOUNTS AS AN AID TO MANAGEMENT

As we have already seen in Chapter 4, control accounts provide important information for the manager of a business. For example, from purchases ledger control account, the manager can find out quickly the figure for creditors without having to go through the subsidiary (purchases) ledger and add up the balances of the individual creditors' accounts. With a computer accounting system control accounts can be printed out at any time.

Other benefits of control accounts include:

- fraud is made more difficult because fraudulent transactions have to be entered in both the control account and the subsidiary account

- locating errors is made easier because the control account is able to demonstrate the arithmetical accuracy of the subsidiary accounts which it controls

PURCHASES LEDGER CONTROL ACCOUNT AND BOOK-KEEPING

The usual way of using control accounts is to incorporate them into the double-entry book-keeping system. This means that purchases ledger control account is in the main ledger while the individual accounts of creditors are held as subsidiary accounts in the subsidiary (purchases) ledger.

The diagram on the opposite page illustrates this.

From time-to-time, the balances of the subsidiary accounts are agreed with the balance of the control account, and any discrepancies investigated. When a purchases ledger control account is in use and journal entries are made (eg for correction of errors – see Chapter 20), transactions involving creditors' accounts must be recorded in

- the purchases ledger control account in the main ledger
- the subsidiary (purchases) ledger

the role of control accounts

Now that we have studied the two control accounts for purchases ledger and sales ledger, it is worth taking a few moments to confirm the position of control accounts in relation to double-entry book-keeping.

The way in which we have used control accounts (and also the usual way in which you will find them in Examinations) is for the control accounts to be part of double-entry book-keeping. Thus, when we look at the trial balance (in Chapter 20), it is the balance of the control account that is used to give us the trial balance figures for debtors and creditors. As control accounts are part of double-entry book-keeping – in the main ledger – then it follows that the subsidiary ledgers for purchases and sales are not part of double-entry book-keeping. Nevertheless, the subsidiary ledgers are important because they tell us the balances of each individual debtor and creditor account. Also, it is good accounting practice to reconcile (agree) the balance of each control account to its subsidiary ledger balances at regular intervals.

■ Purchases ledger control account incorporated into the double-entry book-keeping system

■ Creditors' accounts in the subsidiary (purchases) ledger

Chapter Summary

- The traditional 'T' account needs to be balanced at regular intervals – often the month-end.

- The 'balance b/d' is the account balance at the start of the next period.

- Purchases ledger control account acts as a totals account for the creditors of a business.

- Transactions are recorded on the same side of the control account as on the subsidiary accounts.

- Set-off/contra entries occur when one person has an account in both subsidiary ledgers – sales ledger and purchases ledger – and it is agreed to set-off one balance against the other to leave a net balance. This usually results in the following control account entries:
  - *debit* purchases ledger control account
  - *credit* sales ledger control account

- Control accounts are an aid to management:
  - they give up-to-date information on the total of creditors (or debtors)
  - by making fraud more difficult
  - in helping to locate errors

- Control accounts are normally incorporated into the main ledger of the double-entry book-keeping system. The subsidiary accounts, eg for creditors, are in a separate subsidiary ledger – subsidiary (purchases) ledger.

Key Terms

balance of account	the running total of the account to date
control account	a 'master' account which controls a number of subsidiary accounts
purchases ledger control account	account which acts as a totals account for the creditors of a business
set-off/contra entries	where balances in the subsidiary (sales) ledger and the subsidiary (purchases) ledger are to be set-off against one another

Student Activities

11.1 Balance the following accounts at 30 November 2007, bringing down the balance on 1 December:

Dr		Purchases Account	Cr	
2007		£	2007	£
1 Nov	Balance b/d	64,287		
30 Nov	Purchases Day Book	6,720		

Dr		Purchases Returns Account		Cr
2007		£	2007	£
			1 Nov Balance b/d	1,349
			30 Nov Purchases Returns Day Book	160

Dr		Value Added Tax Account		Cr
2007		£	2007	£
30 Nov	Purchases Day Book	1,176	1 Nov Balance b/d	644
			30 Nov Purchases Returns Day Book	28

Dr		Ryan and Company		Cr
2007		£	2007	£
			1 Nov Balance b/d	348
			4 Nov Purchases	427
			19 Nov Purchases	311
			24 Nov Purchases	256

Dr		Murray Limited		Cr
2007		£	2007	£
1 Nov	Balance b/d	15	8 Nov Purchases	230
11 Nov	Purchases Returns	42	16 Nov Purchases	315
			24 Nov Purchases	171

11.2 You have the following information:

- opening creditor balances at start of month   £15,300
- credit purchases for month   £8,100
- purchases returns for month   £200

What is the figure for closing creditor balances at the end of the month?

(a)   £7,000

(b)   £7,400

(c)   £23,200 ✓

(d)   £23,600

Answer (a) or (b) or (c) or (d)

11.3 Prepare a purchases ledger control account for the month of April 2007 from the following information:

2007		£
1 Apr	Credit balance brought down	14,275
30 Apr	Credit purchases for month	36,592
	Purchases returns	653
	Payments made to creditors	31,074
	Transfer of credit balances to sales ledger	597

The creditors figure at 30 April is to be entered as the balancing figure.

11.4 The main ledger of Rowcester Traders contains the following accounts on 1 February 2007:

purchases, balance £4,397.21 debit

purchases returns, balance £456.29 credit

Value Added Tax, balance £524.86 credit

The subsidiary (purchases) ledger contains the following accounts on 1 February 2007:

Apple Supplies Limited, balance £1,843.22 credit

Beatty Brothers, £51.47 debit

J Johnson, £675.38 credit

Myford Limited, balance £478.29 credit

Newtown Equipment Limited, balance £684.86 credit

W Wright, balance £987.20 credit

The following transactions, which have been authorised by the accounts supervisor took place during February 2007 (note that Rowcester Traders gives each invoice and credit note received its own unique number):

3 Feb	Bought goods on credit from Apple Supplies Limited £1,027.98 + VAT, invoice no 6434
5 Feb	Bought goods on credit from Beatty Brothers £150.68 + VAT, invoice no 6435
6 Feb	Bought goods on credit from J Johnson £328.22 + VAT, invoice no 6436
10 Feb	Returned goods to Apple Supplies Limited £157.20 + VAT, credit note no 145
14 Feb	Bought goods on credit from W Wright £476.38 + VAT, invoice no 6437
17 Feb	Returned goods to Newtown Equipment Limited £105.68 + VAT, credit note no 146
24 Feb	Bought goods on credit from Apple Supplies Limited £849.36 + VAT, invoice no 6438
27 Feb	Transfer of debit balance of £154.27 in the subsidiary (sales) ledger to Myford Limited's account in the subsidiary (purchases) ledger

You are to:

(a) prepare the accounts in the main ledger – including a purchases ledger control account – and subsidiary (purchases) ledger of Rowcester Traders and record the balances at 1 February

(b) enter the above purchase invoices and credit notes in Rowcester Traders' purchases day book and purchases returns day book for February 2007

(c) from the books of prime entry, record the accounting entries – together with the set-off – in the main ledger and subsidiary (purchases) ledger, balancing all accounts at the month-end

(d) reconcile the control account balance with the subsidiary accounts at 1 February and 28 February 2007

12 Making payments

This chapter explains the different ways in which payments are prepared and made by an organisation; it sets out the procedures followed to make sure that all payments are authorised and that confidentiality is maintained. The chapter covers the areas of:

• making payments by cheque

• making payments by inter-bank transfer: giro credits, CHAPS and BACS (computer) payments such as standing orders, direct debits and autopay systems

Two other forms of making payment are covered by separate chapters:

• payroll payments and accounting records are explained in Chapter 14.

• petty cash payments and accounting records are explained in Chapter 16.

This chapter explains the manual completion of documents. Processing payment transactions using computer accounting is dealt with in is dealt with in Osborne Books' **Accounting Work Skills Tutorial** for Unit 31 (Chapter 15).

PERFORMANCE CRITERIA COVERED

unit 30: INTRODUCTORY ACCOUNTING

element 30.2

process purchases and payments

G   calculate supplier payments from source documents

H   schedule payments, and types of payment, as per company policy

OUTGOING PAYMENTS

If you work for an organisation, you will readily appreciate that there are different types of payments involved; some will involve the issue of cheques or cash, some will involve paying money from the organisation's bank account direct to the recipient's bank account, other will involve paying wages and salaries. Here are some typical examples of these different forms of payment:

issue of cheques

- paying suppliers by cheque for goods and services against invoices and statements
- paying for 'one-off' items of *capital* expenditure, eg a computer system
- paying bills (*revenue* expenditure) by cheque and bank giro credit
- making small one-off 'cash' purchases

paying through the bank account

- paying wages
- paying regular suppliers for goods and services
- paying bills, for example business rates

PAYING TRADE SUPPLIERS

internal procedures

Each business or organisation will have its own policies and regulations laid down to ensure that payments to suppliers of goods and services are only made when the goods and services have been received as ordered. A supplier of goods and services is therefore paid when:

- the documents relating to the transaction – the purchase order, delivery note (or goods received note) and invoice have been checked against each other (they are normally filed together)
- any credit due, eg for returned goods, has been received in the form of a credit note
- all discounts, whether *settlement (cash) discount* (for early payment) or *trade discount* or *bulk discount* have been identified and allowed for
- the payment has received the necessary authorisation – often in the form of a supervisor's initials on the invoice, or a rubber stamp

timescales – when to pay?

Each business or organisation will also have its own policies and regulations dictating *when* payment is to be made.

payment on invoice – diary system

Businesses or organisations often pay strictly according to the *due date of the invoice*. Each invoice (and all the accompanying documentation), when it is received will be marked with the due date of payment – eg 30 days after the invoice issue date – and placed in a diary system. With this system a business may make individual payments to different suppliers on any number of days of the month. The system is best suited to small businesses which do not have too many payments to make.

payment runs – based on statements

Another widely adopted system is for suppliers to be paid regularly on the basis of the monthly statement issued rather than in response to individual invoices. A business using this system will set up *payment runs* – ie days on which payments will be made during the month. This might be once a month on the last day of the month, or it could be on the second and last Friday of the month – it is up to the business to decide. On each payment run date the supplier statements will be examined and outstanding items paid (unless they are disputed). This system is easy to manage, particularly if the payments are computerised (see below) as only a limited number of payment runs are needed each month to originate either computer-printed cheques or BACS (inter-bank) payments.

payment schedule and remittance advices

We have already seen that the remittance advice tells the supplier what is being paid, either:

- by *cheque,* in which case the remittance advice accompanies the payment, or

- by *BACS* (inter-bank computer payment), in which case the remittance advice is sent separately by post, fax, or by e-mail

If your job is to make payments and prepare remittance advices, you will probably have a *schedule* of payments to work from, with the payment amount already decided upon and authorised by a supervisor.

paying by cheque

If you are paying a supplier you should attach the cheque to the remittance advice. This may be a tear-off slip attached to the supplier's statement of account, or it may be a standard form used within your organisation. An example of the latter is illustrated on the next page and an example of a cheque on page 236. You should note that the following details are shown:

- the date of the payment
- the amount of the cheque
- the details – ie the reference number ('your reference') and date – of the invoice(s) being paid
- the details (reference number and date) of any credit notes deducted
- the purchaser's order number ('our reference')
- the account number of the buyer (from the sales ledger of the seller)

In addition the remittance advice may show further details such as the cheque number and the amount of any settlement (cash) discount deducted for early settlement (there is none in the illustration).

	REMITTANCE ADVICE		
TO		FROM	
Cool Socks Limited Unit 45 Elgar Estate, Broadfield, BR7 4ER		**Trends** **4 Friar Street** **Broadfield** **BR1 3RF** Tel 01908 761234 Fax 01908 761987 VAT REG GB 0745 8383 56	
Account 3993	31 October 2007		
date	your reference	our reference	payment amount
01 10 07 10 10 07	INVOICE 787923 CREDIT NOTE 12157	47609 47609	277.30 (27.73)
		CHEQUE TOTAL	249.57

a remittance advice accompanying a cheque payment

payment of suppliers by BACS

The use of BACS, the inter-bank computer payment system, will be dealt with in detail later in the chapter. All BACS payments must be communicated to the supplier by means of a posted, faxed, or emailed remittance advice, otherwise the supplier will not know that payment has been made until the bank statement is received, and even then it may be difficult to identify the origin of the payment. If the supplier does not know payment has been received, he or she may start chasing up the debt, which could prove embarrassing!

A BACS remittance advice is illustrated on page 101.

ISSUING OF CHEQUES

Cheques may be either completed manually, or printed out on a computer printer.

When writing out (using ink, not pencil) or typing out the cheque you should take care to complete the

- correct date
- name of the payee (person receiving the money)
- amount in words
- amount in figures (which should be the same!)
- authorised signature (it may be your signature, it may be that of a supervisor or manager)
- counterfoil (date, amount, payee)

No room should be left on the cheque for possible fraudulent additions or alterations; any blank spaces should be ruled through. If any errors are made when you are writing out the cheque, they should be corrected and an authorised signature placed close to the alteration in order to tell the bank that it is an approved correction.

tear off
cheque
here

Date *31/10/03*	
Pay	
Cool Socks Limited	
£ *249.57*	
238628	

counterfoil

Albion Bank PLC
7 The Avenue
Broadfield BR1 2AJ

Date *31 October 2007*   90 47 17

Pay   *Cool Socks Limited* _____

*Two hundred and forty nine pounds 57p*____ A/c payee only ____   £ *249.57* —

TRENDS

V Williams

238628   90 47 17   11719512

cheque

Computer cheque printing is increasingly used by organisations which use computer accounting programs with a purchase ledger facility. The computer will automatically indicate payments that are due and, subject to authorisation, print out the remittance advice and cheque together, ready for posting. Clearly the computer involved must be closely controlled – and probably password protected – in order to prevent unauthorised access and fraudulent payments.

PAYING FOR 'ONE-OFF' ITEMS – CHEQUE REQUISITION FORMS

So far we have looked at the payment of trade suppliers who supply on a regular basis for the normal activities of an organisation, eg merchants who supply potatoes for crisps manufacturers. The procedure for the issue of cheques in this case is reasonably straightforward. There will be times, however, when a cheque is needed for a 'one-off' purpose, for example:

- purchase of an item of equipment, authorised by the organisation
- reimbursement of 'out-of-pocket' expenses incurred by an employee
- payment of a pro-forma invoice (a pro-forma invoice is a request for payment to be made before the supply of the goods or services – contrast this with a normal invoice when payment follows supply)

The normal procedure in these cases is the completion of a cheque requisition form by the person who needs the cheque, as shown below.

Mercia Pumps Limited
CHEQUE REQUISITION FORM

Required by ..**Tom Paget**.............................. Department.**Marketing**......

CHEQUE DETAILS
date for cheque..**31 March 2007**...........
payable to ..**Media Promotions Limited**......
amount £ ....**360.00**......
despatch to (if applicable)..**Media Promotions Limited, 145 High Street, Mereford, MR1 3TF**.....

reason...**Advert in trade journal**.......nominal code..**7556**......

DOCUMENTATION
invoice attached/to follow..**invoice 24516**......
receipt attached/to follow.........
other.........

AUTHORISATION ..*Andrew Wimbush, Marketing Director*.....date..*31 March 2007*.....

a cheque requisition form

Note the following details on the cheque requisition form:

- the cheque has been ordered by Tom Paget, but is to be sent direct to Media Promotions Limited

- the requisition is authorised by Andrew Wimbush, the Marketing Director

- the invoice is attached

- the nominal ledger code is included – this is the category of expense for which an account is maintained in the computer accounting system of the business – 7556 is the computer account number for 'advertising account'; if the business did not have a computer accounting system the name of the account in the main ledger – 'advertising' – would be entered

CONTROL AND AUTHORISATION OF PAYMENTS

spending limits

In order to avoid fraud or unchecked spending within an organisation, all payments must be controlled and authorised. We have seen that incoming invoices must normally be stamped, and signed or initialled by an authorised person before being passed for payment. This is part of an overall system whereby no payment can be made without the necessary authority. The system will vary from organisation to organisation, but the following elements will be usually be found:

- the larger the payment, the more senior the person who needs to authorise it; often each level of management has a money limit imposed – for example a new vehicle will need to be authorised by senior management

- when an item of expenditure is authorised, the person giving their authority will sign or initial and date the supporting document, eg an invoice, a cheque requisition form

cheque signatures

While an organisation will have an internal system of signing for and authorising expenditure, it will also have a written agreement with the bank – a bank mandate – which will set out who can sign cheques. A limited company or partnership may, for example, allow one director or partner to sign cheques up to £5,000, but will require two to sign cheques in excess of £5,000. It is common to have a number of different signatories to allow for partners and directors going on holiday, going sick and being otherwise unavailable for signing cheques.

cash payments and wages

Most organisations will keep a cash float – petty cash – to allow for small everyday items of expenditure such as taxi fares and coffee for customer reception. The operation of the petty cash system is strictly controlled and documented, and will be dealt with in Chapter 16. Organisations are also likely to use cash, cheques and/or BACS for the payment of wages; this will be dealt with in the next chapter.

PAYING BY BANK GIRO CREDIT

We have already seen in Chapter 6 how money can be paid into a bank account by means of a bank paying-in slip. So far we have looked at an organisation which pays in at its own branch, and receives the money in the account on the same day. The banking system also allows for a *bank giro credit* to be paid in at one branch and processed through a three day clearing system (like the cheque clearing system) to another bank or branch. The bank credit clearing system is widely used for:

- paying bills (electricity, gas, telephone)
- settling credit card accounts

The preprinted bank giro credit is usually a tear-off slip at the bottom of a bill. The person or business paying the bill will fill in:

- the amount of the payment
- the date that the payment is being made at the bank
- in some cases the signature of the person paying in the credit at the bank

The bill is then taken to the bank and paid in, together with a cheque for the appropriate amount. A water bill is shown below.

It should be noted that the practice of a business using blank giro credits for 'one-off' payments or for paying suppliers and wages has now largely been discontinued, because of the amount of fraud that was taking place.

BACS PAYMENTS

Bankers Automated Clearing Services (BACS) is a computer transfer payment system owned by the banks. It is widely used for regular payments such as insurance premiums, settlement of trade debts, wages and salaries. BACS is a cheap and efficient means of payment because, instead of a piece of paper having to be prepared and despatched, the transfer is set up on a computer file and transferred between the banks' computers – the payment goes direct from account to account.

The payment cycle is three working days. If a business wants its suppliers or employees to have the money in their accounts on Friday, the money must leave the employer's account on Wednesday. The payment instructions will need to be received by the end of Wednesday, so the accounts department will need to observe this deadline.

STANDING ORDER

The business that needs to make regular payments, eg a loan repayment, completes a written authority (a mandate – see below) instructing the bank what payments to make, to whom, and when. The bank then sets up the instructions on its computer, and the payments are made automatically by computer link on the due dates.

STANDING ORDER MANDATE

To _National_ Bank

Address _45 High Street, Hightown, HT1 7FG_

PLEASE PAY TO

Bank _Western_ Branch _Radstock_ Sort code | 33 09 87 |

Beneficiary _Mendip Loan Brokers_ Account number | 29384729 |

The sum of | £ 100.00 | Amount in words _one hundred pounds only_

Date of first payment _1 April 2007_ Frequency of payment _1st monthly_

Until _1 March 2007_ Reference _FTL294231_

Account to be debited | _Janus Limited_ | Account number | 22472434 |

SIGNATURE(S) _Archie Rice_

If it is a business which is setting up the standing order, it is important that the mandate form is signed by a person (or persons) authorised to do so – it will often be the person(s) authorised to sign cheques.

BACS 'autopay' systems

Businesses often need to make regular payments of variable amounts, for example:

- paying wages on pay day
- making payments to established suppliers at the end of each month

The banks have established a BACS system whereby they set up standing orders to these regular beneficiaries. This has now superseded the practice of completing *blank* bank giro credits for making payments in bulk.

setting up an 'autopay' system

To set up an 'autopay' system the bank needs written instructions from the customer before the amounts can be deducted from the account. What it does, in effect, is to set up a series of standing orders.

The details needed by the bank are:

- the name of the 'beneficiary' – the organisation or person that is to receive the money, eg supplier, employee, insurance company, hire purchase company, etc
- the details of the beneficiary's bank:
  - bank branch
  - sort code number
  - bank account number
- a unique reference number for each beneficiary which is used each time payment is to be made

operating an 'autopay' system

At the end of each month, for example, the accounts department will draw up a list of the suppliers to be paid and a payroll schedule (see the next chapter). Clearly these details will need careful checking and authorisation before instructions are given to the bank. All the business has to do each time payment is to be made is to complete and send to the bank a schedule setting out the payment date, the people who are to receive the money and the amounts. The bank will then process these details through its computers, and payments will be made automatically via the BACS system on the due date. The details may be sent in by post, fax, telephone, or more commonly these days by online instructions.

PAYING SUPPLIERS BY 'AUTOPAY'

City Traders is a shop based in Mereford. In an attempt to cut administrative costs the Accounts Department has decided to pay suppliers through the BACS system. The bank has suggested its AutoCredit System. City Traders has supplied the banking details (sort code and account number) of its suppliers in advance for the bank to put in its own computer. City Traders then writes the monthly payment details on the bank schedule shown below, which is faxed to the bank by Monday 24 September. The suppliers will be paid on Wednesday 26 September.

Mercian Bank PLC
AutoCredit Schedule

Bank branch... Mereford

Originator name. City Traders ... reference... 07246

Date .. 24-9-07

Branch	Account no	Name	Payee no	Amount
45-45-62	10386394	Trendsetters	234	250.00
56-67-23	22347342	FitMan Delivery Co	344	129.76
40-47-07	42472411	Jamesons Ltd	634	450.67
76-87-44	56944491	John Proctor	123	409.79
33-00-77	23442413	Red Skin Company	264	305.78
59-99-01	46244703	Tatters Ltd	197	560.85
		PAYMENT TOTAL		2106.85

Please make the above payments to reach the payees on ....26-9-07.............(date)

Please debit account no......87620261..........with the sum of £...2106.85..............

authorised signature.....*J.Craig*........................

DIRECT DEBIT

The direct debit system is useful for organisations such as insurance companies that receive a large number of variable payments:

- direct debits can be used for either fixed and variable amounts and/or where the time intervals between payments vary
- it is the receiver (beneficiary) of the payment who prepares the computer instructions that request the payer's bank account for payment through the banking system; a direct debit is like a standing order operating backwards

paper-based direct debit instructions

The traditional procedure for setting up a direct debit was for the customer making payment to complete and sign a written authority (mandate) prepared by the beneficiary (the person getting the money, eg an insurance company); this was then returned to the beneficiary (eg the insurance company). The payment details were then posted off to the beneficiary's bank so that the computer instructions could be set up. The original form was then returned to the payer's bank. An example of a direct debit mandate is shown below.

DIRECT Debit

Tradesure Insurance Company
PO Box 134, Helliford, HL9 6TY

Originator's Identification Number 914208

Reference (to be completed by Tradesure Insurance) .... 03924540234 ....

Please complete the details and return this form to Tradesure Insurance

name and address of bank/building society

| National Bank plc |
| Market Street |
| Netherway |
| MR7 9YT |

account name

| Grecian Travel Services |

instructions to bank/building society

- I instruct you to pay direct debits from my account at the request of Tradesure Insurance Company.
- The amounts are variable and may be debited on various dates.
- I understand that Tradesure Insurance Company may change the amounts and dates after giving me prior notice.
- I will inform the bank/building society if I wish to cancel this instruction.
- I understand that of any direct debit is paid which breaks the terms of this instruction, the bank/building society will make a refund.

account number	sort code	signature(s)	date
10318736	76 54 29	M Callapolos	1 April 2007

problems with paper-based direct debits

As you can see, setting up a paper-based direct debit was a protracted and expensive process, open to error and delay. As a consequence the decision was taken by BACS to allow the direct debit payment instructions to be sent electronically by a system known as AUDDIS (Automated Direct Debit Instruction Service).

AUDDIS – the paperless direct debit

A customer wanting to set up a direct debit through AUDDIS (Automated Direct Debit Instruction Service) does not have to sign anything. The instructions (including bank account number, account name and bank sort code) can be provided by the customer over the telephone or on-line over the internet (see screen details below).

This is useful, for example, if a business wants to arrange finance for an item purchased and needs to set up repayments straightaway. A business subscribing to a service can also give similar repayment instructions – nothing need be in writing.

The organisation setting up the 'paperless' direct debit can then enter the details (the amounts, dates, paying bank) into its computer system and send them electronically to the bank making the payments.

an internet screen for accepting AUDDIS instructions

COMPANY CREDIT CARDS, BANK DRAFTS AND CHAPS

company credit cards

Many organisations, particularly those which employ travelling sales representatives, set up a company credit card scheme. This convenient and useful scheme allows company representatives to have credit cards for paying expenses related to the company's business, eg rail tickets, accommodation and food. The credit card bill is settled by the company which is then able to monitor the expenses incurred by its employees.

bank drafts

An organisation may have to make a large purchase – for example new vehicles – and be asked to pay by bank draft. A bank draft is a bank cheque, a guaranteed means of payment which is as good as cash, but without the security risks. In legal terms the bank is both drawer (issuer) and drawee (issuing bank) of the cheque.

CHAPS

The CHAPS (Clearing House Automated Payments System) payment system is for high value payment sent by the banks through their computer networks. It is used extensively by solicitors when they are arranging the purchase and sale of property for their clients. Businesses use it for high value, same day, transfers.

A similar system exists for making payments abroad through the banks' computer network. The banks provide forms for setting up these payments which are sometimes known as IMT's (International Money Transfers).

ONLINE BANKING

With the growth of the use of the internet, many banks are encouraging their customers to manage their payments online. Electronic banking schemes such as Hexagon from HSBC allow customers:

- to get balances and view past transactions
- to make payments from one account to another
- to set up standing orders
- to make CHAPS and international payments

This makes day-to-day management of the finances of a business much simpler. The bank accounts can be monitored 24 hours a day, and greater control can be exercised over payments and receipts.

Chapter Summary

- Outgoing payments made by an organisation include payments to suppliers, payment of bills, cash payments, 'one-off' items and wages.
- Before paying a supplier an organisation must see that all procedures and timescales are observed.
- Businesses often pay suppliers at the end of the month, they pay on receipt of the statement rather than in response to individual invoices.
- When making payment by cheque or by BACS a business will normally send the supplier a remittance advice.
- Care must be taken when issuing cheques to ensure that the details are correct and that no room is left on the cheque for fraudulent alterations.
- If an employee needs a cheque for a 'one-off' payment, he or she will need to have a cheque requisition form completed and authorised.
- The issue of cheques should be strictly controlled through a system of signing 'limits'; normally the larger the amount, the more senior the signatory and the greater number of signatures.
- Payments may be made through the inter-bank transfer system either in paper form or through computer links.
- Bank giro credits, which take three working days to reach their destination account, are preprinted and are used for paying bills and settling credit card accounts.
- Bank computer-based payments are made through Bankers Automated Clearing Services (BACS). These also take three working days to clear.
- A standing order is authorised by the customer in writing and instructs the bank to make regular BACS payments to the beneficiary.
- If a business needs to send a number of BACS payments on a regular basis but with differing amounts each time – eg when paying regular suppliers – it can ask the bank to set up an 'autopay' system. All it needs to do each month is to complete a bank schedule listing the amounts due and the accounts to which they have to be sent.
- A direct debit is authorised by the customer in writing, over the telephone or the internet and instructs the bank to allow the beneficiary to take sums of money through the BACS from the customer's bank account.
- Other methods of payment include:
  - company credit cards for use by employees for expenses
  - bank drafts (bank cheques which are 'as good as cash')
  - CHAPS (computer inter-bank same day payments, usually for large amounts)
- The growth of internet banking has given businesses greater control and flexibility over making payments, and at the same time has allowed them to monitor their bank accounts more closely.

Key Terms		
	remittance advice	a document sent by the buyer to the supplier to advise the details of payment being made
	cheque requisition form	an internal form which is completed and authorised when a cheque needs to be issued, normally for a 'one-off' payment
	bank giro credit	a paper slip (used largely for paying bills) which passes through the bank clearing system to the bank of the organisation receiving payment
	BACS	the BACS system (Bankers Automated Clearing Services) passes payments through the banking system by computer transfer
	beneficiary	the person or organisation who gets the money placed in his/her bank account
	standing order	a BACS payment where the person paying the money sets up a regular series of payments through his/her bank
	direct debit	A BACS payment where the person paying the money authorises the supplier's bank to take money from their bank account
	AUDDIS	AUDDIS (Automated Direct Debit Instruction Service) allows the customer to authorise a direct debit by telephone or on-line and the beneficiary to send those instructions electronically to the payer's bank
	autopay system	a system whereby periodic payments can be made to a number of suppliers through the BACS system – the payer completes a schedule setting out the amounts and beneficiaries and passes it to the bank
	company credit card	a credit card – in the name of the company – issued to a company employee and used for paying expenses
	bank draft	a cheque issued by a bank (and drawn on the bank) purchased by a customer as a payment which is 'as good as cash'
	CHAPS	a CHAPS payment (CHAPS = Clearing House Automated Payments System) is a high-value same-day inter-bank computer payment – often used for vehicle and property purchase payments

Student Activities

12.1   The BACS remittance advice is normally attached to the cheque sent in settlement of an account. True or false?

12.2   Why should a cheque not be completed in pencil?

12.3   A cheque requisition form is used for which *one* of the following purposes?

    (a)   ordering a new cheque book

    (b)   stopping a cheque

    (c)   providing specimen signatures to the bank

    (d)   requesting a cheque within an organisation

12.4   Explain why a partnership or limited company business has to sign a bank mandate.

12.5   (a)   What is the difference between a standing order and a direct debit?

    State whether a standing order or a direct debit is the better method for the following payments, and why:

    (b)   A repayment of a fixed loan: £125 per month for five years

    (c)   A monthly insurance premium which is likely to increase over the years.

12.6   Name two commonly-used methods suitable for making high value 'one-off' payments:

    (a)   a paper-based payment

    (b)   a computer-based payment

12.7   Company credit cards are a popular means of making payment.

    (a)   State one advantage to the employee of the company credit card.

    (b)   State one advantage to the employer of the company credit card.

For the remainder of the Activities in this chapter you are to take the role of an assistant in the Accounts Department of Nimrod Drainage Limited (a VAT-registered company). Part of your day's work is the preparation of remittance advices and cheques for payments to suppliers. You are not required to sign the cheques. The date is 30 April 2007.

12.8   Your supervisor, Ivor Cash, hands you a list of authorised invoices from Jaeger Building Supplies to pay this month. Calculate the amount of the cheque you will have to make out to send with the remittance advice. You do not need to complete any documents. The date is 30 April 2007.

invoice date	payment terms	invoice total (£)
31 March	30 days	125.89
2 April	30 days	14,658.95
3 April	2.5% cash discount for settlement within 7 days	345.50
9 April	30 days	125.00

12.9 Your Supervisor hands you a statement from Mercia Wholesalers, Unit 12 Riverside Industrial Park, Mereford MR2 7GH, with a note, indicating the following invoices to be paid, and a credit note to be set off against payment:

Invoice 8765 dated 12 March 2007, your order number 5517, £765.25

Invoice 8823 dated 2 April 2007, your order number 5792, £3,567.80

Credit note CN 3420 dated 25 April 2007 (your ref R/N 5168), £250.00

Complete the remittance advice and cheque set out below. Note that the total of the credit note should be shown in the money column in brackets, indicating that it is a deduction from the payment.

REMITTANCE ADVICE

TO

FROM

Nimrod Drainage
Unit 6, Riverside Park
Mereford
MR4 5TF
Tel 01908 761200 Fax 01908 761900
VAT REG GB 0745 8383 46

Cheque no.   **Date**

date	your reference	our reference	payment amount

CHEQUE TOTAL

Date   **National Bank PLC**   Date   **35 09 75**
Mereford Branch
10 Cathedral Street, Mereford, MR1 5DE

Pay   only

£   —

A/c payee only

NIMROD DRAINAGE LIMITED
Director   Director

£

000451   000451   35 09 75   12034875

12.10 As an accounts assistant at Nimrod Drainage Limited you have to process the documentation for a wide variety of payments to employees, suppliers and for other business expenses such as one-off purchases, travel costs and bills.

What method of payment would you <u>normally</u> expect to use for the following:

(a)   paying wages

(b)   paying the electricity bill which is sent to the business quarterly

(c)   buying a new car for the Managing Director

(d)   paying travelling expenses for sales representatives

(e)   sending £200,000 to a firm of solicitors for the purchase of new premises

12.11 You have just started work as an accounts assistant and are not authorised to sign cheques or other payment instructions.

The date is 30 April 2007. Your supervisor, Ivor Cash, hands you two documents (shown on the next page):

• a blank standing order form provided by the bank

• a direct debit instruction received from Tradesure Insurance Company

He is in rather a rush and asks you to process the two documents, and to return them to the appropriate address with a compliments slip. He also leaves you a piece of paper with written instructions:

Note from: Ivor   30 April 2007

Hire Purchase Payments

12 monthly instalments of £350 to Broadbent Finance from 15 May 2007, under reference BE/6637.

Bank details Barclays, Eveshore, 30 98 15, Account 72627161.
Debit our Account 12034875

You are to:

(a)   complete the forms as required (look at a Nimrod Drainage cheque for your banking details)

(b)   state to which address you will send them

(c)   comment on any other procedure which you may have to carry out before sending off the forms

STANDING ORDER MANDATE

To _____ Bank

Address _____

PLEASE PAY TO

Bank _____ Branch _____ Sort code [ ]

Beneficiary   Account number [ ]

The sum of £ [ ]   Amount in words _____

Date of first payment _____ Frequency of payment _____

Until _____ Reference _____

Account to be debited [ ]   Account number [ ]

SIGNATURE(S)   ....

.... date.......................

DIRECT Debit

Tradesure Insurance Company
PO Box 134, Helliford, HL9 6TY

Originator's Identification Number 914208

Reference (to be completed by Tradesure Insurance) ...... 03924540234 ....

Please complete the details and return this form to Tradesure Insurance

name and address of bank/building society

instructions to bank/building society

- I instruct you to pay direct debits from my account at the request of Tradesure Insurance Company.
- The amounts are variable and may be debited on various dates.
- I understand that Tradesure Insurance Company may change the amounts and dates after giving me prior notice.
- I will inform the bank/building society if I wish to cancel this instruction.
- I understand that if any direct debit is paid which breaks the terms of this instruction, the bank/building society will make a refund.

account name

account number   sort code   signature(s)   date

13 Payroll payments

this chapter covers . . .

This chapter describes the important process of making payroll payments to employees. The stress is on the accounting and payment aspects of payroll rather than the complex procedures of payroll calculations. The chapter includes:

- a brief introduction to the way in which wages and salaries are calculated

- an explanation of what appears on a typical payslip

- explanations of the double-entry accounting entries involved when making payroll payments, using a wages and salaries control account

PERFORMANCE CRITERIA COVERED

unit 30: INTRODUCTORY ACCOUNTING

element 30.2

process purchases and payments

K   make payments to employees and record those payments

WHAT IS PAYROLL?

payroll

Payroll is a system set up by an individual or an organisation employing people which:

- records the personal details of the employees

- records wages or salaries together with any other payments due to them

- arranges for the money to be paid

- calculates appropriate deductions to be made, eg income tax, National Insurance Contributions, student loan repayments

- arranges for the deductions to be paid to the appropriate authority, eg income tax and National Insurance Contributions to HM Revenue & Customs

It goes without saying that a payroll system must be *accurate* and be kept *confidential.* Employees need to be paid the right amount and they need to be sure that the details of their pay are not circulated to all their colleagues.

manual and computer records

Payroll records may either be maintained manually (on paper) or on a computer-based system. There are a number of commercially available computer systems such as Sage. If a computer system is used it is essential that it has been approved by HM Revenue & Customs. You can normally assume that commercially available systems have been approved for use.

Any payroll system – manual or computer-based – must meet the needs of:

- the organisation's internal record keeping – its accounting system and employee records

- the employees – paying them promptly and accurately

- outside agencies to which returns have to be made, eg HM Revenue & Customs

Payroll records should be kept for a minimum of three years after the end of the year of a tax assessment; some organisations keep them for longer periods, eg six years. They should be filed in an organised way as they may be needed not only by the organisation but also by external auditors. They may also be the subject of inspection by HM Revenue & Customs.

the need for accuracy

The accuracy of the payroll records is essential. Staff must be paid for work done and external authorities such as HM Revenue & Customs must be paid the correct amount. Input of information into the payroll system (eg hours worked, rates of pay) must be carefully checked and authorised.

the need for security

The system must be organised to minimise the risk of information being corrupted or interfered with. Practical considerations include:

- information must not be processed without authorisation
- information must be checked, whether held manually or input into a computer system
- duties must be separated where possible – different people should carry out the various stages of payroll processing – if just one person did everything, carrying out fraud would become easier

When computers are used, care must be taken that data does not fall into the wrong hands. Practical precautions include:

- ensuring that the payroll program has been exited when the computer is unattended, eg lunchtimes, so that passers-by cannot see confidential data
- changing computer passwords regularly (and not writing them down where they can be seen!)

TYPES OF INCOME

salaries and wages – gross and net pay

An annual **salary** is agreed between employer and employee and a proportionate amount is usually paid in weekly or monthly amounts.

Wages are normally paid weekly. A payment rate for each hour worked is agreed and the employee will be paid for the number of hours worked.

Gross pay is the total amount earned by an employee. It is the basic wage or salary plus any additional payments such as overtime and bonuses.

Net pay is the amount the employee receives after the employer has made tax deductions and voluntary deductions such as pensions.

types of gross pay

Most pay is **basic rate** pay, ie payment for the hours that the employee is contracted to work. There are, however, other components of gross pay, which you may come across:

- **Overtime** involves extra payments given to staff who work unsocial hours because of the demands of shift working.
- A **bonus** scheme is an incentive to employees to reach and exceed set targets.

- **Commission** payments are normally made to employees engaged in selling goods or services. The commission is usually paid as a percentage of the total sales made and is generally added to a fixed net salary.
- **Piece rate** payment is another form of incentive to employees to work more quickly. The employer will agree a rate of pay for each article produced or operation completed and the employees will be paid only for the work that they have completed.

tax credits

Another form of income which passes through the payroll process is not part of earnings but a form of State benefit known as a tax credit. There are two types of benefit which now appear in the 'wage packet' as tax credits:

- Working Families' Tax Credit (WFTC)
- Disabled Person's Tax Credit (DPTC)

This money which is paid to employees does not come out of the employer's pocket (that would hardly be fair!) but comes from a reduction in the amount of tax which the employer collects from employees and pays to HM Revenue & Customs. This is why it is called a 'tax credit'.

DEDUCTIONS FROM PAY

There are a number of deductions an employer is likely to make from gross pay. Some are *compulsory* and some are *voluntary*.

compulsory deductions from gross pay

An employer must deduct two government taxes as and when they are due:

- income tax
- National Insurance Contributions

Student Loan repayments may also be made from gross pay. If an employee used to be a student and took out a loan under the government scheme when studying, that loan will have to be repaid from earnings. When the student gets a job, HM Revenue & Customs (often abbreviated to HMRC) will issue a notice to the employer with all the details so that deductions can be made.

voluntary deductions

An employer may deduct the following at the request of the employee:

- payments to charity by means of a Payroll Giving scheme – deducted *before* the tax calculations are made (not shown above)

- pensions (superannuation) scheme payments, stakeholder pensions
- union fees (not shown above)
- SAYE (Save as You Earn) Sharesave Schemes for employees who wish to buy shares in the company that employs them

Study the diagram shown below which summarises potential income to an employee and possible deductions made from that income.

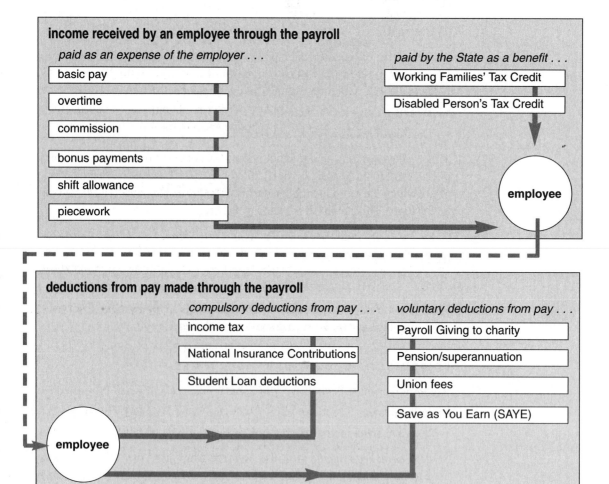

PAY AS YOU EARN – PAYE

what is PAYE?

Pay As You Earn, abbreviated and commonly referred to as *PAYE,* is the arrangement whereby an employer deducts income tax and National

Insurance from an employee's gross pay on each pay day. This money is paid to HM Revenue & Customs by the employer who effectively *collects* the tax for the government.

the tax year

PAYE operates whether the employee is paid weekly, monthly or for any other time period. The income tax and National Insurance collected is normally paid to HM Revenue & Customs monthly, but can be paid quarterly if the amounts are low.

Tax calculations are based on amounts due on earnings during the course of a 'tax' year – which is *not* the same as a calendar year. The tax year runs from April 6 in one year to April 5 in the next year.

income tax and tax allowances

Income tax is a tax on the income received by an individual. 'Income' for tax purposes means wages and salaries, tips, bonuses, and benefits such as a company car.

Employees do not, fortunately, have to pay tax on all their income. In order to help the lower paid, the Government gives a *tax allowance* known as the *personal allowance*, an amount which can be earned during the tax year on which no tax is paid at all. This tax-free income is known as *Free Pay*.

The amount of the personal allowance varies, depending on factors such as whether employees are over a certain age. Additional *tax allowances* are also available for items such as the purchase of special work clothing.

taxable income

Income which *is* liable to tax is known as *taxable income*. Taxable income is calculated by deducting the tax allowances (eg the personal allowance) from gross income. For any tax year therefore:

taxable income = gross income minus the tax allowance

National Insurance

National Insurance Contributions (NIC) are also deducted by the employer under the PAYE system. All employees, except those under 16 and those over 60 (females) and over 65 (males) are liable to pay National Insurance. The purpose of NICs is to provide funds for state pensions and other benefits The employer also has to make National Insurance Contributions (NIC).

National Insurance is essentially just another tax.

THE PAYSLIP

Employees must by law be given a *payslip* showing gross pay and the deductions made to arrive at net pay. There is no set format for a payslip. Some organisations will write or type out the details on a printed form, other organisations may use a computer payroll program which will calculate all the figures and automatically print out the payslip. A typical payslip for an employee paid monthly is shown below.

OSBORNE ELECTRONICS		Pay Advice	June 2007
payments		**deductions**	
	£		£
Basic pay	918.75	Income tax	132.87
Overtime	100.00	National Insurance	70.80
Bonus	20.00	Pension	32.08
TOTAL GROSS PAY	1038.75	Student Loan deduction	20.00
		TOTAL DEDUCTIONS	255.75
Gross pay to date	3427.88		
		TOTAL NET PAY	783.00
Date	**Employee**	Income tax to date	467.00
30.06.07	J Smithers	National insurance to date	244.00

details on the payslip

As noted above, there is no set format for a payslip. The details that will normally be found – if appropriate – are:

essential details	optional details
employer name	tax code
employee name	payroll number
gross pay	National Insurance number
statutory sick pay	method of payment
statutory maternity pay	
tax credits	
deductions made, eg	
– tax for the period	
– tax and NI to date	
– NI for the period	
– Student Loan deductions	
– employee's pension payment	
net pay	

PAYING THE WAGES

Calculating the net pay is the first part of the payroll process. The wages or salaries then have to be paid. There are a number of different ways of paying:

- by cash
- issuing a cheque
- direct to an account by electronic transfer (BACS)

We will deal with each of these in turn.

cash and the need for security

The traditional way of paying wages is by cash, and it is still popular despite the increasing number of people with bank and building society accounts. An employer paying wages in cash can either sub-contract the work to a security firm which will make up the wage packets, or it can be completed by the company's own staff. Preparing wage packets involves collecting sufficient notes and coins from the bank to make up the exact amount for each pay packet.

It is normal practice to telephone the bank in advance to tell them the exact denominations of notes and coins needed. Organisations using online banking services can give these instructions electronically. Employees collecting wages cash from the bank are a obvious target for robbery, so common security measures include using two people to collect the money, and for them to vary the route from the bank.

The cash is placed inside a wage packet marked with the name and pay reference or clock number of the employee. Details showing how the payment is made up and the deductions that have been made are provided to each employee. These details can be shown on a separate pay slip or written on the wage packet itself. The office in which this is carried out should be kept secure – for obvious reasons. Employees should sign for the cash wages when they are received.

The total number of notes and coins needed from the bank is worked out on a form known as a *cash analysis*. An important internal security check for the employer is to ensure that the total of the cash analysis is the same as the amount of the cheque given to the bank to cover the wages. A typical cash analysis is illustrated on the next page.

why pay cash wages?

There are a number of reasons why wages are still paid in cash:

- employees like cash in hand
- some employees may not have bank accounts

cash analysis for week ending..................

name	£50	£20	£10	£5	£2	£1	50p	20p	10p	5p	2p	1p	total
W Rowberry	1	2	1		2			2		1			104.45
D Stanbury	1	1	1		1	1	1	1	1				83.80
K Peters		2		1	1		1		2		1		47.72
O Robinson	2	2	1	1	1	1		2		1		1	158.46
M Richardson	1	1	2	1			1	1		1	1	1	95.78
NUMBER	5	8	5	3	5	2	3	6	3	3	2	2	
TOTAL (£.p)	250.00	160.00	50.00	15.00	10.00	2.00	1.50	1.20	0.30	0.15	0.04	0.02	490.21

a cash analysis

PAYMENT OF WAGES BY CHEQUE

Another traditional method of payment of wages and salaries is the issue of cheques. This avoids the complexities and security problems involved in the paying of cash wages.

The employee can either cash the cheque at the employer's bank, or, more commonly, pay it into a bank or building society account.

manual and computerised systems

If the employer uses a *manual* payroll system this will involve the person doing the payroll writing out individual cheques made payable to each employee for the net pay earned. This cheque will then be enclosed with the payslip in a sealed envelope.

If a *computerised* payroll system is used, it will commonly print out the payment cheque for each employee, together with the payslip (which may be physically attached to the cheque).

issue of pay cheques – manual payroll

A number of security and authorisation procedures need to be followed:

- the cheques need to be kept in a secure place
- the cheques have to be written out carefully – the details (name, date, words and figures) have to be checked carefully against the payroll analysis
- the cheques have to be signed by the required number of authorised signatories (some cheques may be rubber stamped with signatures by authorised staff, or be passed through a 'cheque signing' machine)
- additional controls can include:
  - checking the cheque amounts against the payslips
  - adding up the cheque amounts on a tally-roll calculator and agreeing the total with the payroll analysis total for employees paid by cheque

Although the security risk is not as great as it is with handling cash wages, employers who pay employees by cheque need to ensure that internal checks exist to prevent staff from fraudulently altering amounts on cheques.

A typical pay cheque is illustrated at the top of the next page. Note that:

- the words and figures agree
- lines are drawn after the payee's name and the amount in words – this is to deter fraud
- the cheque is signed by two authorised signatories – directors of the company

Northern Bank PLC
Mereford Branch
28 High Street, Mereford MR1 8FD

date   *25 July 2007*   22-01-59

Pay   *W Rowberry*   only

One hundred and eighty pounds 50p only

Account payee only

£   *180.50*

OSBORNE ELECTRONICS LIMITED

T. Osborne   O. Hardy

Director   Director

402874   22 01 59   37637148

a typical pay cheque

BACS PAYMENTS AND PAYROLL

We saw in the last chapter that the Bankers Automated Clearing Services (BACS) is a computer transfer payment system owned by the banks. It is widely used for regular payments such as

- insurance premiums
- settlement of trade debts
- paying wages and salaries

BACS is a cheap and efficient means of payment because, instead of a piece of paper having to be prepared and despatched, the transfer is set up on a computer file and transferred between the banks' computers – the payment goes direct from account to account.

Sometimes the organisation *receiving* the money, such as an insurance company, will set up the computer data itself for the BACS system to process – this is a *direct debit*.

Sometimes the organisation *sending* the money will set up the computer data, or will get the bank to set it up. When an organisation wants to send a group of payments to different beneficiaries – such as employees – it will set up *automated credits* using the BACS system.

The payment cycle is three working days. If an organisation is paying its wages through BACS and wants its employees to have their money on account on Friday, the money must leave the employer's account on Wednesday. The payment instructions will need to be received by the end of Wednesday, so the payroll department will need to observe this deadline.

PROCESSING PAYROLL THROUGH BACS

Payment of wages and salaries through the BACS system can be made in two different ways:

1 **direct dealing with BACS**

   The organisation paying the wages and salaries sets up the data on computer file *itself* and sends the data on disk (or direct on-line) to BACS – this is often the system used by large organisations which have thousands of wages and salary payments to make each week and month. With this system, the organisation's bank is not directly involved, except to the extent that the total of all the payments will be debited (deducted) from the organisation's bank account.

2 **bank 'automated credit' systems**

   The principle of this system is that the organisation provides the data to its *bank,* which then sets up the computer transfers.

   When an organisation sets up this 'automated credit' system in the first place it will have to provide the banking details of the employees so that the bank can input them into its computer. These details are:

   • the name of the employee

   • the bank sort code

   • the account number

   Once these details have been provided to the bank, the bank will allocate a reference number to each payee/employee. This reference is the 'payee number' shown on the schedule on the opposite page.

   When each payroll date approaches, the payment details are written on a schedule (see opposite page) and sent or faxed to the bank, which then inputs them into its own computer. Organisations with online banking facilities can set up the payroll details over the internet.

   Inevitably, an organisation will want to change the employee details from time-to-time: employees will leave and new staff will be taken on. Amendments can easily be made to the employee records set up on the bank computer. Banks provide amendment forms which enable records to be deleted and new ones added.

   It is important to appreciate that if you are operating an automated credits system, every instruction to the bank is authorised by an authorised signature, which must be obtained if the instructions are to be validated.

   You should also note that this 'automated credit' system is very useful for *smaller* organisations, not only for payroll but also for making payments to suppliers (see page 241).

Case Study

WAGES BY BACS AUTOMATED CREDIT

City Insurance is an insurance broking firm, based in Mereford. In an attempt to cut administrative costs the Finance Manager has decided to pay employees through the BACS system. The bank has suggested its AutoCredit System. City Insurance has supplied the banking details (sort code and account number) of its employees in advance for the bank to put in its own computer. The weekly pay details are then written on the schedule shown below by City Insurance and faxed to the bank on Wednesday 26 September. The employees will be paid on Friday 28 September.

Northern Bank PLC
AutoCredit System

Bank branch...Mereford...........................

Originator name.City Insurance Co........................reference...07246...................

Date..26-9-07................

Branch	Account no	Name	Payee no	Amount
45–45–62	10386394	Smithson H	347	250.00
56–67–23	22347342	Smith M	456	129.76
40–47–07	42472411	Olivier L	209	450.67
76–87–44	56944491	O'Casey S	492	409.79
33–00–77	23442413	French W	385	305.78
59–99–01	46244703	Jones R	546	560.85
		PAYMENT TOTAL		2106.85

Please make the above payments to reach the payees on ....28-9-07............(date)

Please debit account no......37637927..........with the sum of £...2106.85...............

authorised signature.....*S. Laurel*.....................................

---

procedures for the schedule

Note that:

- the employer has a reference – 07246 – which is quoted on all instructions
- each employee also a reference number, which is also quoted on all instructions
- the form is totalled to provide the amount which will be taken from the employer's bank account
- the form is signed by an authorised signatory within the organisation – the data cannot be processed without this signature
- it is common for a form of this type to be in two parts: the bank is given the top copy, and the bottom copy is retained by the organisation making payment

It is essential therefore that before the schedule is handed to the bank it is carefully checked for accuracy. The net pay amounts must tally with the figures on the payroll analysis and the authorised signature must be present.

PAYMENTS TO HM REVENUE & CUSTOMS

Organisations operating PAYE collect income tax and National Insurance Contributions each time the payroll is run. This money must then be paid to HM Revenue & Customs. For most organisations this means a monthly payment sent within fourteen days of the end of the tax month, using a bank giro credit (see below). As the tax month ends on the 5th, this means that the money must by sent by the 19th. The payments will comprise:

- income tax collected from employees
- employees' and employer's National Insurance Contributions
- less any tax credits reclaimable from HM Revenue & Customs

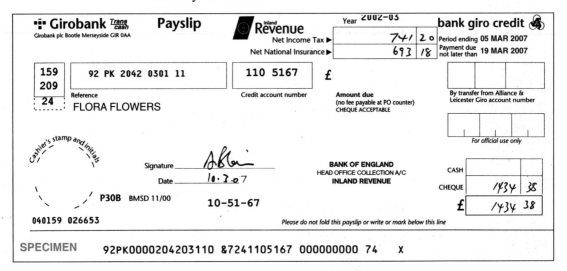

PAYROLL AND THE DOUBLE-ENTRY ACCOUNTING SYSTEM

types of accounting system

Payroll accounting systems will either be paper-based, or computerised. Many 'off-the-shelf' payroll accounting packages are now available, such as the widely-used Sage programs. In this chapter, however, we will use a paper-based system to illustrate the accounting entries generated by the operation of payroll so that you will understand the double-entry principles involved.

types of accounts used

Wages and salaries are a major *expense* for any organisation, but remember that the net pay received by employees is not the same as the *gross pay*, the expense to the employer. The wages and salaries expenses figure that appears in the trial balance of the organisation – the expenses that the employer will have to pay – will be the result of a number of adjustments:

- calculated in the payroll process
- entered in the double-entry accounts of the organisation

There is no 'hard-and-fast' rule which states what accounts have to be set up. The accounts used in this chapter are fairly typical, but you may well find that practice varies from organisation to organisation. The main accounts to be used will be:

- in the cash book (for bank transactions)
- in the main (general) ledger (expenses)

The types of transaction which need entering in the accounts include:

- income tax collected by the employer under PAYE and paid to HM Revenue & Customs by the 19th of the month *after* the payroll has been processed

- employees' National Insurance Contributions collected by the employer under PAYE and paid to HM Revenue & Customs by the 19th of the month *after* the payroll has been processed

- employer's National Insurance Contributions paid to HM Revenue & Customs

- employees' pension contributions deducted from employees' pay and paid to pension funds

- pension contributions provided by the *employer* and paid to pension funds

The double-entry accounts commonly used include:

Bank this is in the cash book and records:

- payment of cash wages, wages cheques and BACS wages transfers – ie the *net pay* of employees
- payment of cheques to outside agencies, eg the monthly payment of deductions to HM Revenue & Customs and payments to pension funds

Wages & Salaries this is in the main ledger and records:

- employees' *gross pay*
- employer's National Insurance Contributions
- employer's pension contributions (if there are any)

– in short, it is the employer's *expense* account for paying employees

HM Revenue & Customs this is in the main ledger and records amounts payable to HM Revenue & Customs (PAYE deductions)

Pension Fund this is in the main ledger and records amounts payable to external pension funds: the employer's and employees' contributions as appropriate (with some schemes the employer and employee make a contribution, with others it is just the employee that contributes)

A common practice is to put all the entries through a Wages and Salaries Control account.

wages and salaries control account

You may already have studied the *control accounts* used by businesses for purchases and sales. They are covered in Chapters 4 and 11 of this book.

A *control account* is a 'master' account which 'controls' a number of other subsidiary ledger accounts. It is used to record the total of transactions passing through the subsidiary accounts. The balance of the control account should always be equal to the total balances of the subsidiary accounts.

For example, the sales ledger *control account* will give the total of the debtors of an organisation and the purchases ledger *control account* will give the total of the creditors. This provides useful information for the management: they will be able to see how much the business is owed by its customers and the amount it owes to its suppliers.

A *wages and salaries control account* is also a master account: all the entries to the various accounts set up to deal with payroll transactions pass through the control account.

The diagram below shows the structure of the control account and subsidiary accounts. Note that the bank account is not shown here – it is involved in many of the transactions, as we will see in the Case Study which follows, but it is not strictly speaking 'subsidiary'.

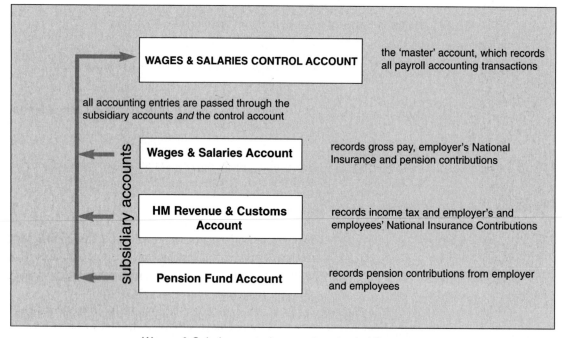

Wages & Salaries control account and subsidiary accounts

Case Study

FLUFFIES: WAGES & SALARIES CONTROL ACCOUNT

Fluffies is a small knitwear business employing five staff. It operates a monthly payroll which is run on the last day of the month. Payroll figures for November 2007 are:

gross pay	£5,500
net pay received by employees	£3,875
income tax deducted by PAYE	£900
NIC (employees' contribution)	£450
NIC (employer's contribution)	£550
pension: paid by the employees by deduction from pay	£275
pension: employer's contribution	£275

What are the payments that are due, and to whom are they payable?

payments due to HM Revenue & Customs (HMRC)

Income tax deducted from employees' pay	£900
Employees' National Insurance Contributions	£450
Employer's National Insurance Contributions	£550
	£1,900

payments due to the pension fund, Allied Life PLC

Employees' contributions, deducted from pay	£275
Employer's contributions	£275
	£550

payments due to the employees

Gross pay	£5,500
less	
Income tax	£900
National Insurance	£450
Pension contributions	£275
Net pay due	£3,875

payments total

£6,325

These four amounts, shown here in the right-hand column, are recorded in the payroll records and have to be entered into the ledger accounts. This is done as follows:

Step 1

Transfer the total of the payments (here £6,325) to Wages & Salaries Account (this is the cost to the employer) and to Wages & Salaries Control Account

debit Wages & Salaries Account
credit Wages & Salaries Control Account

Dr		**Wages & Salaries Account**		Cr
2007	£	2007		£
30 Nov	Wages & salaries 6,325 Control Account			

Dr			**Wages & Salaries Control Account**		Cr
2007		£	2007		£
			30 Nov Wages & salaries		6,325

You will see that this total agrees with the *total monthly payroll expense to the business*: gross pay (£5,500) *plus* employer's National Insurance (£550) *plus* employer's pension contribution (£275) *equals* £6,325.

Step 2
Make entries for the payment of wages (the net pay paid from the bank)

debit   Wages & Salaries Control Account
credit   Bank Account

Dr			**Wages & Salaries Control Account**		Cr
2007		£	2007		£
30 Nov	Bank	3,875	30 Nov Wages & salaries		6,325

Dr			**Bank Account**		Cr
2007		£	2007		£
			30 Nov Wages & Salaries Control Account		3,875

Step 3
Transfer the amount due to HM Revenue & Customs to HMRC Account

debit   Wages & Salaries Control Account
credit   HM Revenue & Customs Account (HMRC Account) (a 'creditor' account
             until the amount is paid in December and 'clears' the account back to zero)

The 'amount due' is £1,900 and comprises income tax (£900) and National Insurance contributions (employer's [£550] and employees' [£450]).

Dr			**Wages & Salaries Control Account**		Cr
2007		£	2007		£
30 Nov	Bank	3,875	30 Nov Wages & salaries		6,325
30 Nov	HMRC	1,900			

Dr	HM Revenue & Customs (HMRC) Account	Cr
2007	£	2007	£
		30 Nov Wages & Salaries Control Account	1,900

Step 4
Transfer the amount due to the pension fund, Allied Life PLC

The amount due is £550 (employer's contribution £275, employee's contribution £275)

debit   Wages & Salaries Control Account
credit   Pension Fund Account (which will become a 'creditor' account until the amount is paid in December and 'clears' the account back to zero)

Dr		Wages & Salaries Control Account		Cr
2007		£	2007	£
30 Nov	Bank	3,875	30 Nov Wages & salaries	6,325
30 Nov	HMRC	1,900		
30 Nov	Pension Fund	550		
		6,325		6,325

Dr	Pension Fund Account	Cr
2007	£	2007	£
		30 Nov Wages & Salaries Control Account	550

conclusion
You will see from the double-entry book-keeping entries shown above that the Wages & Salaries Control Account acts as a 'master' account for all the payroll accounting transactions carried out each time the payroll is run. At the end of the process the control account balance reverts to zero – you will see above that the total of both sides after the pension fund transfer is £6,325 – ie the balance is nil.

The double-entry book-keeping also shows:

• *Wages & Salaries Account:* the cumulative cost during the year of paying the employees – this includes the gross pay, employer's National Insurance and any pension contributions paid by the employer; this is the figure that will appear in the organisation's profit statement – it is the expense borne by the employer

• in HM *Revenue & Customs Account* and *Pension Fund Account* any amounts owing – for example at the end of the month before payments are passed to these agencies – these will be *creditor* accounts

- Payroll records – which are highly confidential – must be maintained accurately and securely.

- Employees' income from the employer, which may be termed 'wages' or 'salary' can be made up of a number of elements: basic pay, overtime, shift allowance, bonus payments, commission, piece rate.

- The payroll is also used to pay certain forms of State benefit – Working Families' Tax Credit and Disabled Person's Tax Credit.

- Compulsory deductions from gross pay include income tax, National Insurance Contributions and any Student Loan repayments which are due to be made.

- Voluntary deductions from gross pay include Payroll Giving schemes, pensions (superannuation), Union fees, and Save as You Earn (SAYE) Sharesave schemes.

- The tax year runs from 6 April in one year until 5 April in the next and is divided into numbered tax weeks and tax months.

- Employees are given tax allowances – amounts of earnings which are free of tax. Taxable income is income on which tax has to be paid; it is gross income less the total tax allowance.

- The tax allowance of an employee is notified by HM Revenue & Customs by means of a tax code – the amount of the tax allowance less the final digit.

- National Insurance is a tax on earnings paid by employers and employees

- All income items and deductions are shown on the employee's payslip together with 'year-to-date' figures.

- Wages can be paid in cash, by cheque or by BACS. The breakdown of notes and coins for cash wages is calculated on a cash analysis form.

- Payments of income tax and National Insurance Contributions to HM Revenue & Customs are made on a bank giro credit form.

- Payroll transactions are recorded in the double-entry accounting records of the business – normally using a control account to record the total of transactions passing through the accounts involved in payroll.

Key Terms		
	gross pay	the total amount earned by an employee
	net pay	the total amount earned by an employee less deductions, ie what the employee 'gets'
	tax credit	a form of State benefit paid through the payroll and reclaimable by the employer
	income tax	a tax, based on the level of an employee's income, collected by HM Revenue & Customs
	National Insurance	(NI) – a tax based on an employee's earnings, collected by HM Revenue & Customs on behalf of the Department of Social Security
	PAYE	Pay As You Earn is a cumulative tax collection system operated by employers on behalf of HM Revenue & Customs
	tax allowance	an amount of income earned by an employee on which tax does not have to be paid
	tax code	a numeric code (plus a letter) which enables the employer to calculate the amount of tax due – it is the tax allowance less the final digit
	taxable income	the income earned by an employee which is subject to income tax (gross income minus the tax allowance)
	payslip	a document given to the employee when the payroll is run, setting out income and deductions
	cash analysis	a form setting out the details of notes and coin needed from the bank by an employer when paying wages in cash
	control account	a double-entry account which acts as a 'master' account for other 'subsidiary' accounts

Student Activities

13.1 The payslip below shows a number of income items and deductions. Study it carefully.

OSBORNE ELECTRONICS		**Pay Advice**	June 2007
payments		**deductions**	
	£		£
Basic pay	918.75	Income tax	122.87
Overtime	100.00	National Insurance	70.80
Bonus	20.00	Pension	32.08
TOTAL GROSS PAY	1038.75	Student Loan deduction	10.00
		TOTAL DEDUCTIONS	235.75
Gross pay to date	3427.88		
		TOTAL NET PAY	803.00
Date	**Employee**	Income tax to date	467.00
30.06.00	B Elliott	National insurance to date	244.00

(a) Write short explanatory notes on the income items (including any cumulative items).

(b) Write short explanatory notes on the deduction items (including any cumulative items). Identify in your notes the compulsory deductions and the voluntary deductions.

(c) What is the meaning of 'TOTAL GROSS PAY' and 'TOTAL NET PAY'?

The following data will form the basis for multiple-choice questions 13.2 to 13.4. In each case, choose one option from (a) to (d)

The payroll system of Home Fires Limited has recorded the following totals for the month of July:

gross pay	£350,780
income tax deducted by PAYE	£69,500
NIC (employees' contribution)	£31,450
NIC (employer's contribution)	£35,085
pension: paid by the employees by deduction from pay	£7,500
pension: employer's contribution	£7,500

13.2 The total payment to HM Revenue & Customs for the month will be

(a) £100,950   (b) £104,585   (c) £15,000   (d) £136,035

13.3 The total wages & salaries expense to the employer will be

(a) £350,780   (b) £462,865   (c) £393,365   (d) £308,195

13.4 The total net pay to employees will be:

(a) £242,330   (b) £249,830   (c) £389,730   (d) £350,780

13.5 Pegasus Limited has recorded the following payroll totals for the month of October 2007:

gross pay	£101,500
income tax deducted by PAYE	£20,500
NIC (employees' contribution)	£9,860
NIC (employer's contribution)	£10,150
pension: employer's contribution (non-contributory pension)	£7,500

(a) Calculate the total payroll cost to the employer

(b) Calculate the payment due to the HM Revenue & Customs

(c) Calculate the net pay due to employees

(d) Draw up double-entry accounts for Wages & Salaries, HM Revenue & Customs, Pension Fund, Bank, and Wages & Salaries Control and enter the relevant entries. Assume a nil opening balance for each account. You do not need to balance the accounts.

13.6 Jasons Wool Shop has recorded the following payroll totals for the month of October 2007:

gross pay	£50,000
income tax deducted by PAYE	£11,110
NIC (employees' contribution)	£4,985
NIC (employer's contribution)	£5,010
pension: paid by the employees by deduction from pay	£1,100
pension: employer's contribution	£1,100

(a) Calculate the total payroll cost to the employer

(b) Calculate the payment due to the HM Revenue & Customs

(c) Calculate the amount due to the Pension Fund

(d) Calculate the net pay due to employees

(e) Draw up double-entry accounts for Wages & Salaries, HM Revenue & Customs, Pension Fund, Bank, and Wages & Salaries Control and enter the relevant entries. Assume a nil opening balance for each account. You do not need to balance the accounts.

Cash book – recording payments

In this chapter we examine the way in which the cash book records payments in the form of cash, cheques and other bank transfers.

As well as recording the money side of book-keeping transactions, the cash book is part of the double-entry system. This chapter focuses on the payments (credit) side of the cash book and we will see also how the opposite debit entry is recorded in creditors' and other accounts.

Also in this chapter we explain the authorisation and payment of expenses claims – a task which is often carried out by a firm's cashier.

PERFORMANCE CRITERIA COVERED

unit 30: INTRODUCTORY ACCOUNTING

element 30.2

process purchases and payments

I   enter payments in cash book and ledgers

USES OF THE CASH BOOK

The payments (credit) side of the cash book brings together:

- cash transactions – most payments for cash, except for low-value expense payments (which are paid through petty cash book – see next chapter)
- bank transactions – all payments through the bank (including the withdrawal of cash from the bank)

We have already seen in Chapter 7 (which dealt with the receipts side of the cash book) how the cash books – ie cash book and petty cash book – combine the roles of books of prime entry and double-entry book-keeping.

Cash books are:

- books of prime entry for cash and bank transactions
- double-entry accounts for cash and bank accounts

RECORDING PAYMENTS – LAYOUT OF THE CASH BOOK

The payments (credit) side of the cash book can be set out in a variety of formats to suit the requirements of a particular business. The columnar cash book is a format which incorporates several money columns. An example of the payments side of a three-column cash book (with three money columns) is shown below:

Credit		Cash Book: Payments				CBP
Date	Details		Folio	Discount received	Cash	Bank
				£	£	£

This is an almost identical layout to that already seen in Chapter 7, page 133. The only differences are that:

- the cash book payments (CBP) is the credit side
- discount received column relates to any settlement or cash discount received by the firm in respect of prompt payments made to creditors

Remember that a business can set out its cash book in the format that best suits its requirements. As we saw in Chapter 7, not all businesses use a cash column. This is most commonly used by businesses that have a high volume of cash transactions (see Case Study below).

book-keeping and the cash book

As the cash book is part of the double-entry system, each entry on the payments side (the credit side) of the cash and bank columns must have an opposite entry on the debit side of another account elsewhere. Note that the discount received column is not part of the double-entry system – it is used in the cash book as a listing device or memorandum column (we will see later in this chapter how amounts from this column are transferred into the double-entry system).

Case Study

SEVERN TRADING COMPANY – CASH BOOK PAYMENTS

situation

The cashier at the firm for which you work, Severn Trading Company, is away on a course this week. You are required, in her absence, to take over as cashier. The following payments are to be entered into the firm's cash book, which has columns for discount received, cash payments and bank:

2007

5 Apr   Paid E Lee & Son, a creditor, £160 by cheque no 101261

6 Apr   Paid Hayes Limited, a creditor, £200 by standing order

6 Apr   Paid S Crane, a creditor, £145 by cheque no 101262 – he has allowed £5 settlement discount

7 Apr   Cash purchases £94 (including VAT of £14)

8 Apr   Cash purchases £282 (including VAT of £42), paid for by cheque no 101263

9 Apr   Paid cheque no 101264 for £70 to S Ford, a creditor, in full settlement of our account of £75

solution

Credit	Cash Book: Payments					CBP 24
Date	Details		Folio	Discount received	Cash	Bank
				£	£	£
2007						
5 Apr	E Lee & Co	101261	PL 804			160
6 Apr	Hayes Limited	SO	PL 752			200
6 Apr	S Crane	101262	PL 610	5		145
7 Apr	Purchases		ML 5001/ 2200		94	
8 Apr	Purchases	101263	ML 5001/ 2200			282
9 Apr	S Ford	101264	PL 698	5		70
				10	94	857

notes

- The cash book payments page is numbered – here 'CBP 24'.

- The cash book forms a part of the double-entry book-keeping system. The payments side of the cash book records the credit entry for cash and bank transactions – in the section which follows we shall see how the debit entry for each transaction is recorded to complete double-entry. (The discount received column is not part of double-entry – we will see how it is transferred into the accounts in the next section.)

- The details column includes a note of the cheque number of each cheque drawn, together with standing orders and direct debits – this information will help when the firm's bank statement is received.

- The folio column has been completed to show in which division of the ledger and to which account number(s) the opposite book-keeping entry appears:

  ML = main ledger

  PL = purchases ledger, ie subsidiary (purchases) ledger

- For cash purchases, the amount of cash (or cheques) paid and recorded in the cash book includes VAT; when recording the debit entries we need to distinguish between the purchases amount and VAT – see the section which follows. This is the reason why two main ledger account numbers are shown in the folio column against cash purchases – the first number refers to purchases account, the second to VAT account.

- The money columns of the cash book have been sub-totalled – this helps as we take information forward into other accounts within the double-entry system, and also when we balance the cash book (see Chapter 18).

COMPLETING DOUBLE-ENTRY TRANSACTIONS

The Case Study has shown us how the credit side of the cash book is used to record payments in the form of cash or through the bank account. In this section we look at how to complete double-entry accounts for:

- cash purchases
- payments made to creditors
- contra entries

recording cash purchases

By 'cash purchases' we mean the purchase of goods (with the intention that they should be resold at a profit) from a supplier, with payment made immediately either in cash or by cheque (or other payment method such as BACS, debit card, credit card). The double-entry book-keeping entries are:

- payment made in cash
    - *debit* purchases account
    - *debit* VAT account (with the amount of VAT)
    - *credit* cash column of the cash book
- payment made by cheque (or other banking payment method)
    - *debit* purchases account
    - *debit* VAT account
    - *credit* bank column of the cash book

Note that such 'cash' suppliers do not have credit accounts.

The debit entries from the Case Study for the cash purchases transactions of 7 April and 8 April are recorded in the double-entry accounts as follows:

MAIN LEDGER

Dr		**Purchases Account** (account no 5001)			Cr
2007			£	2007	£
7 Apr	Cash	CBP 24	80		
8 Apr	Bank	CBP 24	240		

Dr		**Value Added Tax Account** (account no 2200)			Cr
2007			£	2007	£
7 Apr	Cash	CBP 24	14		
8 Apr	Bank	CBP 24	42		

recording payments to creditors

When payment is made to creditors for goods that have been bought from them on credit, the method of payment is:

- either by cheque, or other payment method such as BACS, debit card, credit card
- or, less commonly, in cash

The double-entry book-keeping entries are:

- payment made by cheque (or other banking method)
    - *debit* purchases ledger control account (in the main ledger)
    - *credit* bank column of the cash book
    - and a debit to the creditor's account in the subsidiary (purchases) ledger
- payment made in cash
    - *debit* purchases ledger control account (in the main ledger)
    - *credit* cash column of the cash book
    - and a debit to the creditor's account in the subsidiary (purchases) ledger

As well as the debit to purchases ledger control account, remember that a debit must be recorded on the creditors account in the subsidiary (purchases) ledger. No entry is needed in VAT account when payment is made to creditors – the VAT entry will have been made when the credit purchase was recorded in the accounting system (see Chapter 10).

When cash discount for prompt settlement has been received from the creditor, ie settlement discount has reduced the amount of the payment, entries must be made in the double-entry system as follows:

- *debit* purchases ledger control account
- *credit* discount received account (in the main ledger)
- and a debit to the creditor's account in the subsidiary (purchases) ledger

The debit entries from the Case Study for the payments to creditors are as follows, starting with the subsidiary (purchases) ledger. It is suggested that you 'tick back' each transaction.

Note: for illustrative purposes an amount for purchases has been credited to each creditor's account (with the cross-reference to PDB 67).

SUBSIDIARY (PURCHASES) LEDGER

Dr				E Lee & Co (account no 804)			Cr
2007			£	2007			£
5 Apr	Bank	CBP 24	160	22 Mar	Purchases	PDB 67	300

Dr				**Hayes Limited** (account no 752)			Cr
2007			£	2007			£
6 Apr	Bank	CBP 24	200	22 Mar	Purchases	PDB 67	540

Dr				**S Crane** (account no 610)			Cr
2007			£	2007			£
6 Apr	Bank	CBP 24	145	22 Mar	Purchases	PDB 67	150
6 Apr	Discount Received	ML 6502	5				

Dr				**S Ford** (account no 698)			Cr
2007			£	2007			£
9 Apr	Bank	CBP 24	70	22 Mar	Purchases	PDB 67	75
9 Apr	Discount Received	ML 6502	5				

Notes:

• Amounts for purchases have been shown in the above accounts for illustrative purposes – see Chapter 10, which covers accounting for purchases

• In order to complete double-entry book-keeping, discount received amounts, which have been debited to the creditors' accounts, must also be credited to discount received account in the main ledger (the discount column in the cash book is not part of the double-entry system, but is a memorandum column only). The account is completed by entering the total of the discount column from the cash book, as follows:

MAIN LEDGER

Dr	**Discount Received Account** (account no 6502)			Cr
2007	£	2007		£
		9 Apr	Cash Book CBP 24	10

• Purchases ledger control account (see below) is credited with the amount of discount received.

• Once the total of discount received has been taken from the cash book, the discount column 'starts again' (ie the amount of £10, above, for this week will not be included in next week's transfer).

- Purchases ledger control account is written up as follows at 9 April (the end of the week):

MAIN LEDGER

Dr				Purchases Ledger Control Account	(account no 6002)		Cr
2007			£	2007			£
9 Apr	Bank	CBP 24	**575	22 Mar Purchases	PDB67	*1,065	
9 Apr	Discount Received						
		ML6502	10				

*   As the purchases day book is not shown here, the purchases figure is the total of the credits to the subsidiary creditors' accounts, ie £300 + £540 + £150 + £75.

** the total bank receipts of £575 comprises cheques and bank transfers to creditors, ie £160 + £200 + £145 + £70 (the amount does not include payments for cash purchases, here £282). Later in this chapter – page 311– we will see how an analysed cash book can be used to obtain more easily the total of payments to creditors.

treatment of VAT – cash and credit purchases

When carrying out the book-keeping entries for payments for cash purchases and payments to creditors, the treatment of VAT is quite different. It is important to bear these differences in mind. Remember:

The double-entry for a payment made for **cash purchases** is:

- *debit* purchases account
- *debit* VAT account (with the amount of VAT)
- *credit* bank column of the cash book (or cash column if it is used)

The double-entry for a payment made for a **credit purchase** (ie to a creditor) is :

- *debit* purchases ledger control account (in the main ledger)
- *credit* bank column of the cash book

There is no entry for VAT here because the VAT has already been accounted for when the purchase was first made (see Chapter 10). The entries will then have been: *debit* purchases account, *debit* VAT account and *credit* creditor's account

The diagram on the next page illustrates the book-keeping entries for the payments for purchases, as described in this section of the chapter.

book-keeping entries for payments for purchases

PAYMENTS FOR PURCHASES

methods used:

- cash
- debit card
- BACS
- cheque
- credit card
- other bank transfers

CASH PURCHASES
Debit	Credit

CREDIT PURCHASES
Debit	Credit

MAIN LEDGER

accounts debited;

purchases
net amount

VAT
VAT amount

CASH BOOK

credit cash column
total amount

or

credit bank column
total amount

MAIN LEDGER

accounts debited:

purchases ledger control
total of payments for credit purchases

total of settlement (cash) discount received

CASH BOOK

credit cash or bank column

settlement (cash) discount received recorded in memorandum column

SUBSIDIARY LEDGER

accounts debited:

creditors' accounts
payments for credit purchases

and

settlement (cash) discount received

MAIN LEDGER

credit: discount received account

total of memorandum column from cash book (payments)

REMEMBER!

When money is paid to creditors as payment for credit purchases, there is no debit to VAT account, because the VAT was recorded when the credit purchase was made. There is, however, an entry to VAT account for cash purchases made.

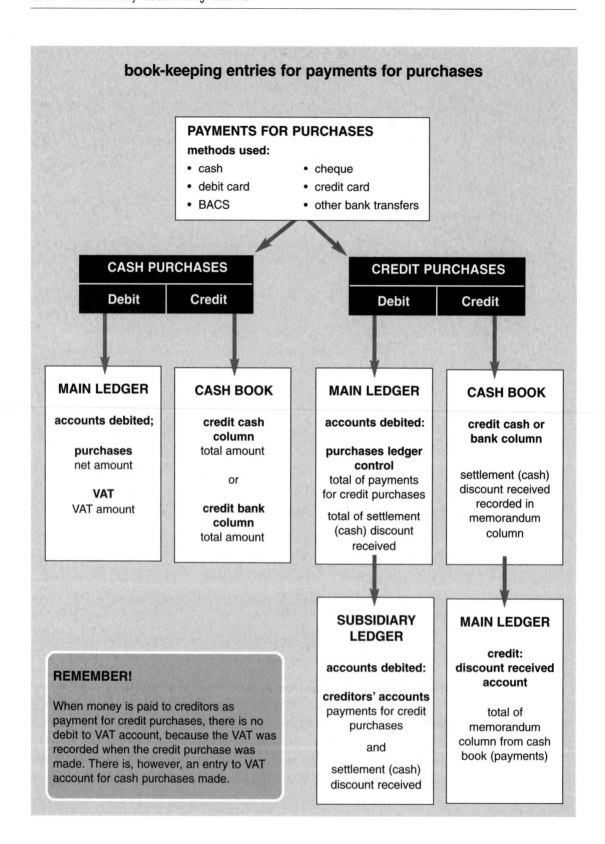

BATCH CONTROL SYSTEMS

Businesses that have a large number of payments to creditors will often use batched data entry in order to enter such transactions into the accounts in one 'run'. As we have seen previously in Chapter 10 (page 210), a batch of transactions for a day, week or month is pre-listed on a batch control form, for example:

Batch Control: cheques paid to creditors

Supplier				Debit	Credit	Credit
Date	Account no	Name	Cheque no	Creditors control	Bank	Discount received
				£	£	£
2007						
5 Apr	PL 804	E Lee & Co	101261	160.00	160.00	–
6 Apr	PL 610	S Crane	101262	150.00	145.00	5.00
9 Apr	PL 698	S Ford	101265	75.00	70.00	5.00
			Check list totals	385.00	375.00	10.00

Prepared by   Neil Ford   Date   9 Apr 2007

Checked by   *Barbara Smith*   Date   *9 Apr 2007*

Posted by   *Dan Ryan*   Date   *9 Apr 2007*

Note that payments to suppliers by bank credit and by standing order have not been shown on the batch control form – only cheques paid are listed. Where a business has large numbers of payments – using methods such as bank credit, standing order, credit and debit cards – it can use batch control systems for each type of payment.

Totals are taken from the batch control form and transferred to purchases ledger control account – it is probably better practice to debit the two separate amounts, ie £375.00 and £10.00, rather than the total debit of £385.00. Payments made other than by cheque – such as bank transfers, standing orders and debit/credit card payments will also be debited to purchases ledger control account.

THE CASH BOOK IN THE ACCOUNTING SYSTEM

The cash book performs two functions within the accounting system:

- it is the book of prime entry for cash/bank transactions

- it forms part of the double-entry system (note that the cash book can, alternatively, be represented in the main ledger by a cash control account – see page 387)

For the payments side of the cash book these functions are illustrated below:

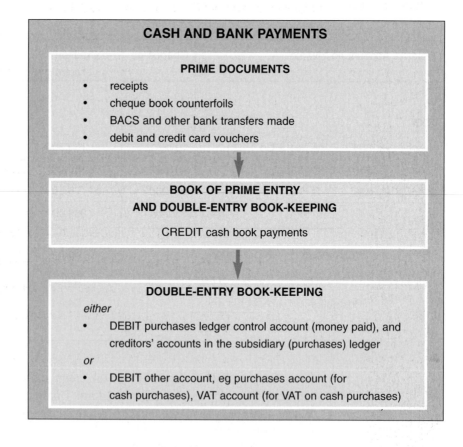

CASH AND BANK PAYMENTS

PRIME DOCUMENTS
- receipts
- cheque book counterfoils
- BACS and other bank transfers made
- debit and credit card vouchers

BOOK OF PRIME ENTRY
AND DOUBLE-ENTRY BOOK-KEEPING

CREDIT cash book payments

DOUBLE-ENTRY BOOK-KEEPING

either
- DEBIT purchases ledger control account (money paid), and creditors' accounts in the subsidiary (purchases) ledger

or
- DEBIT other account, eg purchases account (for cash purchases), VAT account (for VAT on cash purchases)

CASH BOOK – ALTERNATIVE LAYOUTS

A cash book can be adapted to suit the needs of a business – earlier in this chapter we have seen how a three-column cash book incorporates a memorandum column for settlement discount. Two further layouts often used are:

- a cash book which incorporates a money column for VAT

- an analysed cash book which divides both receipts (see Chapter 7) and payments between a number of categories; for example payments could be divided between:
    - the main sections of a business, eg, for an audio/video shop, (1) compact discs, (2) video tapes, and (3) DVDs
    - (1) discount received, (2) Value Added Tax, (3) cash purchases (4) purchases ledger, ie payments to creditors, (5) sundry payments

Examples of these further cash book layouts are shown in the two Case Studies which follow: the first is for a cash book which incorporates a VAT column, the second is for an analysed cash book.

Case Study

CASH BOOK INCORPORATING VAT

situation

The following payments transactions are to be recorded in the cash book of Eveshore Growers for the week commencing 7 June 2007. Assume the VAT rate is 17.5%. The cash book has columns for discount received, VAT and bank.

7 Jun	Paid £235 by cheque to a creditor, Brooklyn Traders
7 Jun	Paid insurance premium of £130 by cheque (no Value Added Tax)
8 Jun	Paid for office stationery by cheque £47, including Value Added Tax
8 Jun	Paid an invoice for £100 from A–Z Supplies, a creditor, by cheque after deducting £5 cash discount
9 Jun	Cash purchase of £188, including Value Added Tax, paid for by cheque
9 Jun	Paid wages of £305, by cheque.

As cashier to Eveshore Growers, you are to:

- write up page 54 of the payments side of the book for the week commencing 7 June 2007, using separate columns for discount, VAT and bank (note that no cash column is required in this cash book)

- sub-total the cash book at 11 June 2007

- explain how the totals for the discount and VAT columns will be entered in the main ledger of Eveshore Growers

solution

Credit	Cash Book: Payments				CBP 54
Date	Details	Folio	Discount received	VAT	Bank
2007			£	£	£
7 Jun	Brooklyn Traders	PL			235
7 Jun	Insurance	ML			130
8 Jun	Office stationery	ML		7	47
8 Jun	A-Z Supplies	PL	5		95
9 Jun	Purchases	ML		28	188
9 Jun	Wages	ML			305
			5	35	1,000

notes:

- The folio columns have been completed as follows (account numbers not shown):

  ML = main ledger

  PL = purchases ledger, ie subsidiary (purchases) ledger

- For transactions involving purchases ledger (eg Brooklyn Traders), no amount for VAT is shown in the VAT columns. This is because VAT has been charged on invoices received and was recorded in the VAT account (through the purchases day book) when the purchase was made.

- VAT on cash purchases, and other transactions, is recorded in the VAT analysis column.

- Payments to creditors (eg Brooklyn Traders) are debited to purchases ledger control account in the main ledger, and to the creditors' accounts in the subsidiary (purchases) ledger.

The discount and VAT columns:

- discount received column – the total of £5 will be credited to discount received account in the main ledger, debited to purchases ledger control account in the main ledger and to the account of A-Z Supplies in the subsidiary (purchases) ledger

- VAT column – the total of £35 will be debited to VAT account in the main ledger (alternatively the individual amounts of £7 and £28 could be debited)

Note that, in the cash book, the discount received and VAT columns 'start again' from zero after the totals have been transferred to the main ledger accounts.

Case Study	# ANALYSED CASH BOOK

situation

Wyvern Auto Spares Limited buys car parts from manufacturers. The company is registered for VAT. The business uses a cash book which analyses payments as follows:

> **PAYMENTS**
> * discount received
> * VAT
> * cash purchases
> * purchases ledger, ie subsidiary (purchases) ledger
> * sundry payments

The following payments transactions are to be entered on page 31 of the payments side of the cash book for the first week of December 2007:

6 Dec	Purchases for cash, £120 + VAT
6 Dec	Paid £235 by cheque to a creditor, Wyvern Electronics
7 Dec	Paid rent on premises, £325 (no VAT) by cheque
7 Dec	Paid an invoice for £250 from Boxhall Supplies Limited (a creditor) by cheque for £240, £10 discount being received for prompt settlement
8 Dec	Paid for office stationery in cash, £40 + VAT
9 Dec	Paid for urgently needed spares in cash, £80 + VAT
9 Dec	Paid an invoice for £155 from Vord Supplies (a creditor) by cheque for £150, £5 discount being received for prompt settlement
10 Dec	Paid wages £385 in cash

The rate of Value Added Tax is 17.5%

solution

Credit				Cash Book: Payments					CBP 31	
Date	Details	Folio	Cash	Bank	Discount received	VAT	Cash purchases	Purchases ledger	Sundry
2007			£	£	£	£	£	£	£
6 Dec	Purchases	ML	141			21	120		
6 Dec	Wyvern Electronics	PL		235				235	
7 Dec	Rent paid	ML		325					325
7 Dec	Boxhall Supplies Limited	PL		240	10			240	
8 Dec	Office stationery	ML	47			7			40
9 Dec	Purchases	ML	94			14	80		
9 Dec	Vord Supplies	PL		150	5			150	
10 Dec	Wages	ML	385						385
			667	950	15	42	200	625	750

notes

- The payments side of the cash book analyses each payment between a number of headings. A business will adapt the cash book and use whatever analysis columns suit it best for its payments.

- References to the ledger sections have been shown in the folio column.

- For transactions involving purchases ledger, no amount for VAT is shown in the VAT columns. This is because VAT has been charged on invoices received and was recorded in the VAT account (through the purchases day book) when the purchase was made.

- The columns are sub-totalled at the end of the week and the totals of the analysis columns are transferred to other accounts as follows:

  – discount received column total of £15 is credited to discount received account in the main ledger and debited to purchases ledger control account in the main ledger

  – Value Added Tax column, the total of £42 is debited to VAT account in the main ledger

  – cash purchases column total of £200 is debited to purchases account in the main ledger

  – purchases ledger column, the total of £625 is debited to purchases ledger control account in the main ledger

- Individual amounts of payments to creditors and discount received are debited to creditors' accounts in the subsidiary (purchases) ledger.

- Sundry payments are dealt with individually by debiting the appropriate account (eg rent paid, office stationery, wages): see section below.

OTHER PAYMENTS

In addition to payments to creditors and for cash purchases, the credit side of the cash book is used to record other payments of the business. These include:

- drawings withdrawn from the business by the owner
- loan repayments made by the business to the loan provider
- expenses of running the business, such as wages, telephone
- purchase of fixed assets (items bought for use in the business on a semi-permanent basis, eg buildings, vehicles, office equipment)

Each of these will be considered in further detail in Chapter 17 where we will see where they fit into the double-entry system. For the moment we will see how they are recorded in the double-entry system of cash book and ledger accounts:

- **owner's drawings**

  – *debit* drawings account

  – *credit* cash book

  The owner of the business withdraws money from the business in the form of cash or a cheque.

- **loan repayments**

  – *debit* loan account

  – *credit* cash book

  The amount of the loan repayment is recorded in cash book.

- **business expenses**

  – *debit* expenses account (using the appropriate account, eg wages account, telephone expenses account)

  – *credit* cash book

  Business expenses are paid either in the form of cash or through the bank. Also note that low-value business expenses are often paid in cash through the petty cash book – see next chapter.

- **purchase of fixed assets**

  – *debit* fixed asset account (using the appropriate account, eg buildings account, vehicles account, office equipment account)

  – *credit* cash book

  The amount of the cost of fixed assets purchased is paid from cash book.

---

example transactions:

2007

16 Jun   The owner of the business draws £100 from the bank for own use

17 Jun   Made a loan repayment of £750 by direct debit to MBC Bank (no VAT)

18 Jun   Paid telephone bill of £282 (including VAT) by cheque

21 Jun   Bought new computer for use in the office, £1,175 (including VAT) paid by cheque

---

The cash book (payments) records these transactions as follows:

Credit	Cash Book: Payments					CBP 10
Date	Details		Folio	Discount received	Cash	Bank
2007				£	£	£
16 Jun	Drawings		ML			100
17 Jun	Loan: MBC Bank		ML			750
18 Jun	Telephone expenses		ML			282
21 Jun	Computer		ML			1,175

Note: alternative layouts of the cash book (payments) could be used; in particular, a layout incorporating the VAT column is especially useful on the payments side.

The debit entries are shown in the main ledger (which contains all of these accounts) as follows:

MAIN LEDGER

Dr				Drawings Account		Cr
2007			£	2007		£
16 Jun	Bank	CBP 10	100			

Dr				Loan Account : MBC Bank		Cr
2007			£	2007		£
17 Jun	Bank	CBP 10	750			

Dr				Telephone Expenses Account		Cr
2007			£	2007		£
18 Jun	Bank	CBP 10	240			

Dr				Value Added Tax Account		Cr
2007			£	2007		£
1 Jun	Bank	CBP 10	42			
21 Jun	Bank	CBP 10	175			

Dr				Computer Account		Cr
2007			£	2007		£
21 Jun	Bank	CBP 10	1,000			

PETTY CASH BOOK

Petty cash book is another type of cash book; it is used for low-value expenses payments made in cash. A particular benefit of the use of a petty cash book is that it takes a lot of small transactions away from the main cashier and reduces the number of transactions passing through the cash book.

We shall look in detail at petty cash book in Chapter 16.

EXPENSES CLAIMS

A further duty of the cashier (or the petty cashier – see Chapter 16) is the checking of *expenses claims*.

Often an employee is required to pay for expenses incurred on behalf of the business or organisation, and then to claim back the amount already paid from the business. Typically, expenses which can be reclaimed include:

- Travel, eg rail, bus, air and taxi fares, mileage allowance where a private car, motorbike or cycle has been used. (Note that the costs of travel to and from work are not paid, except under special circumstances, eg the burglar alarm goes off in the middle of the night and the police request the presence of the keyholder).

- Hotel bills, including meals.

- Subsistence allowance – to cover the costs of working away from the normal place of employment, often paid at a daily rate.

- Other expenses, eg part of the employee's domestic telephone bill.

A business will establish the terms under which it will reimburse an employee. For example, travel claims might have to be at the cheapest form of travel, such as a bus, even if the employee uses his/her private car; first-class travel is likely to be available only to senior employees. Before refunding expenses, the business will usually require proof of the expense, eg a receipt, or the travel ticket.

claims procedure

At regular intervals – perhaps monthly – an employee will be required to submit an expenses claim (see next page). The procedure is likely to be:

- Employee completes and signs expenses claim form.

- Receipts for the expenses are attached to the expenses claim form.

- The form is passed to the employee's manager or section head for authorisation.

- The form is then sent to the accounts department where the amounts will be checked against the company's policies. The calculations on the form will also be checked. The various expenses will then be coded for the appropriate main ledger account, eg travel expenses, telephone expenses, etc. The book-keeping will be:

  – *debit* appropriate expense account (in the main ledger)

  – *credit* cash book payments (cash or bank column, as appropriate)

- The amount will either be paid direct to the employee in cash, by cheque or BACS (small amounts can be paid out of petty cash – see Chapter 16), or the employee's pay will be credited and the amount paid at the next payroll run.

- The firm's main ledger expenses accounts will be debited with the cost. Where an expense includes VAT, a VAT-registered business will debit the appropriate expense account with the net amount of the expense, and debit the VAT to VAT account; in this way, the business claims back the VAT paid on the expense.

income tax and expenses

Most expenses are wholly incurred on behalf of the business or organisation. As such, their reimbursement does not form a part of the employee's salary, and is not subject to income tax. However, some expenses incurred are only partly used on behalf of the business, the other part is a benefit to the employee. Examples include the provision of a company car, or payment of the employee's telephone bill.

HM Revenue & Customs lays down guidelines which, depending on the circumstances, state the employee's liability for income tax, together with the employee's and employer's liability for National Insurance Contributions.

WYVERN TRADERS LIMITED
EXPENSES CLAIM FOR THE MONTH ENDING ....

Name:

Department:

Date	Item	Travelling £	Subsistence £	Entertaining £	Miscellaneous £	Total £	VAT £	Net £
	Total							

OFFICE USE ONLY

Signed:

Date:

Authorised by:

Date:

expenses claim form

Chapter Summary

- The cash book records payments (double-entry credits) made through the bank.

- The basic layout for a cash book (payments) includes a money column for bank transactions, together with a column for discount received. Cash books for businesses which deal with substantial amounts of cash may have a further money column to record cash transactions.

- Another common cash book layout incorporates a VAT column.

- An analysed cash book is used to provide more information: it divides payments between a number of categories.

- The cashier may be responsible for checking expenses claims.

Key Terms

cash book	records both cash and bank transactions; combines the roles of book of prime entry and double-entry book-keeping
columnar cash book	commonly-used layout for cash books which incorporates several money columns, eg for settlement discount, VAT, cash, bank
analysed cash book	cash book which divides payments (and receipts) between a number of categories, eg the main sections of the business
expenses claims	forms used by employees to claim back expenses paid by the employee but incurred on behalf of the business or organisation

Student Activities

14.1 The cash book records:

    (a)   receipts and payments in cash only

    (b)   receipts and payments through the bank only

    (c)   all receipts and payments both in cash and through the bank

    (d)   receipts and payments both in cash (except for low-value expense payments) and through the bank

    Answer (a) or (b) or (c) or (d)

14.2 The following are the payments transactions of Trevellas Traders for February 2007:

   3 Feb   Paid G Wheaton, a creditor, £195 by cheque no 101359

   5 Feb   Paid A Aznar, a creditor, cheque no 101360 for £390 in full settlement of a debt of £400

   10 Feb   Paid wages in cash, £370

   12 Feb   Paid Singh Limited, a creditor, cheque no 101361 for £570 in full settlement of a debt of £585

   17 Feb   Paid telephone account £155 in cash

   19 Feb   Paid Farr and Company, a creditor, cheque no 101362 for £220 in full settlement of a debt of £230

   27 Feb   Paid rent £160 by standing order

You are to:

*   Enter the above payments on page 22 of the three column cash book (which has columns for discount received, cash, and bank) of Trevellas Traders.

*   Sub-total the money columns at 28 February.

Note: entries in the subsidiary (purchases) ledger and main ledger are *not* required.

14.3 The following are the payments transactions of Metro Trading Company for August 2007:

   2 Aug   Cash purchases paid for in cash, £80 + VAT

   5 Aug   Paid T Hall Limited a cheque for £541 in full settlement of a debt of £565

   9 Aug   Paid wages in cash, £254 (no VAT)

   17 Aug   Paid F Jarvis £457 by cheque

   18 Aug   The owner of the business withdraws £200 in cash for own use

   19 Aug   Paid rent by cheque, £275 (no VAT)

   20 Aug   Paid wages in cash, £436 (no VAT)

   24 Aug   Paid J Jones a cheque for £628 in full settlement of a debt of £661

   27 Aug   Cash purchases paid for by cheque, £200 + VAT

   27 Aug   Paid salaries by cheque, £2,043 (no VAT)

   30 Aug   Paid telephone account by cheque, £282 (including VAT)

   30 Aug   Bought office equipment, paying by cheque, £600 + VAT

The rate of Value Added Tax is 17.5%.

Account numbers are to be used – see the next page.

You are to:

*   Enter the above payments on page 45 of the three column cash book of Metro Trading Company. The cash book has columns for discount received, cash and bank.

*   Sub-total the money columns at 31 August.

- Show the entries to be made in the following accounts:

  subsidiary (purchases) ledger

  T Hall Limited (account no 451)

  F Jarvis (account no 510)

  J Jones (account no 643)

  main ledger

  purchases ledger control account (account no 6002)

  discount received account (account no 6502)

  drawings account (account no 7005)

  office equipment account (account no 750)

  purchases account (account no 5001)

  rent paid account (account no 6950)

  telephone expenses account (account no 6212)

  VAT account (account no 2200)

  wages and salaries account (account no 7750)

14.4   The following are the payments transactions of Johnson Brothers for April 2007:

2 Apr	Cash purchases of £47 (including VAT) paid by cheque
2 Apr	Paid travelling expenses of £65 (no VAT) by cheque
5 Apr	Paid the telephone bill of £235 (including VAT) by cheque
6 Apr	Loan repayment of £500 made to ABC Bank by direct debit (no VAT)
9 Apr	The owners of the business withdrew £600 by cheque for own use
13 Apr	Paid an invoice for £190 from M Hughes (a creditor) by cheque for £180, £10 being received for prompt settlement
15 Apr	Bought office stationery £80 + VAT, paying by cheque
16 Apr	Cash purchases of £94 (including VAT) paid by cheque
19 Apr	Bought office equipment, paying by cheque, £400 + VAT
26 Apr	Paid a cheque for £245 to Wilson Limited, a creditor, in full settlement of an invoice for £255
27 Apr	Cash purchases of £120 + VAT, paid by cheque
29 Apr	Paid wages, £350 (no VAT) by cheque
30 Apr	Paid a cheque for £560 to Lucinda Luz, a creditor, in full settlement of an invoice for £580

The rate of Value Added Tax is 17.5%

Account numbers are to be used – see below.

You are to:

- Enter the above payments on page 88 of the cash book of Johnson Brothers, using columns for date, details, discount received, VAT and bank.

- Sub-total the money columns at 30 April.

- Show the entries to be made in the following accounts:

  subsidiary (purchases) ledger

  M Hughes (account no 498)

  Wilson Limited (account no 752)

  Lucinda Luz (account no 601)

  main ledger

  purchases ledger control account (account no 6002)

  discount received account (account no 6502)

  drawings account (account no 7005)

  loan account: ABC Bank (account no 2250)

  office equipment account (account no 750)

  office stationery account (account no 6384)

  purchases account (account no 5001)

  telephone expenses account (account no 6212)

  travelling expenses account (account no 6330)

  VAT account (account no 2200)

  wages and salaries account (account no 7750)

14.5 David Lewis runs a shop selling carpets. He buys his carpets direct from the manufacturers, who allow him credit terms. His business is registered for VAT.

He uses an analysed cash book which has columns for:
- bank
- discount received
- VAT
- purchases
- purchases ledger
- sundry

The following transactions take place during the week commencing 17 May 2007:

17 May   Cash purchases of £75.70 + VAT paid by cheque

17 May   Paid telephone bill of £238.90 (including VAT) by cheque

18 May   Loan repayment of £250.00 made to Wyvern Finance by direct debit (no VAT)

18 May   Paid shop rent by cheque, £255.50 (no VAT)

19 May   Cash purchases of £100.00 (including VAT) paid by cheque

19 May   Paid an invoice for £368.20 from Terry Carpets Limited (a creditor) by cheque for £363.55 and receiving £4.65 discount for prompt settlement

19 May   Paid for stationery by cheque, £28.20 (including VAT)

20 May   David Lewis draws £100.00 from the bank, by cheque, for his own use

20 May   Bought shop fittings £265.00 + VAT, paying by cheque

21 May   Paid an invoice for £295.80 from Longlife Carpets Limited (a creditor), paying £291.50 by cheque, £4.30 discount being received for prompt settlement

21 May   Paid wages, £314.20 by cheque (no VAT)

21 May   Paid a cheque to Trade Supplies (a creditor) for £145.50 in full settlement of an invoice for £149.00

The rate of Value Added Tax is 17.5%

Account numbers are to be used – see below.

You are to:

- Enter the above payments on page 96 of the analysed cash book of David Lewis (VAT amounts should be rounded down to the nearest penny).

- Sub-total the money columns at 21 May.

- Show the entries to be made in the following accounts:

  subsidiary (purchases) ledger

  Terry Carpets Limited (account no 721)

  Longlife Carpets Limited (account no 624)

  Trade Supplies (account no 784)

  main ledger

  purchases ledger control account (account no 6002)

  discount received account (account no 6502)

  drawings account (account no 7005)

  loan account: Wyvern Finance (account no 2270)

  purchases account (account no 5001)

  shop fittings account (account no 740)

  shop rent account (account no 6345)

  stationery account (account no 6382)

  telephone expenses account (account no 6212)

  VAT account (account no 2200)

  wages and salaries account (account no 7750)

14.6 Prepare a purchases ledger control account for the month of April 2007 from the following information:

2007		£
1 Apr	Purchases ledger balances	14,275
30 Apr	Credit purchases for month	36,592
	Purchases returns	653
	Payments made to creditors	31,074
	Settlement discount received	1,048
	Transfer of credit balances to sales ledger	597

The creditors figure at 30 April is to be entered as the balancing figure.

15 Communicating with suppliers

This chapter explains how a business communicates in writing with its suppliers to resolve discrepancies in invoices received from them. It covers the different forms of written communication – notes, letters, emails.

The format of the various forms of communication have already been covered in Chapter 8, 'Customer communications and legal issues'. If you have not read this earlier chapter you are advised to do so before starting this one.

PERFORMANCE CRITERIA COVERED

unit 30: INTRODUCTORY ACCOUNTING

element 30.2

process purchases and payments

J   write to suppliers to resolve discrepancies in invoices

COMMUNICATING WITH SUPPLIERS

We have already seen in Chapter 8 that your course requires that you communicate politely and effectively with people to whom you sell goods or services.

Although in many organisations, 'customer care' is generally given more emphasis than dealing with suppliers, you should bear in mind that the principle of dealing politely and efficiently applies equally to customers and to suppliers.

raising queries with suppliers

Suppliers sell goods and services to the organisation or business for which you work. They may supply on credit or on a cash basis. They may supply materials and stock or they may provide services such as computer maintenance or 24 hour courier delivery. Most communications with suppliers involve queries such as:

- when are the goods arriving?
- when will the service be provided?
- problems with the delivery of incorrect goods
- the wrong amount charged
- an incorrect discount on an invoice
- a credit note which has not been sent

When situations such as this arise, there are various channels of communication that can be used:

oral communications

These are communications by word of mouth. In other words, if you have a simple query, the most efficient way of contacting the supplier may be by telephone or by speaking to the supplier face-to-face. The message can be delivered quickly and an appropriate response received.

If you are unfortunate enough to deal with a supplier that has a telephone system which plays you classical music for fifteen minutes and then connects you to a voicemail, you may have to leave a message.

Please note: you will not be assessed on oral communications in your exam.

written communications

Written communications have been dealt with in detail in Chapter 8. The main methods used when dealing with suppliers are:

- **letter** – used for formal communications, eg complaints, asking for an increase in a credit limit, asking for an increase in trade discount
- **fax** – used for more informal requests, eg sending a purchase order, asking for a copy of an invoice or statement, sending a copy of a incorrect document from the supplier
- **email** – used increasingly for sending orders, raising queries about delivery dates, notifying the supplier about shortages in delivery (not enough goods sent), damaged stock, requesting permission to return goods

Case Study

VALLEYMORE FOODS LIMITED

situation

Valleymore Foods Limited produces a variety of foodstuffs – pies, desserts, and ready-made meals. You work in the Accounts Department of the company and spend some of your time dealing with supplier queries relating to prices, financial documents and purchase ledger accounts. Your name is Patsy Cornish.

This Case Study shows some of the queries and tasks you had to deal with in one working day and provides examples of how you dealt with them.

queries and tasks

1   Your supervisor, Sue Flay, asks you to fax Tasty Fillings Limited who have overcharged you on their invoice 29841 dated 1 July 2007. They have charged £1.10 per kilo for mixed fruit filling rather than £1.05, the price on the last consignment.

2   Later in the day you receive a telephone call from the Tasty Fillings Sales Department stating that £1.10 is the latest price quoted on their website, and so the invoice is correct. You are to write a note to your supervisor, passing on this message.

3   You are checking invoice 8745 received from Tropical Fruits for 50 kilos of passion fruit purée. The price on the invoice is 80p per kilo, but they have entered £80 in the total column and added on VAT of £14. You refer the mistake to your supervisor, Sue Flay, who suggests you send them an email asking for a new invoice.

4   You sent a purchase order to Wessex Meats for 100 kilos of lambs kidneys ten days ago, but have not received the goods. You telephone their Sales Office but they say the purchase order has not arrived; they ask you to fax a copy.

5   Sue Flay has been looking through the supplier discounts your company is given. She asks you to draft the text of a letter asking Tasty Fillings Limited for an increase in trade discount from 15% to 25% in view of the increased business you have given them over the last twelve months.

1 faxed query

To Sales Ledger, Tasty Fillings LImited   Subject: Invoice 29841

Hello

Please note that on your invoice 29841, the mixed fruit filling is charged at £1.10 per kilo rather than at £1.05, which is what we were charged last time. Please can you look into this for me and get back to me. Thank you.

Regards

Patsy Cornish, Purchases Ledger, Valleymore Foods Limited.

2 the internal note

To Sue Flay

4 July 2007   14.10

Re Tasty Fillings Invoice 29841
Tasty Fillings say that the price of the mixed fruit filling has gone up to £1.10 since we last ordered. Their website is showing £1.10 a kilo and so I guess we will have to accept the invoice.

Patsy Cornish

3 email request

To: accounts@tropicalfruits.com
From: accounts@valleymorefoods.com
Time: 4 July 2007 14.55.23
Subject: your invoice 8745

We note that we have been charged £80 instead of £40 (excluding VAT) for 50 kilos of passion fruit purée on invoice 8745. Please can you issue a new invoice for this consignment. Many thanks.

Regards
Patsy Cornish
Accounts (Purchase Ledger), Valleymore Foods Limited

4 faxed order

facsimile transmission header

To: Josie, Sales Office, Wessex Meats
Fax number: 01475 333692
Number of pages including this header: 2   Date: 4 July 2007

message

Purchase Order 12124

Further to our telephone conversation today we are faxing our Purchase Order for lambs kidneys. As the original order appears to have been lost in the post we shall be grateful if you will kindly treat this order as very urgent. Many thanks.

Patsy Cornish, Accounts (Purchase Ledger)

5 a formal letter

Valleymore Foods Limited
Martley Road, St Gregorys, MR2 5GT
Tel 01908 675234 Fax 01908 675332 email foods@valleymore.com

Accounts Manager, Sales Ledger
Tasty Fillings Limited
Unit 12 Moor Park
Newcastle
NE4 7YT

3 July 2007

Dear Sir

Trade Discount

We have been reviewing our records and note that the total of our purchases made from your company increased by 50% during the last twelve months to a total of £56,750.
You currently give us 15% trade discount. We shall be grateful if you would kindly consider increasing this rate to 25% in view of the increased business we have given you.

I look forward to hearing from you.

Yours faithfully

Lionel Edger, Accounts Manager

Chapter Summary

- Businesses need to communicate regularly with their suppliers, who provide goods and services on credit and on a cash basis.
- Communications can be oral – face-to-face meetings and telephone conversations.
- Communications can be also be written – emails, faxes, letters.
- The choice of communication method will depend on the context and the urgency of the message. Typical communications are enquiries, complaints and requests.

Note: there are no Key Terms in this chapter. All the relevant terms are defined in Chapter 8, page 176.

Student Activities

In these three activities you work as an Accounts Assistant for Omnisupplies Limited, an office furniture wholesaler. Use your own name and the current date and make up any other details, such as addresses, which may be needed in each activity.

15.1 Omnisupplies Limited, an office furniture wholesaler, has received delivery of an order placed with Parker Hill Limited for five luxury office chairs in burgundy cloth, catalogue code 2982B. When you receive the invoice (No 24622) you notice that the order code is 2982GL. This code is for the same type of chair, but in green leather. The leather chairs cost £75 more than the cloth-covered chairs and this extra cost has substantially increased the amount of the invoice.

You are to email the Accounts Department of Parker Hill, the supplier. Write down the text of the message that you would leave.

15.2 You receive an invoice (No 3241) from one of your suppliers, Clifton Trading Company, clifton@cliftontrading.co.uk. You are normally given a 2.5% settlement (cash) discount and a 20% trade discount, but these are not included on this invoice.

Write the text of an email pointing this out, as you want to settle the invoice as soon as possible to take advantage of the discount. The goods total before any discounts is £500, plus VAT.

15.3 You receive a statement of account from one of your suppliers, Mordern Stationery, which still operates a manual accounting system and has been known to make mistakes in the past. The statement does not show a credit note for £345.00, reference 2346, received from the company in the last month. Your supervisor suggests faxing the document to Mordern Stationery.

Write a suitable fax message to Mordern Stationery explaining why you are faxing the credit note.

16 Petty cash book

this chapter covers . . .

A petty cash book is used to record low-value cash payments for various small purchases and expenses incurred by a business or other organisation.

An amount of cash is handed by the cashier to a member of staff, the petty cashier, who:

- *is responsible for security of the petty cash money*
- *makes cash payments against authorised petty cash vouchers*
- *records the payments made, and analyses them, in a petty cash book*

Towards the end of the chapter we will see how a petty cash book is balanced, and the way in which it fits into the double-entry book-keeping system.

PERFORMANCE CRITERIA COVERED

unit 30: INTRODUCTORY ACCOUNTING

element 30.3

process petty cash, reconcile accounts and prepare an initial trial balance

A   *operate a petty cash system, including imprest system*

B   *reconcile petty cash control account with cash in hand and petty cash book*

THE PETTY CASH PROCEDURE

The petty cash book is used to record low-value cash payments for purchases and expenses – such as small items of stationery, postages – items which it would not be appropriate to enter in the cash book. Instead, an amount of cash is handed by the cashier to a member of staff, the petty cashier, who is responsible for all aspects of the control of petty cash, principally:

- security of the petty cash money
- making cash payments against authorised petty cash vouchers
- recording the payments made, and analysing them, in a petty cash book

In order to operate the petty cash system, the petty cashier needs the following:

- a *petty cash book* in which to record and analyse transactions
- a *lockable cash box* in which to keep the money
- a stock of blank *petty cash vouchers* (see page 313) for claims on petty cash to be made
- a *lockable desk drawer* in which to keep these items

making a claim

As an employee you are most likely to encounter the petty cash system when making claims for money for small purchases you have made. Before studying the form-filling procedures in detail, read the summary of a typical petty cash transaction set out below:

your supervisor asks you to go and buy a box of computer disks from an office supplies shop

you go to the shop and buy the computer disks; having paid for them, you retain the receipt (for £5.50) which you hand to the petty cashier on your return to the office

the petty cashier authorises a petty cash voucher which contains details of the purchase

the petty cashier gives you £5.50 in cash

the petty cashier attaches the receipt to the petty cash voucher and enters the details in the petty cash book

WHAT ITEMS CAN BE PASSED THROUGH PETTY CASH BOOK?

Petty cash is used to make small cash payments for purchases and expenses incurred by the business. Examples of the type of payments made from petty cash include:

- stationery items
- small items of office supplies
- casual wages
- window cleaning
- bus, rail and taxi fares (incurred on behalf of the business)
- meals and drinks (incurred on behalf of the business)
- postages
- tips and donations

Petty cash should not be used to pay for private expenses of employees, eg tea, coffee, and milk, unless the business has agreed these in advance.

All payments made through petty cash must be supported by relevant documentation. Such documentation includes:

- receipt from a shop
- post office receipt for postage
- rail or bus ticket
- restaurant bill
- receipt from taxi company
- receipt from window cleaning firm

The petty cashier is usually able to authorise petty cash transactions up to a maximum value – for example, up to £25 for any one expense item is a common figure. Larger amounts can often be paid from petty cash provided the expense is authorised by the accounts supervisor.

Case Study

TYAX ENGINEERING LTD: PETTY CASH EXPENSES

situation

You work in the accounts office of Tyax Engineering Limited. One of your duties is that of petty cashier; you are able to authorise transactions up to £25. Which of the following expenses would you allow to be paid out of petty cash?

- envelopes for use in the office, £2.50
- postage on an urgent parcel of engineering parts, £3.75
- bus fare to work claimed by secretary, £1.20
- car mileage to work of office manager called in late at night when the burglar alarm went off (false alarm!), £5.50

- tea and coffee for use in the office, £3.70
- office window cleaning, £2.80
- plant bought for reception area, £5.50
- computer disks, £35.00
- donation to local charity by the business, £5.00
- meal allowance paid to a member of staff required to work during the lunch hour, £3.50

Note: you may assume that all expenses are supported by relevant documentation, such as receipt from a shop, post office etc.

solution

For most expenses it is clear whether or not they can be drawn from petty cash. However, there are points to consider for some of the expenses.

Envelopes	pay from petty cash
Postage	pay from petty cash
Bus fare to work	this is a personal expense and cannot be drawn from petty cash
Car mileage	travel to work is a personal expense, as seen with the previous item; however, as this expense was a special journey in the middle of the night in order to resolve a business problem, it can be paid from petty cash
Tea and coffee	this is a personal expense of employees and cannot normally be paid out of petty cash; however, if the ingredients were used to make drinks for official visitors and customers, it can be paid from petty cash
Window cleaning	pay from petty cash
Plant	pay from petty cash (but plants for the general office cannot be bought with the company's money)
Computer disks	this is a business expense but, in view of the amount (above the authorised limit of the petty cashier) it should be referred to the supervisor or manager for authorisation
Donation	pay from petty cash, subject to authorisation by supervisor
Meal allowance	pay from petty cash, provided that it is company policy to make an allowance in these circumstances

Notes to the Case Study

- If the petty cashier is unable to resolve whether or not an expense can be paid from petty cash, the item should be referred to the accounts supervisor for a decision.
- Before payments can be made for petty cash expenses, they must be:
    - within the authorisation limit of the petty cashier (for example, £25 maximum for any one expense item)

–   supported by documentary evidence, such as a receipt or a rail/bus ticket

–   authorised by the petty cashier, or referred to the appropriate supervisor or manager

• Some businesses allow amounts above the authorisation limit of the petty cashier to be paid from petty cash provided that the expense is authorised by the accounts supervisor.

THE IMPREST METHOD

Most petty cash books operate using the imprest method. With this method the petty cashier starts each week (or month) with a certain amount of money – the imprest amount. As payments are made during the week (or month) the amount of money will reduce and, at the end of the period, the cash will be made up by the main cashier to the imprest amount. For example:

Started week with imprest amount	£100.00
Total of petty cash amounts paid out during week	£80.50
Cash held at end of week	£19.50
Amount drawn from cashier to restore imprest amount	£80.50
Cash at start of next week, ie imprest amount	£100.00

If, at any time, the imprest amount proves to be insufficient, further amounts of cash can be drawn from the cashier. Also, from time-to-time, it may be necessary to increase the imprest amount so that regular shortfalls of petty cash are avoided.

THE NON-IMPREST METHOD

Where a petty cash book is *not* kept on the imprest method, the petty cashier has a float of cash which is replenished by the cashier whenever it runs low. Thus, unlike the imprest method where the cash float is replenished at regular intervals eg weekly or monthly, the float of the non-imprest method is 'topped up' only as and when required.

PETTY CASH VOUCHER

Payments out of petty cash are made only against correct documentation – usually a petty cash voucher (see next page). Petty cash vouchers are completed as follows:

• details and amount of expenditure

- signature of the person making the claim and receiving the money
- signature of the person authorising the payment to be made – usually the petty cashier for amounts within the authorisation limit; larger amounts will be authorised by the accounts supervisor or manager
- additionally, most petty cash vouchers are numbered, so that they can be controlled, the number being entered in the petty cash book
- relevant documentation, such as a receipt from a shop or post office etc, should be attached to the petty cash voucher

petty cash voucher		Number *807*
		date *8 October 2007*

description			amount	
			£	p
C5 Envelopes			*2*	*35*
Photocopier paper			*4*	*70*
			7	*05*

signature *T Harris*

authorised *R Singh*

Petty cash vouchers are the *source documents* for the petty cash book.

LAYOUT OF A PETTY CASH BOOK

Petty cash book is usually set out as follows:

Receipts	Date	Details	Voucher No	Total Payment	Analysis columns				
					VAT	Postages	Stationery	Travel	Ledger
£				£	£	£	£	£	£

The layout shows that:

- receipts from the main cashier are entered in the column on the extreme left
- there are columns for the date and details of all receipts and payments

- there is a column for the petty cash voucher number
- the total payment (ie the amount paid out on each petty cash voucher) is in the next column
- then follow the analysis columns which analyse each transaction entered in the 'total payment' column (note that VAT may need to be calculated – see below)

A business or organisation will use whatever analysis columns are most suitable for it and, indeed, there may be more columns than shown in the example. It is important that expenses are analysed to the correct columns so that the contents show a true picture of petty cash expenditure.

PETTY CASH AND VAT

Value Added Tax is charged by VAT-registered businesses on their taxable supplies. Therefore, there will often be VAT included as part of the expense paid out of petty cash. However, not all expenses will have been subject to VAT. There are four possible circumstances:

- VAT has been charged at the standard rate
- VAT has not been charged because the supplier is not VAT-registered
- the zero rate of VAT applies, eg food and drink (but not meals which are standard-rated), books, newspapers, transport (but not taxis and hire cars)
- the supplies are exempt (eg financial services, postal services)

Often the indication of the supplier's VAT registration number on a receipt or invoice will tell you that VAT has been charged at the standard rate.

Where VAT has been charged, the amount of tax might be indicated separately on the receipt or invoice. However, for small money amounts it is quite usual for a total to be shown without indicating the amount of VAT. An example of a receipt which does not show the VAT content is illustrated below. The receipt is for a box of envelopes purchased from Wyvern Stationers. It shows:

- the name and address of the retailer

- the date and time of the transaction

- the VAT registration number of the retailer

- the price of the item – £4.70

- the amount of money given – a £10 note

- the amount of change given – £5.30

```
        Wyvern Stationers
        25 High St Mereford
          08 10 07   16.07
        VAT Reg 454 7106 34

Salesperson Rashid

Stationery            4.70

TOTAL                 4.70
CASH                 10.00
CHANGE                5.30
```

What it does not show, however, is the VAT content of the purchase price – it only shows the price after the VAT has been added on.

How do we calculate purchase price before the VAT is added on?

The formula, with VAT at 17.5%, is:

price including VAT ÷ 1.175 = price before VAT is added on

in this case ...

£4.70 ÷ 1.175 = £4.00 = price before VAT is added on

The VAT content is therefore

£4.70 less £4.00 = 70p

Here £0.70 will be entered in the VAT column in the petty cash book, £4.00 in the appropriate expense column, and the full £4.70 in the total payment column.

Remember when calculating VAT amounts that fractions of a penny are ignored, ie the tax is rounded *down* to a whole penny.

Case Study

WYVERN TRADERS: PETTY CASH BOOK

situation

You work in the accounts office of Wyvern Traders. One of your tasks is to keep the petty cash book, which is operated on the imprest method. There are a number of transactions which you have authorised (all transactions, unless otherwise indicated, include VAT at 17.5%) to be entered for the week on page 30 of the petty cash book:

2007

5 Apr	Started the week with an imprest amount of £50.00
5 Apr	Paid stationery £3.76 on voucher no 47
5 Apr	Paid taxi fare £2.82 on voucher no 48
6 Apr	Paid postages £0.75 (no VAT) on voucher no 49
7 Apr	Paid taxi fare £4.70 on voucher no 50
7 Apr	Paid J Jones, a creditor, £6.00 (no VAT shown in petty cash book – amount will be on VAT account already) on voucher no 51
8 Apr	Paid stationery £3.76 on voucher no 52
8 Apr	Paid postages £2.85 (no VAT) on voucher no 53
9 Apr	Paid taxi fare £6.11 on voucher no 54

solution

The petty cash book is written up as follows:

Receipts	Date	Details	Voucher No	Total Payment	VAT	Postages	Stationery	Travel	Ledger
							Analysis columns		
£ 50.00	2007			£	£	£	£	£	£
	5 Apr	Balance b/d							
	5 Apr	Stationery	47	3.76	0.56		3.20		
	5 Apr	Taxi fare	48	2.82	0.42			2.40	
	6 Apr	Postages	49	0.75		0.75			
	7 Apr	Taxi fare	50	4.70	0.70			4.00	
	7 Apr	J Jones	51	6.00					6.00
	8 Apr	Stationery	52	3.76	0.56		3.20		
	8 Apr	Postages	53	2.85		2.85			
	9 Apr	Taxi fare	54	6.11	0.91			5.20	
				30.75	3.15	3.60	6.40	11.60	6.00

Petty Cash Book — PCB 30

Notes to the Case Study

Each page of the petty cash book is numbered – here 'PCB 30' – this helps with cross-referencing in the accounts system.

- For each petty cash item, the analysis columns add up to the amount shown in the 'total payment' column
- The totals of the analysis columns add up to the total payment
- The petty cashier will give the firm's book-keeper a posting sheet (see page 319) giving details of the total of each analysis column so that the amounts can be recorded in the double-entry accounts system
- Total payments are £30.75 and, as the petty cash book is kept using the imprest method, this is the amount of cash which will need to be drawn from the cashier in order to restore the imprest
- We shall see how the petty cash book is balanced in the next section (below).

BALANCING PETTY CASH BOOK

A petty cash book is balanced by comparing the receipts and payments columns – just like other double-entry accounts. Where a petty cash book is operated using the imprest method, a further receipt will be the amount of cash received from the main cashier to restore the imprest amount – this is equal to the total paid out during the week.

The following shows how the petty cash book seen in the Case Study above is balanced at the end of the week:

Receipts	Date	Details	Voucher No	Total Payment		Analysis columns				
					VAT	Postages	Stationery	Travel	Ledger
£	2007			£	£	£	£	£	£
50.00	5 Apr	Balance b/d							
	5 Apr	Stationery	47	3.76	0.56		3.20		
	5 Apr	Taxi fare	48	2.82	0.42			2.40	
	6 Apr	Postages	49	0.75		0.75			
	7 Apr	Taxi fare	50	4.70	0.70			4.00	
	7 Apr	J Jones	51	6.00					6.00
	8 Apr	Stationery	52	3.76	0.56		3.20		
	8 Apr	Postages	53	2.85		2.85			
	9 Apr	Taxi fare	54	6.11	0.91			5.20	
				30.75	3.15	3.60	6.40	11.60	6.00
30.75	9 Apr	Cash received							
	9 Apr	Balance c/d		50.00					
80.75				80.75					
50.00	9 Apr	Balance b/d							

Petty Cash Book — PCB 30

Note that, here, the imprest amount has been restored at the end of the week and before the petty cash book has been balanced. An alternative method, depending on the policy of the company, is to balance the petty cash book *before* restoring the imprest amount – in the above example, this will give a balance brought down on 9 April of £19.25 (ie £50.00 minus £30.75); the money received from the cashier (£30.75) will then be recorded in the receipts column.

Where the petty cash book is operated *not* using the imprest method, it is balanced at regular intervals by comparing the receipts and payments columns. Whenever cash is received from the cashier, it is recorded in the receipts column.

The petty cashier prepares a posting sheet giving details of the total of each analysis column so that the amounts can then be recorded in the double-entry system by the book-keeper.

PETTY CASH AND THE ACCOUNTING SYSTEM

Petty cash book has two uses within the accounting system:

- it is the book of prime entry for low value expense payments
- it forms part of the double-entry system (note that the petty cash book can, alternatively, be represented in the main ledger by a petty cash control account – see page 323)

Petty cash book, as well as being a book of prime entry, is usually incorporated into the double-entry system, as is shown in the diagram below.

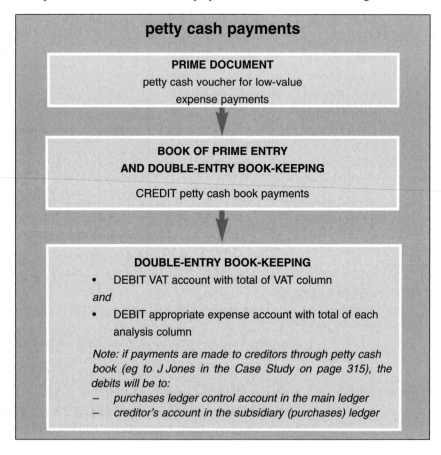

The double-entry book-keeping entries from petty cash book are either posted direct to the main ledger accounts – VAT account and expenses accounts – or often a posting sheet (see below) is used.

At regular intervals – weekly or monthly – the petty cashier prepares a posting sheet which gives the firm's book-keeper details of the totals from the analysis columns of the petty cash book. The posting sheet for the transactions from the Case Study is as follows:

WYVERN TRADERS				
Posting sheet: Petty Cash				
account name	account number	debit	credit	reference
		£	£	
VAT	ML 2200	3.15		PCB 30
Postages	ML 6348	3.60		PCB 30
Stationery	ML 7290	6.40		PCB 30
Travel expenses	ML 7755	11.60		PCB 30
Purchases ledger control	ML 6002	6.00		PCB 30
Bank	CBP		30.75	PCB 30
TOTAL		30.75	30.75	

Prepared by	*Jane Watkins*	Date	*9 April 2007*
Checked by	*Natalie Wilson*	Date	*9 April 2007*
Posted by	Mark Hopwood	Date	9 April 2007

The posting sheet shows:

- *debits* to VAT and expenses accounts in the main ledger in respect of the total of each analysis column
- *debits* in respect of the ledger column amounts (eg J Jones in the Case Study) to:
  - purchases ledger control account
  - subsidiary (purchases) ledger
- *credit* to bank account, being the total amount of expenses paid from petty cash during the period and the amount that will need to be withdrawn from the bank in order to restore the imprest amount of petty cash

From the Case Study, above, and posting sheet, main ledger accounts will be written up as follows at the end of the week (9 April):

MAIN LEDGER

Dr	**Value Added Tax Account** (account no 2200)		Cr	
2007		£	2007	£
9 Apr	Petty cash book PCB 30	3.15		

Dr	**Postages Account** (account no 6348)		Cr
2007	£	2007	£
9 Apr	Petty cash book PCB 30	3.60	

Dr	**Stationery Account** (account no 7290)		Cr
2007	£	2007	£
9 Apr	Petty cash book PCB 30	6.40	

Dr	**Travel Expenses Account** (account no 7755)		Cr
2007	£	2007	£
9 Apr	Petty cash book PCB 30	11.60	

Dr	**Purchases Ledger Control Account** (account no 6002)		Cr
2007	£	2007	£
9 Apr	Petty cash book PCB 30	*6.00	

* this transaction will also be debited to the account of the creditor – here J Jones – in the subsidiary (purchases) ledger.

To restore the imprest amount (or to top-up petty cash when the non-imprest method is used), the petty cashier will complete a cheque requisition form either for the cash itself, or for a cheque made payable to cash. The petty cashier will take the cheque to the bank and obtain the cash. An example of a cheque requisition is shown below:

CHEQUE REQUISITION	
Amount	*£30.75*
Payee	*Cash*
Date	*9 April 2007*
Details	*Reimbursement of petty cash*
Signature	*Jane Watkins, petty cashier*
Authorised by	*Natalie Wilson, supervisor*
Cheque no	*017234*

cheque requisition form

The double-entry book-keeping entries to record this reimbursement are:

– *debit* petty cash book

– *credit* cash book, ie the payments side

For example, the amount of £30.75 cash received when balancing the petty cash book seen earlier (page 317) is recorded in the cash book as follows:

Credit	Cash Book: Payments				CBP
Date	Details	Folio	Discount received	Cash	Bank
2007			£	£	£
9 Apr	Petty cash book 017234	PCB 30			30.75

After this reimbursement, the imprest amount is restored and petty cash book has a balance brought down of £50.00 on 9 April. The petty cash book is now ready for next week's transactions.

CONTROL OF PETTY CASH

The petty cashier is usually responsible to the accounts supervisor for control of the petty cash and for correct recording of authorised petty cash transactions.

Most businesses and organisations set out in writing the procedures to be followed by the petty cashier. This is of benefit not only for the petty cashier to know the extent of his or her duties, but also to help the person who takes over at holiday or other times.

The main procedures for the operation and control of petty cash are:

- On taking over, the petty cashier should check that the petty cash book has been balanced and that the amount of cash held agrees with the balance shown in the book. If there is any discrepancy, this should be referred to the accounts supervisor immediately.

- When the petty cash book is kept under the imprest method, ensure that each week is started with the imprest amount of cash which has been agreed with the accounts supervisor.

- The petty cash is to be kept securely in a locked cash book, and control kept of the keys.
- Petty cash vouchers (in number order) are to be provided on request.
- Petty cash is paid out against correctly completed petty cash vouchers after checking that:
    - the voucher is signed by the person receiving the money
    - the voucher is signed by the person authorising payment (a list of authorised signatories will be provided)
    - a receipt (or other supporting evidence) is attached to the petty cash voucher, and that receipt and petty cash voucher are for the same amount
    - the amount being claimed is within the authorised limit of the petty cashier
- The petty cash book is written up (to include calculation of VAT amounts when appropriate); it is important that the petty cash book is accurate.
- Completed petty cash vouchers are stored safely – filed in numerical order. The vouchers will need to be kept for at least six years. They may be needed by the auditors or in the event of other queries. Completed petty cash books will also need to be retained.
- A surprise check of petty cash will be made by the accounts supervisor – at any one time the cash held plus amounts of petty cash vouchers should equal the imprest amount.
- At the end of each week (or month) the petty cash book is to be balanced.
- Details of the totals of each analysis column are given to the book-keeper – usually on a posting sheet – so that the amount of each expense can be entered into the double-entry system.
- Where the imprest method is used, an amount of cash is drawn from the cashier equal to the amount of payments made, in order to restore the imprest amount.
- The petty cash book and cash in hand are to be presented to the accounts supervisor for checking.
- Any discrepancies are to be dealt with promptly; these may include:
    - petty cash claims that have not been authorised
    - insufficient supporting evidence (eg receipt) attached to the petty cash voucher
    - amounts being claimed which exceed the authorised limit of the petty cashier
    - a receipt and petty cash voucher total differing – the matter should be queried with the person who made the purchase
    - a difference between the totals of the analysis columns and the total payments column in the petty cash book – check the addition of the

columns, the figures against the vouchers, the VAT calculations (does the VAT plus the analysis column amount equal the total payment amount?)

– a difference between the cash in the petty cash box and the balance shown in the petty cash book – if this is not an arithmetic difference it may be a case of theft, and should be reported promptly to the accounts supervisor

– where discrepancies and queries cannot be resolved, they should be referred to the accounts supervisor

• All aspects of petty cash are confidential and should not be discussed with others.

THE USE OF PETTY CASH CONTROL ACCOUNT

This chapter has explained how petty cash book forms part of the double-entry system, The *disadvantage* of this procedure is that petty cash book, from which the postings are made, may have many transactions, and so could contain errors. As the balance of petty cash book is used whenever a trial balance (covered in Chapter 20) is prepared, any error in the petty cash book balancing could 'feed through' into the trial balance and cause problems.

An alternative procedure is to treat petty cash book as a subsidiary ledger, with a *petty cash control account* in the main ledger as part of double-entry – shown on right-hand side of the diagram below. The *advantage* here is that petty cash book – the subsidiary ledger – will be reconciled (agreed) with petty cash control account, in the main ledger (reconciliation is explained on pages 388-390). With this method, errors should be found and corrected before a trial balance is prepared, as it is the balance of petty cash control account rather than the petty cash book totals that is used in the trial balance.

---

petty cash: alternative methods of book-keeping

petty cash book as part of double-entry book-keeping

DOUBLE-ENTRY BOOK-KEEPING:

- petty cash book totals
- VAT and expense accounts

using a petty cash control account

DOUBLE-ENTRY BOOK-KEEPING:

- petty cash control account
- VAT and expense accounts

SUBSIDIARY LEDGER

- petty cash book

The format of petty cash control account, using figures from the petty cash book seen earlier (page 317) is as follows:

Dr			Petty Cash Control Account (account no 925)			Cr
2007		£	2007			£
5 Apr	Balance b/d	50.00	9 Apr	Petty cash book		
9 Apr	Cash book CBP	30.75		PCB 30		30.75
		___	9 Apr	Balance c/d		50.00
		80.75				80.75
9 Apr	Balance b/d	50.00				

Notes:

- The debit 'balance b/d' on 5 April is the same as the opening balance in petty cash book – see page 317. For a petty cash book using the imprest method, as here, this is the imprest amount.

- The credit entry for 'petty cash book PCB 30' on 9 April is the total of the analysis columns (VAT and expenses) from petty cash book. These amounts are debited to their respective accounts in the main ledger as already seen as pages 319 and 320.

- The debit entry for 'Cash book CBP' on 9 April is the reimbursement of petty cash in order to restore the imprest amount. The cheque requisition for this is shown on page 320.

- Finally, the 'balance c/d' on 9 April (and also brought down) is the new balance on petty cash book, ready for next week's transactions. The balance is reconciled with the amount of cash held in the petty cash box.

- The petty cash book records payments for a variety of low-value business expenses. It is both a book of prime entry and is usually incorporated into the double-entry system.

- The person responsible for maintaining the petty cash book is the petty cashier, who is responsible for security.

- Payment can only be made from the petty cash book against correct documentation – usually a petty cash voucher, which must be signed by the person authorising payment.

- Where a business is registered for Value Added Tax, it must record VAT amounts paid on petty cash purchases in a separate column in the petty cash book.

- When petty cash book is a subsidiary account, petty cash control account is used as the main ledger account.

- At regular intervals – weekly or monthly – the petty cash book will be balanced; the total of each analysis column will be debited to the relevant account in the main ledger, and the cashier will restore the imprest amount of cash.

Key Terms		
	petty cash book	book of prime entry usually incorporated into the double-entry system; used for low-value cash payments for business expenses
	petty cashier	person responsible for the petty cash system
	imprest method	where the money held in the petty cash float is restored to the same amount for the beginning of each week or month
	non-imprest method	where the petty cashier has a float of cash which is replenished by the cashier whenever it runs low
	petty cash voucher	prime document used to claim amounts from petty cash
	petty cash control account	main ledger account used when petty cash book is a subsidiary ledger; it shows the total payments made by the petty cashier during the week or month, and records receipts of cash from the cash book

Student Activities

16.1 Most petty cash books operate using the imprest method. This means that:

(a) the petty cashier draws money from the main cashier as and when required

(b) the main cashier has to authorise each petty cash payment

(c) a copy has to be kept of each petty cash voucher

(d) the petty cashier starts each week or month with a fixed amount of money

Answer (a) or (b) or (c) or (d)

16.2 You work as an accounts clerk in the office of Temeside Printers Limited. One of your duties is that of petty cashier; you are able to authorise transactions up to £30 each. Which of the following expenses will you allow to be paid out of petty cash?

(a) postage on a parcel of printing sent to a customer, £3.85

(b) a rubber date stamp bought for use in the office, £4.60

(c) rail fare to work claimed by the office manager's secretary, £2.50

(d) donation to charity, £5.00

(e) tea and coffee for use by office staff, £5.50

(f) mileage allowance claimed by works foreman who had to visit a customer, £4.80

(g) meal allowance paid to assistant who had to work her lunch hour, £4.00

(h) window cleaning, £3.50

(i) purchase of shelving for the office, £55.00

(j) taxi fare claimed for delivering an urgent parcel of printing to a customer, £6.25

Note: you may assume that all expenses are supported by relevant documentation.

Explain any expenses that you will refer to the accounts supervisor.

16.3 As petty cashier, prepare petty cash vouchers under today's date for signature by the person making the claim. You are able to authorise payments up to £10.00 each. A blank voucher is shown below. Alternatively you can download blank documents from www.osbornebooks.co.uk

• £4.45 claimed by Jayne Smith for postage (no VAT) on an urgent parcel of spare parts sent to a customer, Evelode Supplies Limited.

• £2.35, including VAT, claimed by Tanya Howard for air mail envelopes bought for use in the office.

• £8.60, including VAT, claimed by Toni Wyatt for a taxi fare used on a business visit to a customer, Jasper Limited.

Number the vouchers, beginning with number 851

What documentation will you require to be attached to each voucher?

petty cash voucher		No. 851
	date	
description		amount (£)
	VAT	
signature		
authorised		

16.4 The business for which you work is registered for VAT. The following petty cash amounts include VAT at 17.5% and you are required to calculate the amount that will be shown in the VAT column and the appropriate expense column (remember that VAT amounts should be rounded down to the nearest penny):

(a) £9.40
(b) £4.70
(c) £2.35
(d) £2.45
(e) £5.60
(f) £3.47
(g) £8.75
(h) 94p
(i) 99p
(j) £9.41

16.5 The petty cashier of the company where you work as an accounts assistant is away on holiday. The accounts supervisor asks you to balance the petty cash book at 31 August. The petty cash book uses the imprest method and the imprest amount is £75.00.

You are to:

- restore the imprest amount of petty cash to £75.00, making appropriate entries in the petty cash book

- balance the petty cash book at 31 August 2007 and bring down the balances on 1 September

Petty Cash Book

Receipts	Date	Details	Voucher No	Total Payment	VAT	Postages	Travel	Meals	Office Sundries
£	2007			£	£	£	£	£	£
75.00	1 Aug	Balance b/d							
	4 Aug	Postages	223	7.20		7.20			
	6 Aug	Travel expenses	224	4.50			4.50		
	9 Aug	Postages	225	2.54		2.54			
	12 Aug	Envelopes	226	4.70	0.70				4.00
	13 Aug	Window cleaning	227	7.05	1.05				6.00
	17 Aug	Taxi fare	228	7.52	1.12		6.40		
	20 Aug	Postages	229	8.56		8.56			
	23 Aug	Meals	230	6.35				6.35	
	27 Aug	Envelopes	231	6.58	0.98				5.60

16.6 On returning from holiday, you are told to take charge of the petty cash book of Carr Trading. This is kept using the imprest method, the float being £75.00 at the beginning of each month. Analysis columns are used for VAT, travel, postages, stationery, meals, and miscellaneous.

There are a number of transactions for the month which you authorise (all transactions, unless otherwise indicated, include VAT at 17.5%). You are to enter the transactions for the month on page 42 of the petty cash book.

2007

1 Aug	Balance of cash £75.00
4 Aug	Voucher no 39: taxi fare £3.80
6 Aug	Voucher no 40: parcel postage £2.35 (no VAT)
9 Aug	Voucher no 41: pencils £1.26
11 Aug	Voucher no 42: travel expenses £5.46 (no VAT)
12 Aug	Voucher no 43: window cleaner £8.50 (no VAT)
16 Aug	Voucher no 44: large envelopes £2.45
18 Aug	Voucher no 45: donation to charity £5 (no VAT)
19 Aug	Voucher no 46: rail fare £5.60 (no VAT); meal allowance £5.00 (no VAT)
20 Aug	Voucher no 47: recorded delivery postage £0.75 (no VAT)
23 Aug	Voucher no 48: roll of packing tape £1.50
25 Aug	Voucher no 49: excess postage paid £0.55 (no VAT)
27 Aug	Voucher no 50: taxi fare £5.40

You are to:

• Total the analysis columns and prepare a posting sheet which shows the entries to be recorded in the main ledger at the end of the month, on 31 August. Account numbers need not be shown.

• Restore the imprest amount of petty cash book to £75.00 by transfer from the cash book.

• Balance the petty cash book at 31 August 2007 and bring down the balance on 1 September.

16.7 Prepare a petty cash book for Tyax Systems Limited with analysis columns for VAT, postages, travel, meals, and sundry office expenses. Enter the following authorised transactions for the week on page 18 of the petty cash book. The voucher amounts include VAT at 17.5% unless indicated.

2007

7 June Balance of cash £100.00

7 June Postages £6.35 (no VAT), voucher no 123

8 June Travel expenses £3.25 (no VAT), voucher no 124

8 June Postages £1.28 (no VAT), voucher no 125

9 June Envelopes £4.54, voucher no 126

9 June Window cleaning £5.50, voucher no 127

10 June Taxi fare £4.56, meals £10.85, voucher no 128

10 June Postages £8.56 (no VAT), packing materials £3.25, voucher no 129

10 June Taxi fare £4.50, meals £7.45, voucher no 130

11 June Marker pens £2.55, envelopes £3.80, voucher no 131

You are to:

- Total the analysis columns and prepare a posting sheet which shows the entries to be recorded in the main ledger at the end of the week, on 11 June. Account numbers need not be shown.

- Restore the amount of petty cash to £100.00 by transfer from the cash book.

- Balance the petty cash book and bring down the balance at 11 June 2007.

this chapter covers . . .

So far we have studied the principles of double-entry book-keeping and applied them to transactions for sales, purchases, returns, receipts and payments.

In this chapter, we examine in detail the double-entry aspects of a number of transactions (some of which we have seen briefly in earlier chapters):

- capital
- fixed assets
- expenses
- income
- drawings
- loans
- stock
- bad debts written off

The importance of the distinction between capital expenditure and revenue expenditure is discussed later in the chapter. Firstly though, we study in detail the division of the ledger, and the types of accounts found in the book-keeping system.

PERFORMANCE CRITERIA COVERED

unit 30: INTRODUCTORY ACCOUNTING

element 30.2

process purchases and payments

I   enter payments in cash book and ledgers

Note

This chapter covers a wide variety of accounting issues and is therefore included at this stage of the book. It inevitably covers an area wider than that strictly required by Element 30.3

DIVISION OF THE LEDGER

In previous chapters we have already made use of the division of the ledger, whereby separate ledgers are kept, each containing different classes of account. The ledger of a business is usually divided into four sections:

- *subsidiary (sales) ledger*, containing the accounts of the firm's debtors (customers)
- *subsidiary (purchases) ledger*, containing the accounts of the firm's creditors (suppliers)
- *cash book*, containing bank and cash records of the receipts and payments of the business
- *main ledger*, containing all other accounts

When computers are used for accounting, the physical ledger books do not exist. However, the principles of manual and computerised accounting are the same, and the term 'ledgers' is used in computer accounting systems. Accounting software is available for each of the ledgers mentioned above, usually combined into one integrated computer program. The four divisions of the ledger are illustrated in full on the next page.

TYPES OF ACCOUNT

Within a book-keeping system there are different types of accounts: a distinction is made between personal and impersonal accounts. Personal accounts are in the names of people or businesses, eg the accounts for debtors and creditors. Impersonal accounts are non-personal accounts; these are usually divided between real accounts, which represent things such as cash, bank balance, computers, motor vehicles, machinery, etc, and nominal accounts, which record income and expenses such as sales, purchases, wages, etc. The diagram below distinguishes between the different types of account.

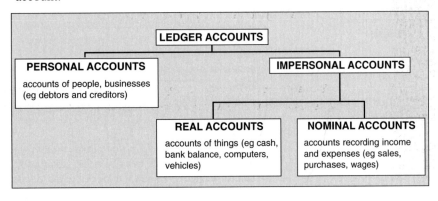

DIVISION OF THE LEDGER

subsidiary (sales) ledger

Subsidiary (sales) ledger contains the accounts of debtors, and records:
- sales made on credit to customers of the business
- sales returns by customers
- payments received from customers
- cash discount allowed for prompt settlement

Cash sales are not recorded in this ledger.

Subsidiary (sales) ledger contains an account for each debtor and records the transactions with that debtor. The total of the subsidiary (sales) ledger account balances should agree with the balance of sales ledger control account in the main ledger.

subsidiary (purchases) ledger

Subsidiary (purchases) ledger contains the accounts of creditors, and records:
- purchases made on credit from suppliers of the business
- purchases returns made by the business
- payments made to suppliers
- cash discount received for prompt settlement

Cash purchases are not recorded in this ledger.

Subsidiary (purchases) ledger contains an account for each creditor and records the transactions with that creditor. The total of the subsidiary (purchases) ledger account balances should agree with the balance of purchases ledger control account in the main ledger.

cash books

The cash books comprise:
- Cash Book
  - records all transactions for bank account and cash account
  - cash book is also often used for listing the amounts of settlement (cash) discount received and allowed, and for recording Value Added Tax

Note that, alternatively, cash book can be represented in the main ledger by a cash control account (see page 387)

- Petty Cash Book
  - records low-value cash payments too small to be entered in the cash book

Note that, alternatively, petty cash book can be represented in the main ledger by a petty cash control account (see page 323)

main ledger

The main ledger contains the other accounts of the business:
- Nominal Accounts
  - sales account (cash and credit sales)
  - purchases account (cash and credit purchases)
  - sales returns, purchases returns
  - expenses and income
  - loan
  - capital, drawings
  - Value Added Tax (where the business is VAT-registered)

- Real Accounts
  - fixed assets, eg premises, computers, motor vehicles
  - other assets, eg cash, bank balance, stock, petty cash
  - control accounts, eg sales ledger, purchases ledger

In previous chapters we have used accounts to record transactions for purchases, sales, returns, receipts and payments. In order to complete our study of double-entry accounts for Introductory Accounting we will look in detail at a number of transactions (some of which have been seen briefly in earlier chapters):

- capital
- fixed assets
- expenses
- income
- drawings
- loans
- stock
- bad debts written off

Note that aspects of Value Added Tax (VAT) are considered later in the chapter (pages 338-339).

CAPITAL ACCOUNT

Capital is the amount of money invested in the business by the owner (or owners). The amount is owed by the business to the owner, although it is unlikely to be repaid immediately as then the business would be unable to operate. A capital account is used to record the amount(s) paid into the business; the book-keeping entries are:

- **capital introduced**
    - *debit* cash book (bank or cash columns as appropriate)
    - *credit* capital account

The dual aspect (see page 50) of this transaction is that cash book (bank or cash columns) has gained value and has been debited; capital account records a liability (to the owner) and is credited. Remember that book-keeping entries look at transactions from the point of view of the business or organisation.

The introduction of capital into a business is often the very first transaction to be entered into the accounts.

Sometimes capital is introduced into the business in forms other than in cash or by cheque. For example, the owner might transfer property or other fixed assets (see below) into the business as capital; the book-keeping entries are:

- *debit* property account (or other account as appropriate)
- *credit* capital account

FIXED ASSETS

Fixed assets are items purchased by a business for use on a permanent or semi-permanent basis. Examples are buildings, machinery, motor vehicles and office equipment. All of these are bought by a business with the intention that they will be used for some time in the business. When a business buys fixed assets, the expenditure is referred to as *capital expenditure* (don't confuse the word capital here with the owner's capital). Capital expenditure means that items have been bought for use in the business for some years to come. By contrast, revenue expenditure is where the items bought will be used by the business quite quickly. For example, the purchase of a car is capital expenditure, while the cost of petrol or diesel for the car is revenue expenditure. The importance of distinguishing between capital and revenue expenditure is discussed on pages 349-350.

When fixed assets are bought, a separate account for each type of fixed asset is used, eg buildings account, machinery account, motor vehicles account, etc. The book-keeping entries are:

*   **purchase of a fixed asset**
    *   – *debit* fixed asset account (using the appropriate account)
    *   – *credit* cash book (bank or cash column, as appropriate)

Here the fixed asset account, which has gained value, is debited. The account which has given value – cash book (bank or cash column) – is credited.

Sometimes fixed assets are returned to the supplier because they do not work, or are unsuitable. When the returns transaction has been agreed with the supplier it will be recorded in the accounts as:

*   **return of unsuitable fixed assets**
    *   – *debit* cash book* (bank or cash column, as appropriate)
    *   – *credit* fixed asset account (using the appropriate account)
    *   * assuming that a bank/cash payment is received for the return

As you will see, such a transaction is the opposite of the original purchase.

Often fixed assets are bought on credit terms (rather than immediate payment by cheque or in cash). The book-keeping entries are:

*   **purchase of a fixed asset on credit**
    *   – *debit* fixed asset account
    *   – *credit* creditor's account

The creditor's account shows the amount the business owes, which will be subsequently paid by cheque or in cash.

EXPENSES

Businesses and other organisations pay various running expenses, such as rent, wages, electricity, telephone, vehicle running expenses, etc. These day-to-day expenses are referred to as *revenue expenditure*. A separate account is used in the accounting system for each main class of revenue expenditure, eg rent account, wages account, etc.

The book-keeping entries are:

- **payment of an expense**
  - *debit* expense account (using the appropriate account)
  - *credit* cash book (bank or cash column as appropriate)

Here the expense account is debited because the business has gained value – for example, with rent paid the business has had the use of the premises for a certain time. The account which gives value, cash book (bank or cash column), is credited.

Often with expenses, there may be a period of credit allowed. For example, the electricity bill may be received today stating that payment is to be made by the end of the month. The business will treat the electricity supplier as a creditor and makes the following accounting entries:

- *debit* electricity account
- *credit* creditor's subsidiary account (in the name of the electricity supplier)

When payment is due it can then be made through the cash book as follows:

- *debit* creditor's subsidiary account (electricity supplier)
- *credit* cash book

Also, entries will need to be made in the purchases ledger control account in the main ledger.

INCOME

From time-to-time a business or organisation may receive amounts of income apart from its normal sales income.

Examples of such 'other income' include rent received, commission received, or fees received. These are recorded in separate accounts for each category of income, eg rent received account, commission received account. The book-keeping entries are:

- **receipt of income**
    - – *debit* cash book (bank or cash column as appropriate)
    - – *credit* income account (using the appropriate account)

The account which has gained value, cash book, is debited; the account which has given value, eg rent received, is credited.

OWNER'S DRAWINGS

Drawings is the term used when the owner takes money, in cash or by cheque (or sometimes goods), from the business for personal use. A drawings account is used to record such amounts; the book-keeping entries for withdrawal of money are:

- **owner's drawings**
    - – *debit* drawings account
    - – *credit* cash book (bank or cash column)

When the owner of the business takes some of the goods in which the business trades for his or her own use, the book-keeping entries are:

- – *debit* drawings account
- – *credit* purchases account

Note that where a business is VAT-registered, VAT must be accounted for on goods taken by the owner.

LOANS

When a business or organisation receives a loan, eg from a relative or the bank, it is the cash account or bank account which gains value, while a loan account (in the name of the lender) records the liability.

- **loan received**
    - – *debit* cash book (bank or cash column)
    - – *credit* loan account (in name of the lender)

Interest paid to the lender is recorded by means of an expenses account called loan interest paid account. Repayment of the loan, or part of the loan by instalments, is recorded in the accounts as:

- **loan repayment**
    - – *debit* loan account
    - – *credit* cash book (bank or cash column)

STOCK

We have seen in earlier chapters how businesses use separate purchases and sales accounts to record when the goods in which they trade are bought and sold. The reason for using separate accounts for purchases and sales is because there is usually a difference between the buying price and the selling price – the latter is higher and gives the business its profit. At least once a year, however, a business values the stock it has on the shelves of the shop, for example, or in the warehouse (the techniques of stock valuation are covered at later levels of your Diploma Pathway studies). As stock is an asset of a business, the valuation is debited to stock account; the credit transaction is to trading account (part of the profit and loss account) where it is used to assist in the calculation of profit.

To summarise, stock account is used only when the stock of a business is valued – at least once a year at the end of the financial year. The book-keeping entries to record the valuation in the accounts are:

- **stock valuation**
  - *debit* stock account
  - *credit* trading account (part of the profit and loss account)

Thus at the start of each financial year there will, for most businesses, be a debit balance on stock account representing the value of stock held.

BAD DEBTS WRITTEN OFF

A bad debt is a debt owing to a business or organisation which it considers will never be paid.

One of the problems of selling goods and services on credit terms is that, from time-to-time, some customers will not pay. As a consequence, the balances of such accounts have to be written off when they become uncollectable. This happens when all reasonable efforts to recover the amount owing have been exhausted, ie statements and letters have been sent to the debtor requesting payment, and legal action – where appropriate – or the threat of legal action has failed to obtain payment.

In writing off a debtor's account as bad, the business is bearing the cost of the amount due. The debtor's account is closed and the amount (or amounts, where a number of accounts are dealt with in this way) is debited to bad debts written off account. This account stores up the amounts of account balances written off during the year (in much the same way as an expense account).

The book-keeping transactions are:

- **bad debt written off**
  - *debit* bad debts written off account
  - *credit* sales ledger control account, and also credit the debtor's subsidiary account in the subsidiary (sales) ledger

VAT AND DOUBLE-ENTRY ACCOUNTS

When a business is registered for Value Added Tax it is able to claim back VAT paid on purchases of goods, fixed assets, and expenses. At the same time it must charge VAT whenever it supplies goods and services (except for zero-rated and exempt goods and services).

We have already seen in previous chapters how VAT is dealt with for purchases, sales and returns. When a business buys, for example, fixed assets it will enter the amount of VAT direct to the debit side of VAT account.

example transaction

On 16 April 2007, Acme Supplies Limited, a company which is registered for Value Added Tax, buys a new computer at a cost of £600 + VAT (at 17.5%) of £105, paying by cheque.

This is recorded in the double-entry accounts as:

Dr		Computer Account		Cr
2007		£	2007	£
16 Apr	Bank	600		

Dr		Value Added Tax Account		Cr
2007		£	2007	£
16 Apr	Bank	105		

Credit		Cash Book: Payments			CBP
Date	Details	Folio	Discount received	Cash	Bank
2007			£	£	£
16 Apr	Computer				705

The Value Added Tax account in the main ledger records:

Value Added Tax Account

Debits (input tax)	Credits (output tax)
VAT on purchases	VAT on sales and/or services
VAT on purchases of fixed assets (except cars)	VAT on the sale of fixed assets
VAT on expenses	VAT on other income
VAT on sales returns	VAT on purchases returns

Not all goods and services purchased can be assumed to include VAT: as well as zero-rated and exempt goods, the supplier might be a business which is not registered for VAT.

VAT relief on bad debts

A VAT-registered business can reclaim VAT originally charged on debts which are now being written off. However, in order to claim relief, *the debt must be more than six months overdue*, ie more than six months from the date the payment was originally due – a sale made on 30 day terms on 1 January would be due for payment on 31 January; if this sale is written off as a bad debt, VAT relief would be available after 31 July.

businesses not registered for VAT

Where businesses and other organisations are not registered for Value Added Tax, they cannot reclaim VAT paid on purchases, fixed assets and expenses, nor can they charge VAT when they supply goods and services.

Thus, for a non-registered business, expenses which include VAT are entered in the accounts at the full invoice value.

PRIME DOCUMENTS AND BOOKS OF PRIME ENTRY

The types of transactions that we have looked at in this chapter follow the pattern that we have seen earlier:

prime document

↓

book of prime entry

↓

double-entry accounts

prime documents

For each of the transactions we have seen, there will be a prime (source) document. These include:

- *purchase of fixed assets* – receipt or invoice from supplier

- *expenses* – receipt or invoice from supplier

- *income* – copy of receipt or invoice issued to a tenant for rent received, or a statement showing amount of commission earned

- *loans* – details of loan agreement, statement of interest paid, receipts for loan repayments

- *capital introduced* – copy of receipt for the money, or memorandum showing how much capital is being introduced

- *owner's drawings* – receipt signed by the owner, or note showing amount of withdrawal

- *stock* – stock-taking sheets and records

- *bad debt written off* – note or memorandum from accounts supervisor to write off debts

The type of prime document will vary from transaction to transaction. For external transactions (ie those involving outsiders) there will usually be some form of receipt, or invoice, or other document. For internal transactions (ie those taking place within the business, including with the owner), there will be more reliance on notes or memorandums.

books of prime entry: regular transactions

For routine day-to-day transactions which pass through the cash book, such as payment of expenses, the cash book forms *both* the book of prime entry *and* one of the double-entry accounts. Income transactions involving the cash book, if routine in nature, are dealt with in the same way, ie no separate book of prime entry is needed.

Where a period of credit is received from expenses suppliers, the bill is listed in an analysed purchases day book as the book of prime entry and the supplier is recorded in the accounts as a creditor. The purchases day book is easily adapted to give appropriate analysis as shown below with sample transactions.

Purchases Day Book							**PDB 49**
Date	Supplier	Invoice No	Folio	Total	VAT	Purchases	Expenses
2007				£	£	£	£
13 May	Western Electricity	400791	PL 779	235.00	35.00		200.00
14 May	P Bond	1479	PL 125	94.00	14.00	80.00	

books of prime entry: non-regular transactions

For non-regular transactions – such as the introduction of capital to the business, purchase of fixed assets, raising a loan, valuation of stock, writing off bad debts – the book of prime entry is called the *journal*. Like the day books that we have seen in earlier chapters, the journal is used to list transactions before they are recorded in the double-entry accounts.

An example journal entry for the introduction of capital is as follows:

Date	Details	Folio	Dr	Cr
2007			£	£
1 Jul	Bank account	CBR	20,000	
	Capital account	ML		20,000
	Opening capital introduced			

Notes:

- journal entries are prepared from authorised prime documents (which are stored securely for possible future reference)
- the names of the accounts to be debited and credited in the book-keeping system are written in the details column; in a journal entry it is customary to show the debit transaction first
- the money amounts of the debit and credit entries are stated in the appropriate columns
- a journal entry always balances, ie the debit entry is equal to the credit entry
- it is usual to include a brief narrative explaining why the transaction is being carried out

- each journal entry is complete in itself and is ruled off to separate it from the next entry
- journal entries are dealt with in more detail in Chapter 19.

Case Study

DOUBLE-ENTRY ACCOUNTS – GALAXY MEDIA

situation

You are the book-keeper to Galaxy Media, which has just been started by its owner Henry Stardust. The business is an agency which supplies actors and actresses to advertising agencies. The business is registered for Value Added Tax

The transactions for the first month of trading, May 2007, are listed below:

2007

- 3 May   Started in business with capital of £5,000, a cheque from Henry Stardust paid into the business bank account
- 7 May   Paid rent for the office, £500 (no VAT) by cheque
- 10 May   Bought office equipment for £2,000 + VAT, paying by cheque
- 12 May   Received a loan of £1,000 (no VAT) from Mike Way by cheque
- 14 May   Received commission of £200 + VAT by cheque
- 17 May   Received electricity bill of £80 + VAT from Western Electric to be paid by 31 May
- 18 May   Withdrew £100 from the bank for own use (drawings)
- 21 May   Returned some of the office equipment (unsuitable) for £400 + VAT, a refund cheque being received
- 28 May   Paid Western Electric the amount due

Show how the above transactions will be recorded in the double-entry accounts of Galaxy Media. Books of prime entry and account numbers need not be shown.

solution

The double-entry accounts for May 2007 will be entered as follows:

CASH BOOK

Debit	Cash Book: Receipts				CBR
Date	Details	Folio	Discount allowed	Cash	Bank
2007			£	£	£
3 May	Capital				5,000
12 May	Loan: M Way				1,000
14 May	Commission received				235
21 May	Office equipment				470

Credit	Cash Book: Payments				CBP
Date	Details	Folio	Discount received	Cash	Bank
2007			£	£	£
7 May	Rent paid				500
10 May	Office equipment				2,350
18 May	Drawings				100
28 May	Western Electric				94

MAIN LEDGER

Dr		Capital Account			Cr
2007			£	2007	£
				3 May Bank	5,000

Dr		Rent Paid Account			Cr
2007			£	2007	£
7 May	Bank		500		

Dr		Office Equipment Account			Cr
2007			£	2007	£
10 May	Bank		2,000	21 May Bank	400

Dr		Value Added Tax Account			Cr
2007			£	2007	£
10 May	Bank		350	14 May Bank	35
17 May	Western Electric		14	21 May Bank	70

Dr		Loan Account: M Way			Cr
2007			£	2007	£
				12 May Bank	1,000

Dr		Commission Received Account			Cr
2007			£	2007	£
				14 May Bank	200

Dr			Purchases Ledger Control Account			Cr
2007		£	2007			£
28 May	Bank	94	17 May	Electricity		80
			17 May	VAT		14

Dr			Electricity Account		Cr
2007		£	2007		£
17 May	Western Electric	80			

Dr			Drawings Account		Cr
2007		£	2007		£
18 May	Bank	100			

SUBSIDIARY (PURCHASES) LEDGER

Dr			Western Electric			Cr
2007		£	2007			£
28 May	Bank	94	17 May	Electricity		80
			17 May	VAT		14

Notes:

- Account numbers have not been used here for cross referencing
- The book of prime entry for each transaction is as follows:
  - capital introduced, book of prime entry is the *journal*
  - rent paid, book of prime entry is the *cash book*
  - purchase of office equipment, *journal*
  - loan received, *journal or cash book*
  - commission received, *cash book*
  - electricity bill, *analysed purchases day book*
  - drawings, *journal or cash book*
  - office equipment returned, *journal*
  - payment of electricity bill, *cash book*

Remember that:

- cash book is the book of prime entry for regular transactions
- journal is the book of prime entry for non-regular transactions
- analysed purchases day book is the book of prime entry for expenses where credit is received

A list of the double-entry accounting entries for the transactions shown in this Case Study is illustrated in the form of a posting sheet on page 348.

Case Study	

WRITING OFF A BAD DEBT – DON'S DINER

situation

You work as a sales ledger clerk in the accounts department of Severn Catering Supplies Limited. The company, which is VAT-registered, sells kitchen equipment to hotels and restaurants throughout the country. The company's terms of trade are for payment within 30 days of invoice date.

It is December 2007 and the accounts supervisor, Sue Robinson, has been reviewing the debtors' accounts in the subsidiary (sales) ledger before the end of the financial year on 31 December. She has been looking at the following account:

Dr		**Don's Diner** (account no 258)	Cr
2007	£	2007	£
5 Jan Sales	47		

Monthly statements of account and 'chaser' letters have been sent to this debtor – the last letter was dated 28 September and was returned marked 'gone away, not known at this address'.

solution

The accounts supervisor has decided that it is time to write off the account of Don's Diner as a bad debt. The debt outstanding is £47 and it is not worthwhile taking legal action for such an amount. You are given the following memo which authorises you to go ahead with the write off:

MEMORANDUM

TO: Sales Ledger Accounts Clerk

FROM: Accounts Supervisor

DATE: 10 December 2007

SUBJECT: DON'S DINER

Please write off the balance of this account as a bad debt – we have done all we can to collect the amount. As we charged VAT on the original invoice, do not forget to reclaim VAT when writing off the balance.

Thanks

Sue

Sue Robinson

prime document

The memo acts as the authorised prime document for this accounting transaction.

book of prime entry

The book of prime entry for this non-regular transaction is the journal. The journal entry to write off the account of Don's Diner is as follows:

Date	Details	Folio	Dr	Cr
2007			£	£
10 Dec	Bad debts written off account	ML 7000	40	
	Value Added Tax account	ML 2200	7	
	Sales ledger control account	ML 6001		47
	Balance of subsidiary (sales) ledger			
	account of Don's Diner written off as a			
	bad debt, as per memo from accounts			
	supervisor dated 10 December 2007		47	47

Note: journal entries are dealt with in more detail in Chapter 19.

double-entry accounts

The account of Don's Diner is closed off as follows:

SUBSIDIARY (SALES) LEDGER

Dr		Don's Diner (account no 258)		Cr
2007	£	2007		£
5 Jan Sales	47	10 Dec Bad debts written off		40
		10 Dec Value Added Tax		7
	47			47

The balance net of VAT, ie £40, is transferred to the debit of bad debts written off account, (together with any other accounts being written off). The VAT amount, ie £7, (VAT at 17.5%) is transferred to the debit of VAT account.

MAIN LEDGER

Dr		Bad Debts Written Off Account (no 7000)		Cr
2007	£	2007		£
10 Dec Don's Diner	40			

Dr		Value Added Tax Account (no 2200)		Cr
2007	£	2007		£
10 Dec Don's Diner	7			

Dr	**Sales Ledger Control Account** (no 6001)		Cr
2007	£	2007	£
		10 Dec Bad debts written off	40
		10 Dec Value Added Tax	7

Thus the account of Don's Diner is now closed and no further goods will be supplied to this customer on credit terms. To summarise writing off a bad debt:

- *prime document* – memo or other authority from accounts supervisor
- *book of prime entry* – the journal
- *double-entry accounts* (for a VAT-registered business claiming VAT relief)
  - *debit* bad debts written off account with the amount of the bad debt, net of VAT
  - *debit* Value Added Tax account with the VAT part of the debt
  - *credit* sales ledger control account with the amount of the bad debt and the VAT relief, and also credit the debtor's account in the subsidiary (sales) ledger

Remember that the debt must be more than six months overdue before VAT relief can be claimed.

THE USE OF POSTING SHEETS

In a large business or organisation, the various aspects of the accounting function will be allocated to a number of staff. For example, to look more closely at the recording and payment of credit purchases:

- one person may be involved in checking invoices received
- another person may prepare the purchases day book
- another may pass invoices or statements received for payment
- another may prepare remittance advices and cheques for sending to creditors
- another may keep the double-entry accounts up-to-date

These job allocations are given as an example only – as always, it is for the business to organise its accounting function to suit its needs. The essential point, though, is that in a larger business several people may be involved in just one area of record keeping, such as purchases, sales, etc. (In a small business, all of these tasks and more would, most likely, be carried out by just one person.)

One feature of a large business is that use may be made of a posting sheet. This lists transactions that are to be entered (or posted) into the double-entry accounts and will be prepared by a member of the accounts department. For example, a posting sheet for the transactions of Galaxy Media (see case Study, page 342) is prepared as follows:

Posting Sheet			
Account	**Folio**	**Debit** £	**Credit** £
Bank	CBR	5,000	
Capital	ML		5,000
Rent paid	ML	500	
Bank	CBP		500
Office equipment	ML	2,000	
VAT	ML	350	
Bank	CBP		2,350
Bank	CBR	1,000	
Loan: M Way	ML		1,000
Bank	CBR	235	
Commission received	ML		200
VAT	ML		35
Electricity	ML	80	
VAT	ML	14	
Purchases ledger control (West. Electric)	ML		94
Drawings	ML	100	
Bank	CBP		100
Bank	CBR	470	
Office equipment	ML		400
VAT	ML		70
Purchases ledger control (West. Electric)	ML	94	
Bank	CBP		94
TOTALS		9,843	9,843

Prepared by	J Jarvis	Date	31 May 2007
Checked by	N Wilson	Date	31 May 2007
Posted by	S Ahmed	Date	31 May 2007

Notes:

- The posting sheet can be designed in any format to suit the needs of the business.
- It can be used for one day's transactions, or for longer periods such as a week or a month – much depends on the number of transactions to be recorded.
- Essential information includes:
  - name of account
  - folio, usually together with the account number
  - amount of debit entry
  - amount of credit entry
- The posting sheet is totalled – this shows that the money amounts of debit entries are equal to credit entries.

- The name of the person preparing the posting sheet is stated with the date, together with the person checking it and the date.

- The name of the person posting the transactions to the firm's double-entry accounts, together with the date, is given.

CAPITAL EXPENDITURE AND REVENUE EXPENDITURE

In the double-entry book-keeping system, it is important to distinguish between **capital expenditure** and **revenue expenditure**.

capital expenditure

Capital expenditure can be defined as expenditure incurred on the purchase, alteration or improvement of fixed assets. For example, the purchase of a car for use in the business or organisation is capital expenditure. Included in capital expenditure are such costs as:

- delivery of fixed assets

- installation of fixed assets

- improvement (but not repair) of fixed assets

- legal costs of buying property

revenue expenditure

Revenue expenditure is expenditure incurred on running expenses. For example, the cost of petrol or diesel for the car (above) is revenue expenditure. Included in revenue expenditure are the costs of:

- maintenance and repair of fixed assets

- administration

- selling and distributing the goods or products in which the business or organisation trades

capital expenditure and revenue expenditure – the differences

In the accounting system, it is important to classify correctly capital expenditure and revenue expenditure. An error at the double-entry book-keeping stage will give problems later on when the profit and loss account and balance sheet (both of these are covered at later levels of the Diploma Pathway) are prepared. For example, if the cost of the car was shown as an expense instead of as a fixed asset, the profit and loss account would show a much lower profit (or even record a net loss), while the balance sheet would not show the car as a fixed asset – clearly this is incorrect as the business or organisation owns the asset.

Study the following examples: they show the differences between capital expenditure and revenue expenditure.

- **£30,000 cost of building an extension to the factory, which includes £1,000 for repairs to the existing factory**
    - capital expenditure £29,000
    - revenue expenditure £1,000 (because it is for repairs to an existing fixed asset)

- **a plot of land has been bought for £20,000, the legal costs are £750**
    - capital expenditure £20,750 (the legal costs are included in the capital expenditure, because they are the cost of acquiring the fixed asset, ie the legal costs are 'capitalised')

- **the business' own employees are used to install a new air conditioning system: wages £1,000, materials £1,500**
    - capital expenditure £2,500 (an addition to the property); note that, in cases such as this, revenue expenditure, ie wages and materials purchases, will need to be reduced to allow for the transfer to capital expenditure

- **own employees used to repair and redecorate the premises: wages £500, materials £750**
    - revenue expenditure £1,250 (repairs and redecoration are running expenses)

- **purchase of a new machine £10,000, payment for installation and setting up £250**
    - capital expenditure, £10,250 (costs of installation of a fixed asset are capitalised)

Only by allocating capital expenditure and revenue expenditure correctly in the accounting system can the profit and loss account and balance sheet reflect accurately the financial state of the business.

- Ledger accounts are classified between:
  - personal accounts
  - impersonal accounts (which are further classified between real accounts and nominal accounts)

- Entries in the cash book are:
  - debit money in
  - credit money out

- Other accounts are opened in the book-keeping system for:
  - capital
  - fixed assets
  - expenses
  - income
  - drawings
  - loans
  - stock
  - bad debts written off

- Posting sheets are used to list transactions to be entered in the double-entry accounts.

- Expenditure is classified between capital expenditure and revenue expenditure.

Key Terms

personal accounts — accounts in the names of people or businesses, eg the accounts for debtors and creditors

impersonal accounts — non-personal accounts, usually divided between real accounts and nominal accounts

real accounts — accounts which represent things, such as cash, bank balance, computers, motor vehicles, machinery

nominal accounts — accounts which record income and expenses, such as sales, purchases, wages

capital account	records the amount of money invested in the business by the owner (or owners)
fixed assets	items purchased by a business for use on a permanent or semi-permanent basis, such as buildings, machinery, motor vehicles, office equipment
expenses	the running expenses of a business, such as rent, wages, electricity, telephone, vehicle running expenses
drawings	amount of money taken by the owner in cash, or by cheque (or sometimes goods), from the business for personal use
stock account	an asset of the business, stock is valued usually at the end of the financial year and the amount is debited to stock account
bad debt	a debt owing to a business or organisation which it considers will never be paid
bad debts written off account	the account to which the amounts of account balances written off as bad are transferred
journal	book of prime entry for non-regular transactions
posting sheets	a list of transactions to be entered in the double-entry accounts
capital expenditure	expenditure incurred on the purchase, alteration or improvement of fixed assets
revenue expenditure	expenditure incurred on running expenses

Student Activities

17.1 Subsidiary (sales) ledger contains:

(a)   creditors' accounts

(b)   sales account

(c)   debtors' accounts

(d)   sales returns account

Answer (a) or (b) or (c) or (d)

17.2 Which one of the following is not a division of the ledger?

(a)   main ledger

(b)   sales account

(c)   subsidiary (sales) ledger

(d)   cash book

Answer (a) or (b) or (c) or (d)

17.3 A friend has recently set up in business. To help him, you have written up the first month's double-entry accounts. Your friend asks you to reply to the following points:

• "I bought a computer, but you've shown it on the debit side. Surely it must go on the credit side? You must be wrong."

• "Why is the transaction for my capital on the credit side of capital account. I've paid in capital, so surely this is the account which has gained value?"

Write your answer to your friend.

17.4 James Anderson set up in business on 1 March 2007 and registered for Value Added Tax. During the first month he has kept the cash book up-to-date as follows:

Debit	Cash Book: Receipts			CBR
Date	Details	Folio	Discount allowed	Bank
2007			£	£
1 Mar	Capital			7,500
15 Mar	Bank loan			2,500
19 Mar	Commission received*			141

Credit	Cash Book: Payments				CBP
Date	Details	Folio	Discount received		Bank
2007			£		£
5 Mar	Computer*				2,350
8 Mar	Rent paid				500
12 Mar	Wages				425
23 Mar	Drawings				200
26 Mar	Wages				380
29 Mar	Van*				5,875

The items with asterisks (*) include Value Added Tax.

James Anderson has not got around to the other double-entry accounts.

You are to draw up the other accounts for James Anderson, and to make the appropriate entries.

Notes:

• Use the current rate of Value Added Tax (17.5% at the time of writing)

• Account numbers need not be used

• Separate books of prime entry need not be shown

17.5   The following are the business transactions of Tony Long, who is registered for Value Added Tax, for the month of May 2007:

3 May	Started a business with capital of £6,000 in the bank
4 May	Bought a machine* for £2,350, paying by cheque
7 May	Bought office equipment* for £2,820, paying by cheque
10 May	Paid rent £350, by cheque
13 May	Obtained a loan of £1,000 from a friend, Lucy Warner, and paid her cheque into the bank
14 May	Paid wages £250, by cheque
18 May	Commission received* £188, by cheque
21 May	Drawings £85, by cheque
28 May	Paid wages £135, by cheque

The items with asterisks (*) include Value Added Tax

You are to:

(a)   write up Tony Long's cash book receipts and cash book payments (his cash book has a bank column and no cash column)

(b)   complete the double-entry book-keeping transactions

Notes:

•   Use the current rate of Value Added Tax (17.5% at the time of writing)

•   Account numbers need not be used

•   Separate books of prime entry need not be shown

17.6   Enter the following transactions into the double-entry book-keeping accounts of Jean Lacey, who is registered for Value Added Tax. Include a cash book with a column for bank.

2007

2 Aug	Started in business with capital of £5,000 in the bank
3 Aug	Bought a computer for £1,800 + VAT, paying by cheque
6 Aug	Paid rent £100, by cheque
10 Aug	Received commission £200 + VAT, by cheque
13 Aug	Bought office fittings £2,000 + VAT, paying by cheque
16 Aug	Received a loan £1,000, by cheque from a friend, Sally Orton
17 Aug	Drawings £100, by cheque
20 Aug	Returned some of the office fittings (unsuitable) and received a refund cheque of £240 + VAT
24 Aug	Received commission £160 + VAT, by cheque
27 Aug	Made a loan repayment to Sally Orton of £150, by cheque

Notes:

•   Use the current rate of Value Added Tax (17.5% at the time of writing)

•   Account numbers need not be used

•   Separate books of prime entry need not be shown

17.7 You work as an assistant in the accounts department of Fleet Sales Limited, a VAT-registered company.

The subsidiary (sales) ledger includes the following account:

Dr			**Dailey Trading Company** (account no 754)		Cr
2007		£	2007		£
15 Jan	Sales	94			

Monthly statements of account and 'chaser' letters have been sent to this debtor – the last letter was dated 10 September 2007 and was returned marked 'gone away, not known at this address'.

Today, 29 November 2007, the accounts supervisor gives you the following memo:

MEMORANDUM

TO: Sales Ledger Accounts Clerk

FROM: Accounts Supervisor

DATE: 29 November 2007

SUBJECT: DAILEY TRADING COMPANY

Please write off the balance of this account as a bad debt — we have done all we can to collect the amount. As we charged VAT on the original invoice, do not forget to reclaim VAT when writing off the balance.

Thanks.

Lucinda

Lucinda Luz

You are to show:

- the journal entry made on 29 November
- the transactions on Dailey Trading Company's account in the subsidiary (sales) ledger
- bad debts written off account in the main ledger
- VAT account in the main ledger
- sales ledger control account in the main ledger

Note: account numbers need not be used

17.8 Classify the following costs as either *capital expenditure* or as *revenue expenditure*

(a) purchase of vehicles

(b) rent paid on premises

(c) wages and salaries

(d) legal fees relating to the purchase of property

(e) redecoration of the office

(f) installation of air-conditioning in the office

(g) wages of own employees used to build extension to the stockroom

(h) installation and setting up of a new machine

Balancing the cash book and bank reconciliation

this chapter covers . . .

In previous chapters we have looked at the receipts side of the cash book (Chapter 7) and at the payments side (Chapter 14). In this chapter we see how cash book is totalled and balanced at the end of the week or month in order to give a figure for cash and bank balances.

We then see what to do when the bank statement is received:

– the comparison of individual items on the bank statement and in the bank columns of the cash book

– the identification of discrepancies

Using the discrepancies, a bank reconciliation statement can be prepared. This provides a link between the balance shown on the bank statement and the balance at bank shown in the cash book of the book-keeping system. The bank reconciliation statement forms part of the check and control process of book-keeping – the regular checking of the bank statement balance against the cash book balance.

PERFORMANCE CRITERIA COVERED

unit 30: INTRODUCTORY ACCOUNTING

element 30.3

process petty cash, reconcile accounts and prepare an initial trial balance

E   *update cash book from source documents*

F   *balance cash book and compare with bank statement*

G   *reconcile bank statement*

BALANCING THE CASH BOOK

The cash book is the book of prime entry and the ledger for cash and bank transactions and, like other accounts, needs to be balanced at regular intervals. (Note that the cash book can, alternatively, be represented in the main ledger by a cash control account – see page 387.)

As we have seen in earlier chapters, the debit (receipts) and credit (payments) sides of the cash book include columns for bank transactions; other columns – such as discount allowed, discount received, Value Added Tax and cash transactions – may also be incorporated.

Remember that a business adapts its cash book layout to suit its needs. If a business does not deal much in cash, it is unlikely to have a cash column. This will help the book-keeper, as it will make balancing much easier!

Shown below and on the top of the next page are the receipts and payments pages from a sample cash book with columns for bank, cash, and discounts allowed and received. If you want to refresh your memory about these two sides of the cash book, they are covered in Chapters 7 and 14 respectively.

In handwritten book-keeping systems the debit (receipts) side forms the left-hand page of cash book, while the credit (payments) side is detailed on the right-hand page. If you look at the bottom of the next page you will see that the debit and credit columns can be put side-by-side to form the full cash book. In this illustration the columns are balanced after the week's transactions.

Debit		Cash Book: Receipts				CBR 24
Date	Details		Folio	Discount allowed	Cash	Bank
2007				£	£	£
5 Apr	Balances brought down				300	1,550
5 Apr	Sales		ML 4001/ 2200		235	
6 Apr	S Wright		SL 295	2		98
6 Apr	Peter Singh Limited (CR)		SL 147			205
7 Apr	J Jones		SL 86	4		76
7 Apr	Sales		ML 4001/ 2200			94
9 Apr	D Whiteman Limited		SL 278	3		45
9 Apr	Natasha Lloyd and Co (SO)		SL 121			110
				9	535	2,178

cash book: debit side

Credit	Cash Book: Payments					CBP 24
Date	Details		Folio	Discount received	Cash	Bank
2007				£	£	£
5 Apr	E Lee & Co	101261	PL 804			160
6 Apr	Hayes Limited	SO	PL 752			200
6 Apr	S Crane	101262	PL 610	5		145
7 Apr	Purchases		ML 5001/ 2200		94	
8 Apr	Purchases	101264	ML 5001/ 2200			282
9 Apr	S Ford		PL 698	5		70
				10	94	857

cash book: credit side

cash book: receipts side (debits)   **cash book: payments side (credits)**

Dr						Cash Book					Cr
Date	Details	Folio	Discount allowed	Cash	Bank	Date	Details	Folio	Discount received	Cash	Bank
2007			£	£	£	2007			£	£	£
5 Apr	Balances b/d			300	1,550	5 Apr	E Lee & Co				160
5 Apr	Sales			235		6 Apr	Hayes Ltd (SO)				200
6 Apr	S Wright		2		98	6 Apr	S Crane		5		145
6 Apr	Peter Singh Ltd (CR)				205	7 Apr	Purchases			94	
						8 Apr	Purchases				282
7 Apr	J Jones		4		76	9 Apr	S Ford		5		70
7 Apr	Sales				94						
9 Apr	D Whiteman Ltd		3		45						
9 Apr	Natasha Lloyd and Co (SO)				110						
			9	535	2,178				10	94	857
						11 Apr	Balances c/d			441	1,321
			9	535	2,178				10	535	2,178
12 Apr	Balances b/d			441	1,321						

full cash book: debit and credit sides combined

Note that in the 'side-by-side' cash book at the bottom of the previous page, details from the folio columns and cheque numbers have not been shown (they are shown in the separate debit and credit sections seen earlier).

The cash and bank columns are balanced using the sub-totals, as follows:

- for the cash columns compare the two subtotals, ie £535 and £94

- deduct the lower figure from the higher (here payments from receipts) to give the balance of cash remaining (£535 – £94 = £441)

- the higher total is recorded at the bottom of both cash columns in a totals 'box' (£535)

- the balance of cash remaining (£441) is entered as a balancing item above the totals box (on the credit side), and is brought down underneath the total on the debit side as the opening balance for next week (£441)

- the two bank columns are dealt with in the same way (£2,178 – £857 = £1,321)

Notice that, in the cash book shown above, the cash and bank balances have been brought down on the debit side. It may happen that the balance at bank is brought down on the credit side: this occurs when payments exceed receipts, and indicates a bank overdraft. It is very important to appreciate that the bank columns of the cash book represent the firm's own records of bank transactions and the balance at bank – the bank statement may well show different figures (see the next page).

At the end of the month, each discount column is totalled separately – no attempt should be made to balance them. At this point, amounts recorded in the columns and the totals are not part of the double-entry system. However, the two totals are transferred to the double-entry system as follows:

- the total on the debit side (£9 in the example above) is debited to discount allowed account in the main ledger (see Chapter 7, page 138)

- the total on the credit side (£10 in the example) is credited to discount received account, also in the main ledger (see Chapter 14, page 282)

The opposite book-keeping entries will have been entered already in the debtors' and creditors' accounts respectively – see Chapters 7 and 14.

CHECKING THE CASH BOOK

As the cash book forms such an integral part of a firm's book-keeping system, it is essential that balances are calculated correctly at regular intervals, eg weekly or monthly – depending on the needs of the business. How can the cash book be checked for accuracy?

cash columns

To check the cash columns is easy. It is simply a matter of counting the cash in the cash till or box, and agreeing it with the balance shown by the cash book. In the example above there should be £441 in the firm's cash till at 11 April 2007. If the cash cannot be agreed in this way, the difference needs to be investigated urgently and any discrepancy referred to the accounts supervisor or other appropriate person.

bank columns

How are these to be checked? We could, perhaps, enquire at the bank and ask for the balance at the end of each week or month, or we could arrange for a bank statement to be sent to us at the end of each week or month. However, the balance of the account at the bank may well not agree with that shown by the bank columns of the cash book.

The reasons why the cash book and bank statement may differ are because there are:

- timing differences caused by
  - unpresented cheques
  - outstanding lodgements
- updating items for the cash book

We will now look at these two differences in the section which follows.

RECEIVING THE BANK STATEMENT

When the bank statement is received it must be matched or compared with the cash book in order to identify any differences or discrepancies. These are:

- timing differences
- updating items for the cash book

timing differences

The two main timing differences or discrepancies between the bank columns of the cash book and the bank statement are:

- *unpresented cheques*, ie cheques drawn, not yet recorded on the bank statement
- *outstanding lodgements*, ie amounts paid into the bank, not yet recorded on the bank statement

The first of these – unpresented cheques – is caused because, when a cheque is written out, it is immediately entered on the payments side of the cash book, even though it may be some days before the cheque passes through the bank clearing system and is recorded on the bank statement. Therefore, for a few days at least, the cash book shows a lower balance than the bank statement in respect of this cheque. When the cheque is recorded on the bank statement, the difference will disappear. We have looked at only one cheque here, but a business will often be issuing many cheques each day, and the difference between the cash book balance and the bank statement balance may be considerable.

With the second timing difference – outstanding lodgements – the firm's cashier will record a receipt in the cash book as he or she prepares the bank paying-in slip. However, the receipt may not be recorded by the bank on the bank statement for a day or so, particularly if it is paid in late in the day (when the bank will put it into the next day's work), or if it is paid in at a bank branch other than the one at which the account is maintained. Until the receipt is recorded by the bank the cash book will show a higher bank account balance than the bank statement. Once the receipt is entered on the bank statement, the difference will disappear.

For these two timing differences the cash book must *not be altered* because, as we have seen, they will correct themselves on the bank statement as time goes by.

updating the cash book

Besides the timing differences described above, there may be other discrepancies between the bank columns of the cash book and the bank statement, and *these do need to be entered* in the cash book to bring it up-to-date. For example, the bank might make an automatic standing order payment on behalf of a business – such an item is correctly debited by the bank, and it might be that the bank statement acts as a reminder to the business cashier of the payment: it should then be entered in the cash book.

Examples of items that show in the bank statement and need to be entered in the cash book include:

receipts

- standing order and BACS (Bankers' Automated Clearing Services) receipts credited by the bank, eg payments from debtors (customers)

- bank giro credit (credit transfer) amounts received by the bank, eg payments from debtors (customers)

- dividend amounts received by the bank

- interest credited by the bank

payments

- standing order and direct debit payments

- bank charges and interest

- unpaid cheques debited by the bank (ie cheques from debtors paid in by the business which have 'bounced' and are returned by the bank marked 'refer to drawer')

For each of these items, the cashier needs to check to see if they have been entered in the cash book; if not, they need to be recorded (provided that the bank has not made an error). If the bank has made an error, it must be notified as soon as possible and the incorrect transactions reversed by the bank in its own accounting records.

THE BANK RECONCILIATION STATEMENT

This forms the link between the balances shown in the bank statement and the cash book.

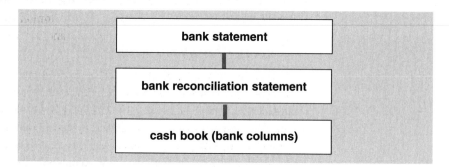

Upon receipt of a bank statement, reconciliation of the two balances is carried out in the following way:

- tick off the items that appear in both cash book and bank statement

- the unticked items on the bank statement are entered into the bank columns of the cash book to bring it up-to-date (provided none are errors made by the bank)

- the bank columns of the cash book are now balanced to find the revised figure

- the remaining unticked items from the cash book will be the timing differences

- the timing differences are used to prepare the bank reconciliation statement, which takes the following format (with example figures):

XYZ TRADING LIMITED
Bank Reconciliation Statement as at 31 October 2007

		£	£
Balance at bank as per bank statement			245
Less: unpresented cheques *(Receipt) +*			
J Lewis	cheque no 0012378	60	
ABC Limited	cheque no 0012392	100	
Eastern Oil Company	cheque no 0012407	80	
			240
			5
Add: outstanding lodgements *(Payment) —*		220	
		300	
			520
Balance at bank as per cash book			525

notes:

- The layout shown above starts from the bank statement balance, and works towards the cash book balance. A common variation of this layout is to start with the cash book balance and to work towards the bank statement balance (see page 369).
- If a bank overdraft is involved, brackets should be used around the numbers to indicate this for the bank statement or cash book balance. The timing differences are still added or deducted, as appropriate.
- Once the bank reconciliation statement agrees, it should be filed because it proves that the bank statement and cash book were reconciled at a particular date. If, next time it is prepared, it fails to agree, the previous statement is proof that reconciliation was reached at that time.

Case Study

BANK RECONCILIATION STATEMENT

situation

The cashier of Severn Trading Company has written up the firm's cash book for the month of February 2007, as shown on the next page.

Note that the cheque number is shown against payments.

Dr					Cash Book			Cr
Date 2007	Details	Cash £	Bank £	Date 2007	Details	Cash £	Bank £	
2 Feb	Balances b/d	250.75	1,340.50	3 Feb	Appleton Ltd 123456		675.25	
6 Feb	A Abbott		208.50	5 Feb	Wages	58.60		
10 Feb	Sales	145.25		12 Feb	Rent 123457		125.00	
16 Feb	Sales		278.30	17 Feb	D Smith & Co 123458		421.80	
20 Feb	Sales	204.35		24 Feb	Stationery	75.50		
23 Feb	D Richards Ltd		162.30	25 Feb	G Christie 123459		797.55	
26 Feb	Sales		353.95		Balances c/d	466.25	586.25	
27 Feb	P Paul Ltd		262.30					
		600.35	2,605.85			600.35	2,605.85	
	Balances b/d	466.25	586.25					

The cash balance of £466.25 shown by the cash columns at the month-end has been agreed with the cash held in the firm's cash box. The bank statement for February 2007 has just been received:

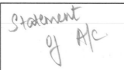

National Bank plc

Branch ..Bartown...............

TITLE OF ACCOUNT ....Severn Trading Company...................

ACCOUNT NUMBER ....67812318.................................

STATEMENT NUMBER 45

DATE	PARTICULARS	PAYMENTS £	RECEIPTS £	BALANCE £
2007				
2 Feb	Balance brought forward			1340.50 Cr
7 Feb	Credit		208.50	1549.00 Cr
10 Feb	Cheque 123456	675.25		873.75 Cr
17 Feb	Credit		278.30	1152.05 Cr
17 Feb	Cheque 123457	125.00		1027.05 Cr
24 Feb	Credit		162.30	1189.35 Cr
24 Feb	BACS J Jarvis Ltd		100.00	1289.35 Cr
26 Feb	Cheque 123458	421.80		867.55 Cr
26 Feb	Direct debit A-Z Finance	150.00		717.55 Cr
27 Feb	Credit		353.95	1071.50 Cr
27 Feb	Bank charges	10.00		1061.50 Cr

solution

Note that the bank statement is prepared from the bank's viewpoint: thus a credit balance shows that the customer is a creditor of the bank, ie the bank owes the balance to the customer. In the customer's own cash book, the bank is shown as a debit balance, ie an asset.

As the month-end balance at bank shown by the cash book, £586.25, is not the same as that shown by the bank statement, £1,061.50, it is necessary to compare individual items in the cash book and on the bank statement for accuracy. The steps are:

1   Tick off the items that appear in both cash book and bank statement.
2   The unticked items on the bank statement are entered into the bank columns of the cash book to bring it up-to-date. These are:
   *   receipt   24 Feb   BACS credit, J Jarvis Limited £100.00
   *   payments   26 Feb   Direct debit, A-Z Finance £150.00
                    27 Feb   Bank Charges, £10.00
In double-entry book-keeping, the other part of the transaction will need to be recorded in the accounts.

3   The cash book is now balanced to find the revised balance:

Dr			Cash Book (bank columns)		Cr
2007		£	2007		
	Balance b/d	586.25	26 Feb	A-Z Finance	150.00
24 Feb	J Jarvis Ltd	100.00	27 Feb	Bank Charges	10.00
			28 Feb	Balance c/d	526.25
		686.25			686.25
1 Mar	Balance b/d	526.25			

4   The remaining unticked items from the cash book are:

   *   receipt 27 Feb – P Paul Limited £262.30

   *   payment 25 Feb – G Christie (cheque no 123459) £797.55

These items are timing differences, which should appear on next month's bank statement. They will be used in the bank reconciliation statement.

5   The bank reconciliation statement is now prepared, starting with the bank statement balance of £1,061.50 and using the unticked items from the cash book which were noted above.

SEVERN TRADING COMPANY	
Bank Reconciliation Statement as at 28 February 2007	
	£
Balance at bank as per bank statement	1,061.50
Less: unpresented cheque, no 123459	797.55
	263.95
Add: outstanding lodgement, P Paul Limited	262.30
Balance at bank as per cash book	526.25

This statement has been produced which starts with the bank statement balance, and finishes with the amended balance from the cash book, ie the two figures are reconciled.

notes on the case study

- The *unpresented cheque* is deducted from the bank statement balance because, until it is recorded by the bank, the bank statement shows a higher balance than the cash book.

- The *outstanding lodgement* is added to the bank statement balance because, until it is recorded by the bank, the bank statement shows a lower balance than the cash book.

PREPARING A BANK RECONCILIATION STATEMENT

In order to help you with the Student Activities at the end of the chapter, here is a step-by-step summary of the procedure. Reconciliation of the bank statement balance with that shown in the cash book should be carried out in the following way:

1 From the bank columns of the cash book tick off, in both cash book and bank statement, the receipts that appear in both.

2 From the bank columns of the cash book tick off, in both cash book and bank statement, the payments that appear in both.

3 Identify the items that are unticked on the bank statement and enter them in the cash book on the debit or credit side, as appropriate. (If, however, the bank has made a mistake and debited or credited an amount in error, this should not be entered in the cash book, but should be notified to the bank for them to make the correction. The amount will need to be entered on the bank reconciliation statement.)

4 The bank columns of the cash book are now balanced to find the up-to-date balance.

5 Start the bank reconciliation statement with the final balance figure shown on the bank statement.

6 In the bank reconciliation statement *deduct* the unticked payments shown in the cash book – these will be unpresented cheques.

7 In the bank reconciliation statement, *add* the unticked receipts shown in the cash book – these are outstanding lodgements.

8 The resultant money amount on the bank reconciliation statement is the balance at bank as per the cash book.

The layout which is often used for the bank reconciliation statement is that shown on page 365. The layout starts with the bank statement balance and finishes with the cash book balance. However, there is no reason why it should not commence with the cash book balance and finish with the bank statement balance: with this layout it is necessary to:

- *add* unpresented cheques
- *deduct* outstanding lodgements

The bank reconciliation statement of Severn Trading Company (see page 367) would then appear as:

SEVERN TRADING COMPANY
Bank Reconciliation Statement as at 28 February 2007

	£
Balance at bank as per cash book	526.25
Add: unpresented cheque, no 123459	797.55
	1,323.80
Less: outstanding lodgement, P Paul Limited	262.30
Balance at bank as per bank statement	1,061.50

DEALING WITH UNUSUAL ITEMS ON BANK STATEMENTS

The following are some of the unusual features that may occur on bank statements. As with other accounting discrepancies, where they cannot be resolved they should be referred to a supervisor for guidance.

out-of-date cheques

These are cheques that are more than six months old. The bank will not pay such cheques, so they can be written back in the cash book, ie debit cash book (and credit the other double-entry account involved).

returned cheques

A cheque received by a business is entered as a receipt in the cash book and then paid into the bank, but it *may be returned* by the drawer's (issuer's) bank to the payee's bank because:

- the drawer (the issuer) has stopped it
- the drawer has no money (the cheque may be returned 'refer to drawer')
  – ie the cheque has 'bounced'

370 introductory accounting tutorial

A cheque returned in this way should be entered in the book-keeping system:

- as a payment in the cash book on the *credit* side
- as a *debit* to the account of the drawer of the cheque in the subsidiary (sales) ledger (if it is a credit sale), and also a *debit* to sales ledger control account

On the other hand, if the business itself stops a cheque, the cheque drawn by the business will have been entered as a payment in the cash book (a *credit*). It should now be entered as

- a receipt on the *debit* side
- a *credit to* the account of the payee, most probably in the subsidiary (purchases) ledger (if it is a credit purchase), and also a *credit* to purchases ledger control account

bank errors

Errors made by the bank can include:

- A cheque debited to the bank account which has not been drawn by the business – look for a cheque number on the bank statement that is different from the current cheque series: care, though, as it could be a cheque from an old cheque book.
- A BACS payment (or other credit) shown on the bank statement for which the business is not the correct recipient. If in doubt, the bank will be able to give further details of the sender of the credit.
- Standing orders and direct debits paid at the wrong time or for the wrong amounts. A copy of all standing order and direct debit mandates sent to the bank should be kept by the business for reference purposes.

When an error is found, it should be queried immediately with the bank. The item and amount should not be entered in the firm's cash book until the issue has been resolved.

bank charges and interest

From time-to-time the bank will debit business customers' accounts with an amount for:

- service charges, ie the cost of operating the bank account
- interest, ie the borrowing cost when the business is overdrawn

Banks usually notify customers in writing before debiting the account.

IMPORTANCE OF BANK RECONCILIATION STATEMENTS

1   A bank reconciliation statement forms an important part of the check and control process of the accounting system. When you prepare it the transactions in the bank columns of the cash book are compared with those recorded on the bank statement. In this way, any errors in the cash book or bank statement will be found and can be corrected (or advised to the bank, if the bank statement is wrong).

2   The bank statement is an independent accounting record, therefore it will assist in deterring fraud by providing a means of verifying the cash book balance.

3   By writing the cash book up-to-date, the business has an amended figure for the bank balance to be shown in the trial balance (see Chapter 20).

4   It is good business practice to prepare a bank reconciliation statement each time a bank statement is received. The reconciliation statement should be prepared as quickly as possible so that any discrepancies – either with the bank statement or in the firm's cash book – can be resolved. Many firms will specify to their accounting staff the timescales for preparing bank reconciliation statements – as a guideline, if the bank statement is received weekly, then the reconciliation statement should be prepared within five working days.

Chapter Summary

- Cash book is balanced at regular intervals – often at the month-end – in order to give a figure for cash and bank balances.

- A bank reconciliation statement is used as part of the check and control process of the accounting system to agree the balance shown by the bank statement with that shown by the bank columns of the cash book.

- Certain differences between the two are timing differences. The main timing differences are:
  - unpresented cheques
  - outstanding lodgements

  These differences will be corrected by time and, most probably, will be recorded on the next bank statement.

- Certain differences appearing on the bank statement need to be entered in the cash book to bring it up-to-date. These include:

Receipts   – standing order and BACS receipts credited by the bank

– bank giro credit amounts received by the bank

– dividend amounts received by the bank

– interest credited by the bank

Payments   – standing order and direct debit payments

– bank charges and interest

– unpaid cheques debited by the bank

- The bank reconciliation statement makes use of the timing differences.

- Once prepared, a bank reconciliation statement is proof that the bank statement and the cash book (bank columns) were agreed at a particular date.

Key Terms

balance of account	the total of the account to date
bank reconciliation statement	forms the link between the balances shown in the bank statement and the cash book
timing differences	discrepancies between the bank statement and the cash book that will be corrected over time, such as unpresented cheques and outstanding lodgements
unpresented cheques	cheques drawn, but not yet recorded on the bank statement
outstanding lodgements	amounts paid into the bank, but not yet recorded on the bank statement

Student Activities

18.1 The cashier of the company where you work as an accounts assistant has asked you to balance the cash book at 31 August. You are aware that the company has a bank overdraft facility of £2,500.

The cash book is as follows:

Dr											Cr
						Cash Book					
Date	Details	Folio	Discount allowed	Cash	Bank	Date	Details	Folio	Discount received	Cash	Bank
2007			£	£	£	2007			£	£	£
1 Aug	Balances b/d			325	925	6 Aug	Crane & Co		35		845
4 Aug	S Quesne		2		98	12 Aug	Wages			275	
17 Aug	J Ahmed		4	76		16 Aug	T Lewis		15		285
23 Aug	D Lloyd		3		45	27 Aug	S Ford		5	70	

You are to:

- balance the cash book at 31 August 2007 and bring down the balances on 1 September

- explain the meaning of the cash and bank balances brought down in the cash book on 1 September

18.2 When preparing a bank reconciliation statement, which one of the following is a timing difference?

(a) unpresented cheques

(b) direct debit payments

(c) bank charges and interest

(d) BACS receipts

Answer (a) or (b) or (c) or (d)

less

18.3 A firm's bank statement shows a balance of £400. Unpresented cheques total £350; outstanding lodgements total £200. What is the balance at bank shown by the cash book?

(a) £100

(b) £200

(c) £250 *C*

(d) £400

Answer (a) or (b) or (c) or (d)

18.4 The bank columns of Tom Reid's cash book for December 2007 are as follows:

2007	Receipts		£	2007	Payments		£
1 Dec	Balance b/d		280	9 Dec	W Smith	345123	40
13 Dec	P Jones		30	13 Dec	Rent	345124	50
17 Dec	H Homer		72	16 Dec	Wages	345125	85
29 Dec	J Hill		13	20 Dec	B Kay	345126	20
				31 Dec	Balance c/d		200
			395				395

He then received his bank statement which showed the following transactions for December 2007:

BANK STATEMENT		Payments £	Receipts £	Balance £
2007				
1 Dec	Balance brought forward			280 CR
13 Dec	Credit		30	310 CR
15 Dec	Cheque no 345123	40		270 CR
17 Dec	Cheque no 345124	50		220 CR
22 Dec	Credit		72	292 CR
23 Dec	Cheque no 345125	85		207 CR

You are to prepare a bank reconciliation statement which agrees the bank statement balance with the cash book balance.

18.5 The bank columns of P Gerrard's cash book for January 2007 are as follows:

2007	Receipts	£	2007	Payments		£
1 Jan	Balance b/d	800.50	2 Jan	A Arthur Ltd	001351	100.00
6 Jan	J Baker	495.60	9 Jan	C Curtis	001352	398.50
30 Jan	G Shotton Ltd	335.75	13 Jan	Donald & Co	001353	229.70
			14 Jan	Bryant & Sons	001354	312.00
			23 Jan	P Reid	001355	176.50

He received his bank statement which showed the following transactions for January 2007:

BANK STATEMENT		Payments	Receipts	Balance
2007		£	£	£
1 Jan	Balance brought forward			800.50 CR
6 Jan	Cheque no 001351	100.00		700.50 CR
6 Jan	Credit		495.60	1,196.10 CR
13 Jan	BACS credit: T K Supplies		716.50	1,912.60 CR
20 Jan	Cheque no 001352	398.50		1,514.10 CR
23 Jan	Direct debit: Omni Finance	207.95		1,306.15 CR
26 Jan	Cheque no 001353	229.70		1,076.45 CR

You are to:

(a) check the items on the bank statement against the items in the cash book and update the cash book accordingly; total the cash book and show the balance carried down at 31 January 2007

(b) prepare a bank reconciliation statement at 31 January 2007 which agrees the bank statement balance with the cash book balance

18.6 The bank columns of Jane Doyle's cash book for May 2007 are as follows:

2007	Receipts	£	2007	Payments		£
1 May	Balance b/d	300	3 May	P Stone	867714	28
7 May	Cash	162	14 May	Alpha Ltd	867715	50
17 May	C Brewster	89	28 May	E Deakin	867716	110
27 May	Cash	60				
28 May	Cash	40				

She received her bank statement which showed the following transactions for May 2007:

BANK STATEMENT		Payments	Receipts	Balance
2007		£	£	£
1 May	Balance brought forward			300 CR
5 May	Cheque no 867714	28		272 CR
7 May	Credit		162	434 CR
17 May	Standing order: A-Z Insurance	25		409 CR
19 May	Credit		89	498 CR
20 May	Cheque no 867715	50		448 CR
26 May	Credit		60	508 CR
31 May	Bank Charges	10		498 CR

You are to:

(a)   write the cash book up-to-date at 31 May 2007, and show the balance carried down

(b)   prepare a bank reconciliation statement at 31 May 2007 which agrees the bank statement balance with the cash book balance

18.7 On 4 June Milestone Motors received a bank statement which showed the following transactions for May 2007:

BANK STATEMENT		Paid out	Paid in	Balance
2007		£	£	£
1 May	Balance brought forward			3,652 C
10 May	Cheque no 451762	751		2,901 C
11 May	Cheque no 451763	268		2,633 C
13 May	Cheque no 451765	1,045		1,588 C
14 May	BACS credit: Perran Taxis		2,596	4,184 C
18 May	Direct debit: Wyvern Council	198		3,986 C
20 May	Direct debit: A1 Insurance	1,005		2,981 C
25 May	Direct debit: Okaro and Company	254		2,727 C
25 May	Bank charges	20		2,707 C
D = Debit C = Credit				

The cash book of Milestone Motors as at 31 May 2007 is shown below:

CASH BOOK

Date	Details	Bank	Date	Cheque no	Details	Bank
2007		£	2007			£
1 May	Balance b/f	3,652	4 May	451762	Smith and Company	751
26 May	J Ackland	832	4 May	451763	Bryant Limited	268
28 May	Stamp Limited	1,119	7 May	451764	Curtis Cars	1,895
			7 May	451765	Parts Supplies	1,045

You are to:

(a)   check the items on the bank statement against the items in the cash book

(b)   update the cash book as needed

(c)   total the cash book and show clearly the balance carried down at 31 May and brought down at 1 June

(d)   prepare a bank reconciliation statement at 31 May 2007 which agrees the bank statement balance with the cash book balance

Using the journal and reconciling control accounts

The journal is the book of prime entry for non-regular transactions, eg purchase of fixed assets on credit, correction of errors, writing off bad debts. The journal – like the other day books (journals) that we have seen – is used to list transactions before they are entered into the double-entry system.

We have already seen how accounts are totalled and balanced at regular intervals – this is an important part of the process towards producing an initial trial balance, which provides a check on the double-entry book-keeping.

As a part of the checking process, we focus in this chapter on the use of control accounts – where a main ledger account controls a number of subsidiary accounts. We review the use of sales ledger and purchases ledger control accounts, petty cash control account, and cash control account. The reconciliation of the control account with the total of the subsidiary ledger provides an important check of the book-keeping process.

PERFORMANCE CRITERIA COVERED

unit 30: INTRODUCTORY ACCOUNTING

element 30.3

process petty cash, reconcile accounts and prepare an initial trial balance

C   *make adjustments through the journal*

D   *reconcile sales and purchase ledger control accounts with subsidiary ledgers*

USE OF THE JOURNAL

The journal completes the accounting system by providing the book of prime entry for non-regular transactions which are not recorded in any other book of prime entry. The categories of such non-regular transactions include:

- opening entries
- purchase and sale of fixed assets on credit
- correction of errors
- other non-regular transactions or adjustments

The reasons for using a journal are:

- to provide a book of prime entry for non-regular transactions
- to eliminate the need for remembering why non-regular transactions were put through the accounts – the journal acts as a notebook
- to reduce the risk of fraud, by making it difficult for unauthorised transactions to be entered in the accounting system
- to reduce the risk of errors, by listing the transactions that are to be put into the double-entry accounts
- to ensure that entries can be traced back to an authorised prime document, providing an audit trail for non-regular transactions (note that documentation is stored securely for future reference, but only for access to authorised personnel, in order to maintain confidentiality)

THE JOURNAL – A BOOK OF PRIME ENTRY

The journal is a book of prime entry; it is not, therefore, part of the double-entry book-keeping system. The journal is used to list the transactions that are to be put through the accounts. The accounting system for non-regular transactions is as follows:

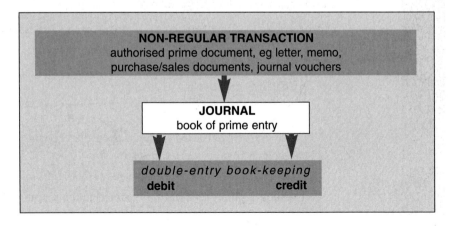

Look at the way the journal is set out with a sample transaction, and then read the notes that follow:

Date	Details	Folio	Dr	Cr
2007			£	£
1 Jul	Bank account	CBR	20,000	
	Capital account	ML		20,000
	Opening capital introduced			

Notes:

- journal entries are prepared from authorised prime (source) documents – which are stored securely for possible future reference
- the names of the accounts to be debited and credited in the book-keeping system are written in the details column; it is customary to show the debit transaction first
- the money amount of each debit and credit is stated in the appropriate column
- the folio column cross-references to the division of the ledger where each account is found (it can also include an account number)
- a journal entry always balances, ie debit and credit entries are for the same amount or total
- it is usual to include a brief narrative explaining why the transaction is being carried out, and making reference to the prime document whenever possible (in Skills Tests and Examinations you should always include a narrative unless specifically told otherwise)
- each journal entry is complete in itself and is ruled off to separate it from the next entry

Remember that, when a business uses control accounts which are incorporated into the double-entry accounts, the transactions from the journal involving sales ledger and purchases ledger must be recorded in the respective control accounts *and* in the subsidiary accounts for debtors or creditors.

OPENING ENTRIES

These are the transactions which open the accounts of a new business. For example, a first business transaction is:

1 Jan 2007 Started in business with £10,000 in the bank

This non-regular transaction is entered in the journal as follows:

Date	Details	Folio	Dr	Cr
2007			£	£
1 Jan	Bank account	CBR	10,000	
	Capital account	ML		10,000
	Opening capital introduced			

After the journal entry has been made, the transaction can be recorded in the double-entry accounts.

Here is another opening entries transaction to be recorded in the journal:

1 Feb 2007   Started in business with cash £100, bank £5,000, stock £1,000, machinery £2,500, creditors £850

The journal entry is:

Date	Details	Folio	Dr	Cr
2007			£	£
1 Feb	Cash account	CBR	100	
	Bank account	CBR	5,000	
	Stock account	ML	1,000	
	Machinery account	ML	2,500	
	Purchases ledger control account	ML		850
	Capital account*	ML		7,750
			8,600	8,600
	Assets and liabilities			
	at the start of business			

* Assets – liabilities = capital

Notes:

- capital is, in this example, the balancing figure, ie assets minus liabilities
- the journal is the book of prime entry for all opening entries, including cash and bank; however the normal book of prime entry for other cash/bank transactions is the cash book
- the amounts for the journal entry will now need to be recorded in the double-entry accounts, and in the subsidiary (purchases) ledger

PURCHASE AND SALE OF FIXED ASSETS ON CREDIT

The purchase and sale of fixed assets are non-regular business transactions which are recorded in the journal as the book of prime entry. Only *credit* transactions are entered in the journal (because cash/bank transactions are recorded in the cash book as the book of prime entry). However, a business (or an Examination question) may choose to journalise cash entries: strictly, though, this is incorrect as two books of prime entry are being used.

15 Apr 2007   Bought a machine for £1,000 plus VAT (at 17.5%) on credit from Machinery Supplies Limited, purchase order no 2341.

Date	Details	Folio	Dr	Cr
2007			£	£
15 Apr	Machinery account	ML	1,000	
	VAT account	ML	175	
	Purchases ledger control account*	ML		1,175
	Purchase of machine from creditor, Machinery Supplies Limited: order 2341		1,175	1,175

20 May 2007   Car sold for £2,500 on credit to Wyvern Motors Limited (no VAT chargeable)..

Date	Details	Folio	Dr	Cr
2007			£	£
20 May	Sales ledger control account*	ML	2,500	
	Car account	ML		2,500
	Sale of car, registration Y787 KAB, to debtor Wyvern Motors Limited			

* Instead of entering the above two transactions in the subsidiary purchases and sales ledgers, an alternative treatment would be to open main ledger accounts for the creditor and the debtor. This would avoid confusion with trade creditors and trade debtors in the subsidiary ledgers.

OTHER TRANSFERS

Any other non-regular transactions need to be recorded in the journal. Examples of such transactions include:

* correction of errors – this topic is covered in the next chapter.
* bad debts written off
* expenses charged to owner's drawings
* goods for the owner's use

bad debts written off

We have already seen, in Chapter 17, the double-entry book-keeping entries to write off a debtor's account:

- *debit* bad debts written off account
- *debit* Value Added Tax account (if VAT relief is available)
- *credit* sales ledger control account (and credit the account of the debtor in the subsidiary ledger)

15 Dec 2007   *Write off the account of Don's Diner which has a balance of £47, as a bad debt (VAT relief is available)*

The journal entry is:

Date	Details	Folio	Dr	Cr
2007			£	£
15 Dec	Bad debts written off account	ML	40	
	Value Added Tax account	ML	7	
	Sales ledger control account	ML		47
			47	47
	Balance of subsidiary (sales) ledger account of Don's Diner written off as a bad debt, as per memo from accounts supervisor dated 10 December 2007			

expenses charged to the owner's drawings

Sometimes the owner of a business uses business facilities for private use, eg telephone, or car. The owner will agree that part of the expense shall be charged to him or her as drawings, while the other part represents a business expense. The book-keeping entry to record the adjustment is:

- *debit* drawings account
- *credit* expense account, eg telephone

31 Dec 2007   *The balance of telephone account is £600; of this, one-quarter is the estimated cost of the owner's private usage*

The journal entry to show the transfer of private usage is:

Date	Details	Folio	Dr	Cr
2007			£	£
31 Dec	Drawings account	ML	150	
	Telephone account	ML		150
	Transfer of private use to drawings account			

goods for the owner's use

When the owner of a business takes some of the goods in which the business trades for his or her own use, the double-entry book-keeping is:

– *debit* drawings account
– *credit* purchases account

15 Oct 2007   Owner of the business takes goods for own use, £105

The journal entry is:

Date	Details	Folio	Dr	Cr
2007			£	£
15 Oct	Drawings account	ML	105	
	Purchases account	ML		105
	Goods taken for owner's use			

Note: where a business is VAT-registered, VAT must be accounted for on goods taken by the owner.

BALANCING ACCOUNTS

The topic of balancing accounts has been studied already in Chapters 4 and 11. We have seen that accounts are totalled and balanced at regular intervals – often at the end of each month – in order to show the amounts, for example:

• owing to each creditor
• owing by each debtor
• of sales
• of purchases
• of sales returns
• of purchases returns
• of expenses incurred by the business or organisation
• of fixed assets – eg premises, machinery – owned by the business or organisation
• of capital and drawings of the owner of the business
• of other liabilities, eg loans

At this point you may wish to look again at the processes involved in balancing accounts. These are covered on pages 69-72 and 219-221. Remember that, when accounts are produced using a computer accounting system, there is no need to balance each account – the balance is calculated automatically after each transaction.

Balancing accounts is an important part of the process towards producing an initial trial balance (see Chapter 20). The initial trial balance uses the balances of accounts in order to provide a check on the double-entry book-keeping. In this chapter we will see how this checking process can be started by focusing on the reconciliation of control accounts with the totals of the balances in the subsidiary ledger.

CONTROL ACCOUNTS

The use of control accounts has been incorporated into all but the earliest transactions we have seen for recording receipts and payments. The idea behind control accounts is that a main ledger account controls a number of subsidiary accounts. This is illustrated by the sales ledger control account, as follows:

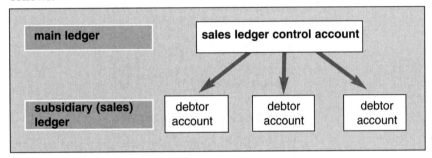

Clearly there can be almost any number of subsidiary accounts under a control account. However, if the number of subsidiary accounts was to become very large, it might be appropriate to divide the accounts between another (or more) control accounts, eg sales ledger control A-K, sales ledger control L-Z.

The principle of control accounts is that they record – usually in the form of totals – the amounts of transactions passing through the subsidiary accounts. For example, if sales for the week to three credit customers were £100, £200 and £300 the individual accounts in the subsidiary ledger will be debited with the separate amounts, while sales ledger control account will be debited with the total credit sales of £600. Taking this principle further, if the total of the opening balances for subsidiary accounts is known, together with the total of amounts increasing these balances, and the total of amounts decreasing these balances, then the total of the closing balances for the subsidiary accounts can be calculated. for example:

	£
Total of opening balances	50,000
Add increases	10,000
	60,000
Less decreases	12,000
Total of closing balances	48,000

TYPES OF CONTROL ACCOUNT

sales ledger control account

This control account has been studied already in Chapter 4 (pages 75-77). The diagram on the previous page shows the link between sales ledger control account in the main ledger and the debtors' accounts in the subsidiary (sales) ledger. An example of sales ledger control account is as follows:

NOHI Account

Dr				Sales Ledger Control Account			Cr
2007			£	2007			£
1 Jan	Balance b/d		500	31 Jan	Bank		443
31 Jan	Sales		700	31 Jan	Discount allowed		7
				31 Jan	Sales returns		70
				31 Jan	Balance c/d		680
			1,200				1,200
1 Feb	Balance b/d		680				

purchases ledger control account

This control account – which has been studied already in Chapter 11 (pages 221-223) – can be illustrated diagrammatically as follows:

Note the link between purchases ledger control account in the main ledger and the creditors accounts in the subsidiary (purchases) ledger. An example of purchases ledger control account is as follows:

Purchase
balance b/d

Dr			Purchases Ledger Control Account			Cr
2007		£	2007			£
31 Jan	Purchases returns	150	1 Jan	Balance b/d		1,000
31 Jan	Bank	594	31 Jan	Purchases		1,700
31 Jan	Discount received	6				
31 Jan	Balance c/d	1,950				
		2,700				2,700
			1 Feb	Balance b/d		1,950

petty cash control account

This control account – which has been explained already in Chapter 16 (pages 323-324) – can be illustrated diagrammatically as follows:

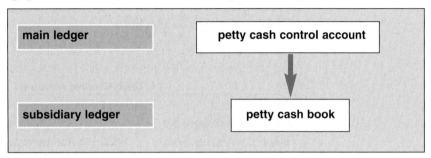

An example of a petty cash control account is as follows:

Dr			Petty Cash Control Account			Cr
2007		£	2007			£
5 Apr	Balance b/d	50.00	9 Apr	Petty cash book		30.75
9 Apr	Cash book	30.75	9 Apr	Balance c/d		50.00
		80.75				80.75
9 Apr	Balance b/d	50.00				

Note that, above, the credit entry on 9 April for £30.75 is the total for the period of payments (including VAT) made out of petty cash. The debit entry on 9 April for £30.75 reimburses the petty cashier from the cash book for the amount paid out, so restoring the float of petty cash to £50.00.

cash control account

This control account can be illustrated diagrammatically as follows:

Here the cash book is treated as a subsidiary ledger with a *cash control account* in the main ledger. The advantage is that cash book – the subsidiary ledger – will be reconciled with cash control account in the main ledger. With this method, errors should be found and corrected before a trial balance is prepared, as it is the balance of cash control account rather than the cash book totals that is used in the trial balance.

An example of a cash control account (using the figures from the cash book shown on page 360) is as follows:

Dr		£	Cash Control Account		Cr
2007		£	2007		£
5 Apr	Cash balance b/d	300	11 Apr	Cash payments for week	94
5 Apr	Bank balance b/d	1,550	11 Apr	Bank payments for week	857
11 Apr	Cash receipts for week	235	11 Apr	Cash balance c/d	441
11 Apr	Bank receipts for week	628	11 Apr	Bank balance c/d	1,321
		2,713			2,713
12 Apr	Cash balance b/d	441			
12 Apr	Bank balance b/d	1,321			

RECONCILING CONTROL ACCOUNTS

One of the advantages of using control accounts is that, for each control account in the main ledger, there are a number (often a large number) of accounts in the subsidiary ledger. Thus the main ledger is not cluttered up with the accounts of individual debtors and creditors – this is illustrated by the diagram below which shows four accounts in the main ledger representing several accounts in the subsidiary ledgers. (In practice, the subsidiary sales and purchases ledgers are likely to contain many more accounts than are shown here.)

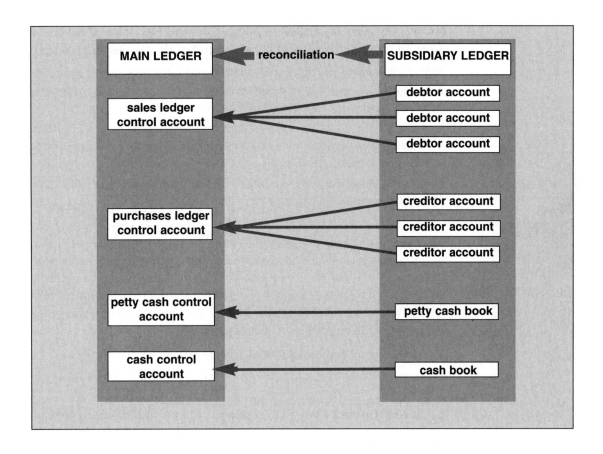

From time-to-time, the book-keeper is able to check that the balance of the control account is the same as the total of the balances of the individual subsidiary accounts which it controls. This reconciliation process is carried out by a listing similar to the following example:

Reconciliation of sales ledger control account		
	1 January 2007	*31 January 2007*
	£	£
A Ackroyd	100	150
B Barnes	200	200
C Cox	50	180
D Douglas	150	150
Sales ledger control account	500	680

The sales ledger control account illustrated earlier in this chapter (page 386) shows how the reconciliation has been made with the balance on the control account at the beginning and end of the month. It is for the user of the accounting system to decide how often to reconcile the control account with the subsidiary accounts – weekly, monthly, quarterly or annually.

Any discrepancy between control account and subsidiary ledger should be investigated immediately and the error(s) traced. Discrepancies for sales ledger and purchases ledger control accounts can include:

- errors in the double-entry book-keeping, particularly in the subsidiary ledger, eg transactions not recorded, transactions recorded on the wrong side of the subsidiary account

- errors in calculating or recording the balance, eg a discrepancy of £1,000 in the reconciliation might be caused by a balance of £500 being recorded as debit when it should in fact be credit

With petty cash control account (see pages 323-324), the main purpose of reconciliation is to ensure that the balance of the control account agrees with both a physical count of the cash and with the balance of the petty cash book. (Note that, between balancing dates, cash held plus amounts of petty cash vouchers should reconcile with the imprest amount – which will also be the balance showing on petty cash control account.)

Discrepancies for petty cash control account can include:

- errors in recording transactions, eg transactions not recorded, wrong amounts

- difference between the analysis columns and the total payments column, particularly where there are VAT calculations (does VAT plus the analysis column amount equal the total payment amount?)

- difference between the cash held and the balance of the petty cash book; if this cannot be resolved, it may be a case of theft, and should be reported promptly to the accounts supervisor

Where discrepancies and queries cannot be resolved, they should be referred to the accounts supervisor or other appropriate person.

Case Study

RECONCILING PURCHASES LEDGER CONTROL ACCOUNT: AGGIESURF LIMITED

situation

Aggiesurf Limited sells a range of high quality clothes and accessories which are popular for wear (on dry land) with both surfers and non-surfers. The company buys from manufacturers – some of which are abroad – and sells to specialist surfing shops and other retailers in the popular surfing areas, particularly the south west of England. You work as an accounts assistant for Aggiesurf Limited. Today the accounts supervisor has asked you to reconcile the purchases ledger control account with the total of the subsidiary (purchases) ledger accounts. The information which follows is available to you.

Entries recorded in the subsidiary (purchases) ledger in July 2007:

	£
Balance of creditors at 1 July 2007	47,100
Goods purchased on credit	26,325
Payments to creditors	29,650
Discount received	800
Goods returned to suppliers	1,300

The following balances were in the subsidiary (purchases) ledger at 31 July 2007:

	£	
Wyvern Manufacturing Company	9,150	credit
Clothes by Design Limited	8,975	credit
Mereford Textiles	12,320	credit
Lazydays and Company	4,680	credit
Beachwear Limited	500	debit*
Sunglass Manufacturing Company	2,890	credit
Carrick and Company	3,160	credit

Note that the balance of Beachwear Limited is debit

solution

The first thing to do is to prepare a purchases ledger control account for July 2007 from the details above. The account is balanced at 31 July to show the balance carried down to next month.

Dr			Purchases Ledger Control Account			Cr
2007		£	2007			£
31 Jul	Bank	29,650	1 Jul	Balance b/d		47,100
31 Jul	Discount received	800	31 Jul	Purchases		26,325
31 Jul	Purchases returns	1,300				
31 Jul	Balance c/d	41,675				
		73,425				73,425
			1 Aug	Balance b/d		41,675

Reconciliation of the purchases ledger control account with the total of the subsidiary ledger is as follows:

	£
Purchases ledger control account balance as at 31 July 2007	41,675
Total of subsidiary (purchases) ledger accounts at 31 July 2007*	40,675
Difference	1,000

* see previous page: £9,150 + £8,975 + £12,320 + £4,680 – £500 + £2,890 + £3,160

As a discrepancy of £1,000 has been identified, you must either resolve it or refer it to the appropriate person – here the accounts supervisor. It is possible that there has been an error in posting transactions to the accounts and the debit balance of £500 for Beachwear Limited may in fact be a credit balance – this needs to be investigated.

Chapter Summary

- The journal is used to list non-regular transactions.

- The journal is a book of prime entry – it is not a double-entry account.

- Journal entries are prepared from authorised prime documents, which are stored securely for possible future reference.

- The journal is used for:
  - opening entries
  - purchase and sale of fixed assets on credit
  - correction of errors
  - other transfers

- Accounts are totalled and balanced at regular intervals – an important part of the process towards producing an initial trial balance.

- The idea behind control accounts is that a main ledger account controls a number of subsidiary accounts.

- The main control accounts used in the accounting system are:
  - sales ledger control account
  - purchases ledger control account
  - petty cash control account
  - cash control account

- At regular intervals control accounts are reconciled with the totals of the balances in the subsidiary ledger – any discrepancy should be investigated immediately and the error(s) traced.

Key Terms		
	journal	the book of prime entry for non-regular transactions
	opening entries	the transactions which open the accounts of a new business
	goods for the owner's use	goods taken by the owner of a business for personal use
	sales ledger control account	main ledger account which controls the subsidiary (sales) ledger
	purchases ledger control account	main ledger account which controls the subsidiary (purchases) ledger
	petty cash control account	main ledger account which controls the petty cash book
	cash control account	main ledger account which controls the cash book
	reconciliation of control accounts	process of agreeing the balance of the control account with the total of the balances in the subsidiary ledger

Student Activities

19.1 Which one of the following will not be recorded in the journal?

(a) credit purchase of a fixed asset

(b) cash sale of goods

(c) write off of a bad debt

(d) expenses charged to owner's drawings

Answer (a) or (b) or (c) or (d)

19.2 Which business transaction goes with which book of prime entry?

business transaction	book of prime entry
• credit sale of a fixed asset (1)	• petty cash book (7)
• credit purchase of goods from a supplier (2)	• sales day book (6)
• returned credit purchases to the supplier (3)	• purchases day book (2)
• customer returns goods sold on credit (4)	• sales returns day book (4)
• cheque received from a debtor (5)	• purchases returns day book (3)
• credit sale of goods to a customer (6)	• journal (1)
• expense paid out of petty cash (7)	• cash book (5)

19.3 Henry Lewis is setting up the book-keeping system for his new business, which sells office stationery. He decides to use the following books of prime entry:

- Journal
- Sales Day Book
- Purchases Day Book
- Sales Returns Day Book
- Purchases Returns Day Book
- Cash Book

His book-keeping system comprises a main ledger, with a subsidiary (sales) ledger and a subsidiary (purchases) ledger.

The following business transactions take place:

(a) He receives an invoice from Temeside Traders for £956 for goods supplied on credit.

(b) He issues an invoice to Malvern Models for £176 of goods.

(c) He buys a computer for use in his business for £2,000 on credit from A-Z Computers Limited.

(d) He issues a credit note to Johnson Brothers for £55 of goods.

(e) A debtor, Melanie Fisher, settles the balance of her account, £107, by cheque.

(f) He makes cash sales of £25.

(g)   Henry Lewis withdraws cash £100 for his own use.

(h)   He pays a creditor, Stationery Supplies Limited, the balance of the account, £298, by cheque.

(i)   A debtor, Jim Bowen, with an account balance of £35 is to be written off as a bad debt.

(j)   A credit note for £80 is received from a creditor, Ian Johnson.

You are to take each business transaction in turn and state:

*   the name of the book of prime entry

*   the name of the account to be debited

*   the name of the account to be credited

Note: VAT is to be ignored.

19.4   You work as an accounts assistant for Chapelporth Limited. The company manufactures kitchen units which are sold on credit to DIY chains, kitchen and cookware shops, and kitchen fitters.

Today the accounts supervisor has asked you to reconcile the sales ledger control account with the total of the subsidiary (sales) ledger. The information which follows is available to you.

Summary of transactions with credit customers in March 2007:

	£
Balance of debtors at 1 March 2007	142,830
Credit sales	105,350
Money received from credit customers	97,247
Discount allowed	840
Sales returns from credit customers	2,890
Bad debt written off	250

The following balances were shown in the subsidiary (sales) ledger at 31 March 2007:

	£	
Q & B Group plc	50,118	debit
House Base Stores plc	35,297	debit
Vickes Limited	37,386	debit
Perran Mills Limited	10,943	debit
Portreath Home and Garden	250	debit
Bradley and Company	9,651	debit
Towan Traders	3,558	debit

You are to:

(a)   Prepare a sales ledger control account for March 2007 from the details above. The account is to be balanced at 31 March 2007 to show the balance carried down to next month.

(b)   Reconcile the sales ledger control account with the total of the subsidiary ledger in the format shown on the next page.

	£
Sales ledger control account balance as at 31 March 2007	
Total of subsidiary (sales) ledger accounts as at 31 March 2007	
Difference	_____

(c)   If there is a difference calculated in (b) above, what do you think might have caused it?

19.5   The following entries were recorded in the subsidiary (purchases) ledger of Trevaunance Limited during the month of October 2007:

	£
Balance of creditors at 1 October 2007	35,105
Goods purchased on credit	23,294
Paid creditors	28,070
Discount received	430
Goods returned to suppliers	1,270

The following balances were in the subsidiary (purchases) ledger at 31 October 2007:

	£	
C Morgan	3,852	credit
Raven and Company	5,631	credit
Newbeach plc	10,854	credit
Hawke Supplies	350	debit
Packet Traders	752	credit
Durning Limited	4,175	credit
TR Limited	3,015	credit

You are to:

(a)   Prepare a purchases ledger control account for October 2007 from the details above. The account is to be balanced at 31 October 2007 to show the balance carried down to next month.

(b)   Reconcile the purchases ledger control account with the total of the subsidiary ledger in the following format:

	£
Purchases ledger control account balance as at 31 October 2007	
Total of subsidiary (purchases) ledger accounts as at 31 October 2007	
Difference	_____

(c)   If there is a difference calculated in (b) above, what do you think might have caused it?

19.6 Jennings and Company keeps a petty cash control account in the main ledger and the petty cash book is the subsidiary account. Petty cash book is kept on the imprest method, and the imprest amount is £250.

In April 2007, £176 was spent from petty cash and, at the end of the month, the imprest amount was restored from the bank.

You are to:

(a) Enter the transactions for April 2007 into the petty cash control account below, showing clearly the balance carried down.

Dr		Petty Cash Control Account		Cr
2007		£	2007	£
1 Apr	Balance b/d	250		

(b) State *one* other check you would carry out to ensure that the petty cash book is correct.

Initial trial balance and correction of errors

We have already seen how it is necessary to balance the traditional form of account (the 'T' account) from time-to-time, according to the needs of the business. In this chapter we list the balance of each account from the ledger, distinguishing between those accounts which have debit balances and those which have credit balances. The total of these two lists forms the initial trial balance which, if it balances, proves that the accounting records are arithmetically correct.

A trial balance does not prove the complete accuracy of the accounting records and there may well be errors. These fall into two groups:

- errors not shown by a trial balance
- errors shown by a trial balance

In this chapter, we look at the types of errors within each of these groups and, when they are found, we explain how to correct them using journal entries.

Note that this chapter shows how to extract a trial balance manually. In **Accounting Work Skills Tutorial**, when we deal with computer accounting, you will see how the computer prints out a trial balance automatically as a report, thus saving much time and trouble.

PERFORMANCE CRITERIA COVERED

unit 30: INTRODUCTORY ACCOUNTING

element 30.3

process petty cash, reconcile accounts and prepare an initial trial balance

H   *prepare an initial trial balance*

I   *create a suspense account when necessary and subsequently clear it*

BALANCING THE ACCOUNTS

Before an initial trial balance can be extracted, it is necessary to balance each account in the main ledger, together with the cash book. The balance brought down needs to be calculated correctly and shown on the correct side of the account. It is the balance brought down figure that is used in the initial trial balance.

Before going to the initial trial balance stage it is important to check that control accounts reconcile to their respective subsidiary ledgers. This then demonstrates the arithmetical accuracy of a subsidiary ledger section – although there still could be a number of errors (which we will look at later in this chapter).

Before moving on to the extraction of an initial trial balance, do make sure that you are able to balance accounts accurately – please refer back to Chapters 4 and 11 if you wish to review this process.

EXTRACTING AN INITIAL TRIAL BALANCE

The book-keeper extracts an initial trial balance from the accounting records in order to check the arithmetical accuracy of the double-entry book-keeping, ie that the debit entries equal the credit entries.

A trial balance is a list of the balances of every account from the ledger, distinguishing between those accounts which have debit balances and those which have credit balances.

A trial balance is extracted at regular intervals – often at the end of each month – and the balances are set out in two totalled columns, a debit column and a credit column.

Read the three bullet point notes set out below and refer at the same time to the example trial balance shown on the next page.

*   The debit and credit columns are totalled and the totals should agree. In this way the trial balance proves that the accounting records are arithmetically correct. (But note that a trial balance does not prove the complete accuracy of the accounting records – see page 402.)
*   The balance for each account listed in the trial balance is the amount brought down after the accounts have been balanced.
*   As well as the name of each account, it is quite usual to show in the trial balance the account number. Most accounting systems give numbers to accounts and these can be listed in a separate 'folio' or 'reference' column. For sake of simplicity these details are not shown here.

Trial balance of Ace Suppliers as at 31 January 2007

Name of account	Dr £	Cr £
Purchases	7,500	
Sales		16,000
Sales returns	250	
Purchases returns		500
Sales ledger control	1,550	
Purchases ledger control		900
Rent paid	1,000	
Wages	1,500	
Heating and lighting	1,250	
Office equipment	5,000	
Machinery	7,500	
Stock at 1 Jan 2007	2,500	
Cash	500	
Bank	4,550	
Value Added Tax		1,200
J Williams: loan		7,000
Capital		10,000
Drawings	2,500	
	35,600	35,600

DEBIT AND CREDIT BALANCES – GUIDELINES

Certain accounts always have a debit balance, while others always have a credit balance. You should already know these, but the lists set out below will act as a revision guide, and will also help in your understanding of trial balances.

Debit balances include:

- cash account and petty cash account
- purchases account
- sales returns account
- fixed asset accounts, eg premises, motor vehicles, machinery, office equipment, etc
- stock account – the stock valuation at the beginning of the year
- expenses accounts, eg wages, telephone, rent paid, etc

- drawings account
- sales ledger control account *debtors*

Credit balances include:

- sales account
- purchases returns account
- income accounts, eg rent received, commission received, fees received
- capital account
- loan account
- purchases ledger control account *creditors*

Notes:

- Bank account can be either debit or credit – it will be debit when the business has money in the bank, and credit when it is overdrawn.

- Value Added Tax account can be either debit or credit – it will be debit when VAT is due to the business and credit when the business owes VAT to HM Revenue & Customs.

IF THE INITIAL TRIAL BALANCE DOESN'T BALANCE . . .

If the initial trial balance fails to balance, ie the two totals are different, there is an error (or errors):

- *either* in the addition of the trial balance
- *and/or* in the double-entry book-keeping

The accounts supervisor needs to be informed if the trial balance does not balance; he or she will give guidance as to what is to be done.

The procedure for finding the error(s) is as follows:

- check the addition of the trial balance
- check that the balance of each account has been correctly entered in the trial balance, and under the correct heading, ie debit or credit
- check that the balance of every account in the ledger has been included in the trial balance
- check the calculation of the balance on each account
- calculate the amount that the trial balance is wrong, and then look in the accounts for a transaction for this amount: if one is found, check that the double-entry book-keeping has been carried out correctly

- halve the amount by which the trial balance is wrong, and look for a transaction for this amount: if it is found, check the double-entry book-keeping
- if the amount by which the trial balance is wrong is divisible by nine, then the error may be a reversal of figures, eg £65 entered as £56, or £45 entered as £54
- if the trial balance is wrong by a round amount, eg £10, £100, £1,000, the error is likely to be in the calculation of the account balances
- if the error(s) is still not found, it is necessary to check the book-keeping transactions since the date of the last trial balance, by going back to the prime documents and books of prime entry

ERRORS NOT SHOWN BY A TRIAL BALANCE

As mentioned earlier, a trial balance does not prove the complete accuracy of the accounting records.

There are six types of errors that are not shown by a trial balance. These are explained below.

1 error of omission

Here a business transaction has been completely omitted from the accounting records, ie both the debit and credit entries have not been made.

2 reversal of entries

With this error, the debit and credit entries have been made in the accounts but on the wrong side of the two accounts concerned. For example, a cash sale has been entered wrongly as debit sales account, credit cash account. (This should have been entered as a debit to cash account, and a credit to sales account.)

3 mispost/error of commission

Here, a transaction is entered to the wrong person's account. For example, a sale of goods on credit to A T Hughes has been entered as debit to A J Hughes' account, credit sales account. Double-entry book-keeping has been completed and the sales ledger control account will reconcile with the subsidiary (sales) ledger. However, when A J Hughes receives a statement of account, he or she will soon complain about being debited with goods not ordered or received.

4   error of principle

This is when a transaction has been entered in the wrong type of account. For example, the cost of fuel for vehicles has been entered as debit motor vehicles account, credit bank account. The error is that motor vehicles account represents fixed assets, and the transaction should have been debited to the expense account for motor vehicle running expenses.

5   error of original entry (or transcription)

Here, the correct accounts have been used, and the correct sides: what is wrong is that the amount has been entered incorrectly in both accounts. This could be caused by a 'bad figure' on an invoice or a cheque, or it could be caused by a 'reversal of figures', eg an amount of £45 being entered in both accounts as £54. Note that both debit and credit entries need to be made incorrectly for the trial balance still to balance; if one entry has been made incorrectly and the other is correct, then the error will be shown.

6   compensating error

This is where two errors cancel each other out. For example, if the balance of purchases account is calculated wrongly at £10 too much, and a similar error has occurred in calculating the balance of sales account, then the two errors will compensate each other, and the trial balance will not show the errors.

Correction of errors is covered fully later in this chapter (pages 403-409).

IMPORTANCE OF THE TRIAL BALANCE

A business will extract a trial balance on a regular basis to check the arithmetic accuracy of the book-keeping. However, the trial balance is also used as the starting point in the production of the financial statements (or final accounts) of a business. These are produced once a year (often more frequently) and comprise:

• profit and loss account

• balance sheet

The final accounts show the owner(s) how profitable the business has been, what the business owns, and how the business is financed. The preparation of final accounts is an important aspect of accountancy. Final accounts will be assessed at later levels of your Diploma Pathway studies. For the moment, we can say that extraction of a trial balance is an important exercise in the accounting process: it proves the book-keeper's accuracy, and also lists the account balances which form the basis for the final accounts of a business.

CORRECTION OF ERRORS

In any book-keeping system there is always the possibility of an error. Ways to avoid errors, or ways to reveal them sooner, include:

- division of the accounting function between a number of people, so that no one person is responsible for all aspects of a business transaction
- regular circulation of statements of account to debtors, who will check the transactions on their accounts and advise any discrepancies
- checking of statements of account received from creditors against the accounting records
- extraction of a trial balance at regular intervals
- the checking of bank statements and preparing bank reconciliation statements
- checking cash and petty cash balances against cash held
- the use of control accounts
- the use of a dedicated computer accounting program

Despite all of these, errors will still occur from time-to-time and, in this section, we will look at:

- correction of errors not shown by a trial balance
- correction of errors shown by a trial balance, using a suspense account

CORRECTION OF ERRORS NOT SHOWN BY A TRIAL BALANCE

Earlier in this chapter we listed the types of errors in a book-keeping system that are not revealed by a trial balance. These are:

- error of omission
- reversal of entries
- mispost/error of commission
- error of principle
- error of original entry (or transcription)
- compensating error

Although these errors are not shown by a trial balance, they are likely to come to light if the procedures suggested in the previous section, above, are followed. For example, a debtor will soon let you know if their account has been debited with goods they did not buy.

When an error is found, it needs to be corrected by means of a journal entry which shows the book-keeping entries that have been passed. Remember that all journal entries are prepared from authorised prime documents – these could take the form of a memorandum or email from the accounts supervisor; such documents, together with any other paperwork, should be stored securely for possible future reference.

We will now look at an example of each of the errors not shown by a trial balance, and will see how it is corrected by means of a journal entry.

hint!

A practical hint which may help in correcting errors is to write out the double-entry accounts as they appear with the error; then write in the correcting entries and see if the result has achieved what was intended.

error of omission

Credit sale of goods, £200 plus VAT (at 17.5%) on invoice 4967 to H Jarvis completely omitted from the accounting system; the error is corrected on 12 May 2007

Date	Details	Folio	Dr	Cr
2007			£	£
12 May	Sales ledger control	ML	235	
	Sales	ML		200
	VAT	ML		35
			235	235
	Invoice 4967 omitted from accounts: in the subsidiary (sales) ledger – debit H Jarvis £235			

This type of error can happen in a very small business – often where the book-keeping is done by one person. For example, an invoice, when produced, is 'lost' down the back of a filing cabinet. Where a computer accounting system is used, it should be impossible for this error to occur. Also, if documents are numbered serially, then none should be mislaid.

reversal of entries

A payment, on 3 May 2007 by cheque for £50 to a creditor, S Wright (receipt no 93459), has been debited in the cash book and credited to purchases ledger control account; this is corrected on 12 May 2007

Date	Details	Folio	Dr	Cr
2007			£	£
12 May	Purchases ledger control	ML	50	
	Bank	CBP		50
	Purchases ledger control	ML	50	
	Bank	CBP		50
			100	100
	Correction of £50 reversal of entries (cheque no 93459): in the subsidiary (purchases) ledger			
	– debit S Wright £50			
	– debit S Wright £50			

To correct this type of error it is best to reverse the entries that have been made incorrectly (the first two journal entries), and then to put through the correct entries. Although it will correct the error, it is wrong to debit £100 to purchases ledger control account and to credit £100 to bank account. This is because there was never a transaction for this amount – the original transaction was for £50.

As noted earlier, it is often an idea to write out the accounts, complete with the error, and then to write in the correcting entries. As an example, the two accounts involved in this last error are shown with the error made on 3 May, and the corrections made on 12 May indicated by the shading:

Dr				**Purchases Ledger Control Account**		Cr
2007		£		2007		£
12 May	Bank	50		3 May Bank		50
12 May	Bank	50				

Dr				**Cash Book** (bank columns)		Cr
2007		£		2007		£
3 May	S Wright	50		12 May S Wright		50
				12 May S Wright		50

The accounts now show a net debit transaction of £50 on purchases ledger control account, and a net credit transaction of £50 on bank account, which is how this payment to a creditor should have been recorded in the first place.

mispost/error of commission

Credit sales of £47, including VAT (at 17.5%) on invoice no 321 have been debited to the account of J Adams, instead of the account of J Adams Ltd; the error is corrected on 17 May 2007

Date	Details	Folio	Dr	Cr
2007			£	£
17 May	Sales ledger control	ML	47	
	Sales ledger control	ML		47
	Correction of mispost (invoice 5321):			
	in the subsidiary (sales) ledger			
	– debit J Adams Limited £47			
	– credit J Adams £47			

This type of error can be avoided, to some extent, by the use of account numbers, and by persuading the customer to quote the account number or reference on each transaction. All computer accounting systems use numbers/references to identify accounts, but it is still possible to post a transaction to the wrong account.

error of principle

The cost of diesel fuel, £30 (excluding VAT) on receipt no 34535, has been debited to vehicles account; the error is corrected on 20 May 2007

Date	Details	Folio	Dr	Cr
2007			£	£
20 May	Vehicle running expenses	ML	30	
	Vehicles	ML		30
	Correction of error: voucher no 647			

This type of error is similar to a mispost except that, instead of the wrong person's account being used, it is the wrong class of account.

In the above example, the vehicle running costs must be kept separate from the cost of the asset (the vehicle), otherwise the expense and asset accounts will be incorrect, leading to profit for the year being overstated and the fixed asset being shown in the balance sheet at too high a figure.

error of original entry (or transcription)

Postages of £45 paid by cheque entered in the accounts as £54; the error is corrected on 27 May 2007

Date	Details	Folio	Dr	Cr
2007			£	£
27 May	Bank	CBP	54	
	Postages	ML		54
	Postages	ML	45	
	Bank	CBP		45
			99	99
	Correction of error: postages of £45 entered into the accounts as £54; cheque no 93617			

This error could have been corrected by debiting bank and crediting postages with £9, being the difference between the two amounts. However, there was no original transaction for this amount, and it is better to reverse the wrong transaction and put through the correct one. A reversal of figures either has a difference of nine (as above), or an amount divisible by nine. An error of original entry can also be a 'bad' figure on a cheque or an invoice, entered wrongly into both accounts.

compensating error

Rates account is overcast (ie it is overadded) by £100; sales account is also overcast by the same amount; the error is corrected on 31 May 2007

Date	Details	Folio	Dr	Cr
2007			£	£
31 May	Sales	ML	100	
	Rates	ML		100
	Correction of overcast on rates account and sales account			

Here, an account with a debit balance – rates – has been overcast; this is compensated by an overcast on an account with a credit balance – sales. There are several permutations on this theme, eg two debit balances, one overcast, one undercast; a debit balance undercast, a credit balance undercast.

important notes to remember

We have just looked at several journal entries in connection with the correction of errors. Remember:

- The journal is the book of prime entry for non-regular transactions. The journal entries must then be recorded in the book-keeping system.
- For all the journal entries shown above which involve sales ledger or purchases ledger, we have assumed that control accounts are used, which are incorporated into the main ledger of the accounting system; remember that the transactions must also be recorded in the appropriate subsidiary ledger – subsidiary (sales) ledger or subsidiary (purchases) ledger.

TRIAL BALANCE ERRORS: USE OF SUSPENSE ACCOUNT

There are many types of errors which are revealed by a trial balance:

- omission of one part of the double-entry transaction
- recording two debits or two credits for a transaction
- recording a different amount for a transaction on the debit side from the credit side
- errors in the calculation of balances (not compensated by other errors)
- error in transferring the balance of an account to the trial balance
- error of addition in the trial balance

When errors are shown, the trial balance is 'balanced' by recording the difference in a suspense account, as shown in the Case Study below.

Case Study

SUSPENSE ACCOUNT: TEMESIDE TRADERS:

situation

The book-keeper of Temeside Traders is unable to balance the trial balance on 31 December 2006. As the error or errors cannot be found quickly, the trial balance is balanced by recording the difference in a suspense account:

	Dr £	Cr £
Trial balance totals	100,000	99,850
Suspense account		150
	100,000	100,000

A suspense account is opened in the main ledger with, in this case, a credit balance of £150:

Dr	Suspense Account		Cr
2006	£	2006	£
		31 Dec Trial balance difference	150

A detailed examination of the book-keeping system is now made in order to find the errors. As errors are found, they are corrected by means of a journal entry. The journal entries will balance, with one part of the entry being either a debit or credit to suspense account. In this way, the balance on suspense account is eliminated by book-keeping transactions. Using the above suspense account, the following errors are found and corrected on 14 January 2007:

- sales account is undercast by £100   *add the sales by £100*
- a payment to a creditor, A Wilson, for £65, has been recorded in the bank as £56
- telephone expenses of £55 have not been entered in the expenses account
- stationery expenses £48 have been debited to both the stationery account and the bank account

These errors are corrected by journal entries shown below. Note that the journal narrative includes details of cheque numbers and dates taken from the records of the business.

Date	Details	Folio	Dr	Cr
2007			£	£
14 Jan	Suspense account	ML	100	
	Sales account	ML		100
	Undercast on 23 December 2006 now corrected			
14 Jan	Bank account	CBR	56	
	Suspense account	ML		56
	Suspense account	ML	65	
	Bank account	CBP		65
			121	121
	Payment to A Wilson for £65 (cheque no 783726) on			
	30 December 2006 entered in bank as £56 in error			
14 Jan	Telephone expenses account	ML	55	
	Suspense account	ML		55
	Omission of entry in expenses account:			
	paid by cheque no 783734			
14 Jan	Suspense account	ML	48	
	Bank account	CBP		48
	Suspense account	ML	48	
	Bank account	CBP		48
			96	96
	Correction of error: payment by cheque no 783736			
	debited in error to bank account			

After these journal entries have been recorded in the accounts, suspense account appears as:

Dr			Suspense Account		Cr
2007		£	2006		£
14 Jan	Sales	100	31 Dec	Trial balance difference	150
14 Jan	Bank	65	2007		
14 Jan	Bank	48	14 Jan	Bank	56
14 Jan	Bank	48	14 Jan	Telephone expenses	55
		261			261

Thus all the errors have now been found, and suspense account has a nil balance.

Chapter Summary

- Taking the balance of each account in the ledger, an initial trial balance can be extracted.

- A trial balance does not prove the complete accuracy of the accounting records; errors not shown by a trial balance are:
  - error of omission
  - reversal of entries
  - mispost/error of commission
  - error of principle
  - error of original entry
  - compensating error

- Errors shown by a trial balance include: omission of one part of the book-keeping transaction, recording two debits/credits for a transaction, recording different amounts in the two accounts, calculating balances incorrectly, transferring wrong balances to the trial balance.

- Correction of errors is always a difficult topic to put into practice: it tests knowledge of book-keeping procedures and it is all too easy to make the error worse than it was in the first place! The secret of dealing with this topic well is to write down – in account format – what has gone wrong. It should then be relatively easy to see what has to be done to put the error right.

- All errors are non-regular transactions and need to be corrected by means of a journal entry: the book-keeper then records the correcting transactions in the accounts.

- When error(s) are shown by a trial balance, the amount of the error is placed in a suspense account. As the errors are found, journal entries are made which 'clear out' the suspense account.

Key Terms		
	trial balance	list of the balances of every account from the ledger, distinguishing between those accounts which have debit balances and those which have credit balances
	error of omission	business transaction completely omitted from the accounting records
	reversal of entries	debit and credit entries made on the wrong side of the accounts
	mispost/error of commission	transaction entered to the wrong person's account
	error of principle	transaction entered in the wrong type of account
	error of original entry	wrong amount entered incorrectly in accounts
	compensating error	where two errors cancel each other
	suspense account	account in which is placed the amount of an error shown by the initial trial balance, pending further investigation

Student Activities

20.1   Which one of the following accounts always has a debit balance?

(a)   capital account

(b)   purchases account

(c)   sales account

(d)   purchases returns account

Answer (a) or (b) or (c) or (d)

20.2   Which one of the following accounts always has a credit balance?

(a)   sales returns account

(b)   premises account

(c)   capital account

(d)   wages account

Answer (a) or (b) or (c) or (d)

20.3   Andrew Jarvis started in business on 1 April 2007.

During the month he had the following transactions:

2007

1 Apr	Paid £1,000 into business bank account as opening capital	
2 Apr	Bought goods for resale, paying by cheque, £255	
5 Apr	Paid for advertising by cheque, £60	
7 Apr	Sold goods, £195, a cheque being received	
8 Apr	Paid rent by cheque, £125	
9 Apr	Sold goods, £248, a cheque being received	
12 Apr	Drawings £100 by cheque	
14 Apr	Bought goods for resale, paying by cheque, £240	
16 Apr	Received a loan from J Couchman, £1,000 by cheque	
19 Apr	Sold goods, £220, a cheque being received	
21 Apr	Bought shop fittings, £1,250, paying by cheque	
23 Apr	Bought goods for resale, paying by cheque, £180	
26 Apr	Paid for advertising by cheque, £90	
28 Apr	Sold goods, £312, a cheque being received	
29 Apr	Paid rent by cheque, £125	
30 Apr	Drawings £125 by cheque	

You are to:

(a)   record the transactions in his cash book (which has a money column for bank only)

(b)   record the transactions in his other double-entry accounts

(c)   balance all the accounts that have more than one transaction at 30 April 2007

(d)   draw up a trial balance at 30 April 2007

Notes:
- *day books are not required*
- *Andrew Jarvis is not registered for VAT*

20.4 Produce the trial balance of Jane Greenwell as at 28 February 2007. She has omitted to open a capital account. You are to fill in the missing figure in order to balance the trial balance.

	£
Bank overdraft	1,250
Purchases	850
Cash	48
Sales	1,940
Purchases returns	144
Creditors	1,442
Equipment	2,704
Van	3,200
Stock at 1 Jan 2007	1,210
Sales returns	90
Debtors	1,174
Wages	1,500
Capital	?

20.5 The following errors have been made in the accounting records of Beacon Traders:

(a) An entry for a credit purchase has been made in purchases and VAT accounts, but has been omitted from purchases ledger control account.

(b) A sales invoice has been omitted from all accounting records. Error of omission

(c) A purchases invoice has been entered to the account of B Ryan instead of D Ryan. Error of commission

(d) The amount of VAT on a sales invoice has been calculated incorrectly.

You are to state which of these errors will cause an imbalance in the trial balance.

20.6 An amount has been entered into the book-keeping system as £65 instead of £56. The error is called:

(a) compensating error

(b) mispost

(c) error of principle

(d) error of original entry

Answer (a) or (b) or (c) or (d)

20.7 A trial balance fails to agree by £75 and the difference is placed to a suspense account. Later it is found that a credit sale for this amount has not been entered in the sales account. Which one of the following journal entries is correct?

(a) debit suspense account £75; credit sales account £75

(b) debit suspense account £150; credit sales account £150

(c) debit sales account £75; credit suspense account £75

(d) credit sales account £75

Answer (a) or (b) or (c) or (d)

20.8 The following errors have been made in the main ledger of Mereford Manufacturing:

(a) £100 has been debited to rent paid account instead of to rates account.

(b) Sales returns have been entered into the accounting records as £96 instead of the correct amount of £69. (Note: ignore VAT)

(c) A debtor, Zelah Stores, has ceased trading. The amount outstanding on the account of £200 plus VAT has been written off as a bad debt in the subsidiary (sales) ledger, but no entries have been made in the main ledger.

(d) Purchases returns of £175 have been debited to purchases returns account and credited to purchases ledger control account.

(e) Diesel fuel for vehicles of £45 has been debited to vehicles account. (Note: ignore VAT)

You are to record the journal entries to correct the errors shown above in the main ledger (narratives are not required).

20.9 The trial balance of Thomas Wilson balanced. However, a number of errors have been found in the book-keeping system:

(a) Credit sale of £150 to J Rigby has not been entered in the accounts.

(b) A payment by cheque for £125 to H Price Limited, a creditor, has been recorded in the account of H Prince.

(c) The cost of a new delivery van, £10,000, has been entered to vehicle expenses account.

(d) Postages of £55, paid by cheque, have been entered on the wrong sides of both accounts.

(e) Both purchases account and purchases returns account have been undercast by £100.

(f) A payment for £89 from L Johnson, a debtor, has been entered in the accounts as £98.

You are to take each error in turn and:

• state the type of error

• show the correcting journal entry

Notes:

• *the accounting system comprises a main ledger (which includes purchases ledger and sales ledger control accounts), and subsidiary purchases and sales ledgers*

• *VAT is to be ignored*

• *use today's date for the journal entries*

20.10 Jeremy Johnson extracts a trial balance from his book-keeping records on 30 September 2007. Unfortunately the trial balance fails to balance and the difference, £19 debit, is placed to a suspense account pending further investigation.

The following errors are later found:

(a) A cheque payment of £85 for office expenses has been entered in the cash book but no entry has been made in the office expenses account.

(b) A payment for photocopying of £87 by cheque has been correctly entered in the cash book, but is shown as £78 in the photocopying account.

(c) Sales returns account has been overcast by £100.

(d) Commission received of £25 has been entered twice in the account.

You are to:

• make journal entries to correct the errors

• show the suspense account after the errors have been corrected

Note: VAT is to be ignored.

20.11 You work as an accounts assistant for Durning Supplies. The accounts supervisor hands you the company's trial balance as at 28 February 2007 (see below). Unfortunately the trial balance did not balance and the accounts supervisor has placed the difference in a suspense account until the error(s) can be found.

Trial balance as at 28 February 2007

	Dr £	Cr £
Purchases	122,500	
Sales		239,850
Rent paid	5,220	
Wages	96,310	
Office equipment	6,000	
Machinery	12,000	
Heating and lighting	3,510	
Telephone expenses	2,054	
Stock at 1 March 2006	24,740	
Bank	8,230	
Sales ledger control	22,840	
Purchases ledger control		15,680
Value Added Tax		5,320
Capital		58,500
Drawings	15,900	
Suspense	46	
	319,350	319,350

The accounts supervisor asks you to investigate the difference and to prepare journal entries to correct the error(s). During investigations, you find the following errors:

(a)   Sales account has been overcast by £100.

(b)   Rent paid of £205 has been entered twice in the account.

(c)   A payment for telephone expenses of £56 has been correctly entered in the cash book, but is shown as £65 in telephone expenses account.

(d)   A payment for heating of £160 has been entered in the cash book but no entry has been made in the heating and lighting account.

You are to:

•   make journal entries to correct the errors (narratives are not required)

•   show the suspense account after the errors has been corrected

•   rewrite the trial balance after correcting the errors

Note: VAT is to be ignored.

21 Using the trial balance

this chapter covers . . .

This chapter links together the books of prime entry, the double-entry accounts system and the trial balance.

It shows how the accounting system operates and illustrates this by means of two fully-worked Case Studies, one for credit purchases (page 424) and one for credit sales (page 432).

PERFORMANCE CRITERIA COVERED

unit 30: INTRODUCTORY ACCOUNTING

element 30.3

process petty cash, reconcile accounts and prepare an initial trial balance

H   prepare an initial trial balance

THE ACCOUNTING SYSTEM

As we have seen so far, businesses need to record financial transactions for practical reasons:

- they need to quantify transactions such as purchases, sales, expenses
- they need to present the figures in a meaningful way in order to measure the success of the business or organisation

The accounting system can be complex and this chapter seeks to summarise and bring together the key elements that we have studied so far. The process of accounting follows a number of distinct stages which are illustrated in the diagram on the next page.

The rest of this chapter summarises the stages of the accounting system and brings together all that we have seen so far. Included in the chapter are two fully-worked Case Studies which illustrate, firstly, accounting for credit purchases (page 424) and, secondly, accounting for credit sales (page 432); the Case Studies incorporate the use of control accounts, together with some journal entries.

PRIME DOCUMENTS

Business transactions generate prime (source) documents, and we have already studied the key documents in depth in Chapters 2 and 9.

sale and purchase of goods and services

When a business or organisation buys or sells goods or services the seller prepares an invoice stating

- the amount owing
- when it should be paid
- details of the goods sold or service provided

cash sales and credit sales – debtors and creditors

An invoice is prepared by the seller for

- **cash sales** – where payment is immediate, whether in cash, by cheque, by debit card or by credit card (Note that not all cash sales will require an invoice to be prepared by the seller – shops, for instance, normally issue a receipt for the amount paid.)
- **credit sales** – where payment is to be made at a later date (often 30 days later)

the accounting system

PRIME DOCUMENTS

invoices – issued and received

credit notes – issued and received

bank paying-in slips

cheques issued

BACS documents

sources of accounting information

BOOKS OF PRIME ENTRY

day books

journal

cash books (also used in double-entry – see below)

gathering and summarising accounting information

DOUBLE-ENTRY ACCOUNTS

main ledger

- 'nominal' accounts for sales, purchases, expenses, capital, loans etc, and control accounts
- 'real' accounts for items, eg fixed assets

cash books

- cash book for cash and bank transactions
- petty cash book

subsidiary ledgers

- for sales ledger, purchases ledger, petty cash and non-trade debtors

recording the dual aspect of accounting transactions in the ledgers of the accounting system

TRIAL BALANCE

a summary of the balances of all the accounts at the end of the accounting period

arithmetic checking of double-entry book-keeping

FINANCIAL STATEMENTS*

- profit and loss account

- balance sheet

account which measures the profit (or loss) for an accounting period

statement of assets, liabilities and capital at the end of an accounting period

A debtor is a person who owes you money when you sell on credit.

A creditor is a person to whom you owe money when you buy on credit.

return of goods – the credit note

If the buyer returns goods which are bought on credit (they may be faulty or incorrect) the seller will prepare a credit note (see page 28 for an example) which is sent to the buyer, reducing the amount of money owed. The credit note, like the invoice, states the money amount and the goods or services to which it relates.

banking transactions

Businesses and organisations, like anyone else with a bank account, need to pay in money, and draw out cash and make payments. Paying-in slips, cheques and BACS transfers are used frequently in business as prime documents for bank account transactions. 'BACS' stands for Bankers Automated Clearing Services, which provide electronic transfer of amounts from one bank account to another.

RECORDING OF TRANSACTIONS

Many businesses and organisations issue and receive large quantities of invoices, credit notes and banking documents, and it is useful for them to list these in summary form. These summaries are known as books of prime entry.

The books of prime entry include:

- **sales day book** – a list of credit sales made, compiled from invoices issued
- **purchases day book** – a list of credit purchases made, compiled from invoices received
- **sales returns day book** – a list of 'returns in', ie goods returned by credit customers, compiled from credit notes issued
- **purchases returns day book** – a list of 'returns out', ie goods returned to credit suppliers, compiled from credit notes received
- **cash book** – the business' record of the cash and bank transactions compiled from receipts, paying-in slips, cheques and BACS documents
- **petty cash book** – a record of low-value purchases, compiled from petty cash vouchers
- **journal** – a record of non-regular transactions, which are not recorded in any other book of prime entry

The books of prime entry provide the information for the double-entry book-keeping system.

DOUBLE-ENTRY ACCOUNTS: THE LEDGER

The basis of the accounting system is the double-entry book-keeping system which is embodied in a series of records known as the ledger. This is divided into a number of separate accounts.

double-entry book-keeping

Double-entry book-keeping involves making two entries in the accounts for each transaction. With a manual accounting system the two entries are made by hand; with a computer accounting system one entry is made on the keyboard, and the computer operator indicates to the machine where the other entry is to be made by means of a code.

accounts

The sources for the entries are the books of prime entry. The ledger into which the entries are made is normally a bound book (in a non-computerised system) divided into separate accounts, eg a separate account for sales, purchases, each type of business expense, each debtor, each creditor, and so on. Each account will be given a specific name, and a number for reference purposes (or input code, with a computer system).

division of the ledger

Because of the large number of accounts involved, the ledger is traditionally divided into a number of sections. These same sections are used in computer accounting systems.

- **Cash book** – comprising cash account and bank account; also a petty cash book (which may be a subsidiary ledger) for low-value purchases. Note that cash books are also books of prime entry.
- **Main ledger** – the remainder of the accounts: nominal accounts, eg sales, purchases, expenses, real accounts for items owned by the business, and control accounts.
- **Subsidiary ledgers** – for sales ledger, purchases ledger, petty cash, and non-trade debtors.

INITIAL TRIAL BALANCE

The initial trial balance lists the balances of all the double-entry accounts, distinguishing between those with debit balances and those with credit balances. The total of the debit and credit columns should be equal, which means that the trial balance 'balances'.

An initial trial balance is prepared or extracted (from the double-entry accounts) at regular intervals – weekly, fortnightly or monthly – depending on the requirements of the business or organisation. One will always be prepared at the end of the financial year, which may vary between businesses and organisations – although 31 December (end of the calendar year) and 31 March (near the end of the tax year) are popular. The heading of a trial balance gives the name of the business or organisation whose accounts have been listed and the date it was extracted, eg 'as at 31 December 2007'.

Whilst the trial balance acts as an arithmetic check on the double-entry book-keeping, there can still be a number of errors within the accounts system. As we have seen in Chapter 20, there may be:

- errors not shown by a trial balance
- errors shown by a trial balance

As well as being a check on the book-keeping, the trial balance is a valuable source of information used to help in the preparation of financial statements.

FINANCIAL STATEMENTS

The financial statements or 'final accounts' comprise:

- profit and loss account, which shows the profit (or loss) for an accounting period such as a year
- balance sheet, which lists the assets, liabilities and capital at the end of the accounting period

Financial statements are assessed at later levels of the Diploma Pathway.

CASE STUDIES

To conclude this part of the book and to bring together the book-keeping system, there now follow two case studies, based on a common scenario:

- **Case Study 1** (on the next page) focuses on accounting for credit purchases, commencing with the books of prime entry – purchases day book and purchases returns day book – together with some aspects of cash book. The Case Study comprises entry of opening balances into accounts, recording of transactions from the day books and cash book, balancing accounts and transfer of balances (including additional balances) to a trial balance. The debit and credit columns of the trial balance are then totalled and shown to be equal.
- **Case Study 2** (on page 432) focuses on accounting for credit sales. As well as the books of prime entry – sales day book and sales returns day book –

it includes aspects of cash book and journal entries. Opening balances are entered into the accounts, transactions are recorded from the day books, and cash book and journal, and the accounts are then balanced. The balances are transferred (together with additional balances) to a trial balance, the debit and credit columns of which are totalled and shown to be equal.

WYVERN NURSERIES – ACCOUNTING FOR CREDIT PURCHASES

situation

You work as an accounts assistant for Wyvern Nurseries.

The company runs a garden centre in Wyvern, and buys in plants and other garden and leisure products from suppliers. At its nurseries it grows the 'specialist' range of plants which are also sold to shops and other garden centres in the area. Wyvern Nurseries is registered for VAT.

Your job in the accounts department is principally concerned with the subsidiary purchases and sales ledgers and also with aspects of the main ledger. Main ledger contains purchases ledger and sales ledger control accounts, which form part of the double-entry. Individual accounts of creditors and debtors are kept in subsidiary ledgers.

Today is 1 May 2007 and you are working on the subsidiary (purchases) ledger and main ledger sections of the accounting system.

Books of prime entry
Day books have been written up by a colleague (the rate of VAT is 17.5%) as follows:

	Purchases Day Book					
Date	Details	Invoice No	Total	VAT	Purchases	Stationery
2007			£	£	£	£
1 May	Garden Supplies Ltd	5439	470	70	400	
1 May	Woodcraft & Co	A471	705	105	600	
1 May	Office Direct	9579	235	35		200
1 May	Pershore Pots	754	329	49	280	
1 May	Pete's Plants	427	188	28	160	
1 May	Garden Supplies Ltd	5459	376	56	320	
	TOTALS		2,303	343	1,760	200

Purchases Returns Day Book						
Date	Details	Credit Note No	Total	VAT	Purchases returns	Stationery returns
2007			£	£	£	£
1 May	Garden Supplies Ltd	CN194	94	14	80	
1 May	Office Direct	C4571	47	7		40
1 May	Pershore Pots	CN761	141	21	120	
	TOTALS		282	42	200	40

Account balances

The following accounts are relevant and the balances shown are at the start of the day on 1 May 2007:

	£
Credit suppliers:	
Garden Supplies Limited	13,254
Office Direct	5,729
Pershore Pots	1,068
Pete's Plants	2,901
Woodcraft & Co	2,784
Purchases ledger control	25,736
Purchases	325,172
Purchases returns	4,850
Stationery	1,379
Discount received	454
VAT (credit balance)	6,274
Cash	260
Bank (debit balance)	14,170

Include a reconciliation of the balance of purchases ledger control account with the subsidiary accounts.

Cash book: payments

Payments made on 1 May 2007 are to be entered into the accounts:

	Total	VAT	Net
	£	£	£
• Pete's Plants (paid by cheque)	354		
• Woodcraft & Co (paid by cheque)	1,750		
(in full settlement of a debt of £1,800)			
• Stationery (paid by cheque)	94	14	80

Trial balance

After writing up the double-entry accounts you are asked to prepare a trial balance at the close of business on 1 May 2007. The following account balances are to be incorporated (there have been no transactions on these accounts on 1 May):

	£
Sales ledger control	62,851
Sales	735,450
Sales returns	6,020
Discount allowed	475
General expenses	73,284
Wages and salaries	119,477
Bank charges	354
Bad debts written off	496
Equipment and vehicles	194,646
Stock at 1 Jan 2007	55,270
Capital	100,000
Drawings	18,910

solution

Subsidiary (purchases) ledger

This contains the creditors' accounts and is written up in the following steps:

- enter the opening balances
- enter the amounts from purchases day book (using the total figure)
- enter the amounts from purchases returns day book (using the total figure)
- record the amounts of payments from the cash book, including any settlement (cash) discount received

The accounts are balanced and the balances carried down on 1 May 2007. The balances are then brought down on 2 May 2007.

SUBSIDIARY (PURCHASES) LEDGER

Garden Supplies Limited

Date	Details	Amount	Date	Details	Amount
2007		£	2007		£
1 May	Purchases returns	94	1 May	Balance b/d	13,254
1 May	Balance c/d	14,006	1 May	Purchases	470
			1 May	Purchases	376
		14,100			14,100
			2 May	Balance b/d	14,006

Office Direct

Date	Details	Amount	Date	Details	Amount
2007		£	2007		£
1 May	Stationery returns	47	1 May	Balance b/d	5,729
1 May	Balance c/d	5,917	1 May	Stationery	235
		5,964			5,964
			2 May	Balance b/d	5,917

Pershore Pots

Date	Details	Amount	Date	Details	Amount
2007		£	2007		£
1 May	Purchases returns	141	1 May	Balance b/d	1,068
1 May	Balance c/d	1,256	1 May	Purchases	329
		1,397			1,397
			2 May	Balance b/d	1,256

Pete's Plants

Date	Details	Amount	Date	Details	Amount
2007		£	2007		£
1 May	Bank	354	1 May	Balance b/d	2,901
1 May	Balance c/d	2,735	1 May	Purchases	188
		3,089			3,089
			2 May	Balance b/d	2,735

Woodcraft & Co

Date	Details	Amount	Date	Details	Amount
2007		£	2007		£
1 May	Bank	1,750	1 May	Balance b/d	2,784
1 May	Discount received	50	1 May	Purchases	705
1 May	Balance c/d	1,689			
		3,489			3,489
			2 May	Balance b/d	1,689

Reconciliation of purchases ledger control account

	1 May 2007	2 May 2007
	£	£
Garden Supplies Limited	13,254	14,006
Office Direct	5,729	5,917
Pershore Pots	1,068	1,256
Pete's Plants	2,901	2,735
Woodcraft & Co	2,784	1,689
Purchases ledger control account (see below)	25,736	25,603

Main ledger

Main ledger contains all the other accounts of the business, except for cash book (see below). Purchases ledger control account is included in main ledger and records the same transactions as have been entered in the subsidiary (purchases) ledger accounts.

Amounts are transferred to main ledger from purchases day book, purchases returns day book and cash book.

MAIN LEDGER
Purchases Ledger Control Account

Date	Details	Amount	Date	Details	Amount
2007		£	2007		£
1 May	Purchases Returns Day Book	282	1 May	Balance b/d	25,736
1 May	Bank	*2,104	1 May	Purchases Day Book	2,303
1 May	Discount received	50			
1 May	Balance c/d	25,603			
		28,039			28,039
			2 May	Balance b/d	25,603

* £354 + £1,750

Purchases Account

Date	Details	Amount	Date	Details	Amount
2007		£	2007		£
1 May	Balance b/d	325,172	1 May	Balance c/d	326,932
1 May	Purchases Day Book	1,760			
		326,932			326,932
2 May	Balance b/d	326,932			

Purchases Returns Account

Date	Details	Amount	Date	Details	Amount
2007		£	2007		£
1 May	Balance c/d	5,050	1 May	Balance b/d	4,850
			1 May	Purchases Returns Day Book	200
		5,050			5,050
			2 May	Balance b/d	5,050

Stationery Account

Date	Details	Amount	Date	Details	Amount
2007		£	2007		£
1 May	Balance b/d	1,379	1 May	Purchases Returns Day Book	*40
1 May	Purchases Day Book	200			
1 May	Bank	80	2 May	Balance c/d	1,619
		1,659			1,659
2 May	Balance b/d	1,619			

* This returns item could, alternatively, be credited to a stationery returns account

Discount Received Account

Date	Details	Amount	Date	Details	Amount
2007		£	2007		£
1 May	Balance c/d	504	1 May	Balance b/d	454
			1 May	Cash Book	50
		504			504
			2 May	Balance b/d	504

Value Added Tax Account

Date	Details	Amount	Date	Details	Amount
2007		£	2007		£
1 May	Purchases Day Book	343	1 May	Balance b/d	6,274
1 May	Cash Book	14	1 May	Purchases Returns	
1 May	Balance c/d	5,959		Day Book	42
		6,316			6,316
			2 May	Balance b/d	5,959

Tutorial note: only the main ledger accounts with transactions on 1 May have been shown here.

Cash book

Cash book contains both cash and bank account. It performs two functions:

- book of prime entry for cash and bank transactions
- part of the double-entry accounts system

CASH BOOK

Date	Details	Discount allowed	Cash	Bank	Date	Details	Discount received	Cash	Bank
2007		£	£	£	2007		£	£	£
1 May	Balances b/d		260	14,170	1 May	Pete's Plants			354
					1 May	Woodcraft & Co	50		1,750
					1 May	Stationery			94*
					1 May	Balances c/d		260	11,972
		−	260	14,170			50	260	14,170
2 May	Balances b/d		260	11,972					

* £80 stationery + £14 VAT

Trial balance

The balance of each account in the double-entry system is listed according to whether it is debit or credit.

Wyvern Nurseries

Trial balance as at 1 May 2007

	Dr	Cr
	£	£
Name of account		
Purchases ledger control		25,603
Purchases	326,932	
Purchases returns		5,050
Stationery	1,619	
Discount received		504
Value Added Tax		5,959
Cash	260	
Bank	11,972	
Sales ledger control	62,851	
Sales		735,450
Sales returns	6,020	
Discount allowed	475	
General expenses	73,284	
Wales and salaries	119,477	
Bank charges	354	
Bad debts written off	496	
Equipment and vehicles	194,646	
Stock at 1 Jan 2007	55,270	
Capital		100,000
Drawings	18,910	
	872,566	872,566

Tutorial notes to the trial balance:

- debit balances include cash, purchases, sales returns, sales ledger control, expenses, fixed assets, stock, drawings
- credit balances include sales, purchases returns, purchases ledger control, income, capital, loans
- bank account can be either debit or credit – debit when there is money in the bank, credit when overdrawn
- VAT account can be either debit or credit – debit when VAT is due to the business, credit when the business owes money to HM Revenue & Customs
- a trial balance which balances is not proof of the complete accuracy of the accounting records

**Case
Study**

WYVERN NURSERIES – ACCOUNTING FOR CREDIT SALES

This Case Study is a continuation of the Case Study on the previous eight pages. You work as an accounts assistant for Wyvern Nurseries. The scenario is set out in full at the beginning of the Case Study on page 424.

situation

Today is 2 May 2007 and you are working on the subsidiary (sales) ledger and main ledger sections of the accounting system.

Books of prime entry

Day books have been written up by a colleague (the rate of VAT is 17.5%) as follows:

Sales Day Book					
Date	Details	Invoice No	Total	VAT	Net
2007			£	£	£
2 May	Beeching and Sons	SI9075	658	98	560
2 May	The Potting Shed	SI9076	188	28	160
2 May	Beech Ltd	SI9077	282	42	240
2 May	Tranter & Co	SI9078	1,222	182	1,040
2 May	The Potting Shed	SI9079	141	21	120
2 May	Green Fingers Ltd	SI9080	423	63	360
	TOTALS		2,914	434	2,480

Sales Returns Day Book					
Date	Details	Credit Note No	Total	VAT	Net
2007			£	£	£
2 May	Tranter & Co	CN454	141	21	120
2 May	Green Fingers Ltd	CN455	94	14	80
	TOTALS		235	35	200

Cash book

The cash book has been written up and balanced by a colleague as follows:

CASH BOOK									
Date	Details	Discount allowed	Cash	Bank	Date	Details	Discount received	Cash	Bank
2007		£	£	£	2007		£	£	£
2 May	Balances b/d		260	11,972	2 May	Vehicle purchase*			5,000
2 May	Beech Ltd	50		950	2 May	Bank charges**			28
2 May	Tranter & Co			357	2 May	Drawings			100
2 May	The Potting Shed			596	2 May	Balances c/d		260	8,747
		50	260	13,875			–	260	13,875
3 May	Balances b/d		260	8,747					

*   the vehicle purchased was a secondhand car – no VAT to reclaim on cars
**   no VAT on bank charges

Journal transactions

The accounts supervisor asks you to make journal entries for the following:

- the subsidiary (sales) ledger account balance in the name of AB Garden Services is to be written off as a bad debt, you are told that VAT relief is available on this debt
- vehicle insurance of £1,550 has been recorded in the equipment and vehicles account instead of general expenses account

Once the journal entries have been checked by the supervisor, they are to be recorded in the double-entry system.

Account balances

The following accounts are relevant and the balances shown are at the start of the day on 2 May 2007:

	£
Credit customers:	
AB Garden Services	47
Beech Limited	12,367
Beeching and Sons	15,847
Green Fingers Limited	11,236
The Potting Shed	15,596
Tranter & Co	7,758
Sales ledger control	62,851
Sales	735,450
Sales returns	6,020
Discount allowed	475
VAT (credit balance)	5,959
General expenses	73,284
Bank charges	354

Bad debts written off	496
Equipment and vehicles	194,646
Drawings	18,910

Include a reconciliation of the balance of sales ledger control account with the subsidiary accounts.

Trial balance

After writing up the double-entry accounts you are asked to prepare a trial balance at the close of business on 2 May 2007. The following balances are to be incorporated (there have been no transactions on these accounts on 2 May):

	£
Purchases ledger control	25,603
Purchases	326,932
Purchases returns	5,050
Stationery	1,619
Discount received	504
Wages and salaries	119,477
Stock at 1 Jan 2007	55,270
Capital	100,000

solution

Journal transactions

The journal entries are as follows:

JOURNAL			
Date	Details	Debit	Credit
2007 2 May	Bad debts written off account Value Added Tax account Sales ledger control account	£ 40 7	£ 47
		47	47
	Balance of subsidiary (sales) ledger account of AB Garden Services written off as a bad debt on instructions of the accounts supervisor		
2 May	General expenses account Equipment and vehicles account	1,550	1,550
	Correction of error of principle on ...		

The journal entries are checked by the supervisor and then recorded in the double-entry system.

Subsidiary (sales) ledger

This contains the debtors' accounts and is written up in the following steps:

- enter the opening balances
- enter the total amounts from sales day book
- enter the total amounts from sales returns day book
- record the amounts of receipts from cash book, including any settlement (cash) discount allowed
- record the journal entry which relates to sales ledger accounts

The accounts are balanced and the balances are carried down on 2 May 2007. The balances are then brought down on 3 May 2007.

SUBSIDIARY (SALES) LEDGER

AB Garden Services

Date	Details	Amount	Date	Details	Amount
2007		£	2007		£
2 May	Balance b/d	47	2 May	Bad debts written off	40
			2 May	Value Added Tax	7
		47			47

Beech Limited

Date	Details	Amount	Date	Details	Amount
2007		£	2007		£
2 May	Balance b/d	12,367	2 May	Bank	950
2 May	Sales	282	2 May	Discount allowed	50
			2 May	Balance c/d	11,649
		12,649			12,649
3 May	Balance b/d	11,649			

Beeching and Sons

Date	Details	Amount	Date	Details	Amount
2007		£	2007		£
2 May	Balance b/d	15,847	2 May	Balance c/d	16,505
2 May	Sales	658			
		16,505			16,505
3 May	Balance b/d	16,505			

Green Fingers Limited

Date	Details	Amount	Date	Details	Amount
2007		£	2007		£
2 May	Balance b/d	11,236	2 May	Sales returns	94
2 May	Sales	423	2 May	Balance c/d	11,565
		11,659			11,659
3 May	Balance b/d	11,565			

The Potting Shed

Date	Details	Amount	Date	Details	Amount
2007		£	2007		£
2 May	Balance b/d	15,596	2 May	Bank	596
2 May	Sales	188	2 May	Balance c/d	15,329
2 May	Sales	141			
		15,925			15,925
3 May	Balance b/d	15,329			

Tranter & Co

Date	Details	Amount	Date	Details	Amount
2007		£	2007		£
2 May	Balance b/d	7,758	2 May	Sales returns	141
2 May	Sales	1,222	2 May	Bank	357
			2 May	Balance c/d	8,482
		8,980			8,980
3 May	Balance b/d	8,482			

Reconciliation of sales ledger control account

	2 May 2007	3 May 2007
	£	£
AB Garden Services	47	–
Beech Limited	12,367	11,649
Beeching and Sons	15,847	16,505
Green Fingers Limited	11,236	11,565
The Potting Shed	15,596	15,329
Tranter & Co	7,758	8,482
Sales ledger control account (see next page)	62,851	63,530

Main ledger

Main ledger contains all the other double-entry accounts, except for cash book (see below). Sales ledger control account is included in main ledger and records the same transactions as have been entered in the subsidiary (sales) ledger accounts.

Amounts are transferred to main ledger from sales day book, sales returns day book, the journal and cash book.

MAIN LEDGER
Sales Ledger Control Account

Date	Details	Amount	Date	Details	Amount
2007		£	2007		£
2 May	Balance b/d	62,851	2 May	Sales Rets Day Book	235
2 May	Sales Day Book	2,914	2 May	Bank	*1,903
			2 May	Discount allowed	50
			2 May	Bad debt written off	40
			2 May	Value Added Tax	7
			2 May	Balance c/d	63,530
		65,765			65,765
3 May	Balance b/d	63,530			

* £950 + £357 + £596

Sales Account

Date	Details	Amount	Date	Details	Amount
2007		£	2007		£
2 May	Balance c/d	737,930	2 May	Balance b/d	735,450
			2 May	Sales Day Book	2,480
		737,930			737,930
			3 May	Balance b/d	737,930

Sales Returns Account

Date	Details	Amount	Date	Details	Amount
2007		£	2007		£
2 May	Balance b/d	6,020	2 May	Balance c/d	6,220
2 May	Sales Returns Day Book	200			
		6,220			6,220
3 May	Balance b/d	6,220			

Discount Allowed Account

Date	Details	Amount	Date	Details	Amount
2007		£	2007		£
2 May	Balance b/d	475	2 May	Balance c/d	525
2 May	Cash Book	50			
		525			525
3 May	Balance b/d	525			

Value Added Tax Account

Date	Details	Amount	Date	Details	Amount
2007		£	2007		£
2 May	Sales Rets Day Book	35	2 May	Balance b/d	5,959
2 May	AB Garden Services	7	2 May	Sales Day Book	434
2 May	Balance c/d	6,351			
		6,393			6,393
			3 May	Balance b/d	6,351

General Expenses Account

Date	Details	Amount	Date	Details	Amount
2007		£	2007		£
2 May	Balance b/d	73,284	2 May	Balance c/d	74,834
2 May	Equipment and vehicles	1,550			
		74,834			74,834
3 May	Balance b/d	74,834			

Bank Charges Account

Date	Details	Amount	Date	Details	Amount
2007		£	2007		£
2 May	Balance b/d	354	2 May	Balance c/d	382
2 May	Bank	28			
		382			382
3 May	Balance b/d	382			

Bad Debts Written Off Account

Date	Details	Amount	Date	Details	Amount
2007		£	2007		£
2 May	Balance b/d	496	2 May	Balance c/d	536
2 May	AB Garden Services	40			
		536			536
3 May	Balance b/d	536			

Equipment and Vehicles Account

Date	Details	Amount	Date	Details	Amount
2007		£	2007		£
2 May	Balance b/d	194,646	2 May	General expenses	1,550
2 May	Bank	5,000	2 May	Balance c/d	198,096
		199,646			199,646
3 May	Balance b/d	198,096			

Drawings Account

Date	Details	Amount	Date	Details	Amount
2007		£	2007		£
2 May	Balance b/d	18,910	2 May	Balance c/d	19,010
2 May	Bank	100			
		19,010			19,010
3 May	Balance b/d	19,010			

Trial balance

The balance of each account in the double-entry system is listed according to whether it is debit or credit.

Wyvern Nurseries
Trial balance as at 2 May 2007

Name of account	Dr	Cr
Purchases ledger control		25,603
Purchases	326,932	
Purchases returns		5,050
Stationery	1,619	
Discount received		504
Value Added Tax		6,351
Cash	260	
Bank	8,747	
Sales ledger control	63,530	
Sales		737,930
Sales returns	6,220	
Discount allowed	525	
General expenses	74,834	
Wages and salaries	119,477	
Bank charges	382	
Bad debts written off	536	
Equipment and vehicles	198,096	
Stock at 1 Jan 2007	55,270	
Capital		100,000
Drawings	19,010	
	875,438	875,438

Note: A trial balance which balances is not proof of the complete accuracy of the accounting records; errors not shown by a trial balance include:

- error of omission
- reversal of entries
- mispost/error of commission
- error of principle (here vehicle insurance recorded in the equipment and vehicles account)
- error of original entry (or transcription)
- compensating error

Chapter Summary

- Businesses record financial transactions in order to
    - quantify transactions
    - present the figures in a meaningful way

- The accounting system follows a number of distinct stages
    - prime (source) documents
    - books of prime entry
    - double-entry book-keeping
    - trial balance
    - financial statements

Key Terms

prime (source) documents sources of accounting information

books of prime entry day books, journal and cash books where accounting information is gathered and summarised

double-entry book-keeping recording the dual aspect of accounting transactions in the ledgers of the accounting system

trial balance arithmetic check of the double-entry book-keeping

financial statements (or final accounts) comprising profit and loss account and balance sheet (both of which are covered fully at later levels of the Diploma Pathway)

Student Activities

The following background information is common to both Student Activities:

You work as an accounts assistant for 'Fashion Traders'. The company buys 'end-of-line' stocks of clothes for men and women in bulk from manufacturers and sells them on to smaller shops and discount stores. Fashion Traders is registered for VAT.

Your job in the accounts department is principally concerned with the subsidiary purchases and sales ledgers and also with aspects of the main ledger. Main ledger contains purchases ledger and sales ledger control accounts, which form part of the double-entry. Individual accounts of creditors and debtors are kept in subsidiary ledgers.

21.1   Today is 1 October 2007 and you are working on the subsidiary (purchases) ledger and main ledger sections of the accounting system.

Transactions

The following transactions have been entered into the relevant books of prime entry as shown below. No entries have yet been made into the ledger system. The VAT rate is 17.5%.

Purchases Day Book						
Date	Details	Invoice No	Total	VAT	Purchases	Stationery
2007			£	£	£	£
1 Oct	Wyvern Clothes	I 4379	1,457	217	1,240	
1 Oct	Jeans-R-Us Ltd	7629	2,820	420	2,400	
1 Oct	One Stop Office	5438	423	63		360
1 Oct	J & S Manufacturing	3941	1,034	154	880	
1 Oct	Wyvern Clothes	I 4385	1,222	182	1,040	
1 Oct	Dalton & Co	A 3691	1,598	238	1,360	
	TOTALS		8,554	1,274	6,920	360

Purchases Returns Day Book						
Date	Details	Credit Note No	Total	VAT	Purchases returns	Stationery returns
2007			£	£	£	£
1 Oct	Jeans-R-Us Ltd	C071	141	21	120	
1 Oct	Dalton & Co	CN764	94	14	80	
1 Oct	One-Stop Office	CN342	47	7		40
	TOTALS		282	42	200	40

CASH BOOK										
Date	Details	Discount allowed	Cash	Bank	Date	Details	Discount received	Cash	Bank
2007		£	£	£	2007		£	£	£
1 Oct	Balances b/d		275	2,054	1 Oct	J & S Manufact .	25		775
1 Oct	Balance c/d			400	1 Oct	Wyvern Clothes	45		1,055
					1 Oct	One-Stop Office			624
					1 Oct	Balance c/d		275	
		–	275	2,454			70	275	2,454
2 Oct	Balance b/d		275		2 Oct	Balance b/d			400

Balances

The following account balances are relevant to you at the start of the day on 1 October 2007:

	£
Credit suppliers:	
Dalton & Co	23,076
Jeans-R-Us Limited	12,120
J & S Manufacturing	13,491
One-Stop Office	9,466
Wyvern Clothes	2,610
Purchases ledger control	60,763
Purchases	428,494
Purchases returns	8,327
Stationery	3,650
Discount received	841
VAT (credit balance)	8,347

You are to:

(a) Enter the opening balances listed above into the following accounts:

Subsidiary (purchases) ledger:	Dalton & Co
	Jeans-R-Us Limited
	J & S Manufacturing
	One-Stop Office
	Wyvern Clothes
Main ledger:	Purchases ledger control
	Purchases
	Purchases returns
	Stationery
	Discount received
	VAT

(b) From the day books and cash book shown on pages 442 and 443, make the relevant entries in the accounts in the subsidiary (purchases) ledger and the main ledger.

(c) Balance the accounts, showing clearly the balance carried down at 1 October 2007 (the closing balance).

(d) Now that you have closed the above accounts, show clearly the balance brought down at 2 October 2007 (the opening balance). Demonstrate a reconciliation of the balance of the purchases ledger control account with the subsidiary accounts.

(e) Prepare a trial balance at the close of business on 1 October 2007 using the balances brought down on the above accounts, cash book, and incorporating the following account balances (on which there have been no transactions on 1 October):

	£
Sales ledger control	100,690
Sales	758,174
Sales returns	12,364
Discount allowed	1,497
General expenses	25,842
Wages and salaries	127,608
Bad debts written off	1,762
Office equipment	7,750
Warehouse equipment	85,250
Stock at 1 Jan 2007	165,940
Bank loan	40,000
Capital	115,324
Drawings	28,600

21.2 Today is 2 October 2007 and you are working on the subsidiary (sales) ledger and main ledger sections of the accounting system.

Transactions

The following transactions have been entered into the relevant books of prime entry as shown below. No entries have yet been made into the ledger system. The VAT rate is 17.5%.

Sales Day Book					
Date	Details	Invoice No	Total	VAT	Net
2007			£	£	£
2 Oct	Bentley Stores Ltd	SI7054	752	112	640
2 Oct	Just Jeans	SI7055	188	28	160
2 Oct	Teme Trading Co	SI7056	329	49	280
2 Oct	Bentley Stores Ltd	SI7057	376	56	320
2 Oct	Southwick Stores	SI7058	470	70	400
2 Oct	Bentley & Co	SI7059	423	63	360
	TOTALS		2,538	378	2,160

Sales Returns Day Book					
Date	Details	Credit Note No	Total	VAT	Net
2007			£	£	£
2 Oct	Teme Trading Co	CN761	94	14	80
2 Oct	Just Jeans	CN762	47	7	40
	TOTALS		141	21	120

CASH BOOK									
Date	Details	Discount allowed	Cash	Bank	Date	Details	Discount received	Cash	Bank
2007		£	£	£	2007		£	£	£
Oct	Balance b/d		275		2 Oct	Balance b/d			400
2 Oct	Bentley & Co			420	2 Oct	Wages & salaries			1,050
2 Oct	Just Jeans	10		240	2 Oct	Drawings			310
2 Oct	Bentley Stores Ltd	45		1,825	2 Oct	Loan repayment			500
					2 Oct	Balances c/d		275	225
		55	275	2,485			–	275	2,485
3 Oct	Balances b/d		275	225					

Balances

The following account balances are relevant to you at the start of the day on 2 October 2007:

	£
Credit customers:	
Bentley & Co	31,095
Bentley Stores Limited	21,870
Just Jeans	10,629
Southwick Stores	16,205
Teme Trading Co	20,797
Victoria's Fashions	94
Sales ledger control	100,690
Sales	758,174
Sales returns	12,364
Discount allowed	1,497
VAT (credit balance)	7,115
Wages and salaries	127,608
Bad debts written off	1,762
Bank loan	40,000
Drawings	28,600

Journal entries

The accounts supervisor asks you to make entries in the journal and the double-entry accounts for the following:

- the subsidiary (sales) ledger account balance in the name of Victoria's Fashions is to be written off as a bad debt; you are told that VAT relief is available on this debt

- a cheque for £220 received on 12 September from a debtor, Bentley & Co, has been entered in the account of Bentley Stores Limited, in error; there was no discount allowed on this receipt

You are to:

(a)   Enter the opening balances listed above into the following accounts:

Subsidiary (sales) ledger:

Bentley & Co

Bentley Stores Limited

Just Jeans

Southwick Stores

Teme Trading Co

Victoria's Fashions

Main ledger:

Sales ledger control

Sales

Sales returns

Discount allowed

VAT

Wages and salaries

Bad debts written off

Bank loan

Drawings

(b) • From the day books and cash book shown on page 445, make the relevant entries in the accounts in the subsidiary (sales) ledger and the main ledger.

• Record the entries in the journal for the transactions mentioned by the accounts supervisor and then enter the transactions into the relevant accounts.

(c) Balance the accounts, showing clearly the balance carried down at 2 October 2007 (the closing balance).

(d) Now that you have closed the above accounts, show clearly the balance brought down on 3 October 2007 (opening balance). Demonstrate a reconciliation of the balance of sales ledger control account with the subsidiary accounts.

(e) Prepare a trial balance at the close of business on 2 October 2007 using the balances brought down on the above accounts, cash book, and incorporating the following account balances (on which there have been no transactions on 2 October):

	£
Purchases ledger control	66,511
Purchases	435,414
Purchases returns	8,527
Stationery	3,970
Discount received	911
Office equipment	7,750
General expenses	25,842
Warehouse equipment	85,250
Stock at 1 Jan 2007	165,940
Capital	115,324

Answers to student activities

CHAPTER 1: INTRODUCTION TO ACCOUNTING

1.1   (c)

1.2   revenue: (a) (c) (d); capital: (b) (e)

1.3   cash: (a) (b) (d) credit: (c) (e)

1.4   See text, pages 11-12.

1.5   Assets minus liabilities equals capital. See pages 15-16. The capital would increase.

1.6   See text, page 15-16.

1.7   (a)   Jo's pay packet, income tax and national insurance will be incorrect; if Jo does not check the payslip, the error may go undetected.

   (b)   The invoice will be incorrect, the customer may exceed the credit limit, the business may lose the customer!

   (c)   The bank account may go overdrawn, the business may be charged extra interest and fees, cheques may be 'bounced' resulting in the withdrawal of credit by suppliers.

CHAPTER 2: DOCUMENTS FOR GOODS AND SERVICES SUPPLIED

2.1   (a)   delivery note   (b)   returns note   (c)   invoice
   (d)   statement   (e)   credit note   (f)   purchase order

2.2

	total £	discount £	net total £	VAT £	invoice total £
(a)	160.00	32.00	128.00	22.40	150.40
(b)	400.00	80.00	320.00	56.00	376.00
(c)	40.00	none	40.00	7.00	47.00
(d)	8000.00	1600.00	6400.00	1120.00	7520.00

2.3

	net total	discount deducted	total after cash discount	VAT	invoice total*
(a)	128.00	3.20	124.80	21.84	149.84
(b)	320.00	8.00	312.00	54.60	374.60
(c)	40.00	1.00	39.00	6.82	46.82
(d)	6400.00	160.00	6240.00	1092.00	7492.00

*Remember that the VAT is normally added to the total before deduction of cash discount.

2.4   Net monthly = payment of net amount one month after the invoice date.

E & OE = Errors and Omissions Excepted (a supplier has the right to correct an invoice after issue).

Carriage paid = Delivery costs paid to the delivery address (contrast with Ex-Works).

2.5   Examples: Purchase order number, delivery note number, invoice number, stock code, account number, credit note number.
The main importance of coding is for accurate cross referencing.

2.6   The problems are the urgency and the need for accuracy. If the wrong goods are sent the problems will be compounded.

Solutions: telephone or e-mail, and fax a copy of the order pointing out the error.

Best and quickest solution - telephone.

Important point – ask for a replacement corrected order to be sent (marked 'confirmation' to avoid duplication), preferably by fax so that a further check can be made. This is to make sure your position is strong, just in case the customer gets it wrong again! This type of problem can be sorted out at assistant level, but should be reported to the supervisor when he/she returns.

2.7   (a)   Incorrect discount rate applied (10%), wrong addition for total. Goods total should be £76.00, VAT £13.30 and final total £89.30.

(b)   Total before discount should be £250.00. VAT has also been rounded up (should have been rounded down to £35.43). Corrected figures: goods total £225.00 (after deduction of 10% discount), VAT £39.37, final total £264.37.

2.8

	Net amount	VAT	Total
	£	£	£
(a)	40.00	7.00	47.00
(b)	34,613.60	6,057.38	40,670.98
(c)	34.03	5.95	39.98
(d)	80.00	14.00	94.00
(e)	0.40	0.07	0.47
(f)	1.03	0.17	1.20

2.9   Statement should be dated 31 July 2007 and addressed to Mr Simpson.
The entries are:

2007		debit £	credit £	balance £
1 July	Balance /bf	58.75		58.75
4 July	Cheque received		58.75	00.00
8 July	Invoice 10982	340.75		340.75
14 July	Credit note 2378		34.07	306.68
			TOTAL	306.68

CHAPTER 3: ACCOUNTING FOR CREDIT SALES AND SALES RETURNS

3.1 (a)

3.2 (a)

3.3 (a) • The prime (source) documents for credit sales transactions are sales invoices or copy invoices, that have been checked and authorised.

• The details and amounts of the invoices are entered into sales day book. In the money columns of sales day book is recorded:

- total column, the final total of each invoice

- VAT column, the VAT amount shown on each invoice

- net column, the net ('goods or services total') amount of each invoice

• After sales day book has been written up for the week or month, it is totalled and the information from it is transferred into the double-entry system.

• The book-keeping entries are:

- the amounts from the total column for each separate transaction are debited to the accounts of the customers in sales (debtors) ledger

- the total of the VAT column is credited to VAT account in the main (general) ledger

- the total of the net column is credited to sales account in the main (general) ledger

(b) • The prime (source) documents for sales returns transactions are credit notes (or copies of credit notes) issued, that have been checked and authorised.

• The details and amounts of the credit notes are entered into sales returns day book. In the money columns of the sales returns day book is recorded:

- total column, the final total of each credit note

- VAT column, the VAT amount shown on each credit note

- net column, the net ('goods or services total') amount of each credit note

• After sales returns day book has been written up for the week or month, it is totalled and the information from it is transferred into the double-entry system.

• The book-keeping entries are:

- the amounts from the total column for each separate transaction are credited to the accounts of the customers in sales (debtors) ledger

- the total of the VAT column is debited to VAT account in the main (general) ledger

- the total of the net column is debited to sales returns account in the main (general) ledger

3.4   (a)

Sales Day Book						SDB 50
Date	Customer	Invoice No	Folio	Total	VAT	Net
2007				£ p	£ p	£ p
2 Apr	Malvern Stores	4578	SL 110	64.62	9.62	55.00
5 Apr	Pershore Retailers	4579	SL 145	76.37	11.37	65.00
7 Apr	E Grainger	4580	SL 55	32.90	4.90	28.00
9 Apr	P Wilson	4581	SL 172	68.15	10.15	58.00
12 Apr	M Kershaw	4582	SL 90	89.30	13.30	76.00
14 Apr	D Lloyd	4583	SL 95	77.55	11.55	66.00
19 Apr	A Cox	4584	SL 32	38.77	5.77	33.00
22 Apr	Dines Stores	4585	SL 48	119.85	17.85	102.00
23 Apr	Malvern Stores	4586	SL 110	55.22	8.22	47.00
26 Apr	P Wilson	4587	SL 172	41.12	6.12	35.00
29 Apr	A Cox	4588	SL 32	96.35	14.35	82.00
30 Apr	Totals for month			760.20	113.20	647.00

(b)   **SALES (DEBTORS) LEDGER**

Dr		**Malvern Stores** (account no 110)		Cr
2007		£ p	2007	£ p
2 Apr	Sales	SDB 50 64.62		
23 Apr	Sales	SDB 50 55.22		

Dr		**Pershore Retailers** (account no 145)		Cr
2007		£ p	2007	£ p
5 Apr	Sales	SDB 50 76.37		

Dr		**E Grainger** (account no 55)		Cr
2007		£ p	2007	£ p
7 Apr	Sales	SDB 50 32.90		

Dr		**P Wilson** (account no 172)		Cr
2007		£ p	2007	£ p
9 Apr	Sales	SDB 50 68.15		
26 Apr	Sales	SDB 50 41.12		

Dr		**M Kershaw** (account no 90)		Cr
2007		£ p	2007	£ p
12 Apr	Sales	SDB 50 89.30		

Dr   **D Lloyd** (account no 95)   Cr

2007			£ p	2007		£ p
14 Apr	Sales	SDB 50	77.55			

Dr   **A Cox** (account no 32)   Cr

2007			£ p	2007		£ p
19 Apr	Sales	SDB 50	38.77			
29 Apr	Sales	SDB 50	96.35			

Dr   **Dines Stores** (account no 48)   Cr

2007			£ p	2007		£ p
22 Apr	Sales	SDB 50	119.85			

MAIN (GENERAL) LEDGER

Dr   **Sales Account** (account no 4001)   Cr

2007		£ p	2007			£ p
			30 Apr	Sales Day Book SDB 50		647.00

Dr   **Value Added Tax Account** (account no 2200)   Cr

2007		£ p	2007			£ p
			30 Apr	Sales Day Book SDB 50		113.20

3.5 (a)

Sales Returns Day Book						SRDB 8
Date	Customer	Credit Note No	Folio	Total	VAT	Net
2007				£ p	£ p	£ p
8 Apr	Pershore Retailers	CN 572	SL 145	23.50	3.50	20.00
12 Apr	E Grainger	CN 573	SL 55	32.90	4.90	28.00
16 Apr	D Lloyd	CN 574	SL 95	38.77	5.77	33.00
28 Apr	Malvern Stores	CN 575	SL 110	23.50	3.50	20.00
30 Apr	A Cox	CN 576	SL 32	47.00	7.00	40.00
30 Apr	Totals for month			165.67	24.67	141.00

(b)

SALES LEDGER

Dr	Pershore Retailers (account no 145)					Cr
2007			£ p	2007		£ p
5 Apr	Sales	SDB 50	76.37	8 Apr Sales Returns SRDB 8		23.50

Dr	E Grainger (account no 55)					Cr
2007			£ p	2007		£ p
7 Apr	Sales	SDB 50	32.90	12 Apr Sales Returns SRDB 8		32.90

Dr	D Lloyd (account no 95)					Cr
2007			£ p	2007		£ p
14 Apr	Sales	SDB 50	77.55	16 Apr Sales Returns SRDB 8		38.77

Dr	Malvern Stores (account no 110)					Cr
2007			£ p	2007		£ p
2 Apr	Sales	SDB 50	64.62	28 Apr Sales Returns SRDB 8		23.50
23 Apr	Sales	SDB 50	55.22			

Dr	A Cox (account no 32)					Cr
2007			£ p	2007		£ p
19 Apr	Sales	SDB 50	38.77	30 Apr Sales Returns SRDB 8		47.00
29 Apr	Sales	SDB 50	96.35			

MAIN (GENERAL) LEDGER

Dr	Sales Returns Account (account no 4010)				Cr
2007		£ p	2007		£ p
30 Apr	Sales Returns Day Book SRDB 8	141.00			

Dr	Value Added Tax Account (account no 2200)				Cr
2007		£ p	2007		£ p
30 Apr	Sales Returns Day Book SRDB 8	24.67	30 Apr Sales Day Book SDB 50		113.20

CHAPTER 4: BALANCING ACCOUNTS AND CONTROL ACCOUNT FOR SALES

4.1

Dr   **Sales Account**   Cr

2007		£	2007		£
30 Apr	Balance c/d	17,195	1 Apr	Balance b/d	12,555
			30 Apr	Sales Day Book	4,640
		17,195			17,195
			1 May	Balance b/d	17,195

Dr   **Sales Returns Account**   Cr

2007		£	2007		£
1 Apr	Balance b/d	527	30 Apr	Balance c/d	727
30 Apr	Sales Returns Day Book	200			
		727			727
1 May	Balance b/d	727			

Dr   **Value Added Tax Account**   Cr

2007		£	2007		£
30 Apr	Sales Returns Day Book	35	1 Apr	Balance b/d	1,233
30 Apr	Balance c/d	2,010	30 Apr	Sales Day Book	812
		2,045			2,045
			1 May	Balance b/d	2,010

Dr   **T Johnson**   Cr

2007		£	2007		£
1 Apr	Balance b/d	496	30 Apr	Balance c/d	1,463
5 Apr	Sales	198			
20 Apr	Sales	467			
26 Apr	Sales	302			
		1,463			1,463
1 May	Balance b/d	1,463			

Dr   **Doyle Traders**   Cr

2007		£	2007		£
1 Apr	Balance b/d	183	14 Apr	Sales Returns	47
8 Apr	Sales	221	30 Apr	Balance c/d	752
22 Apr	Sales	395			
		799			799
1 May	Balance b/d	752			

4.2   (b)

4.3   *Principles of control accounts*

- Control accounts are 'master' accounts which control a number of subsidiary accounts.
- Control accounts use total figures:
  - total of opening balances
  - total of amounts increasing the balances
  - total of amounts decreasing the balances

  In this way, the total of the closing balances for the subsidiary accounts can be calculated and then checked against a separate listing of the balances of the subsidiary accounts to ensure that the two figures agree.
- Two commonly used control accounts are:
  - sales ledger control account, the total of the subsidiary (sales) ledger
  - purchases ledger control account, the total of the subsidiary (purchases) ledger

Control accounts as an aid to management

- The figures for debtors and creditors are available immediately from the appropriate control account – there is no need to add up the balances of all the individual debtors' or creditors' accounts.
- Control accounts can help in locating errors. The balance of the control account can be checked against the separate listing of balances of the subsidiary accounts to ensure that the two figures agree. However, this only proves the arithmetical accuracy of the control account and subsidiary accounts – there could still be errors within the ledger section.
- Fraud is made more difficult when control accounts are used – this especially applies to a manual accounting system. The reason for this is that any fraudulent transaction to be recorded on the subsidiary account of a debtor or creditor must also be entered in the control account. As the control account will be either maintained by a supervisor, or checked regularly by the manager, the control accounts add another level of security within the accounting system.

Control accounts and book-keeping

- A business must decide how to use control accounts in its book-keeping system; the usual way of doing this is to incorporate the control accounts into double-entry book-keeping.
- The control accounts form part of the double-entry system in the main ledger.
- The individual accounts of debtors and creditors are not part of double-entry but are kept as subsidiary accounts which record how much each debtor owes, and how much is owed to each creditor.
- From time-to-time, the balances of the subsidiary accounts are agreed with the balance of the appropriate control account.

4.4

Dr		Sales Ledger Control Account		Cr
2007		£	2007	£
1 Jun	Balance b/d	17,491	30 Jun Sales returns	1,045
30 Jun	Credit sales	42,591	30 Jun Payments received	
			from debtors	39,024
			30 Jun Balance c/d	20,013
		60,082		60,082
1 Jul	Balance b/d	20,013		

4.5 (b) Author's note: Day books are shown before the completed accounts.

Sales Day Book

Date	Customer	Invoice No	Folio	Total	VAT	Net
2007				£ p	£ p	£ p
3 Feb	Arrow Valley Retailers	2731	SL	241.75	36.00	205.75
5 Feb	Mereford Manufact. Co	2732	SL	132.03	19.66	112.37
10 Feb	Wyvern Warehouse Ltd	2733	SL	485.22	72.26	412.96
12 Feb	Redgrove Restorations	2734	SL	303.39	45.18	258.21
19 Apr	B Brick (Builders) Ltd	2735	SL	323.54	48.18	275.36
23 Feb	Redgrove Restorations	2736	SL	240.25	35.78	204.47
28 Feb	Totals for month			1,726.18	257.06	1,469.12

Sales Returns Day Book

Date	Customer	Credit Note No	Folio	Total	VAT	Net
2007				£ p	£ p	£ p
6 Feb	Redgrove Restorations	CN 127	SL	100.93	15.03	85.90
17 Feb	Mereford Manufact. Co	CN 128	SL	53.19	7.92	45.27
27 Feb	B Brick (Builders) Ltd	CN 129	SL	33.37	4.97	28.40
28 Feb	Totals for month			187.49	27.92	159.57

(a) and (c)

MAIN LEDGER

Dr		Sales Account			Cr
2007		£ p	2007		£ p
28 Feb	Balance c/d	6,566.36	1 Feb	Balance b/d	5,097.24
			28 Feb	Sales Day Book	1,469.12
		6,566.36			6,566.36
			1 Mar	Balance b/d	6,566.36

Dr		Sales Returns Account			Cr
2007		£ p	2007		£ p
1 Feb	Balance b/d	346.97	28 Feb	Balance c/d	506.54
28 Feb	Sales Returns Day Book	159.57			
		506.54			506.54
1 Mar	Balance b/d	506.54			

Dr		Value Added Tax Account			Cr
2007		£ p	2007		£ p
28 Feb	Sales Returns Day Book	27.92	1 Feb	Balance b/d	452.31
28 Feb	Balance c/d	681.45	28 Feb	Sales Day Book	257.06
		709.37			709.37
			1 Mar	Balance b/d	681.45

Dr		Sales Ledger Control Account			Cr
2007		£ p	2007		£ p
1 Feb	Balance b/d	2,012.43	28 Feb	Sales returns	187.49
28 Feb	Credit sales	1,726.18	28 Feb	Balance c/d	3,551.12
		3,738.61			3,738.61
1 Mar	Balance b/d	3,551.12			

SUBSIDIARY (SALES) LEDGER

Dr		Arrow Valley Retailers			Cr
2007		£ p	2007		£ p
1 Feb	Balance b/d	826.40	28 Feb	Balance c/d	1,068.15
3 Feb	Sales	241.75			
		1,068.15			1,068.15
1 Mar	Balance b/d	1,068.15			

Dr		B Brick (Builders) Limited			Cr
2007		£ p	2007		£ p
1 Feb	Balance b/d	59.28	27 Feb	Sales returns	33.37
19 Feb	Sales	323.54	28 Feb	Balance c/d	349.45
		382.82			382.82
1 Mar	Balance b/d	349.45			

Dr		Mereford Manufacturing Company			Cr
2007		£ p	2007		£ p
1 Feb	Balance b/d	293.49	17 Feb	Sales returns	53.19
5 Feb	Sales	132.03	28 Feb	Balance c/d	372.33
		425.52			425.52
1 Mar	Balance b/d	372.33			

Dr		Redgrove Restorations			Cr
2007		£ p	2007		£ p
1 Feb	Balance b/d	724.86	6 Feb	Sales returns	100.93
12 Feb	Sales	303.39	28 Feb	Balance c/d	1,167.57
23 Feb	Sales	240.25			
		1,268.50			1,268.50
1 Mar	Balance b/d	1,167.57			

Dr		Wyvern Warehouse Limited			Cr
2007		£ p	2007		£ p
1 Feb	Balance b/d	108.40	28 Feb	Balance c/d	593.62
10 Feb	Sales	485.22			
		593.62			593.62
1 Mar	Balance b/d	593.62			

(d)

Reconciliation of sales ledger control account

	1 February 2007	28 February 2007
	£ p	£ p
Arrow Valley Retailers	826.40	1,068.15
B Brick (Builders) Limited	59.28	349.45
Mereford Manufacturing Company	293.49	372.33
Redgrove Restorations	724.86	1,167.57
Wyvern Warehouse Limited	108.40	593.62
Sales ledger control account	2,012.43	3,551.12

CHAPTER 5: RECEIVING AND RECORDING PAYMENTS

5.1   *Customer*   *Change*   *Notes & coin given in change*

1	£1.50	1 x £1 coin, 1 x 50p coin
2	£6.70	1 x £5 note, 1 x £1 coin, 1 x 50p coin, 1 x 20p coin
3	£2.49	1 x £2 coin, 2 x 20p coins, 1 x 5p coin, 2 x 2p coins
4	£3.21	1 x £2 coin, 1 x £1 coin, 1 x 20p coin, 1 x 1p coin
5	£0.66	1 x 50p coin, 1 x 10p coin, 1 x 5p coin, 1 x 1p coin
6	£3.78	1 x £2 coin, 1 x £1 coin, 1 x 50p coin, 1 x 20p coin, 1 x 5p coin, 1 x 2p coin, 1 x 1p coin
7	£7.24	1 x £5 note, 1 x £2 coin, 1 x 20p coin, 2 x 2p coins
8	£0.58	1 x 50p coin, 1 x 5p coin, 1 x 2p coin, 1 x 1p coin
9	£3.46	1 x £2 coin, 1 x £1 coin, 2 x 20p coins, 1 x 5p coin, 1 x 1p coin
10	£1.92	1 x £1 coin, 1 x 50p coin, 2 x 20p coins, 1 x 2p coin

5.2   £

cash float at start of day   28.71

plus sales made during the day   46.46

equals amount of cash held at end of day   75.17

5.3   (a)   2 x £13.99 = £27.98; 2 x 85p = £1.70; total £29.68 + VAT £5.19 = £34.87
        (b)   £149.95 + 99p = £150.94; add VAT of £26.41 = £177.35
        (c)   2 x £35.99 = £71.98; add VAT of £12.59 = £84.57

5.4   (a)   A & S Systems Ltd (G Brown signs as director – an authorised signatory)
        (b)   Southern Bank PLC
        (c)   Electron Games Limited
        For explanations see page 88.

5.5   A crossed cheque must be paid into a bank account. A cheque without a crossing – an 'open' cheque – may be cashed by the payee. It is therefore a security risk and is very rare.

5.6   (a)   General crossing – the cheque has to be paid into a bank account.
        (b)   Special crossing – the cheque has to be paid in at Barclays Bank, Hanover Square.
        (c)   The same as (a) – the phrase '& co' no longer has any significance.
        (d)   Account payee crossing – the cheque must be paid into the account of the payee.

5.7   The Cheques Act 1992 states that a cheque that is crossed 'account payee' (or similar) is not transferable. The cheque cannot be accepted because the only person who can pay it into a bank account is the payee, Henry Enfield.

5.8   See page 89 of text.

5.9   See page 92 of text.

5.10   Someone else seeing and remembering the PIN number being entered.

5.11   (c)

5.12   The store will need to ask for payment to be made using some other method.

5.13   (b)

5.14   (d)

5.15   See page 99 of text.

5.16   (a) the bank (both)

(b) large purchase where cash or near cash is required, eg car purchase, house purchase

5.17   Cheques received through the post, cash sales at the counter.

CHAPTER 6: PAYING INTO THE BANK

6.1   See page 111 of text.

6.2   See page 111 of text.

6.3   False. Debtor

6.4   False. Creditor

6.5   (a) ... mortgagor ... mortgagee
         (b) ... bailee ... bailor
         (c)   agent

6.6   (a)   Loan account
         (b)   Overdraft
         (c)   Deposit account

6.7   (a)   3 days
         (b)   24 hours (or as long as first class post takes)
         Yes, the business could obtain same day clearance (the two accounts are at the same branch)

6.8   See page 117 of text.

6.9   See page 120 of text.

6.10   (a) credit   (b) debit

6.11   Cheques:

		Cash:		
	£20.00		2 x £20 notes	£40.00
	£18.50		5 x £10 notes	£50.00
	£75.25		8 x £5 notes	£40.00
	£68.95		2 x £1 coins	£2.00
	£182.70		6 x 50p coins	£3.00
			4 x 10p coins	£0.40
			2 x 2p coins	£0.04
				£135.44

Total amount of credit: £318.14

6.12   Total of sales vouchers £396.94 less refund voucher £13.50, total of summary £383.44.

CHAPTER 7: CASH BOOK – RECORDING RECEIPTS

7.1   (d)

7.2   *Main responsibilities of the cashier*
- Preparing remittance lists for cheques received in the post
- Recording receipts and payments through the bank and in cash
- Issuing receipts for cash (and sometimes cheques) received
- Making authorised cash payments (except for low-value expenses payments which are paid by the petty cashier)
- Preparing cheques for authorised payments – to be signed by those permitted to sign on behalf of the company
- Paying cash and cheques received into the bank
- Controlling the firm's cash, in a cash till or cash box
- Issuing cash to the petty cashier who operates the firm's petty cash book
- Ensuring that all transactions passing through the cash book are supported by documentary evidence
- Checking the accuracy of the cash and bank balances at regular intervals
- Checking expenses claims and seeking authorisation before making payment
- Liaising with the other accounts staff – accounts clerks and petty cashier

Qualities of a cashier
- Accuracy – in writing up the cash book, in cash handling, and in ensuring that payments are made only against correct documents and appropriate authorisation
- Security – of cash and cheque books, and correct authorisation of payments
- Confidentiality – that all cash/bank transactions, including cash and bank balances, are kept confidential

7.3

Debit		Cash Book: Receipts			CBR 45
Date	Details	Folio	Discount allowed	Cash	Bank
2007			£	£	£
1 Aug	Balances b/d			276	4,928
3 Aug	Wild & Sons Ltd	SL 843			398
6 Aug	Sales	ML 4001/ 2200		188	
16 Aug	A Lewis Ltd	SL 531	20		1,755
18 Aug	Sales	ML 4001/ 2200		282	
20 Aug	Harvey & Sons Ltd	SL 467			261
23 Aug	Bank loan	ML 2210			750
24 Aug	Sales	ML 4001/ 2200		235	235
26 Aug	Rent received	ML 4951		100	
27 Aug	Wild & Sons Ltd	SL 843	15		595
			35	1,081	8,922

SUBSIDIARY (SALES) LEDGER

Dr		**Wild & Sons Ltd** (account no 843)			Cr
2007	£	2007			£
		3 Aug	Bank	CBR 45	398
		27 Aug	Bank	CBR 45	595
		27 Aug	Discount allowed	ML 6501	15

Dr		**A Lewis Ltd** (account no 531)			Cr
2007	£	2007			£
		16 Aug	Bank	CBR 45	1,755
		16 Aug	Discount allowed	ML 6501	20

Dr	**Harvey & Sons Ltd** (account no 467)			Cr
2007	£	2007		£
		20 Aug	Bank	CBR 45	261

MAIN LEDGER

Dr	**Sales Ledger Control Account** (account no 6001)			Cr
2007	£	2007		£
		31 Aug	Bank	CBR 45	*3,009
		31 Aug	Discount allowed	ML 6501	35
		* £398 + £1,755 + £261 + £595			

Dr	**Discount Allowed Account** (account no 6501)			Cr
2007	£	2007		£
31 Aug Cash Book	CBR 45	35		

Dr	**Bank Loan Account** (account no 2210)			Cr
2007	£	2007		£
		23 Aug	Bank	CBR 45	750

Dr	**Rent Received Account** (account no 4951)			Cr
2007	£	2007		£
		26 Aug	Cash	CBR 45	100

Dr	**Sales Account** (account no 4001)			Cr
2007	£	2007		£
		6 Aug	Cash	CBR 45	160
		18 Aug	Cash	CBR 45	240
		24 Aug	Cash	CBR 45	200
		24 Aug	Bank	CBR 45	200

Dr	**Value Added Tax Account** (account no 2200)			Cr
2007	£	2007		£
		6 Aug	Cash	CBR 45	28
		18 Aug	Cash	CBR 45	42
		24 Aug	Cash	CBR 45	35
		24 Aug	Bank	CBR 45	35

7.4

Debit			Cash Book: Receipts			CBR 88
Date	Details	Folio	Discount allowed	VAT		Bank
2007			£	£		£
1 Apr	Balances b/d					718
8 Apr	J Bowen	SL 117	5			85
9 Apr	Sales	ML 4001/ 2200		70		470
12 Apr	Rent received	ML 4951				250
16 Apr	Sales	ML 4001/ 2200		14		94
19 Apr	J Burrows	SL 125	25			575
20 Apr	Sales	ML 4001/ 2200		28		188
26 Apr	Wilson Ltd	SL 855	10			245
			40	112		2,625

SUBSIDIARY (SALES) LEDGER

Dr			**J Bowen** (account no 117)		Cr
2007			£	2007	£
				8 Apr Bank CBR 88	85
				8 Apr Discount allowed ML 6501	5

Dr			**J Burrows** (account no 125)		Cr
2007			£	2007	£
				19 Apr Bank CBR 88	575
				19 Apr Discount allowed ML 6501	25

Dr			**Wilson Limited** (account no 855)		Cr
2007			£	2007	£
				26 Apr Bank CBR 88	245
				26 Apr Discount allowed ML 6501	10

MAIN LEDGER

Dr			**Sales Ledger Control Account** (account no 6001)		Cr
2007			£	2007	£
				30 Apr Bank CBR 88	*905
				30 Apr Discount allowed ML 6501	40

* £85 + £575 + £245

Dr   **Discount Allowed Account** (account no 6501)   Cr

2007		£	2007		£
30 Apr	Cash Book	CBR 88 40			

Dr   **Rent Received Account** (account no 4951)   Cr

2007		£	2007			£
			12 Apr	Bank	CBR 88	250

Dr   **Sales Account** (account no 4001)   Cr

2007		£	2007			£
			9 Apr	Bank	CBR 88	400
			16 Apr	Bank	CBR 88	80
			20 Apr	Bank	CBR 88	160

Dr   **Value Added Tax Account** (account no 2200)   Cr

2007		£	2007			£
			30 Apr	Cash Book	CBR 88	112

7.5

Debit			Cash Book: Receipts					CBR 96
Date	Details	Folio	Bank	Disc allwd	VAT	Sales	Sales ledger	Sundry
2007			£ p	£ p	£ p	£ p	£ p	£ p
17 May	Balances b/d		825.30					
17 May	Sales	ML 4001	534.62		79.62	455.00		
17 May	Rent received	ML 4951	255.50					255.50
18 May	Sales	ML 4001	164.50		24.50	140.00		
18 May	T Jarvis	SL 497	155.00	2.50			155.00	
19 May	Loan: T Lewis	ML 2200	500.00					500.00
19 May	Sales	ML 4001	752.00		112.00	640.00		
20 May	Sales	ML 4001	264.37		39.37	225.00		
21 May	Capital	ML 3005	1,000.00					1,000.00
21 May	Wyvern District Cncl	SL 924	560.45	5.00			560.45	
			5,011.74	7.50	255.49	1,460.00	715.45	1,755.50

SUBSIDIARY (SALES) LEDGER

Dr				T Jarvis (account no 497)			Cr
2007		£	p	2007			£ p
				18 May	Bank	CBR 96	155.00
				18 May	Discount allowed	ML 6501	2.50

Dr				Wyvern District Council (account no 924)			Cr
2007		£	p	2007			£ p
				21 May	Bank	CBR 96	560.45
				21 May	Discount allowed	ML 6501	5.00

MAIN LEDGER

Dr				Capital Account (account no 3005)			Cr
2007		£	p	2007			£ p
				21 May	Bank	CBR 96	1,000.00

Dr				Sales Ledger Control Account (account no 6001)			Cr
2007		£	p	2007			£ p
				21 May	Cash Book	CBR 96	715.45
				21 May	Discount allowed	ML 6501	7.50

Dr		Discount Allowed Account (account no 6501)			Cr
2007		£ p	2007		£ p
21 May Cash Book	CBR 96	7.50			

Dr				Loan Account: T Lewis (account no 2220)			Cr
2007		£	p	2007			£ p
				19 May	Bank	CBR 96	500.00

Dr				Rent Received Account (account no 4951)			Cr
2007		£	p	2007			£ p
				17 May	Bank	CBR 96	255.50

Dr		Sales Account	(account no 4001)		Cr
2007	£ p	2007			£ p
		21 May	Cash Book	CBR 96	1,460.00

Dr		Value Added Tax Account	(account no 2200)		Cr
2007	£ p	2007			£ p
		21 May	Cash Book	CBR 96	255.49

7.6

Dr		Sales Ledger Control Account		Cr
2007	£	2007		£
1 Dec Balance b/d	38,643	31 Dec	Sales returns	3,210
31 Dec Credit sales	45,419	31 Dec	Payments received from debtors	43,987
		31 Dec	Discount allowed	695
		31 Dec	Balance c/d	36,170
	84,062			84,062
2005		2005		
1 Jan Balance b/d	36,170			

CHAPTER 8: CUSTOMER COMMUNICATIONS AND LEGAL ISSUES

8.1   The cheque will not be accepted by the bank so it should be returned by post with a request that either a new cheque be issued (best solution) or that the figures changed to £550 and countersigned by the appropriate signatories.

8.2   Fax the invoices through to the customer with a reminder on the fax header sheet that the invoices are now due for payment.

8.3   The memorandum should be correctly headed and addressed. The message should be brief and clear. The memorandum can be signed, although this is not essential. The memorandum should include an 'enc.' (enclosure) marker.

8.4   Examples of different types of chaser are reproduced on pages 161-166. The important details to include are invoice amount, number and date (a copy should ideally be enclosed [nb 'enc.' marker]) and terms. The tone should not be too strong – remember that the invoice may even have been lost, or the cheque already be in the post (both common excuses!). The letter should be marked for signature by the Accounts Manager.

8.5   A letter of apology is required here. The error may well be the customer's fault, but on no account should this be suggested in the letter (she is 'a valued customer'). The letter should acknowledge the problem, state what corrective action has been taken and finish on a positive note. The tone should be conciliatory but not 'grovelling' (which sounds insincere). The letter should be correctly addressed and signed off.

8.6   The definition must contain the message that a contract is an agreement that is legally binding and enforceable in a court of law.

8.7   Agreement, bargain, intention to create legal relations. See text on page 168 and following.

8.8   (a)   Yes. A contract can be oral. A purchase order is just part of the paperwork confirming the agreement.

      (b)   Yes. The purchase order and despatch of the goods constitute the agreement, bargain and commercial nature of the transaction.

      (c)   No. When the job was done there was no intention to create legal relations or to involve consideration (payment) – it was done as a favour. The £10 followed the job and was just incidental.

      (d)   Yes. The fact that the person is a friend is not relevant. There was an agreement, consideration and an intention to create legal relations.

8.9   The cashier is right. The price on the shelf is just an invitation to treat. The price is agreed at the till.

8.10   No. The stipulation that the goods are received by 4 April amounts to a counter-offer to the supplier's terms and does not constitute an acceptance. It would only be a valid contract if the supplier had agreed to the revised terms.

8.11   17 March. The postal rule applies – as long as the letter is correctly addressed stamped and posted.

8.12   He is wrong. He is liable under the Sale of Goods Act which states that goods sold must be of 'satisfactory quality … fit for the purpose … as described.' The purchaser is entitled to a replacement or a refund as long as the problem is reported without delay.

8.13   No. The Trades Descriptions Act states that it is illegal to make false statements about goods offered for sale. The chair is advertised as having an adjustable back; if it does not, you are entitled to your money back. You could also report the matter to Trading Standards Department who can pursue the matter.

CHAPTER 9: DOCUMENTS FOR GOODS AND SERVICES RECEIVED

9.1   (a)   purchase order

(b)   delivery note

(c)   goods received note

(d)   remittance advice

(e)   invoice

(f)   returns note

9.2   An unauthorised purchase order cannot be used as the basis for raising an order. The purchase order will have to be returned to the purchaser for signature, or alternatively, if the order is urgent, the purchaser could be contacted and a new order faxed through.

9.3   (d)

9.4   A returns note accompanies any goods returned by the purchaser to the seller; a credit note is issued by the seller when credit has to be given to the purchaser, eg for returned goods. Hence a credit note is usually issued when a returns note is received.

9.5   The buyer would effectively be overcharged. The buyer would request a credit note. Under no circumstances should the invoice be altered.

9.6   The errors are:

(a)   the goods were delivered to the wrong address

(b)   an incorrect customer discount has been applied (10% instead of 15%)

(c)   the wrong goods were sent (product code 4574 instead of 4573)

The total should have been £95 less 15% discount = £80.75 plus VAT of £14.13 = £94.88

The letter should point out these errors and state that the disks are being returned for credit.

9.7   The amount to be paid will be:

£3,650 + £1,200 + £1,945 − £568 = £6,227. The £4,560 invoice will be paid on 12 September.

CHAPTER 10: ACCOUNTING FOR CREDIT PURCHASES AND PURCHASES RETURNS

10.1 (d)

10.2 (a)
- The prime (source) documents for credit purchases transactions are purchases invoices received from suppliers, that have been checked and authorised.
- The details and amounts of the invoices are entered into the purchases day book. In the money columns of purchases day book is recorded:
  - total column, the final total of each invoice
  - VAT column, the VAT amount shown on each invoice
  - net column, the net ('goods or services total') amount of each invoice
- After purchases day book has been written up for the week or month, it is totalled and the information from it is transferred into the double-entry system.
- The book-keeping entries are:
  - the amounts from the total column for each separate transaction are credited to the accounts of the suppliers in purchases (creditors) ledger
  - the total of the VAT column is debited to VAT account in main (general) ledger
  - the total of the net column is debited to purchases account in main (general) ledger

(b)
- The prime (source) documents for purchases returns transactions are credit notes received from suppliers, that have been checked and authorised.
- The details and amounts of the credit notes are entered into purchases returns day book. In the money columns of the purchases returns day book is recorded:
  - total column, the final total of each credit note
  - VAT column, the VAT amount shown on each credit note
  - net column, the net ('goods or services total') amount of each credit note
- After purchases returns day book has been written up for the week or month, it is totalled and the information from it is transferred into the double-entry system.
- The book-keeping entries are:
  - the amounts from the total column for each separate transaction are debited to the accounts of the suppliers in purchases (creditors) ledger
  - the total of the VAT column is credited to VAT account in main (general) ledger
  - the total of the net column is credited to purchases returns account in main (general) ledger

10.3 (a)

Date	Supplier	Invoice No	Folio	Total	VAT	Net
Purchases Day Book						PDB 36
2007				£ p	£ p	£ p
2 Apr	Severn Supplies	6789	PL 721	293.75	43.75	250.00
5 Apr	I Johnstone	A241	PL 604	246.75	36.75	210.00
9 Apr	L Murphy	2456	PL 659	217.37	32.37	185.00
15 Apr	Mercia Manufacturing	X457	PL 627	211.50	31.50	180.00
19 Apr	AMC Enterprises	AMC 456	PL 520	405.37	60.37	345.00
26 Apr	S Green	2846	PL 574	464.12	69.12	395.00
30 Apr	Totals for month			1,838.86	273.86	1,565.00

(b)

PURCHASES (CREDITORS) LEDGER

Dr		**Severn Supplies** (account no 721)		Cr
2007	£ p	2007		£ p
		2 Apr	Purchases	PDB 36 293.75

Dr		**I Johnstone** (account no 604)		Cr
2007	£ p	2007		£ p
		5 Apr	Purchases	PDB 36 246.75

Dr		**L Murphy** (account no 659)		Cr
2007	£ p	2007		£ p
		9 Apr	Purchases	PDB 36 217.37

Dr		**Mercia Manufacturing** (account no 627)		Cr
2007	£ p	2007		£ p
		15 Apr	Purchases	PDB 36 211.50

Dr		**AMC Enterprises** (account no 520)		Cr
2007	£ p	2007		£ p
		19 Apr	Purchases	PDB 36 405.37

Dr		**S Green** (account no 574)		Cr
2007	£ p	2007		£ p
		26 Apr	Purchases	PDB 36 464.12

MAIN (GENERAL) LEDGER

Dr   **Purchases Account** (account no 5001)   Cr

2007			£ p	2007		£ p
30 Apr	Purchases Day Book	PDB 36	1,565.00			

Dr   **Value Added Tax Account** (account no 2200)   Cr

2007			£ p	2007		£ p
30 Apr	Purchases Day Book	PDB 36	273.86			

10.4 (a)

	Purchases Returns Day Book				**PRDB 11**	
Date	Supplier	Credit Note No	Folio	Total	VAT	Net
2007				£ p	£ p	£ p
7 Apr	Severn Supplies	CN225	PL 721	58.75	8.75	50.00
14 Apr	L Murphy	X456	PL 659	94.00	14.00	80.00
21 Apr	AMC Enterprises	C3921	PL 520	146.87	21.87	125.00
29 Apr	S Green	CN/SG247	PL 574	79.90	11.90	68.00
30 Apr	Totals for month			379.52	56.52	323.00

(b)

PURCHASES (CREDITORS) LEDGER

Dr   **Severn Supplies** (account no 721)   Cr

2007			£ p	2007			£ p
7 Apr	Purchases Returns	PRDB 11	58.75	2 Apr	Purchases	PDB 36	293.75

Dr   **L Murphy** (account no 659)   Cr

2007			£ p	2007			£ p
14 Apr	Purchases Returns	PRDB 11	94.00	9 Apr	Purchases	PDB 36	217.37

Dr	**AMC Enterprises** (account no 520)		Cr
2007	£ p	2007	£ p
21 Apr Purchases Returns		19 Apr Purchases PDB 36	405.37
PRDB 11 146.87			

Dr	**S Green** (account no 574)		Cr
2007	£ p	2007	£ p
29 Apr Purchases Returns		26 Apr Purchases PDB 36	464.12
PRDB 11 79.90			

MAIN (GENERAL) LEDGER

Dr	**Purchases Returns Account** (account no 5010)		Cr
2007	£ p	2007	£ p
		30 Apr Purchases Returns	
		Day Book PRDB 11	323.00

Dr	**Value Added Tax Account** (account no 2200)		Cr
2007	£ p	2007	£ p
30 Apr Purchases Day		30 Apr Purchases Returns	
Book PDB 36 273.86		Day Book PRDB 11	56.52

10.5

	Purchases Day Book							PDB 21
Date	Supplier	Invoice No	Folio	Total	VAT	Net	Furniture	Carpets
2007				£ p	£ p	£ p	£ p	£ p
2 Apr	T Table Ltd	2750		1,465.81	218.31	1,247.50	1,247.50	
7 Apr	Eastern Imports	2751		936.24	139.44	796.80		796.80
9 Apr	Minster Carpets Ltd	2752		2,203.40	328.16	1,875.24		1,875.24
14 Apr	Pegasus Ltd	2753		585.30	87.17	498.13	498.13	
16 Apr	United Carpets Ltd	2754		559.55	83.33	476.22		476.22
21 Apr	Gerrard Furniture	2755		977.00	145.51	831.49	831.49	
23 Apr	T Table Ltd	2756		762.45	113.55	648.90	648.90	
28 Apr	Eastern Imports	2757		1,524.33	227.02	1,297.31		1,297.31
30 Apr	Totals for month			9,014.08	1,342.49	7,671.59	3,226.02	4,445.57

CHAPTER 11: BALANCING ACCOUNTS AND CONTROL ACCOUNT FOR PURCHASES

11.1

Dr			Purchases Account			Cr
2007			£	2007		£
1 Nov	Balance b/d		64,287	30 Nov	Balance c/d	71,007
30 Nov	Purchases Day Book		6,720			
			71,007			71,007
1 Dec	Balance b/d		71,007			

Dr		Purchases Returns Account			Cr
2007		£	2007		£
30 Nov	Balance c/d	1,509	1 Nov	Balance b/d	1,349
			30 Nov	Purchases Returns Day Book	160
		1,509			1,509
			1 Dec	Balance b/d	1,509

Dr		Value Added Tax Account			Cr
2007		£	2007		£
30 Nov	Purchases Day Book	1,176	1 Nov	Balance b/d	644
			30 Nov	Purchases Returns Day Book	28
			30 Nov	Balance c/d	504
		1,176			1,176
1 Dec	Balance b/d	504			

Dr		Ryan and Company			Cr
2007		£	2007		£
30 Nov	Balance c/d	1,342	1 Nov	Balance b/d	348
			4 Nov	Purchases	427
			19 Nov	Purchases	311
			24 Nov	Purchases	256
		1,342			1,342
			1 Dec	Balance b/d	1,342

Dr		Murray Limited			Cr
2007		£	2007		£
1 Nov	Balance b/d	15	8 Nov	Purchases	230
11 Nov	Purchases Returns	42	16 Nov	Purchases	315
30 Nov	Balance c/d	659	24 Nov	Purchases	171
		716			716
			1 Dec	Balance b/d	659

11.2   (c)

11.3

Dr	Purchases Ledger Control Account		Cr

2007		£	2007		£
30 Apr	Purchases returns	653	1 Apr	Balance b/d	14,275
30 Apr	Payments made to creditors	31,074	30 Apr	Credit purchases	36,592
30 Apr	Set-off: sales ledger	597			
30 Apr	Balance c/d	18,543			
		50,867			50,867
			1 May	Balance b/d	18,543

11.4   (b)   Author's note: Day books are shown before the completed accounts.

Purchases Day Book						
Date	Supplier	Invoice No	Folio	Total	VAT	Net
2007				£ p	£ p	£ p
3 Feb	Apple Supplies Ltd	6434	PL	1,207.87	179.89	1,027.98
5 Feb	Beatty Brothers	6435	PL	177.04	26.36	150.68
6 Feb	J Johnson	6436	PL	385.65	57.43	328.22
14 Feb	W Wright	6437	PL	559.74	83.36	476.38
24 Feb	Apple Supplies Ltd	6438	PL	997.99	148.63	849.36
28 Feb	Totals for month			3,328.29	495.67	2,832.62

Purchases Returns Day Book						
Date	Supplier	Credit Note No	Folio	Total	VAT	Net
2007				£ p	£ p	£ p
10 Feb	Apple Supplies Ltd	CN145	PL	184.71	27.51	157.20
17 Feb	Newtown Equipment Ltd	CN146	PL	124.17	18.49	105.68
28 Feb	Totals for month			308.88	46.00	262.88

(a) and (c)

MAIN LEDGER

Dr   **Purchases Account**   Cr

2007		£ p	2007		£ p
1 Feb	Balance b/d	4,397.21	28 Feb	Balance c/d	7,229.83
28 Feb	Purchases Day Book	2,832.62			
		7,229.83			7,229.83
1 Mar	Balance b/d	7,229.83			

Dr   **Purchases Returns Account**   Cr

2007		£ p	2007		£ p
28 Feb	Balance c/d	719.17	1 Feb	Balance b/d	456.29
			28 Feb	Purchases Returns	
				Day Book	262.88
		719.17			719.17
			1 Mar	Balance b/d	719.17

Dr   **Value Added Tax Account**   Cr

2007		£ p	2007		£ p
28 Feb	Purchases Day Book	495.67	1 Feb	Balance b/d	524.86
28 Feb	Balance c/d	75.19	28 Feb	Purchases Returns	
				Day Book	46.00
		570.86			570.86
			1 Mar	Balance b/d	75.19

Dr   **Purchases Ledger Control Account**   Cr

2007		£ p	2007		£ p
			1 Feb	Balance b/d	4,617.48
27 Feb	Set off: sales ledger	154.27	28 Feb	Credit purchases	3,328.29
28 Feb	Purchases returns	308.88			
28 Feb	Balance c/d	7,482.62			
		7,945.77			7,945.77
			1 Mar	Balance b/d	7,482.62

SUBSIDIARY (PURCHASES) LEDGER

Dr   **Apple Supplies Limited**   Cr

2007		£ p	2007		£ p
10 Feb	Purchases returns	184.71	1 Feb	Balance b/d	1,843.22
28 Feb	Balance c/d	3,864.37	3 Feb	Purchases	1,207.87
			24 Feb	Purchases	997.99
		4,049.08			4,049.08
			1 Mar	Balance b/d	3,864.37

Dr   **Beatty Brothers**   Cr

2007		£ p	2007		£ p
1 Feb	Balance b/d	51.47	5 Feb	Purchases	177.04
28 Feb	Balance c/d	125.57			
		177.04			177.04
			1 Mar	Balance b/d	125.57

Dr   **J Johnson**   Cr

2007		£ p	2007		£ p
28 Feb	Balance c/d	1,061.03	1 Feb	Balance b/d	675.38
			6 Feb	Purchases	385.65
		1,061.03			1,061.03
			1 Mar	Balance b/d	1,061.03

Dr   **Myford Limited**   Cr

2007		£ p	2007		£ p
27 Feb	Set-off: sales ledger	154.27	1 Feb	Balance b/d	478.29
28 Feb	Balance c/d	324.02			
		478.29			478.29
			1 Mar	Balance b/d	324.02

Dr   **Newtown Equipment Limited**   Cr

2007		£ p	2007		£ p
17 Feb	Purchases returns	124.17	1 Feb	Balance b/d	684.86
28 Feb	Balance c/d	560.69			
		684.86			684.86
			1 Mar	Balance b/d	560.69

Dr		W Wright		Cr
2007	£ p	2007		£ p
28 Feb Balance c/d	1,546.94	1 Feb Balance b/d		987.20
		14 Feb Purchases		559.74
	1,546.94			1,546.94
		1 Mar Balance b/d		1,546.94

(d)   **Reconciliation of purchases ledger control account**

	1 February 2007	28 February 2007
	£ p	£ p
Apple Supplies Limited	1,843.22	3,864.37
Beatty Brothers	*(51.47)	125.57
J Johnson	675.38	1,061.03
Myford Limited	478.29	324.02
Newtown Equipment Limited	684.86	560.69
W Wright	987.20	1,546.94
Purchases ledger control account	4,617.48	7,482.62

*   debit balance

CHAPTER 12: MAKING PAYMENTS

12.1   False. No cheque is involved in a BACS payment.

12.2   For security reasons: to prevent fraudulent alterations.

12.3   (d)

12.4   To establish the legal relationship between the bank and the business. The bank has to know *who* can sign cheques, and for what amounts. It also needs specimen signatures so that it can verify written instructions, eg cheque signatures and other payment instructions.

12.5   (a)   See text pages 240 and 243.   (b) Standing order   (c) Direct debit

12.6   (a)   Bank draft   (b) CHAPS

12.7   (a)   He/she doesn't have to rely on carrying his/her own money; <u>or</u> he/she doesn't have to pay!

(b)   Monitoring of expenditure, <u>or</u> control of expenditure.

12.8   Note that the cash discount is not available – the period has expired. Total £15,255.34. **12.9**   Total £4,083.05

12.10 The most <u>normal</u> methods are:
(a) BACS
(b) bank giro credit
(c) bank draft
(d) company credit card
(e) CHAPS

12.11 standing order

(a) Standing order completed as shown below.

(b) The form will be sent to the National Bank, as they will set up the payments.

(c) The standing order will have to be signed by an authorised signatory (or two) within the business. It should also be noted that details of the due payments will be passed to the person in charge of entering up the cash book as the payments will form part of the double-entry book-keeping of the company.

STANDING ORDER MANDATE

To _____ *NATIONAL* _____ Bank

Address _____ *10 CATHEDRAL STREET MELFORD MR1 5DE* _____

PLEASE PAY TO

Bank *BARCLAYS*   Branch *EVESHORE*   Sort code *30 98 15*

Beneficiary _____ Account number *726 271 61*

The sum of £ *350*   Amount in words *THREE HUNDRED AND FIFTY POUNDS*

Date of first payment *15 MAY 2003*   Frequency of payment *MONTHLY*

Until *15 APRIL 2007*   Reference *BE/ 6637*

Account to be debited *MIMRO DRAINAGE LTD* Account number *1203 4875*

SIGNATURE(S) ....

.... date...................

direct debit

(a) Direct debit form completed as shown below (standing order form above).

(b) The form will be sent to Tradesure Insurance, as they will set up the payments.

(c) The direct debit will have to be signed by an authorised signatory (or two) within the business. It should also be noted that details of the due payments are normally advised by the originator of the direct debit (here the insurance company). These will be passed to the person in charge of entering up the cash book as the payments will form part of the double-entry book-keeping of the company.

——— **direct debit Instruction** ———

Tradesure Insurance Company
PO Box 134, Helliford, HL9 6TY

Originator's Identification Number 914208
03924540234

Reference(to be completed by Tradesure Insurance)..........

Please complete the details and return this form to Tradesure Insurance

name and address of bank/building society

NATIONAL BANK
10 CATHEDRAL STREET
MELFORD
MN 5DE

account name
MIMRO DRAINAGE LIMITED

account number *1203 4875*   sort code *35.09.75*

instructions to bank/building society
• I instruct you to pay direct debits from my account at the request of Tradesure Insurance Company
• The amounts are variable and may be debited on various dates
• I understand that Tradesure Insurance Company may change the amounts and dates only after giving me prior notice
• I will inform the bank/building society if I wish to cancel this instruction
• I understand that if any direct debit is paid which breaks the terms of this instruction, the bank/building society will make a refund.

signature(s)   date

CHAPTER 13: PAYROLL PAYMENTS

13.1   See chapter text, pages 254 to 257

13.2   (d)

13.3   (c)

13.4   (a)

13.5   (a)   £119,150

(b)   £40,510

(c)   £71,140

(d)

account	debit (£)		credit (£)	
Wages & Salaries	Wages & Salaries Control	119,150		
Bank			Wages & Salaries Control	71,140
HM Revenue & Customs			Wages & Salaries Control	40,510
Pension Fund			Wages & Salaries Control	7,500
Wages & Salaries Control	Bank	71,140	Wages & Salaries	119,150
	HM Revenue & Customs	40,510		
	Pension Fund	7,500		

13.6   (a)   £56,110

(b)   £21,105

(c)   £2,200

(d)   £32,805

(e)

account	debit (£)		credit (£)	
Wages & Salaries	Wages & Salaries Control	56,110		
Bank			Wages & Salaries Control	32,805
HM Revenue & Customs			Wages & Salaries Control	21,105
Pension Fund			Wages & Salaries Control	2,200
Wages & Salaries Control	Bank	32,805	Wages & Salaries	56,110
	HM Revenue & Customs	21,105		
	Pension Fund	2,200		

CHAPTER 14: CASH BOOK– RECORDING PAYMENTS

14.1 (d)

14.2

Credit	Cash Book: Payments				CBP 22
Date	Details	Folio	Discount received	Cash	Bank
			£	£	£
2007					
3 Feb	G Wheaton 101359	PL			195
5 Feb	A Aznar 101360	PL	10		390
10 Feb	Wages	ML		370	
12 Feb	Singh Limited 101361	PL	15		570
17 Feb	Telephone	ML		155	
19 Feb	Farr and Company 101362	PL	10		220
27 Feb	Rent SO	ML			160
			35	525	1,535

14.3

Credit			Cash Book: Payments			CBP 45
Date	Details	Folio	Discount received	Cash	Bank	
2007			£	£	£	
2 Aug	Purchases	ML 5001/2200		94		
5 Aug	T Hall Ltd	PL 451	24		541	
9 Aug	Wages	ML 7750		254		
17 Aug	F Jarvis	PL 510			457	
18 Aug	Drawings	ML 7005		200		
19 Aug	Rent paid	ML 6950			275	
20 Aug	Wages	ML 7750		436		
24 Aug	J Jones	ML 643	33		628	
27 Aug	Purchases	ML 5001/2200			235	
27 Aug	Salaries	ML 7750			2,043	
30 Aug	Telephone	ML 6212/2200			282	
30 Aug	Office equipment	ML 750/2200			705	
			57	984	5,166	

SUBSIDIARY (PURCHASES) LEDGER

Dr   **T Hall Limited** (account no 451)   Cr

2007			£	2007	£
5 Aug	Bank	CBP 45	541		
5 Aug	Discount received ML 6502		24		

Dr   **F Jarvis** (account no 510)   Cr

2007			£	2007	£
17 Aug	Bank	CBP 45	457		

Dr   **J Jones** (account no 643)   Cr

2007			£	2007	£
24 Aug	Bank	CBP 45	628		
24 Aug	Discount received ML 6502		33		

MAIN LEDGER

Dr   **Purchases Ledger Control Account** (account no 6002)   Cr

2007			£	2007	£
31 Aug	Bank	CBP 45	*1,626		
31 Aug	Discount received ML 6502		57		

* £541 + £457 + £628

Dr			**Discount Received Account** (account no 6502)			Cr
2007		£	2007			£
			31 Aug Cash Book	CBP 45		57

Dr			**Drawings Account** (account no 7005)		Cr
2007		£	2007		£
18 Aug Cash	CBP 45	200			

Dr			**Office Equipment Account** (account no 750)		Cr
2007		£	2007		£
30 Aug Bank	CBP 45	600			

Dr			**Purchases Account** (account no 5001)		Cr
2007		£	2007		£
2 Aug Cash	CBP 45	80			
27 Aug Bank	CBP 45	200			

Dr			**Rent Paid Account** (account no 6950)		Cr
2007		£	2007		£
19 Aug Bank	CBP 45	275			

Dr			**Telephone Expenses Account** (account no 6212)		Cr
2007		£	2007		£
30 Aug Bank	CBP 45	240			

Dr			**Value Added Tax Account** (account no 2200)		Cr
2007		£	2007		£
2 Aug Cash	CBP 45	14			
27 Aug Bank	CBP 45	35			
30 Aug Bank	CBP 45	42			
30 Aug Bank	CBP 45	105			

Dr			**Wages and Salaries Account** (account no 7750)		Cr
2007		£	2007		£
9 Aug Cash	CBP 45	254			
20 Aug Cash	CBP 45	436			
27 Aug Bank	CBP 45	2,043			

14.4

Credit			Cash Book: Payments			CBP 88
Date	Details	Folio	Discount received	VAT		Bank
2007			£	£		£
2 Apr	Purchases	ML 5001/2200		7		47
2 Apr	Travelling expenses	ML 6330				65
5 Apr	Telephone	ML 6212/2200		35		235
6 Apr	ABC Bank: loan	ML 2250				500
9 Apr	Drawings	ML 7005				600
13 Apr	M Hughes	PL 498	10			180
15 Apr	Office stationery	ML 6384/2200		14		94
16 Apr	Purchases	ML 5001/2200		14		94
19 Apr	Office equipment	ML 750/2200		70		470
26 Apr	Wilson Ltd	PL 752	10			245
27 Apr	Purchases	ML 5001/2200		21		141
29 Apr	Wages	ML 7750				350
30 Apr	L Luz	PL 601	20			560
			40	161		3,581

SUBSIDIARY (PURCHASES) LEDGER

Dr		**M Hughes** (account no 498)				Cr
2007			£	2007		£
13 Apr	Bank	CBP 88	180			
13 Apr	Discount received ML 6502		10			

Dr		**Wilson Limited** (account no 752)				Cr
2007			£	2007		£
26 Apr	Bank	CBP 88	245			
26 Apr	Discount received ML 6502		10			

Dr		**Lucinda Luz** (account no 601)				Cr
2007			£	2007		£
30 Apr	Bank	CBP 88	560			
30 Apr	Discount received ML 6502		20			

MAIN LEDGER

Dr		**Purchases Ledger Control Account** (account no 6002)				Cr
2007			£	2007		£
30 Apr	Bank	CBP 88	*985			
30 Apr	Discount received ML 6502		40			

* £180 + £245 + £560

Dr		**Discount Received Account** (account no 6502)			Cr
2007		£	2007		£
			30 Apr	Cash Book CBP 88	40

Dr   **Drawings Account** (account no 7005)   Cr

2007			£	2007	£
9 Apr	Bank	CBP 88	600		

Dr   **Loan Account: ABC Bank** (account no 2250)   Cr

2007			£	2007	£
6 Apr	Bank	CBP 88	500		

Dr   **Office Equipment Account** (account no 750)   Cr

2007			£	2007	£
19 Apr	Bank	CBP 88	400		

Dr   **Office Stationery Account** (account no 6384)   Cr

2007			£	2007	£
15 Apr	Bank	CBP 88	80		

Dr   **Purchases Account** (account no 5001)   Cr

2007			£	2007	£
2 Apr	Bank	CBP 88	40		
16 Apr	Bank	CBP 88	80		
27 Apr	Bank	CBP 88	120		

Dr   **Telephone Expenses Account** (account no 6212)   Cr

2007			£	2007	£
5 Apr	Bank	CBP 88	200		

Dr   **Travelling Expenses Account** (account no 6330)   Cr

2007			£	2007	£
2 Apr	Bank	CBP 88	65		

Dr   **Value Added Tax Account** (account no 2200)   Cr

2007			£	2007	£
30 Apr	Cash Book	CBP 88	161		

Dr   **Wages and Salaries Account** (account no 7750)   Cr

2007			£	2007	£
29 Apr	Bank	CBP 88	350		

14.5

Credit			Cash Book: Payments					CBP 96
Date	Details	Folio	Bank	Disc recvd	VAT	Purchases	Purchases ledger	Sundry
2007			£ p	£ p	£ p	£ p	£ p	£ p
17 May	Purchases	ML 5001/ 2200	88.94		13.24	75.70		
17 May	Telephone	ML 6212/ 2200	238.90		35.58			203.32
18 May	Wyvern Finance:loan	ML 2270	250.00					250.00
18 May	Shop rent	ML 6345	255.50					255.50
19 May	Purchases	ML 5001/ 2200	100.00		14.89	85.11		
19 May	Terry Carpets Ltd	PL 721	363.55	4.65			363.55	
19 May	Stationery	ML 6382/ 2200	28.20		4.20			24.00
20 May	Drawings	ML 7005	100.00					100.00
20 May	Shop fittings	ML 740/ 2200	311.37		46.37			265.00
21 May	Longlife Carpets Ltd	PL 624	291.50	4.30			291.50	
21 May	Wages	ML 7750	314.20					314.20
21 May	Trade Supplies	PL 784	145.50	3.50			145.50	
			2,487.66	12.45	114.28	160.81	800.55	1,412.02

SUBSIDIARY (PURCHASES) LEDGER

Dr		Terry Carpets Limited (account no 721)			Cr
2007		£ p	2007		£ p
19 May Bank	CBP 96	363.55			
19 May Discount received ML 6502		4.65			

Dr		Longlife Carpets Limited (account no 624)			Cr
2007		£ p	2007		£ p
21 May Bank	CBP 96	291.50			
21 May Discount received ML 6502		4.30			

Dr		Trade Supplies (account no 784)			Cr
2007		£ p	2007		£ p
21 May Bank	CBP 96	145.50			
21 May Discount received ML 6502		3.50			

MAIN LEDGER

Dr   **Purchases Ledger Control Account** (account no 6002)   Cr

2007		£ p	2007		£ p
21 May Cash Book	CBP 96	800.55			
21 May Discount received	CBP 96	12.45			

Dr   **Discount Received Account** (account no 6502)   Cr

2007		£ p	2007		£ p
			21 May Cash Book	CBP 96	12.45

Dr   **Drawings Account** (account no 7005)   Cr

2007		£ p	2007		£ p
20 May Bank	CBP 96	100.00			

Dr   **Loan Account: Wyvern Finance** (account no 2270)   Cr

2007		£ p	2007		£ p
18 May Bank	CBP 96	250.00			

Dr   **Purchases Account** (account no 5001)   Cr

2007		£ p	2007		£ p
21 May Cash Book	CBP 96	160.81			

Dr   **Shop Fittings Account** (account no 740)   Cr

2007		£ p	2007		£ p
20 May Bank	CBP 96	265.00			

Dr   **Shop Rent Account** (account no 6345)   Cr

2007		£ p	2007		£ p
18 May Bank	CBP 96	255.50			

Dr   **Stationery Account** (account no 6382)   Cr

2007		£ p	2007		£ p
19 May Bank	CBP 96	24.00			

Dr   **Telephone Expenses Account** (account no 6212)   Cr

2007		£ p	2007		£ p
17 May Bank	CBP 96	203.32			

Dr   **Value Added Tax Account** (account no 2200)   Cr

2007		£ p	2007		£ p
21 May Cash Book	CBP 96	114.28			

Dr   **Wages and Salaries Account** (account no 7750)   Cr

2007		£ p	2007		£ p
21 May Bank	CBP 96	314.20			

14.6

Dr		Purchases Ledger Control Account			Cr
2007		£	2007		£
30 Apr	Purchases returns	653	1 Apr	Balance b/d	14,275
30 Apr	Payments made to creditors	31,074	30 Apr	Credit purchases	36,592
30 Apr	Discount received	1,048			
30 Apr	Set-off: sales ledger	597			
30 Apr	Balance c/d	17,495			
		50,867			50,867
			1 May	Balance b/d	17,495

CHAPTER 15: COMMUNICATING WITH SUPPLIERS

15.1   Something like: 'Hello. We recently received your invoice 24622 but notice that the five luxury chairs we ordered under code 2982B have been invoiced under code 2982GL. As a result we have been overcharged. Please can you investigate this and email back. Thank you. Regards.'

15.2   The email should point out the omissions and ask for a new invoice to be issued as soon as possible. The new net total should be £400, which would then attract cash discount of £10. VAT is charged on the lower amount but the invoice final total does not include the cash discount.

15.3   Fax the credit note through to Mordern Stationery with a message on the fax sheet that the credit note has been received and should appear on the statement. The total due on the statement as it stands is £345 higher than it should be.

CHAPTER 16: PETTY CASH BOOK

16.1   (d)

16.2   *Allow:* (a), (b), (f), (g), (h), (j) – all supported by an appropriate receipt being attached to the petty cash voucher.

Refer:

(c)   travel to work – not normally a business expense, except for emergency call-outs

(d)   donation to charity – subject to authorisation by supervisor

(e)   staff tea and coffee – check if it is company policy to pay for this personal expense of the office staff

(i)   shelving for the office – this expense is above the authorisation limit of the petty cashier; the item should be referred to the accounts supervisor, who may authorise it for payment through the main cash book.

16.3

petty cash voucher		No. 851
	date *today*	
description		amount (£)
Postage on urgent parcel of spare parts to Evelode Supplies Ltd	4	45
	4	45
VAT		
	4	45
signature *Jayne Smith*		
authorised *A Student*		

Documentation will be a Post Office receipt for £4.45.

petty cash voucher		No. 852
	date *today*	
description		amount (£)
Airmail envelopes	2	00
	2	00
VAT	0	35
	2	35
signature *Tanya Howard*		
authorised *A Student*		

Documentation will be a till receipt from the stationery shop for £2.35.

petty cash voucher   No. 853

date *today*

description		amount (£)	
Taxi fare re visit to Jasper Ltd		7	32
		7	32
	VAT	1	28
		8	60

signature   *Josh Delabole*

authorised   *A Student*

Documentation will be a receipt from the taxi company for £8.60.

16.4

	Expense (excluding VAT)	VAT	Total
	£	£	£
(a)	8.00	1.40	9.40
(b)	4.00	0.70	4.70
(c)	2.00	0.35	2.35
(d)	2.09	0.36	2.45
(e)	4.77	0.83	5.60
(f)	2.96	0.51	3.47
(g)	7.45	1.30	8.75
(h)	0.80	0.14	0.94
(i)	0.85	0.14	0.99
(j)	8.01	1.40	9.41

16.5

Petty Cash Book

Receipts	Date	Details	Voucher No	Total Payment	Analysis columns				
					VAT	Postages	Travel	Meals	Office Sundries
£	2007			£	£	£	£	£	£
75.00	1 Aug	Balance b/d							
	4 Aug	Postages	223	7.20		7.20			
	6 Aug	Travel expenses	224	4.50			4.50		
	9 Aug	Postages	225	2.54		2.54			
	12 Aug	Envelopes	226	4.70	0.70				4.00
	13 Aug	Window cleaning	227	7.05	1.05				6.00
	17 Aug	Taxi fare	228	7.52	1.12		6.40		
	20 Aug	Postages	229	8.56		8.56			
	23 Aug	Meals	230	6.35				6.35	
	27 Aug	Envelopes	231	6.58	0.98				5.60
				55.00	3.85	18.30	10.90	6.35	15.60
55.00	31 Aug	Cash received							
	31 Aug	Balance c/d		75.00					
130.00				130.00					
75.00	1 Sep	Balance b/d							

16.6   **Petty Cash Book**   **PCB 42**

Receipts	Date	Details	Voucher No	Total Payment	VAT	Travel	Postages	Stationery	Meals	Misc
£	2007			£	£	£	£	£	£	£
75.00	1 Aug	Balance b/d								
	4 Aug	Taxi fare	39	3.80	0.56	3.24				
	6 Aug	Parcel post	40	2.35			2.35			
	9 Aug	Pencils	41	1.26	0.18			1.08		
	11 Aug	Travel expenses	42	5.46		5.46				
	12 Aug	Window cleaner	43	8.50						8.50
	16 Aug	Envelopes	44	2.45	0.36			2.09		
	18 Aug	Donation	45	5.00						5.00
	19 Aug	Rail fare/meal allow	46	10.60		5.60			5.00	
	20 Aug	Postage	47	0.75			0.75			
	23 Aug	Tape	48	1.50	0.22			1.28		
	25 Aug	Postage	49	0.55			0.55			
	27 Aug	Taxi fare	50	5.40	0.80	4.60				
				47.62	2.12	18.90	3.65	4.45	5.00	13.50
47.62	31 Aug	Cash received								
	31 Aug	Balance c/d		75.00						
122.62				122.62						
75.00	1 Sep	Balance b/d								

CARR TRADING

Posting sheet: petty cash

account name	account number	debit	credit	reference
		£	£	
VAT	ML	2.12		PCB 42
Travel	ML	18.90		PCB 42
Postages	ML	3.65		PCB 42
Stationery	ML	4.45		PCB 42
Meals	ML	5.00		PCB 42
Miscellaneous	ML	13.50		PCB 42
Bank	CBP		47.62	PCB 42
TOTAL		47.62	47.62	

Prepared by ___*A Student*___   Date ___*31 August 2007*___

Checked by _____   Date _____

Posted by _____   Date _____

16.7   **Petty Cash Book**   **PCB 18**

Receipts	Date	Details	Voucher No	Total Payment	VAT	Postages	Travel	Meals	Sundry Office
£	2007			£	£	£	£	£	£
100.00	7 Jun	Balance b/d							
	7 Jun	Postages	123	6.35		6.35			
	8 Jun	Travel expenses	124	3.25			3.25		
	8 Jun	Postages	125	1.28		1.28			
	9 Jun	Envelopes	126	4.54	0.67				3.87
	9 Jun	Window cleaning	127	5.50	0.81				4.69
	10 Jun	Taxi fare/meals	128	15.41	2.29		3.88	9.24	
	10 Jun	Post/packing	129	11.81	0.48	8.56			2.77
	10 Jun	Taxi fare/meals	130	11.95	1.77		3.83	6.35	
	11 Jun	Pens/envelopes	131	6.35	0.94				5.41
				66.44	6.96	16.19	10.96	15.59	16.74
66.44	11 Jun	Cash received							
	11 Jun	Balance c/d		100.00					
166.44				166.44					
100.00	11 Jun	Balance b/d							

TYAX SYSTEMS LIMITED

Posting sheet: petty cash

account name	account number	debit	credit	reference
		£	£	
VAT	ML	6.96		PCB 18
Postages	ML	16.19		PCB 18
Travel	ML	10.96		PCB 18
Meals	ML	15.59		PCB 18
Sundry office	ML	16.74		PCB 18
Bank	CBP		66.44	PCB 18
TOTAL		66.44	66.44	

Prepared by _A Student_   Date _11 June 2007_

Checked by _____   Date _____

Posted by _____   Date _____

CHAPTER 17: FURTHER ASPECTS OF DOUBLE-ENTRY ACCOUNTS

17.1 (c) **17.2** (b)

17.3 Computer
- The double-entry book-keeping transaction for the purchase of a computer is:
  - *debit* computer account
  - *credit* cash account or bank account
  (This assumes that the computer has been bought as a fixed asset, ie for use in the business, and that it has been paid for either in cash or by cheque.)
- Thus, the computer account records an asset, while cash/bank account has given value.
- The computer, being an asset, is recorded in the accounts by a debit transaction; the method of paying for it is recorded in cash/bank account by a credit transaction.

Capital
- The double-entry book-keeping transaction for the introduction of capital into a business is:
  - *debit* cash account or bank account
  - *credit* capital account
  (This assumes that the capital was in the form of money rather than other assets.)
- Thus, the cash/bank account has gained value, while capital account records a liability to the owner. It is a liability that is unlikely to be repaid immediately as the business would then be unable to operate.

17.4

JAMES ANDERSON

Dr	**Capital Account**		Cr
2007	£	2007	£
		1 Mar Bank	7,500

Dr	**Computer Account**		Cr
2007	£	2007	£
5 Mar Bank	2,000		

Dr	**Rent Paid Account**		Cr
2007	£	2007	£
8 Mar Bank	500		

Dr	**Wages Account**		Cr
2007	£	2007	£
12 Mar Bank	425		
26 Mar Bank	380		

Dr	**Bank Loan Account**		Cr
2007	£	2007	£
		15 Mar Bank	2,500

Dr	**Commission Received Account**		Cr
2007	£	2007	£
		19 Mar Bank	120

Dr	Drawings Account		Cr
2007	£	2007	£
23 Mar Bank	200		

Dr	Van Account		Cr
2007	£	2007	£
29 Mar Bank	5,000		

Dr	Value Added Tax Account		Cr
2007	£	2007	£
5 Mar Bank (computer)	350	19 Mar Bank (commission	
29 Mar Bank (van)	875	received)	21

17.5

TONY LONG

Debit	Cash Book: Receipts			CBR
Date	Details	Folio	Discount allowed	Bank
2007			£	£
3 May	Capital			6,000
13 May	L Warner: loan			1,000
18 May	Commission received			188

Credit	Cash Book: Payments			CBP
Date	Details	Folio	Discount received	Bank
2007			£	£
4 May	Machine			2,350
7 May	Office equipment			2,820
10 May	Rent			350
14 May	Wages			250
21 May	Drawings			85
28 May	Wages			135

Dr	Capital Account		Cr
2007	£	2007	£
		3 May Bank	6,000

Dr	Machinery Account		Cr
2007	£	2007	£
4 May Bank	2,000		

Dr	Office Equipment Account		Cr
2007	£	2007	£
7 May Bank	2,400		

Dr	Rent Paid Account		Cr
2007	£	2007	£
10 May Bank	350		

Dr	Lucy Warner: Loan Account		Cr
2007	£	2007	£
		13 May Bank	1,000

Dr	Wages Account		Cr
2007	£	2007	£
14 May Bank	250		
28 May Bank	135		

Dr	Commission Received Account		Cr
2007	£	2007	£
		18 May Bank	160

Dr	Drawings Account		Cr
2007	£	2007	£
21 May Bank	85		

Dr	Value Added Tax Account		Cr
2007	£	2007	£
4 May Bank (machinery)	350	18 May Bank (commission	
7 May Bank (office equipment)	420	received)	28

17.6 **JEAN LACEY**

Debit	Cash Book: Receipts			CBR
Date	Details	Folio	Discount allowed	Bank
2007			£	£
2 Aug	Capital			5,000
10 Aug	Commission received			
16 Aug	S Orton: loan			1,000
20 Aug	Office fittings			282
24 Aug	Commission received			188

Credit	Cash Book: Payments			CBP
Date	Details	Folio	Discount received	Bank
2007			£	£
3 Aug	Computer			2,115
6 Aug	Rent paid			100
13 Aug	Office fittings			2,350
17 Aug	Drawings			100
27 Aug	S Orton: loan			150

Dr	Capital Account		Cr
2007	£	2007	£
		2 Aug Bank	5,000

Dr	Computer Account		Cr
2007	£	2007	£
3 Aug Bank	1,800		

Dr	Rent Paid Account		Cr
2007	£	2007	£
6 Aug Bank	100		

Dr	Commission Received Account		Cr
2007	£	2007	£
		10 Aug Bank	200
		24 Aug Bank	160

Dr	Office Fittings Account		Cr
2007	£	2007	£
13 Aug Bank	2,000	20 Aug Bank	240

Dr	Sally Orton: Loan Account		Cr
2007	£	2007	£
27 Aug Bank	150	16 Aug Bank	1,000

Dr	Drawings Account		Cr
2007	£	2007	£
17 Aug Bank	100		

Dr	Value Added Tax Account		Cr
2007	£	2007	£
3 Aug Bank (computer)	315	10 Aug Bank (commission recvd)	35
13 Aug Bank (office fittings)	350	20 Aug Bank (office fittings)	42
		24 Aug Bank (commission recvd)	28

17.7

Date	Details	Folio	Dr	Cr
2007			£	£
29 Nov	Bad debts written off account	ML	80	
	Value Added Tax account	ML	14	
	Sales ledger control account	ML		94
			94	94
	Balance of subsidiary (sales) ledger account			
	of Dailey Trading Company written off as a bad			
	debt, as per memo from accounts supervisor			
	dated 29 November 2007			

SUBSIDIARY (SALES) LEDGER

Dr			**Dailey Trading Company** (account no 754)		Cr
2007		£	2007		£
15 Jan	Sales	94	29 Nov Bad debts written off		80
			29 Nov Value Added Tax		14
		94			94

MAIN LEDGER

Dr		**Bad Debts Written Off Account**		Cr
2007		£	2007	£
29 Nov	Dailey Trading Co	80		

Dr		**Value Added Tax Account**		Cr
2007		£	2007	£
29 Nov	Dailey Trading Co	14		

Dr	**Sales Ledger Control Account**		Cr
2007	£	2007	£
		29 Nov Bad debts written off	80
		29 Nov Value Added Tax	14

17.8

		capital expenditure	revenue expenditure
(a)	purchase of vehicles	✓	
(b)	rent paid on premises		✓
(c)	wages and salaries		✓
(d)	legal fees relating to the purchase of property	✓	
(e)	redecoration of office		✓
(f)	installation of air-conditioning in office	✓	
(g)	wages of own employees used to build extension to the stockroom	✓	
(h)	installation and setting up of a new machine	✓	

CHAPTER 18: BALANCING THE CASH BOOK AND BANK RECONCILIATION

18.1

Dr						CASH BOOK					Cr
Date	Details	Folio	Discount allowed	Cash	Bank	Date	Details	Folio	Discount received	Cash	Bank
2007			£	£	£	2007			£	£	£
1 Aug	Balances b/d			325	925	6 Aug	Crane & Co		35		845
4 Aug	S Quesne		2		98	12 Aug	Wages			275	
17 Aug	J Ahmed		4	76		16 Aug	T Lewis		15		285
23 Aug	D Lloyd		3		45	27 Aug	S Ford		5	70	
31 Aug	Balance c/d				62	31 Aug	Balance c/d			56	
			9	401	1,130				55	401	1,130
1 Sep	Balance b/d			56		1 Sep	Balance b/d				62

18.2 (a) **18.3** (c)

18.4

TOM REID

BANK RECONCILIATION STATEMENT AS AT 31 DECEMBER 2007

	£
Balance at bank as per bank statement	207
Less: unpresented cheque:	
B Kay (cheque no 345126)	20
	187
Add: outstanding lodgement:	
J Hill	13
Balance at bank as per cash book	200

18.5 (a)

2007	Receipts		£	2007	Payments		£
1 Jan	Balance b/d		800.50	2 Jan	A Arthur Ltd	001351	100.00
6 Jan	J Baker		495.60	9 Jan	C Curtis	001352	398.50
30 Jan	G Shotton Ltd		335.75	13 Jan	Donald & Co	001353	229.70
13 Jan	TK Supplies	BACS	716.50	14 Jan	Bryant & Sons	001354	312.00
				23 Jan	P Reid	001355	176.50
				23 Jan	Omni Finance	DD	207.95
				31 Jan	Balance c/d		923.70
			2,348.35				2,348.35
1 Feb	Balance b/d		923.70				

(b)

P GERRARD

BANK RECONCILIATION STATEMENT AS AT 31 JANUARY 2007

	£	£
Balance at bank as per bank statement		1,076.45
Less: unpresented cheques:		
Bryant & Sons (001354)	312.00	
P Reid (001355)	176.50	
		488.50
		587.95
Add: outstanding lodgement:		
G Shotton Limited		335.75
Balance at bank as per cash book		923.70

18.6   (a)

Dr			**Cash Book** (bank columns)		Cr
2007		£	2007		£
1 May	Balance b/d	300	3 May P Stone	867714	28
7 May	Cash	162	14 May Alpha Ltd	867715	50
17 May	C Brewster	89	28 May E Deakin	867716	110
24 May	Cash	60	17 May *Standing order: A-Z Insurance*		*25*
28 May	Cash	40	31 May *Bank charges*		*10*
			31 May *Balance c/d*		*428*
		651			*651*
1 Jun	*Balance b/d*	*428*			

(b)

JANE DOYLE

BANK RECONCILIATION STATEMENT AS AT 31 MAY 2007

	£
Balance at bank as per bank statement	498
Less: unpresented cheque:	
E Deakin (867716)	110
	388
Add: outstanding lodgement:	
cash	40
Balance at bank as per cash book	428

18.7 (a) - (c)

CASH BOOK

Date	Details	Bank	Date	Cheque no	Details	Bank
2007		£	2007			£
1 May	Balance b/f	3,652	4 May	451762	Smith and Company	751
26 May	J Ackland	832	4 May	451763	Bryant Limited	268
28 May	Stamp Limited	1,119	7 May	451764	Curtis Cars	1,895
14 May	Perran Taxis	2,596	7 May	451765	Parts Supplies	1,045
			18 May		Wyvern Council	198
			20 May		A1 Insurance	1,005
			25 May		Okaro and Company	254
			25 May		Bank charges	20
			31 May		Balance c/d	2,763
		8,199				8,199
1 Jun	Balance b/d	2,763				

(d)

MILESTONE MOTORS
Bank Reconciliation Statement as at 31 May 2007

	£	£
Balance at bank as per bank statement		2,707
Less: unpresented cheque no 451764		1,895
		812
Add: outstanding lodgements		
J Ackland	832	
Stamp Limited	1,119	
		1,951
Balance at bank as per cash book		2,763

CHAPTER 19: USING THE JOURNAL AND RECONCILING CONTROL ACCOUNTS

19.1   (b)

19.2   *business transaction*
- credit sale of a fixed asset
- credit purchase of goods from a supplier
- returned credit purchases to the supplier
- customer returns goods sold on credit
- cheque received from a debtor
- credit sale of goods to a customer
- expense paid out of petty cash

book of prime entry
- journal
- purchases day book
- purchases returns day book
- sales returns day book
- cash book
- sales day book
- petty cash book

19.3

	book of prime entry	*debit*	*credit*
(a)	purchases day book	purchases a/c	purchases ledger control a/c
(b)	sales day book	sales ledger control a/c	sales a/c
(c)	journal	office equipment a/c	purchases ledger control a/c
(d)	sales returns day book	sales returns a/c	sales ledger control a/c
(e)	cash book	bank a/c	sales ledger control a/c
(f)	cash book	cash a/c	sales a/c
(g)	cash book	drawings a/c	cash a/c
(h)	cash book	purchases ledger control a/c	bank a/c
(i)	journal	bad debts written off a/c	sales ledger control a/c
(j)	purchases returns day book	purchases ledger control a/c	purchases returns a/c

Notes:
- Where control accounts are used, transactions will need to be recorded in the appropriate subsidiary ledger accounts.
- An alternative for (c) is to open a main ledger account for the creditor, A-Z Computers Limited – this will avoid confusion with trade creditors in the subsidiary (purchases) ledger.

19.4   (a)

Dr		£		Cr £
Sales Ledger Control Account				
2007		£	2007	£
1 Mar	Balance b/d	142,830	31 Mar Bank	97,247
31 Mar	Sales	105,350	31 Mar Discount allowed	840
			31 Mar Sales returns	2,890
			31 Mar Bad debt written off	250
			31 Mar Balance c/d	146,953
		248,180		248,180
1 Apr	Balance b/d	146,953		

(b)

	£
Sales ledger control account balance as at 31 March 2007	146,953
Total of subsidiary (sales) ledger accounts as at 31 March 2007	147,203
Difference	250

(c) The bad debt of £250 may not have been written off in the subsidiary (sales) ledger, and could relate to the account of Portreath Home and Garden.

19.5 (a)

Dr		Purchases Ledger Control Account			Cr
2007		£	2007		£
31 Oct	Bank	28,070	1 Oct	Balance b/d	35,105
31 Oct	Discount received	430	31 Oct	Purchases	23,294
31 Oct	Purchases returns	1,270			
31 Oct	Balance c/d	28,629			
		58,399			58,399
			1 Nov	Balance b/d	28,629

(b)

	£
Purchases ledger control account balance as at 31 October 2007	28,629
Total of subsidiary (purchases) ledger accounts as at 31 October 2007	27,929
Difference	700

(c) There may have been a posting error and the debit balance of Hawke Supplies may in fact be a credit balance.

19.6 (a)

Dr		Petty Cash Control Account			Cr
2007		£	2007		£
1 Apr	Balance b/d	250	30 Apr	Petty cash book	176
30 Apr	Cash book	176	30 Apr	Balance c/d	250
		426			426
1 May	Balance b/d	250			

(b) Carry out a physical check of the amount of cash in the petty cash box.

CHAPTER 20: INITIAL TRIAL BALANCE AND CORRECTION OF ERRORS

20.1 (b)

20.2 (c)

20.3 (a)

Dr										Cr
Date	Details	Folio	Discount allowed	Bank	Date	Details	Folio	Discount received		Bank
2007			£	£	2007			£		£
1 Apr	Capital			1,000	2 Apr	Purchases				255
7 Apr	Sales			195	5 Apr	Advertising				60
9 Apr	Sales			248	8 Apr	Rent paid				125
16 Apr	J Couchman: loan			1,000	12 Apr	Drawings				100
19 Apr	Sales			220	14 Apr	Purchases				240
28 Apr	Sales			312	21 Apr	Shop fittings				1,250
					23 Apr	Purchases				180
					26 Apr	Advertising				90
					29 Apr	Rent				125
					30 Apr	Drawings				125
					30 Apr	Balance c/d				425
			–	2,975					–	2,975
1 May	Balance b/d		–	425						

(CASH BOOK — title spans the top)

(b) and (c) **MAIN LEDGER**

Capital Account

Dr			Cr
2007	£	2007	£
		1 Apr Bank	1,000

Purchases Account

Dr			Cr
2007	£	2007	£
2 Apr Bank	255	30 Apr Balance c/d	675
14 Apr Bank	240		
23 Apr Bank	180		
	675		675
1 May Balance b/d	675		

Advertising Account

Dr			Cr
2007	£	2007	£
5 Apr Bank	60	30 Apr Balance c/d	150
26 Apr Bank	90		
	150		150
1 May Balance b/d	150		

Dr		Sales Account				Cr
2007		£	2007			£
30 Apr	Balance c/d	975	7 Apr	Bank		195
			9 Apr	Bank		248
			19 Apr	Bank		220
			28 Apr	Bank		312
		975				975
			1 May	Balance b/d		975

Dr		Rent Paid Account			Cr
2007		£	2007		£
8 Apr	Bank	125	30 Apr	Balance c/d	250
29 Apr	Bank	125			
		250			250
1 May	Balance b/d	250			

Dr		Drawings Account			Cr
2007		£	2007		£
12 Apr	Bank	100	30 Apr	Balance c/d	225
30 Apr	Bank	125			
		225			225
1 May	Balance b/d	225			

Dr		J Couchman: Loan Account			Cr
2007		£	2007		£
			16 Apr	Bank	1,000

Dr		Shop Fittings Account		Cr
2007		£	2007	£
21 Apr	Bank	1,250		

(d)

Trial balance of Andrew Jarvis as at 30 April 2007

Name of account	Dr £	Cr £
Bank	425	
Capital		1,000
Purchases	675	
Advertising	150	
Sales		975
Rent paid	250	
Drawings	225	
J Couchman: Loan		1,000
Shop fittings	1,250	
	2,975	2,975

20.4   **Trial balance of Jane Greenwell as at 28 February 2007**

Name of account	Dr £	Cr £
Bank		1,250
Purchases	850	
Cash	48	
Sales		1,940
Purchases returns		144
Creditors		1,442
Equipment	2,704	
Van	3,200	
Stock at 1 Jan 2007	1,210	
Sales returns	90	
Debtors	1,174	
Wages	1,500	
Capital (missing figure)		6,000
	10,776	10,776

20.5 (a)   will cause an imbalance in the trial balance
         (b)   will not cause an imbalance in the trial balance
         (c)   will not cause an imbalance in the trial balance
         (d)   will not cause an imbalance in the trial balance

20.6 (d)

20.7 (a)

20.8

Date	Details	Folio	Dr £	Cr £
(a)	Rates		100	
	Rent paid			100
(b)	Sales ledger control		96	
	Sales returns			96
	Sales returns		69	
	Sales ledger control			69
			165	165
(c)	Bad debts written off		200	
	Value Added Tax		35	
	Sales ledger control			235
			235	235

Date	Details	Folio	Dr	Cr
			£	£
(d)	Purchases ledger control		175	
	Purchases returns			175
	Purchases ledger control		175	
	Purchases returns			175
			350	350
(e)	Vehicle running expenses		45	
	Vehicles			45

20.9 (a) *error of omission*

Date	Details	Folio	Dr	Cr
			£	£
	Sales ledger control	ML	150	
	Sales	ML		150
	Sales invoice no .... omitted from			
	the accounts: in the subsidiary (sales) ledger –			
	debit J Rigby £150			

(b) *mispost/error of commission*

Date	Details	Folio	Dr	Cr
			£	£
	Purchases ledger control	ML	125	
	Purchases ledger control	ML		125
	Correction of mispost – cheque no .....:			
	in the subsidiary (purchases) ledger			
	– debit H Price Limited			
	– credit H Prince			

(c) *error of principle*

Date	Details	Folio	Dr	Cr
			£	£
	Delivery van	ML	10,000	
	Vehicle expenses	ML		10,000
	Correction of error – vehicle no			
	invoice no			

(d) *reversal of entries*

Date	Details	Folio	Dr	Cr
			£	£
	Postages	ML	55	
	Bank	CBP		55
	Postages	ML	55	
	Bank	CBP		55
			110	110
	Correction of reversal of entries			
	on			

(e) *compensating error*

Date	Details	Folio	Dr	Cr
			£	£
	Purchases	ML	100	
	Purchases returns	ML		100
	Correction of under-cast on purchases			
	account and purchases returns account			
	on ....(date).......			

(f) *error of original entry*

Date	Details	Folio	Dr	Cr
			£	£
	Sales ledger control	ML	98	
	Bank	CBP		98
	Bank	CBR	89	
	Sales ledger control	ML		89
			187	187
	Correction of error – cheque for £89			
	received on ....(date)....: in the subsidiary			
	(sales) ledger			
	– debit L Johnson £98			
	– credit L Johnson £89			

20.10

Date	Details	Folio	Dr	Cr
			£	£
(a)	Office expenses	ML	85	
	Suspense	ML		85
	Omission of entry in office expenses account – payment made by cheque no .... on ....(date)			
(b)	Suspense	ML	78	
	Photocopying	ML		78
	Photocopying	ML	87	
	Suspense	ML		87
			165	165
	Payment for photocopying £87 (cheque no .... on ....) entered in photocopying account as £78 in error			
(c)	Suspense	ML	100	
	Sales returns	ML		100
	Overcast on ...(date)... now corrected			
(d)	Commission received	ML	25	
	Suspense	ML		25
	Commission received on .... entered twice in commission received account, now corrected			

Dr		£		Suspense Account	£	Cr
2007			2007			
30 Sep	Trial balance difference	19	(a)	Office expenses	85	
(b)	Photocopying	78	(b)	Photocopying	87	
(c)	Sales returns	100	(d)	Commission received	25	
		197			197	

20.11

Date	Details	Folio	Dr	Cr
			£	£
(a)	Sales		100	
	Suspense			100
(b)	Suspense		205	
	Rent paid			205
(c)	Suspense		65	
	Telephone expenses			65
	Telephone expenses		56	
	Suspense			56
			121	121
(d)	Heating and lighting		160	
	Suspense			160

answers to student activities **511**

Dr		£	Suspense Account		Cr
2007		£	2007		£
28 Feb	Trial balance difference	46		Sales	100
	Rent paid	205		Telephone expenses	56
	Telephone expenses	65		Heating and lighting	160
		316			316

Note: the net difference on telephone expenses is a £9 debit to suspense account.

Trial balance as at 28 February 2007
after correction of errors

	Dr	Cr
	£	£
Purchases	122,500	
Sales		239,750
Rent paid	5,015	
Wages	96,310	
Office equipment	6,000	
Machinery	12,000	
Heating and lighting	3,670	
Telephone expenses	2,045	
Stock at 1 March 2006	24,740	
Bank	8,230	
Sales ledger control	22,840	
Purchases ledger control		15,680
Value Added Tax		5,320
Capital		58,500
Drawings	15,900	
Suspense	–	
	319,250	319,250

CHAPTER 21: USING THE TRIAL BALANCE

21.1 **SUBSIDIARY (PURCHASES) LEDGER**

Dalton & Co

Date	Details	Amount	Date	Details	Amount
2007		£	2007		£
1 Oct	Purchases returns	94	1 Oct	Balance b/d	23,076
1 Oct	Balance c/d	24,580	1 Oct	Purchases	1,598
		24,674			24,674
			2 Oct	Balance b/d	24,580

Jeans-R-Us Limited

Date	Details	Amount	Date	Details	Amount
2007		£	2007		£
1 Oct	Purchases returns	141	1 Oct	Balance b/d	12,120
1 Oct	Balance c/d	14,799	1 Oct	Purchases	2,820
		14,940			14,940
			2 Oct	Balance b/d	14,799

J & S Manufacturing

Date	Details	Amount	Date	Details	Amount
2007		£	2007		£
1 Oct	Bank	775	1 Oct	Balance b/d	13,491
1 Oct	Discount received	25	1 Oct	Purchases	1,034
1 Oct	Balance c/d	13,725			
		14,525			14,525
			2 Oct	Balance b/d	13,725

One-Stop Office

Date	Details	Amount	Date	Details	Amount
2007		£	2007		£
1 Oct	Stationery returns	47	1 Oct	Balance b/d	9,466
1 Oct	Bank	624	1 Oct	Stationery	423
1 Oct	Balance c/d	9,218			
		9,889			9,889
			2 Oct	Balance b/d	9,218

Wyvern Clothes

Date	Details	Amount	Date	Details	Amount
2007		£	2007		£
1 Oct	Bank	1,055	1 Oct	Balance b/d	2,610
1 Oct	Discount received	45	1 Oct	Purchases	1,457
1 Oct	Balance c/d	4,189	1 Oct	Purchases	1,222
		5,289			5,289
			2 Oct	Balance b/d	4,189

Reconciliation of purchases ledger control account

	1 Oct 2007	2 Oct 2007
	£	£
Dalton & Co	23,076	24,580
Jeans-R-Us Limited	12,120	14,799
J & S Manufacturing	13,491	13,725
One-Stop Office	9,466	9,218
Wyvern Clothes	2,610	4,189
Purchases ledger control account (see below)	60,763	66,511

MAIN LEDGER
Purchases Ledger Control Account

Date	Details	Amount	Date	Details	Amount
2007		£	2007		£
1 Oct	Purchases Returns Day Book	282	1 Oct	Balance b/d	60,763
1 Oct	Bank	*2,454	1 Oct	Purchases Day Book	8,554
1 Oct	Discount received	70			
1 Oct	Balance c/d	66,511			
		69,317			69,317
			2 Oct	Balance b/d	66,511

* £775 + £1,055 + £624

Purchases Account

Date	Details	Amount	Date	Details	Amount
2007		£	2007		£
1 Oct	Balance b/d	428,494	1 Oct	Balance b/d	435,414
1 Oct	Purchases Day Book	6,920			
		435,414			435,414
2 Oct	Balance b/d	435,414			

Purchases Returns Account

Date	Details	Amount	Date	Details	Amount
2007		£	2007		£
1 Oct	Balance c/d	8,527	1 Oct	Balance b/d	8,327
			1 Oct	Purchases Returns Day Book	200
		8,527			8,527
			2 Oct	Balance b/d	8,527

Stationery Account

Date	Details	Amount	Date	Details	Amount
2007		£	2007		£
1 Oct	Balance b/d	3,650	1 Oct	Purchases Returns Day	
1 Oct	Purchases Day Book	360		Book	40
			1 Oct	Balance c/d	3,970
		4,010			4,010
2 Oct	Balance b/d	3,970			

Discount Received Account

Date	Details	Amount	Date	Details	Amount
2007		£	2007		£
1 Oct	Balance c/d	911	1 Oct	Balance b/d	841
			1 Oct	Cash Book	70
		911			911
			2 Oct	Balance b/d	911

Value Added Tax Account

Date	Details	Amount	Date	Details	Amount
2007		£	2007		£
1 Oct	Purchases Day Book	1,274	1 Oct	Balance b/d	8,347
1 Oct	Balance c/d	7,115	1 Oct	Purchases Returns Day	
				Book	42
		8,389			8,389
			2 Oct	Balance b/d	7,115

Fashion Traders
Trial balance as at 1 October 2007

Name of account	Dr £	Cr £
Purchases ledger control		66,511
Purchases	435,414	
Purchases returns		8,527
Stationery	3,970	
Discount received		911
Value Added Tax		7,115
Cash	275	
Bank		400
Sales ledger control	100,690	
Sales		758,174

continued on next page

Sales returns	12,364
Discount allowed	1,497
General expenses	25,842
Wages and salaries	127,608
Bad debts written off	1,762
Office equipment	7,750
Warehouse equipment	85,250
Stock at 1 Jan 2007	165,940
Bank loan		40,000
Capital		115,324
Drawings	28,600	
	996,962	996,962

21.2

JOURNAL

Date	Details	Debit	Credit
2007		£	£
2 Oct	Bad debts written off account	80	
	Value Added Tax account	14	
	Sales ledger control account		94
		94	94
	Balance of subsidiary (sales) ledger account of		
	Victoria's Fashions written off as a bad debt		
	on instructions of the accounts supervisor		
2 Oct	Sales ledger control account	220	
	Sales ledger control account		220
	Correction of mispost on 12 September; in the		
	subsidiary (sales) ledger:		
	– debit Bentley Stores Limited		
	– credit Bentley & Co		

SUBSIDIARY (SALES) LEDGER

Bentley & Co

Date	Details	Amount	Date	Details	Amount
2007		£	2007		£
2 Oct	Balance b/d	31,095	2 Oct	Bank	420
2 Oct	Sales	423	2 Oct	Bentley Stores	220
			2 Oct	Balance c/d	30,878
		31,518			31,518
3 Oct	Balance b/d	30,878			

Bentley Stores Limited

Date	Details	Amount	Date	Details	Amount
2007		£	2007		£
2 Oct	Balance b/d	21,870	2 Oct	Bank	1,825
2 Oct	Sales	752	2 Oct	Discount allowed	45
2 Oct	Sales	376	2 Oct	Balance c/d	21,348
2 Oct	Bentley & Co	220			
		23,218			23,218
3 Oct	Balance b/d	21,348			

Just Jeans

Date	Details	Amount	Date	Details	Amount
2007		£	2007		£
2 Oct	Balance b/d	10,629	2 Oct	Sales returns	47
2 Oct	Sales	188	2 Oct	Bank	240
			2 Oct	Discount allowed	10
			2 Oct	Balance c/d	10,520
		10,817			10,817
3 Oct	Balance b/d	10,520			

Southwick Stores

Date	Details	Amount	Date	Details	Amount
2007		£	2007		£
2 Oct	Balance b/d	16,205	2 Oct	Balance c/d	16,675
2 Oct	Sales	470			
		16,675			16,675
3 Oct	Balance b/d	16,675			

Teme Trading Co

Date	Details	Amount	Date	Details	Amount
2007		£	2007		£
2 Oct	Balance b/d	20,797	2 Oct	Sales returns	94
2 Oct	Sales	329	2 Oct	Balance c/d	21,032
		21,126			21,126
3 Oct	Balance b/d	21,032			

Victoria's Fashions

Date	Details	Amount	Date	Details	Amount
2007		£	2007		£
2 Oct	Balance b/d	94	2 Oct	Bad debts written off	80
			2 Oct	Value Added Tax	14
		94			94

Reconciliation of sales ledger control account

	2 Oct 2007	3 Oct 2007
	£	£
Bentley & Co	31,095	30,878
Bentley Stores Limited	21,870	21,348
Just Jeans	10,629	10,520
Southwick Stores	16,205	16,675
Teme Trading Co	20,797	21,032
Victoria's Fashions	94	–
Sales ledger control account (see below)	100,690	100,453

MAIN LEDGER

Sales Ledger Control Account

Date	Details	Amount	Date	Details	Amount
2007		£	2007		£
2 Oct	Balance b/d	100,690	2 Oct	Sales Returns Day Book	141
2 Oct	Sales Day Book	2,538	2 Oct	Bank	*2,485
			2 Oct	Discount allowed	55
			2 Oct	Bad debt written off	80
			2 Oct	Value Added Tax	14
			2 Oct	Balance c/d	100,453
		103,228			103,228
3 Oct	Balance b/d	100,453			

* £420 + £240 + £1,825

Sales Account

Date	Details	Amount	Date	Details	Amount
2007		£	2007		£
2 Oct	Balance c/d	760,334	2 Oct	Balance b/d	758,174
			2 Oct	Sales Day Book	2,160
		760,334			760,334
			3 Oct	Balance b/d	760,334

Sales Returns Account

Date	Details	Amount	Date	Details	Amount
2007		£	2007		£
2 Oct	Balance b/d	12,364	2 Oct	Balance c/d	12,484
2 Oct	Sales Returns Day Book	120			
		12,484			12,484
3 Oct	Balance b/d	12,484			

Discount Allowed Account

Date	Details	Amount	Date	Details	Amount
2007		£	2007		£
2 Oct	Balance b/d	1,497	2 Oct	Balance c/d	1,552
2 Oct	Cash Book	55			
		1,552			1,552
3 Oct	Balance b/d	1,552			

Value Added Tax Account

Date	Details	Amount	Date	Details	Amount
2007		£	2007		£
2 Oct	Sales Returns Day Book	21	2 Oct	Balance b/d	7,115
2 Oct	Victoria's Fashions	14	2 Oct	Sales Day Book	378
2 Oct	Balance c/d	7,458			
		7,493			7,493
			3 Oct	Balance b/d	7,458

Wages and Salaries Account

Date	Details	Amount	Date	Details	Amount
2007		£	2007		£
2 Oct	Balance b/d	127,608	2 Oct	Balance c/d	128,658
2 Oct	Bank	1,050			
		128,658			128,658
3 Oct	Balance b/d	128,658			

Bad Debts Written Off Account

Date	Details	Amount	Date	Details	Amount
2007		£	2007		£
2 Oct	Balance b/d	1,762	2 Oct	Balance c/d	1,842
2 Oct	Victoria's Fashions	80			
		1,842			1,842
3 Oct	Balance b/d	1,842			

Bank Loan Account

Date	Details	Amount	Date	Details	Amount
2007		£	2007		£
2 Oct	Bank	500	2 Oct	Balance b/d	40,000
2 Oct	Balance c/d	39,500			
		40,000			40,000
			3 Oct	Balance b/d	39,500

Drawings Account

Date	Details	Amount	Date	Details	Amount
2007		£	2007		£
2 Oct	Balance b/d	28,600	2 Oct	Balance c/d	28,910
2 Oct	Bank	310			
		28,910			28,910
3 Oct	Balance b/d	28,910			

Fashion Traders

Trial balance as at 2 October 2007

	Dr	Cr
	£	£
Name of account		
Purchases ledger control		66,511
Purchases	435,414	
Purchases returns		8,527
Stationery	3,970	
Discount received		911
Value Added Tax		7,458
Cash	275	
Bank	225	
Sales ledger control	100,453	
Sales		760,334
Sales returns	12,484	
Discount allowed	1,552	
General expenses	25,842	
Wages and salaries	128,658	
Bad debts written off	1,842	
Office equipment	7,750	
Warehouse equipment	85,250	
Stock at 1 Jan 2007	165,940	
Bank loan		39,500
Capital		115,324
Drawings	28,910	
	998,565	998,565

Index